STUDIES IN EARLY MODER
POLITICAL AND SOCIAL HISTORY

Volume 12

LONDON'S NEWS PRESS AND THE THIRTY YEARS WAR

Studies in Early Modern Cultural, Political and Social History

ISSN: 1476–9107

Series editors
Tim Harris – Brown University
Stephen Taylor – Durham University
Andy Wood – Durham University

LONDON'S NEWS PRESS AND THE THIRTY YEARS WAR

Jayne E. E. Boys

THE BOYDELL PRESS

First published 2011
The Boydell Press, Woodbridge
Reprinted in paperback 2014

ISBN 978 1 84383 677 3 hardback
ISBN 978 1 84383 934 7 paperback

The Boydell Press is an imprint of Boydell & Brewer Ltd
PO Box 9, Woodbridge, Suffolk IP12 3DF, UK
and of Boydell & Brewer Inc.
668 Mt Hope Avenue, Rochester, NY 14620–2731, USA
website: www.boydellandbrewer.com

A catalogue record for this book is available
from the British Library

The publisher has no responsibility for the continued existence or
accuracy of URLs for external or third-party internet websites referred
to in this book, and does not guarantee that any content on
such websites is, or will remain, accurate or appropriate.

This publication is printed on acid-free paper

Contents

Illustrations

Plates

Figures

Acknowledgements

I am grateful to Dr Gerhardt Benecke, my first tutor, whose enthusiasm and encouragement inspired my interest in the Thirty Years War and the news trade. I also want to thank Dr Kenneth Fincham for his support and advice over the years: without his help this would not have been possible. Thanks also go to David Ormrod, Jacqueline Eales, Erin Dooley, Tim Harris and Tom Cogswell for their encouragement, and to the many librarians who have assisted me, particularly at the Bodleian, Cambridge University Library, and also at the British Library where the calm efficiency of the service cannot fail to impress. The Burney Collection contains the best single resource for news reporting in English on the Thirty Years War from the early 1620s through to the 1640s, and its curators have been most helpful.

The notes and dates follow the usual conventions. New Style dating is given and the year is taken to begin on 1 January. Newsbook and coranto dates are given as they appear in the original publications and I discuss dating issues in Chapter 2. Spelling and punctuation in quotations is not modernised unless I am quoting from a secondary source, except that I have used modern conventions for 'j's', 'v's' and 's's'. The place of publication is London unless otherwise stated. The use of false imprints is discussed in Chapter 3. Titles that appear throughout are cited in full in the first instance in each consecutive chapter, except for those that appear in the table of abbreviations. Corantos, currantoes and newsbooks are identified in the footnotes by their date and number in the relevant printed catalogues (STC, N&S or Wing), in the following form; (date), pages, catalogue reference. Some 1640s publications also have Thomason collection shelf marks from the British Library, given as E with the number. References are provided in full in the bibliography.

Abbreviations

Add MS   Additional Manuscripts, British Library
Amussen   S. D. Amussen and M. A. Kishlansky, *Political Culture and Politics in Early Modern England* (Manchester, 1995)
Annual (1993) *Studies in Newspaper and Periodical History; 1993 Annual*, ed. M. Harris (Westport, CT and London, 1993)
Annual (1994) *Studies in Newspaper and Periodical History; 1994 Annual*, ed. M. Harris (Westport, CT and London, 1994)
APC   *Acts of the Privy Council*
Arber   E. Arber, *A Transcript of the Register of the Company of Stationers' of London 1554–1640*, 4 vols (London and Birmingham, 1875–94)
Arblaster   P. Arblaster, 'Current Affairs Publishing in the Habsburg Netherlands 1620–1660 in Comparative European Perspective' (D. Phil. Thesis, University of Oxford, 1999)
Atherton   I. Atherton, 'The Itch Grown a Disease: Manuscript Transmission of News in the Seventeenth Century', in *News, Newspapers, and Society in Early Modern Britain*, ed. J. Raymond (London and Portland, OR, 1999), 39–65
Barnard   J. Barnard and D. F. McKenzie, ed., *The Cambridge History of the Book 1557–1695*, vol. 4 (Cambridge, 2002)
B&B   Butter and Bourne
CandT   *Court and Times of Charles I*, ed. T. Birch, 2 vols (1848)
Chamberlain   *The Letters of John Chamberlain*, ed. N. E. McClure, 2 vols (Philadelphia, PA, 1939)
Cogswell   T. Cogswell, *The Blessed Revolution: English Politics and the Coming of War 1621–24* (Cambridge, 1989)
CSPD   *Calendar of State Papers Domestic*
Cust   R. Cust, 'News and Politics in Early Seventeenth Century England', *PandP*, 112 (1986), 60–90
Dahl   F. Dahl, *A Bibliography of English Corantos and Periodical Newsbooks 1620–42* (1952)
DandB   B. Dooley and S. Baron, ed., *The Politics of Information in Early Modern Europe* (London and New York, 2001)
EHR   *The Economic History Review*
ESR   *European Studies Review* (*European History Quarterly* from 1984)

Fox	A. Fox, 'Rumour, News and Popular Opinion in Elizabethan and Early Stuart England', *Historical Journal*, 40 (1997), 597–620
Frank	J. Frank, *The Beginnings of the English Newspaper* (Cambridge, MA, 1966)
Frearson	M. C. Frearson, 'The English Corantos of the 1620s' (D. Phil. Thesis, University of Cambridge, 1993)
Hanson	L. Hanson, 'English Newsbooks 1620–1641', *The Library*, 4:18 (1938), 355–84
Harl. MS	Harleian Manuscript, British Library
HJ	*Historical Journal*
HLQ	*Huntington Library Quarterly*
Jackson	*Records of the Court of the Stationers' Company 1602–1640*, ed. W. A. Jackson (1957)
JBS	*Journal of British Studies*
Jonson	Ben Jonson, 'The Staple of News', 1625 in *Ben Jonson: The Complete Plays*, 2 vols (Everyman Library, 1910/1970)
JNandPH	*Journal of Newspapers and Periodical History*
Koopmans	J. W. Koopmans, *News and Politics in Early Modern Europe 1500–1800* (Leuven, Paris and Dudley, MA, 2005)
Lake	K. Sharpe and P. Lake, ed., *Culture and Politics in Early Stuart England* (Basingstoke and London, 1994)
Lambert	S. Lambert, 'State Control of the Press in Theory and Practice: The Role of the Stationers' Company before 1640', in *Censorship and the Control of Print in England and France 1600–1910*, ed. R. Myers and M. Harris (Winchester, 1992), 1–32
Levy	F. J. Levy, 'The Decorum of News', in *News, Newspapers, and Early Modern Britain*, ed. J. Raymond (1999), 12–38
Love	H. Love, *Scribal Publication in Seventeenth Century England* (Oxford, 1993)
MB	Mercurius Britannicus
McKenzie	D. F. McKenzie, *Making Meaning: Printers of the Mind and Other Essays*, ed. P. D. McDonald and M. F. Suarez (Amherst and Boston, MA, 2002)
N&S	C. Nelson and M. Seccombe, *British Newspapers and Periodicals: A Short Title Catalogue* (New York, 1987)
ODNB	*Oxford Dictionary of National Biography* (Oxford, 2004)
Patterson	W. B. Patterson, *King James VI and I and the Reunion of Christendom* (Cambridge, 1997)
PandP	*Past and Present*
Plant	M. Plant, *The English Book Trade; An Economic History of the Making and Sale of Books* (1965)
Pory	W. S. Powell, *John Pory 1572–1636: The Life and Letters of Man of Many Parts* (Chapel Hill, NC, 1977)

Proclamations	*Stuart Royal Proclamations*, ed. P. L. Hughes and J. F. Larkin, 2 vols (Oxford, 1973–83)
Raymond	J. Raymond, *The Invention of the Newspaper* (Oxford, 1996)
Reeve	L. J. Reeve, *Charles I and the Road to Personal Rule* (Cambridge, 1989)
Ries	P. Ries, 'The Anatomy of a Seventeenth Century Newspaper', *Daphnis*, 6, Heft 1–2 (1977), 170–232
Rous	*The Diary of John Rous*, ed. M. A. Everett Green (Camden Society, 1·64, 1856)
Schumacher	W. H. Schumacher, 'Vox Populi: The Thirty Years' War in English Pamphlets and Newspapers' (D. Phil. Thesis, University of Princeton, 1975)
Siebert	F. Siebert, *Freedom of the Press in England 1476–1776* (Urbana, IL, 1952)
Shaaber	M. A. Shaaber, *Some Forerunners of the Newspaper in England 1476–1622* (Philadelphia, PA, 1929)
SPDom.	State Papers Domestic, The National Archives
STC	*A Short-Title Catalogue of Books Printed in England, Scotland and Ireland 1475–1640*, ed. A. W. Pollard, G. R. Redgrave and K. F. Pantzer, 3 vols (1991), Vol. 4, Indexes (New York, 1998)
Watt	T. Watt, *Cheap Print and Popular Piety, 1550–1640* (Cambridge, 1991)
Wedgwood	C. V. Wedgwood, *The Thirty Years' War* (1938/1968)
Wing	D. Wing, *Short-Title Catalogue of Books Printed in England, Scotland, Ireland, Wales and British America and of English Books Printed in Other Countries 1641–1700*, rev. ed., 3 vols (New York, 1972–94)

Introduction

'God grant a good and universal Peace'[1]

This prayer concluded a letter from Mainz with news that the Elector of Saxony was treating with the Habsburg emperor for peace at Pirna. It was included inconspicuously towards the end of chapter 4 of a London publication, *The German History Continued* that appeared in the mid-1630s, at a time when, according to conventional historical wisdom, the publication of news in London was subject to a ban that lasted from October 1632 to December 1638. In fact, this *German History* followed upon a dozen or more publications in London covering recent events in the Thirty Years War that appeared after the 1632 ban. Others included *The Swedish Intelligencer … with the Discipline, The History of the Present Warres* and *A True Relacon of the Duke of Ffreidlands death.*[2]

The events reported may now seem far removed from the day-to-day concerns of seventeenth-century Londoners. By the autumn of 1634, the emperor, Ferdinand, was capitalising on success at the Battle of Nordlingen by negotiating from strength for peace within the Empire and England had little say in the matter. Yet many Scottish and English lives were lost at Nordlingen and government reaction in London was swift, and far more draconian than the better-known ban of 1632 that stopped London production of weekly newsbooks only. This was a crackdown on all foreign news reporting that lasted until 1637.[3] Only one further news digest was published in the whole of 1635 and 1636 and this was probably allowed only to correspond with the arrival in England of Charles I's nephew, the new Palatine Elector, Charles Louis, late in November 1635. The November 1635 news digest belatedly recounted details of the Protestant losses at Nordlingen and plainly showed that Peace of Prague, concluded in May 1635, made no provision for the restitution of the Palatinate.[4]

The reason for the government's reaction is not immediately obvious: a prayer for peace was entirely consistent with the foreign policy Charles had settled upon when, following long discussions with Sweden, he deter-

---

[1] *The German History*, Part 7 (1634), 70, STC23525.7.
[2] See pp. 232–5.
[3] An official translation of a treaty was permitted: *The forme of the agreement*, B&B (1634), STC23366.
[4] *The Modern History of the World*, Part 8 (1635), Section 2, 50–1, STC23525.9.

mined not to put his backing behind Gustavus Adolphus's successful military campaign in Germany. But by 1634 Charles was becoming frustrated by lack of progress in his alternative dealings with Spain for the restoration of the Palatinate. He issued his first writs for ship money that October. Specific instructions for the sheriffs went out on 3 December. Intending to strengthen the fleet, ship money was presented as a means of improving defences against piracy as well as the threats of continental neighbours. Charles hoped to give England a stronger negotiating hand and was silencing the press during a time of intense diplomatic activity. While the Prague articles in May 1635 demonstrated just how little England counted by this stage in the affairs of Europe (providing reason enough for a decision to delay its reporting in print in England for as long as possible), Charles was not about to accept this outcome. No longer so committed to peace, he explored a further option – the scope for an alliance with France. The strict embargo on war news only ended when the resulting offensive and defensive treaty with France was prepared. Then Monro, His Expedition (recounting his continental military experiences), a journal of Arundel's embassy to the Habsburgs (relating the experience of journeying through war-torn Germany), and the start of a new news series, The principall passages of Germany, Italy, France, were authorised for publication in early 1637 as part of a carefully orchestrated programme of publications to support and encourage military engagement in the Thirty Years War.[5]

It has been suggested that, had this treaty with France been ratified, it would have brought Charles's kingdoms fully into the Thirty Years War, in opposition to the Counter-Reformation advances of the Habsburgs, and there may have been no domestic conflicts.[6] Enlisted English soldiers would have been fighting in Germany alongside their volunteering Protestant neighbours and Swedish allies. But in 1637 the battle lines were formed instead, with many Scots released from Swedish service in Germany and supported by Swedish supplies shipped via the Baltic in opposition to Charles and his new Scottish Prayer Book. Meanwhile a wide range of London publications encouraged readers further in a belief that not enough had been done by Charles to support either his Palatine relatives or the Protestant cause.

This illustration of the interplay between high domestic politics, international relations and London news publication is just one of many that occurred throughout the 1620s and 1630s, and even into the 1640s. This book brings together these different spheres of interest, so often treated in isolation, demonstrating their interdependence. Throughout the period, events in the Thirty Years War played a far larger role in influencing readers,

5   Arber, Vol. 4, 343, 344, 345; R. Monro, Monro, His Expedition with the worthy Scots Regiment (1637); W. Crowne, A Journall… the Embassee of the Earle of Arundell to the Emperor of Germany (1637); Numb.1. The principall passages of (1637), STC4293.
6   K. Sharpe, The Personal Rule of Charles I (New Haven, CT and London, 1992), 825–8, 953–4.

parliaments and early Stuart decision-making than is generally recognised. Hans Werner has identified fifty-five plays, entertainments and masques with allusions to the Thirty Years War between 1620 and 1642, including ten that were entirely devoted to it, plus up to sixty works of prose and poetry. News coverage was extensive and informative, and surviving journals, commonplace books and the letters of news correspondents in England show that contemporaries took printed war news seriously. Successive failures to assume an effective role in the Thirty Years War, and efforts to resolve the crisis by engaging with Spain in negotiations to restore the Palatinate, undermined confidence in the Crown's commitment to Protestantism. This fuelled anxieties that at times verged upon paranoia about popish conspiracies at home and abroad, and resulted in a generation of soldiers and officers receiving military training and experience on the Continent as volunteers and mercenaries, primarily serving under Swedish, Danish and Dutch banners.[7]

Themes in recent historiography

Interest has grown in the formation of public opinion and what Jürgen Habermas described as the emergence of a 'public sphere', where information about contemporary events was exchanged and discussed. Habermas's work has spurred an upsurge in analysis and reflection on what constitute the essential criteria of a rational, critical and influential public sphere, making this topic steadily more popular and mainstream.[8]

---

[7] C. Hibbard, *Charles I and the Popish Plot* (Chapel Hill, NC, 1983); P. H. Wilson, *Europe's Tragedy: a History of the Thirty Years' War* (2009), 321–2; H. Werner, 'The Hector of Germainie, or The Palsgrave, Prime Elector* and Anglo-German Relations of Early Stuart England: The View from the Popular Stage', in *The Stuart Court and Europe: Essays in Politics and Political Culture*, ed. M. Smuts (Cambridge, 1996), 113; B. Donagan, 'Halcyon Days and the Literature of the War: England's Military Education before 1642', *PandP*, 147 (1995); A. Grosjean, *An Unofficial Alliance: Scotland and Sweden 1569–1654* (Leiden and Boston, MA, 2003), 56–71, 88–95; R. B. Manning, *Swordsmen: The Martial Ethos in the Three Kingdoms* (Oxford, 2003), 10–47, 67, 119, 128–9, 131 135; J. Ohlmeyer, *Civil War and Restoration in the Three Stuart Kingdoms: The Career of Randal MacDonnell, Marquis of Antrim, 1609–1683* (Cambridge, 1993), 154–87.
[8] J. Habermas, *The Structural Transformation of the Public Sphere: An Inquiry into a Category of Bourgeois Society*, trans. T. Burger (Cambridge, MA, 1989), especially 13–17, 20–1; T. C. W. Blanning, *The Culture of Power and the Power of Culture: Old Regime Europe 1660–1789* (Oxford, 2002); D. Freist, *Governed by Opinion; Politics, Religion and the Dynamics of Communication in Stuart London, 1637–45* (London and New York, 1997); M. Kishlansky, 'Turning Frogs into Princes', in *Political Culture and Politics in Early Modern England*, ed. S. D. Amussen and M. A. Kishlansky (Manchester, 1995); P. Lake, 'Constitutional Consensus and Puritan Opposition in the 1620s; Thomas Scott and the Spanish Match', *HJ*, 25 (1982); K. Sharpe, *Reading Revolutions: The Politics of Reading in*

Habermas concentrated upon the role of the Western European intellectual aristocracy, the bourgeoisie and middle classes, prompting questions
about the membership of these groups and their involvement in public debate.
Within this exploration, historians are now examining the characteristics of
the 'middling sort' in seventeenth-century England. Christopher Brooks has
described their distinctive urban culture and Barry Reay has helped place
the readership and market for newsbooks in its cultural context, drawing
out its political and economic relevance. News publishers, as traders and
entrepreneurs who served their apprenticeships in the Stationers' Company,
were also middling sorts operating within these cultural frameworks. Jonathan Barry has described their attitudes, seeing success and failure in terms
of the individual, with an emphasis on industry, thrift, self-discipline, and
most importantly, credit worthiness.[9]

Debate around the development of polarities in public opinion provides a
further context for the story of foreign news reporting. A Protestant version
of events, vital at the time to muster and retain support for resistance to the
Habsburgs, laid foundations for a story that was to have significant long-term
ramifications in Britain and across Europe. It underpinned the nineteenth-
century formation of a unified Protestant Germany and has subsequently
supplied a basis for Whig, Marxist and Habermasian arguments that link the
transformation of news with the transformation of political culture, leading
ultimately to the rise of liberal democracy.

There has been considerable progress in our understanding of the relationships between the dissemination of information and the formation of
public opinion. Manuscript news circulation has been explored along with
questions about the interplay between libels and the cheapest and most
popular publications of the period. This shows how oral news and print
were interrelated so that information could flow between the media, and
news could penetrate throughout all levels of society. Studies of cheap print
and distribution have demonstrated how all regions of Britain could be
connected. We can now appreciate the way and the extent that news travelled, and this has opened up the tantalising prospect that the whole of the
British Isles could have been reached with news of the Thirty Years War.[10]

Early Modern England (New Haven, CT, 2000); D. Zaret, 'Religion, Science and Printing
in the Public Spheres in Seventeenth-century England', in *Habermas and the Public
Sphere*, ed. C. Calhoun (Cambridge, MA and London, 1992).

[9] C. Brooks, 'Apprenticeship and Social Mobility and the Middling Sort', and J. Barry,
'Bourgeoise Collectivism? Urban Association and the Middling Sort', in *The Middling Sort
of People, Culture, Society, and Politics in England 1550–1800*, ed. J. Barry and C. Brooks
(Cambridge, 1991); B. Reay, *Popular Cultures in England 1550–1750* (1998).

[10] P. Croft, 'The Reputation of Robert Cecil: Libels, Political Opinion and Popular
Awareness in the Early Seventeenth Century', *Transactions of the Royal Historical
Society*, 6:1 (1991); P. Croft, 'Libels, Popular Literacy and Public Opinion in Early
Modern England', *Historical Research*, 68 (1995); T. Cogswell, 'Underground Verse and
the Transformation of Early Stuart Political Culture', in *Political Culture*, Amussen and

Historiographical point (handwritten marginal note)

Yet the role of the printed periodical news that covered the war has been relatively neglected. Whig historians suggested the early Stuart media was too censored to be effective. They told a traditional story of the triumph of the press over censorship and though revisionists challenged the Whig account of an escalating constitutional crisis in pre-Civil War England they also discounted the significance of the early press. Post-revisionists have since argued for a more nuanced approach but while this has fed into greater interest in exploring contemporary ephemeral publications such as pamphlets and ballads, it has not, so far, led to a significant growth in the study of foreign news reporting.[11] The dull and abbreviated texts of foreign newsbooks, the need to read many successive issues (scattered in a number of library collections) to detect story lines, and the need for a grasp of the broader European context, may have deterred many from paying them attention, particularly since, as Steven Pincus has suggested, English foreign policy in this period 'has more often been written off than written about'. However, this is changing: there is now a wide recognition that news reports generated excitement and foreign policy was widely discussed outside Parliament in the 1620s, and there is an appreciation of the way this played into anti-popery that was to remain a persistent concern throughout the early Stuart regime.[12] This account of the history of the periodical news reporting of the Thirty Years War is therefore both timely and relevant. Pursuing the

Kishlansky, 277–300; D. Underdown, *A Freeborn People* (1996), 19, 39, 50, 70–1; Love; Watt; A. McShane Jones, 'The Gazet in Metre; Or the Rhiming Newsmonger' The English Broadside Ballad as Intelligencer, a New Narrative', in Koopmans; P. Lake, 'Deeds Against Nature', and A. Bellamy, 'Raylinge Rhymes and Vaunting Verse', in *Culture and Politics in Early Stuart England*, ed. K. Sharpe and P. Lake (Basingstoke and London, 1994); Fox, 607–13, 616, 620; A. Fox, 'Ballads, Libels and Popular Ridicule in Jacobean England', *PandP*, 145 (1995); M. Spufford, *Small Books and Pleasant Histories, Popular Fiction and its Readership in Seventeenth Century England* (Cambridge, 1981); C. S. Clegg, *Press Censorship in Jacobean England* (Cambridge, 2001), especially Ch. 5; Levy, 13, 17, 31–4; H. Pierce, *Unseemly Pictures: Graphic Satire and Politics in Early Modern England* (New Haven, CT and London, 2008).

[11] Frank; Shaaber; M. A. Shaaber, 'The First English Newspaper', *Studies in Philology*, 29 (1932); Dahl; F. Dahl, 'Amsterdam – the Cradle of English Newspapers', *The Library*, 5:4 (1949); F. Dahl, *Amsterdam – the Earliest Newspaper Centre of Western Europe* (The Hague, 1939); F. Dahl, *Dutch Corantos 1618–1650, A Bibliography and an Introductory Essay on Seventeenth Century Stop Press News* (The Hague, 1946); Siebert; Lambert; S. Lambert, 'Coranto Printing in England', *JNandPH*, 8, (1992); Clegg, *Jacobean England*.

[12] S. Pincus, *Protestantism and Patriotism: Ideologies and the Making of English Foreign Policy, 1650–1668* (Cambridge, 1996), 1; Cogswell, 287–8, 325; T. Cogswell, 'The Politics of Propaganda: Charles I and the People in the 1620s', *JBS*, 29 (1990); T. Cogswell, 'The People's Love: The Duke of Buckingham and Popularity', in *Politics, Religion and Popularity in Early Stuart Britain*, ed. T. Cogswell, R. Cust and P. Lake (Cambridge, 2002); C. J. Sommerville, *The News Revolution in England: Cultural Dynamics of Daily Information* (New York and Oxford, 1996), 22–8; R. Cust, *The Forced Loan and English Politics 1626–28* (Oxford, 1989), 317; Hibbard, *Popish Plot*, 4.

story through to the Peace of Westphalia also opens a new line of enquiry into the role of the Thirty Years War in the English domestic context of the 1640s.

Malcolm Smuts has questioned the extent to which England was being 'pushed from behind' by the unfinished business of the Reformation and European religious wars. He points to the 'sense of impending danger' that haunted the Stuart succession and poisoned domestic relationships whenever the influence of Spain was arose. It led to mistrust of anyone at Court who appeared sympathetic to Madrid. His work reminds us of the highly cosmopolitan character of seventeenth-century court societies and demonstrates the ways in which in the late 1630s British politics became 'ominously linked to the larger conflict taking place on the Continent', identifying Charles and Henrietta Maria with Spanish interest. A next step is towards seeing England as an integral, if outlying, part of Europe, and a player and victim of the Thirty Years War. Jonathan Scott argues that the English were absorbed in continental affairs because England's troubles 'were part of, and cannot be understood apart from, the historical experience of Europe'. He has described a single European conflict where the last act was not the Peace of Westphalia but the execution of Charles I. English fear of popery spanned the century, crossed social and political boundaries and was only explicable in a European context.[13] Historians exploring events leading to the Civil War in their British context have also been drawn to a fully international perspective through a growing recognition of the economic, military and cultural relationships between Scotland and Ireland and various parts of Europe.[14] Many now emphasise the importance of political and religious beliefs in these relationships and recognise that the European war affected public opinion from 1618 and applied significant pressure on a government incapable of sustaining a war effort.[15]

This wider European perspective is most evident in the history of the politics of information since the study of the dynamics of communication

[13] M. Smuts, *Culture and Power in England 1585–1685* (1999), 5, 42, 48; M. Smuts, 'Religion, European Politics and Henrietta Maria's Circle, 1625–41', in *Henrietta Maria, Piety, Politics and Patronage*, ed. E. Griffey (Aldershot and Burlington, VT, 2008), 13, 28–33; J. Scott, *England's Troubles: Seventeenth Century English Political Instability in a European Context* (Cambridge, 2000), 15, 21, 27–9, 51, 54.

[14] Grosjean, *An Unofficial Alliance*; A. Grosjean and S. Murdoch, ed., *Scottish Communities Abroad in the Early Modern Period* (Leiden and Boston, MA, 2005); S. Murdoch, *Britain, Denmark-Norway and the House of Stuart, 1603–1660* (East Linton, 2003); D. Worthington, ed., *British and Irish Emigrants and Exiles in Europe 1603–1688* (Leiden and Boston, MA, 2010); S. Murdoch, 'James VI and the Formation of a Scottish-British Military Identity', in *Fighting for Identity: Scottish Military Experience c. 1550–1900*, ed. S. Murdoch and A. Mackillop (Leiden and Boston, MA, 2002), 19–24.

[15] D. Hirst, *England in Conflict 1603–1660, Kingdom, Community, Conflict* (1999); Cogswell, 28, 30, 310; J. Morrill, 'The Religious Context of the English Civil War', in *Nature of the English Revolution* (1993), 68; Reeve, 37–40, 62–5, 70–1.

involves tracking a process of information sharing from city to city, and country to country. By the late sixteenth century information spread the length and breadth of the Continent and in the first half of the seventeenth century everywhere in Europe experienced an increase in the availability of printed news. London was very much a part of a wider diplomatic community, linked to other capital cities; part of a wider trading community, connected through the ports of the Low Countries, the Baltic and the Mediterranean; and part of a confessional community based upon the Protestant brotherhood of churches in northern Europe, and through the Catholic community, to Antwerp, Madrid and Rome. The foreign policies of James and Charles (including both acts and omissions) contributed to the political and military confusion that perpetuated European conflict, allowing it to spread to bring in many nations. Britain was engaged in years of recruitment, wars with Spain and France and many embassies, until the tensions underlying its indecision and ineffectiveness triggered conflicts within the Stuart kingdoms. Meanwhile, the press provided almost weekly accounts of the progress of events and became a vehicle of involvement, along with the newsletters of merchants, army officers, intelligencers and diplomats and the comings and goings of volunteers, mercenaries, traders, migrants and embassies.

Thirty Years War news publications

As Counter-Reformation tensions grew in Europe and Catholic rulers went back on their agreements with Protestants, anxiety in Protestant communities created a significant market for news while the unfolding, geographically dispersed and complex events of the Thirty Years War provided the content. The Stuart Crown was involved from the beginning through Princess Elizabeth's marriage to Frederick of the Palatinate and his decision to accept the Bohemian Crown. From 1619, English readers were able to follow in print the arguments about the Habsburg succession that triggered his decision and, from 1620, there was recruiting in London for Frederick's cause as the champion of Protestantism.

James's attempts to negotiate were followed by his decision to call Parliament in 1621 and foreign powers were allowed to recruit directly into their armies. The drums beat repeatedly, particularly in Scotland and the southeast of England. The English middle classes, supportive of the Protestant cause in Europe and sympathetic to the plight of their princess, watched anxiously. News publications recounted a pertinent story at a time when many were concerned about the commitment and affiliations of the Crown and news coverage became so extensive that readers were able to follow events and relate what they read to their concerns about public affairs at home. For the stationers' trade in London keeping up with the demand for news came with a need to develop new skills of financial management, marketing and negotiation. As they quickly determined to aim for continuity of publication, they walked a tight rope to maintain a working relationship with the authorities. State papers and contemporary correspondence provide evidence that government was influential from an early stage. Foreign news publication was channeled into a series of licensed weekly periodicals run by a syndicate of five publishers from October 1622 with an impressive distribution network radiating out into the country. The format was changed from single newssheets, called 'corantos' after the Dutch publications they first came from, to small quarto books of sixteen or more pages that were called 'newsbooks' when the bibliographical groundwork was established in the 1930s and 1940s.[16] These reported on a wide range of events, initiated an exploration of editorial style, and prompted the development of methods of rapid news distribution. This syndicate was succeeded in 1624 by a partnership of the stationers Nathaniel Butter and Nicholas Bourne who continued approximately weekly periodical publication. They kept going despite lapses, long periods of unsuccessful Protestant campaigns, and the failure of government to engage effectively in the Thirty Years War, until October 1632.

Charles's initial militaristic response was short-lived and unsuccessful, but even after peace with Spain in 1630, many English, Welsh and Scots continued to enlist, especially in the Swedish army, while Catholics from Ireland served the Habsburgs, especially in the Army of Flanders. On the crest of the wave of successes of Gustavus Adolphus, greeted as the saviour of Protestantism in Europe, Butter and Bourne's weekly publications regained popularity and the partnership began a parallel, less frequent, series of highly successful and lengthy news journals named variously *The Swedish Intelligencer* and *The Continuation of the German History*.[17] It was these that were stopped in the mid-1630s. Then, from 1637, the names of these news digests included *Diatelesma* and *Modern History*, and they competed in London with works from other publishers, taking advantage of Charles renewed interest in a more adversarial foreign policy. But Charles's use of ship money, his dalliances and co-operation with Spain, combined with his policies of toleration towards Catholics and efforts to unify and beautify Anglican liturgy, changed the tone of debate. Questions in the early 1620s were about how effective and committed James was to his title as 'Defender' of the Protestant faith, and how much he was being strung along and duped by Gondomar, the Spanish ambassador. By the mid-1630s there were grounds for questioning whether Britain was experiencing the rolling back of Protestantism as witnessed elsewhere, and domestic affairs continued to be influenced much more than is generally recognised by the European conflict and by Charles's response.

[16] Plates, pp. 46, 126 and 132.
[17] Plate, p. 164.

At the end of 1638 Butter and Bourne were given permission to resume the publication of shorter, frequent, news updates. Their 'currantoes', as they were called at this time, were in a slightly larger than quarto format and were four-sided close translations of weekly publications from Frankfurt, Nuremberg and Amsterdam.[18] This gave a frequency of publication of up to three and sometimes four issues a week and a huge output of 200 issues in the first 15 months. In 1640 however, as Charles's troubles escalated, there was a decisive shift in the focus of public attention and the partnership was succeeded by a new generation of news publishers that emerged from the press reporting of the Long Parliament. All sides in the domestic conflicts of this period sought recognition and support from the Continent, and all feared the implications of hostile intervention from abroad. Reporting on the complex interactions of Thirty Years War diplomacy demanded a high level of skills and understanding. John Dillingham's *Moderate Intelligencer* emerged as the weekly publication that most effectively covered the concluding years of negotiations in Munster and Westphalia, and addressed concerns about the implications for Britain of armies disbanding.[19]

A total of more than 400 different periodicals, including reissues and new editions, have survived from London coverage of the Thirty Years War. To these we can add versions of the longer news digests of the 1630s, plus many sermons, plays, broadside ballads, pamphlets and the periodicals of the civil war years that reflected the European conflict. These can be read alongside our knowledge of what was happening, where and when, to place reporting and reactions in their context and to observe the extent to which timely and accurate information was reaching and being disseminated from London.

Little of the foreign news available to seventeenth-century readers was from primary sources though accounts from eyewitnesses became more readily available in the 1630s. Most printed news was compilations of relayed and reedited accounts of events. With improved access to archives in Germany we can now observe the way in which news was gathered, progressively edited and disseminated, with each city feeding the next. It reveals that the bibliographical approach adopted earlier in England, with its almost exclusive focus on a Dutch heritage, was too limiting. A new generation of European media historians are beginning to expand our understanding of the trade, including Paul Reis on news publication networking around the Baltic. Paul Arblaster has provided a European and Catholic perspective of the news trade in 1620s and 1630s, the sourcing of material, its printing and marketing. Several historians are now exploring relationships between the news industries in the Low Countries, London and Edinburgh and the way these reflected religious affiliations. Brendan Dooley and Sabrina Baron

---

[18] Plate, p. 244.
[19] Plate, p. 262.

have brought together articles intended to begin the study of the European political information business using an interdisciplinary approach.[20] This information can now be added to what we know about London and its news networks to create a more complete picture of the early trade.

This book explores the impact the Thirty Years War had through the story of the development of news reporting in London. Many parts of the British Isles had direct links with the Continent. Ports along the south and east coast were in communication with France, the Netherlands and Baltic. They carried correspondence, traded news and imported paper and often illicit printed materials too. Edinburgh booksellers and clergy had links, particularly with the churches and book trade in Amsterdam, Leiden, Veere, Middelburg and Antwerp. A direct connection with George Veseler, the first Dutch printer to have translations of his corantos marketed in London, meant the Scots were not dependent upon London for a supply of Dutch corantos. Spain was more influential in parts of Ireland. Printed material arrived in Ireland from Antwerp, Louvain and Paris as well as from London via Bristol and sometimes Chester, while Wales was connected to the London and Oxford book trades via carriers.[21] However, the focus of this book is on how the trade evolved and how London played its part in news communication networks, and how war news was received by the printing trade, customers and government. As much of the material and evidence of the spread of views in correspondence and commonplace books is from English sources, this English dimension is inevitably reflected in the chapters that follow.

Chapter 1 explores the appetite for and interest in news, the scope and constraints of methods for communicating contemporary events by the early seventeenth century, and the way the start of war was reported. Chapter 2

---

[20] Ries; P. Arblaster, *Antwerp and the World: Richard Verstegan and the International Culture of the Catholic Reformation* (Leuven, 2004); P. Arblaster, 'London, Antwerp and Amsterdam: Journalistic Relations in the First Half of the Seventeenth Century', in *The Bookshop of the World: The Role of the Low Countries in the Book-trade 1473–1941*, ed. L. Hellinga, A. Duke, J. Harskamp and T. Hermans ('t Goy-Houten, The Netherlands, 1999); G. Leth, 'A Protestant Public Sphere: The Early European Newspaper Press', in *Annual* (1993); K. L. Sprunger, *Trumpets from the Tower* (Leiden, New York and Koln, 1994); DandB.

[21] A. J. Mann, *The Scottish Book Trade 1500–1720: Print, Commerce and Print Control in Early Modern Scotland* (East Linton, 2000), 67–84, 90; J. Bevan, 'Scotland', in Barnard, 688–9, 697; Sprunger, *Trumpets*, 28–37, 39, 102, 108, 115–7, 125, 157–64; D. Horsbroch, '"Wish You Were Here?" Scottish Reactions to "Postcards" Home from the "Germane Warres"', in *Scotland and the Thirty Years' War, 1618–1648*, ed. S. Murdoch (Leiden and Boston, MA, 2001), 246–50, 253–5; R. Welch, 'The Book in Ireland', in Barnard, 707–16; P. H. Jones, 'Wales', in Barnard, 729–33; G. Long, *Books Beyond the Pale: Aspects of the Provincial Book Trade in Ireland before 1850* (Dublin, 1996), 3–4, 9; J. Kerrigan, *Archipelagic English: Literature, History and Politics 1603–1707* (Oxford, 2008), 7, 46, 48, 71–6, 225, 227.

provides the European news press context where information was available through an array of periodical publications. They were usually weekly, printed newsbooks and newssheets covering a miscellany of the latest news reports. These appeared in many cities under a variety of contemporary names, including 'relations', 'avisos', 'corantos' and 'zeitungen', and are now referred to generically as 'newspapers'. This chapter looks at what we now know of these sources and assesses the extent to which this material became available in London, its scope, strengths and weaknesses as a source of information, and its growth and diversification as the war progressed.

Chapter 3 shows how periodical news coverage in the English language began. Reviewing the evidence and the debates of bibliographers in the 1930s and 1940s in the light of current knowledge of the European and domestic print industries, it has been possible to provide an up-to-date and more definitive account. This explores the competition, dynamism and innovation of the early period and explains events leading to the licensing arrangements that emerged through relationships between the publishers, the Stationers' Company and the Crown. It includes the reaction of James I to rising public interest in foreign affairs, leaving the broader study of government involvement in the news press to Chapters 7 to 9.

To address questions about political awareness and the evolution of public opinion as England headed toward Civil War, the significance of the periodicity needs be better understood. Chapter 4 expands upon the theme of the pivotal role of publishers in overcoming the unique copy supply, labour, distribution and financial issues that accompanied periodical publication. It explores prints runs and the distribution network to establish the scale, financial viability and reach of the trade to its readers. To maintain periodicity, production and distribution had to be effective. Only when seeing these together is it possible to fully appreciate the significance of the foreign news. Getting these right meant that people everywhere could become aware of the Thirty Years War and start to reflect upon issues of foreign policy. This chapter argues that the innovations of this period merit greater recognition if we are to move beyond seeing the periodicals of the 1620s and 1630s simply as precursors to the domestic newsbooks of the 1640s.[22]

---

[22] J. Raymond, 'Irrational, Impractical and Unprofitable: Reading the News in Seventeenth Century Britain', in *Reading, Society and Politics in Early Modern England*, ed. K. Sharpe and S. N. Zwicker (Cambridge, 2003); J. Raymond, 'The Newspaper, Public Opinion, and the Public Sphere in the Seventeenth Century', and Atherton, in *News, Newspapers, and Society in Early Modern Britain*, ed. J. Raymond (London and Portland, OR, 1999); F. J. Levy, 'How Information Spread among the Gentry, 1550–1640', *JBS*, 21 (1982); Raymond, 7–9, 12–3, 90–4; J. Raymond, *Pamphlets and Pamphleteering in Early Modern Britain* (Cambridge, 2003), 128–38; M. C. Frearson, 'The Distribution and Readership of London Corantos in the 1620's', in *Serials and their Readers 1620–1914* (Winchester and New Castle, 1993); M. C. Frearson, 'London Corantos in the 1620s', *Annual* (1993), 1–25.

Part 2 explores the way editors provided new markets with an education in European politics, the Counter-Reformation and its military implications, and how their readers responded. Editors struggled to overcome the poor reputation of their trade and to substantiate their claim to be the purveyors of 'one truth' and the authority on events as they unfolded. But their news supply was uncertain, rumours abounded and events in Europe were repeatedly challenging established concepts of harmony and order.

As Sharpe argues, a full history of the politics of the English Renaissance state must be based on the study of reading in the context of political culture, addressing how texts were produced, disseminated and received, how they were written and read if we are to understand how a society that appeared to speak in harmony divided in violent conflict. He has shown how social change and reading gave people the opportunity to construct their own interpretations and values, and how Protestants and Catholics defined themselves through their distinctive modes of reading. For Protestants, 'the journey to faith was a continuous process of interiorising the word' and this involved strenuous and purposeful reading and writing.[23] I do not attempt to deconstruct news texts for their symbolic and cultural meaning, nor to delve into the early seventeenth-century world view and philosophy of knowledge, but I demonstrate and assess the significance of the foreign news reporting as reflected through the comments of its readers and of editors responding the reactions of their customers.[24]

Part 3 reflects upon the way this new understanding fits within, and changes, our perspective the high politics of the 1620s and 1630s and considers whether it contributes towards an explanation of the fears and distrust of the monarchy by 1640. It investigates relationships with the authorities from 1622 until, in the mid-1640s, John Dillingham established *The Moderate Intelligencer*. These chapters break new ground in their account of how increasing literacy, licensing, unfolding diplomatic relations and policy influenced the content of the news and contributed to the development of public opinion. They pose questions about how well James and Charles apprehended the nature of the threat to their position that events on the Continent created. Both the Crown and the publishers were influential in the production of the news. This account highlights pragmatism and the part played by trial and error as the relationship evolved in the face

---

[23] Sharpe, *Reading Revolutions*, ix, 5, 8, 15, 19; K. Sharpe, *Remapping Early Modern England: The Culture of Seventeenth-Century Politics* (Cambridge, 2000), 13, 25; Sharpe and Zwicker, *Reading, Society*, 8–11.

[24] J. P. Sommerville, *Royalists and Patriots, Politics and Ideology in England 1603–1640* (London and New York, 1999); K. Sharpe, 'Ideas and Politics in Early Stuart England', *History Today*, 38 (1988); K. Sharpe, 'A Commonwealth of Meanings, Languages, Analogues, Ideas and Politics', in *Politics and Ideas in Early Stuart England* (London, 1989); B. J. Shapiro, *A Culture of Fact: England 1550–1720* (Ithaca, NY and London, 2000).

of a completely new genre, social and political phenomenon. It also shows the extent to which the Crown's attitude to the press was shaped by foreign policies, and the way the Crown and the publishers worked together when their interests coincided, concluding with how the foreign news trade influenced and was integrated into news publishing in the 1640s.

This book follows the story of periodical news publication through both sloughs and periods of heightened interest in the Thirty Years War, offering three decades of print history alongside a thematic development of issues that interwove the domestic and international concerns of this period. Rapid transformation of the media in the early 1620s was tested in the fire of Charles I's confused foreign policies, then evolved in the 1640s into a vociferous press which played a critical role in print battles to sway public opinion in the Civil Wars. We see government involvement with the press and censorship were reflections of the difficulties in steering foreign policy against a backdrop of fiscal and military constraints. This account sheds light upon a range of debates about news sources, accuracy and truth, and the role of the news in political education. News penetrated the country, cutting across social ranks as issues, could be passed by hand, read aloud and discussed, contributing to an expanding awareness of wider European struggles and perpetuating long-standing fears of Catholic plots and Spanish expansionism without exposing the thinking behind events whether in the form of potentially counter-balancing diplomatic considerations or evolving mercantile concerns.

Part One

The Press and the Trade

1

An Appetite for News?
Media and the London News Market
before the Battle of White Mountain

The Thirty Years War began at a time when communications about contemporary issues were growing and diversifying. Newsletter writing became a profession for some dedicated correspondents who provided regular and detailed accounts of recent events, while pamphlet publication expanded. Political criticism circulated, often orally, through verse libels, gossip, rumours, sermons and plays, but also in correspondence, satirical woodcut illustrations and broadsheet ballads. In the sixteenth and the early seventeenth centuries, the word 'news' was no better established than a variety of synonyms, including 'tydings' and 'relations', and was not as clearly defined as it is today, but by the start of the crisis in Bohemia in 1618, news interest was widespread. This chapter describes communications extending outwards from London through the British Isles and shows how political awareness increasingly permeated all levels of society. It begins an exploration of how this was transforming the nature of public discussion of current events and how public interest in the affairs of the Stuart Princess Elizabeth and her husband, Frederick of the Palatinate, turned foreign news coverage into a growing business venture for the stationers' trade in London, leaving a more detailed analysis of the news trade relationship between London and other European cities to the next chapter.

News might begin its circulation in St Paul's Cathedral and churchyard, at St Paul's Cross, the inns, taverns and barber's shops around the City, in Westminster, or at the market places of provincial towns and cities. Chapmen, hawkers and pedlars travelled the country selling smaller books and communicating news, door to door and through inns, markets and fairs. It is difficult to establish just how far off main routes and into the most remote areas of the British Isles they went, though there is evidence of travellers reaching many scattered rural communities throughout England and journeying to and from Scotland and Wales. There is also evidence of trade with bookstores in the far north of England and Edinburgh. The west of England could supply material to customers across the Welsh border and to Ireland; though communications by sea were as likely to be important for Scotland, Ireland and Wales with watermen on the Thames acting as carriers of news from London to Scotland and back.[1]

An enquiry after news was a customary greeting at all levels of society: throughout the early modern period, travellers and traders met on the highways, roads and rivers, at fairs and markets, in alehouses and hostelries. They were greeted with the question, 'What news?' and would relay whatever news and rumour had come to their attention. News penetrated every level of society with people speaking of it at every opportunity and passing on truth and rumour alike. News could come from remote and fantastic places and it seems many people were willing to believe all manner of things were possible. Nonetheless, people could be furnished with up-to-date information and form quite knowledgeable opinions.[2]

Communication by word of mouth, not unlike a continuous Chinese whisper, could spread misinformation and lead to disturbance of the peace and the distress of individuals through defamation and seditious libel. In 1625 Francis Bacon summarised, 'Libels and licentious discourses against the state ... and ... false news often running up and down to the disadvantage of the state ... are amongst the signs of troubles.'[3] Much of the evidence for interest in news comes from the testimonies of those indicted for sedition before courts such as the quarter sessions and assizes. Some of the cases show the hurt and injury a libel could do.[4]

In the essentially oral society of Tudor England political verse and comment could circulate readily by word of mouth, through drama, singing and reading aloud. Manuscript sheets could be posted in public places, handed out at markets and other busy locations, and shared in social groups. Printing provided the maximum form of publicity. Anyone could participate in the production and dissemination of libellous verses: the illiterate could work up a libellous song in an alehouse and get someone else to write it down to spread a story beyond their immediate neighbourhood, while

[1] J. Taylor, *Taylor his Travels ... to ... Prague* (1620), A2, STC23802; A. Fox, *Oral and Literate Culture in England 1500–1700* (Oxford, 2000), 342–4, 346–9, 359–61, 353, 364, 398–9; D. Freist, *Governed by Opinion; Politics, Religion and the Dynamics of Communication in Stuart London, 1637–45* (London and New York, 1997), 110–5; M. Spufford, *Small Books*, Ch. 5; J. Kerrigan, *Archipelagic English: Literature, History and Politics 1603–1707* (Oxford, 2008), 48; B. Reay, *Popular Cultures in England 1550–1750* (New York and Harlow, Essex, 1998), 48–50.

[2] E. H. Shagan, 'Rumours and Popular Politics in the Reign of Henry VIII', in *The Politics of the Excluded, c.1500–1850*, ed. T. Harris (Basingstoke and New York, 2001), 30–59; Fox, *Oral*, 339–41, 345, 352–3, 366; Fox, 612–6, Freist, *Governed*, 177.

[3] Ibid., 609; Fox, *Oral*, 335, 337; A. Bellany, 'The Embarrassment of Libels: Perceptions and Representations of Verse Libelling in Early Stuart England', in *The Politics of the Public Sphere in Early Modern England*, ed. P. Lake and S. Pincus (Manchester, 2007), 145–7; F. Bacon, *The Works of Francis Bacon*, 6 (1874), ed. J. Spedding, R. L. Ellis and D. D. Heath, 407.

[4] Fox, *Oral*, 305, 313, 315.

some of the best writers of the day used verse to add topical satire to stage productions. Cogswell has commented on libels and verse having 'all the delicacy and literary merit of modern graffiti' while acknowledging them as 'a remarkable vehicle for the dissemination of political attitudes', with a frequent focus on the sexual and scandalous sides of Stuart politics. The victims of these libels similarly resorted to the courts resulting in extensive documentation for a considerable body of material that, because of its ephemeral nature, could have otherwise disappeared with trace. The veracity of much of the content might well have been questionable, but Bellany has noted how contemporaries were 'fascinated and politically engaged by them' and 'vaunting verse' found its place in the commonplace books of gentry alongside pamphlet reports and other material. Colcough, for example, traced the work of one poet, John Hoskyns, in people's collections and concluded that commonplace books were used to amass opinion and information 'something like a tool of political analysis', while his study of the commonplace book of Robert Horn, a Shropshire rector, shows the vigour with which Horn gathered contemporary material on the Spanish match. Sharpe's study of Sir William Drake's records of his reading of classical and Renaissance texts demonstrates how Drake revisited texts time and again to shape his thinking on current events. Readers reflected and sifted. Probably most could distinguish good verse from bad, and recognise serious interventions, false charges and legitimate accusations. They could form their own judgement.[5]

Official voices were also heard: proclamations read out in market places and churches could provide vehicles for pronouncements and official news reports, advice on new laws and taxes.[6] By reaching all parishes, sermons had potentially large audiences, and appeals for the poor and for discharged soldiers were delivered from pulpits. The Elizabethan regime was increasingly willing to provide information on military matters in sermons such as *An Homelie against Disobedience and Wylfull Rebellion* (1596) and *A Comfort against the Spaniard* (1596). There were many Jacobean sermons on the sanctity of kings and James used the pulpit to expound his *Book of Sports* in

[5] Watt, 14–23, 30–3, 116–9; P. Lake and M. Questier, *Antichrist's Lewd Hat* (New Haven, CT, 2002), 502–3, 695; Fox, *Oral*, 42, 303, 306–10, 325, 333, 385–6; A. Bellany, '"Raylinge Rhymes and Vaunting Verse": Libellous Politics in Early Stuart England, 1603–1628', in Lake, 285–6, 290–2, 296, 309; T. Cogswell, *The Blessed Revolution: English Politics and the Coming of War 1621–24* (Cambridge, 1989), 325; A. Fox, 'Ballads, Libels and Popular Ridicule in Jacobean England', *PandP*, 145 (1995), 49–52, 54–7, 61, 69–71; Bellany, 'The Embarrassment', 158–62; K. Sharpe, *Reading Revolutions: The Politics of Reading in Early Modern England* (New Haven, CT, 2000), 239–49, 265, 269, 318; D. Colclough, *Freedom of Speech in Early Stuart England* (Cambridge, 2005), 196–250.

[6] K. Sharpe, 'The Kings's Writ: Royal Authors and Royal Authority in Early Modern England', in *Culture and Politics*, ed. Sharpe and Lake, 117; K. Sharpe, *Remapping Early Modern England: The Culture of Seventeenth-Century Politics* (Cambridge, 2000), 141; Fox, *Oral*, 41, 349.

1618. Sermons delivered before assizes and elections were often about issues of concern, calling listeners to act for the common good.[7] But the purpose of a sermon was primarily to provide instruction and invoke godly behaviour. As today, preachers generally used news in their sermons to prove points, inspire an emotional response from the congregation or inform prayers.

Like news exchanged with passers-by, songs and verses, sermons were limited as a means of communicating contemporary events: to keep a congregation up to date on a regular basis, preachers needed first to receive news regularly. Increased demand for information was, by the late sixteenth century, having an effect upon the book trade. London was growing and living standards were rising. A growth in spending power was creating a consumer society in which the 'middling sort' emulated the lifestyles of higher social classes. With more disposable income they had more access to written material and the cost of printed works was falling in real terms. Cressy's analysis of signatures suggested that by the 1640s male literacy in London was as high as seventy to eighty percent and female literacy up to twenty percent. Debate has suggested that, since reading was taught before writing and writing was a poor indicator of the ability to read, figures based on signatures may be viewed as minima. Women were especially likely to be able to read though not write. We are now fairly confident that there was a hierarchy closely associated with trades, social and economic position so that, within London, all but the poorest men could read, including tradesmen, craftsmen and artisans. These became patrons of cheap print. Of course, this means that while we have evidence of reading from the most educated levels of society where they participated in correspondence or recorded their reading in journals and commonplace books, there were large numbers of others who read or heard news but left little evidence.[8]

---

[7] G. Davies, 'English Political Sermons 1603–1640', *HLQ*, 3 (1939), 4, 7; M. Maclure, *The St Paul's Cross Sermons 1534–1642*, 1 (Toronto and Oxford, 1958), 7–8; C. Hill, *Puritanism and Revolution* (1958), 262; G. Davies, *The Early Stuarts 1603–1660* (Oxford, 1959), 76; D. Randall, *Credibility in Elizabethan and Early Stuart Military News* (2008), 31, 45; K. Sharpe, *Image Wars; Promoting Kings and Commonwealths in England, 1603–1660* (New Haven, CT and London, 2010), 54–7; R. Cust, 'The "Public Man" in Late Tudor and Early Stuart England', in *The Politics*, ed. Lake and Pincus, 123–6; T. Claydon, 'The Sermon, the "Public Sphere" and the Political Culture of Late Seventeenth Century England', in *The English Sermon Revised: Religion, Literature and History, 1600–1750*, ed. L. A. Ferrell and P. McCullough (Manchester, 2000), 212–17.

[8] D. Cressy, *Literacy and Social Order: Reading and Writing in Tudor and Stuart England* (Cambridge, 1980); D. Cressy. 'Literacy in Context: Meaning and Measurement in Early Modern England', in *Consumption and the World of Goods*, ed. J. Brewer and R. Porter (1993), 312, 315–6; K. Thomas, 'The Meaning of Literacy in Early Modern England', in *The Written Word: Literacy in Transition*, ed. G. Baumann (Oxford, 1986), 97–131; Fox, 'Ballads, Libels', 60; M. Spufford, 'First Steps in Literacy: The Reading and Writing of the Humblest Seventeenth-century Spiritual Autobiographers', *Social History*, 4 (1979), 407–435.

Beyond London, the populations of England, Scotland and Wales were rural and thinly dispersed with a few cities that were growing. Literacy was increasing more slowly, with perhaps thirty percent of males and ten percent of females able to read. It is more difficult to assess spending power, but we know the dependence of the economy on agriculture meant change was only gradual and linked with increased economic activity in concentrations of population. It seems that, for many, wages lagged behind rises in the cost of food through the sixteenth century. Sudden crises continued to have marked effects upon the economy, including plagues and failed harvests, creating an unpredictable, stop-go economy for non-essential goods like print. To James Raven these underlying conditions explain why book demand grew fastest among the middling and propertied classes. Recovery in the seventeenth century from price inflation and redistribution within the economy benefited the gentry and some yeomanry first, so that a growing book market was 'sited in a landscape of sturdy farmhouses and coaching inns, new town houses and confident city and country gentlemen, burghers and tradesmen'.[9]

As the range of printed material grew, it permeated popular culture. Ballads especially bridged social groups and blurred the boundaries between oral and literate expression. Information that began as gossip could be taken into a letter or a printed text, then passed back into oral circulation through being read aloud in alehouses, market places and in homes. Songs about local events and people could be passed on through a community, then find their way into a printed broadside ballad and then spread more widely. Printed and other written sources continually supplemented and stimulated the oral circulation of news. Neighbours copied out and borrowed letters and rural artisans read news to others. By the end of the sixteenth century because news and current affairs could be spread by reading out reports, through pictures, verse and song and it could shape the attitudes of all levels of society, so that no one lived entirely beyond the reach of the written and printed word.[10]

Broadsheet ballads and proclamations were printed on one side of a folio sheet and were ideal for transporting around the countryside by carriers and for posting in public places. Ballads with woodcut images were probably among the first printed texts to reach cottages of artificers and husbandmen. Reading aloud was the custom, and Scribner suggests that 'looking was given at least as much weight as reading', 'creating a situation of oral interchange' with pictures and their interpretation as a focal point. But while there was

[9]   J. Raven, 'The Economic Context', in Barnard, 572–5.

[10]   J. Barry, 'Literacy and Literature in Popular Culture: Reading and Writing in Historical Perspective', in *Popular Culture in England c1500–1850*, ed. T. Harris (1995), 81–2; Fox, *Oral*, 19, 340–1, 44, 50, 301–02, 322–4.

a Jacobean upsurge in the woodcut trade, the picture was not used on the same large scale as in Germany.[11]

It is often difficult to draw political and social conclusions from English ballads because of difficulties in dating them and placing them in context. Most were not entered into the Stationers' Company registers, so these only tell us something of their sporadic production and reflect some of the contemporary issues that caught the imagination of the public. Angela McShane noted that we have a record of about 10,000 ballads printed in the seventeenth century (extant or known titles), but this is only a minimum. They had four traditional topics: royal events, war, treason and threats to Protestantism at home and abroad. For example, ten ballads on the accession of James I were recorded in the register, the deaths of Prince Henry and Anne of Denmark were covered, as was the marriage of Elizabeth and Frederick. Nine ballads were registered on the Gunpowder Plot and these proved so successful that they were produced until the beginning of the eighteenth century. They mocked, explained and entertained using events that were already known through other news media as exemplars of wider truths or as warnings.[12]

London also developed a market for ephemeral, cheap print, about miracles, monsters, witches and murders. Moralistic pamphlets, providential news and prodigy pamphlets were sold alongside heavily stylised and predictable stories of murder, retribution and repentance. Many aimed to shock, titillate with the bizarre, bloodthirsty and gruesome accounts, while censuring deviant behaviours and arguing that sin must be controlled. News of court pageantry was also popular. Pamphlets, for example, reported the awarding of honours and royal entertainments, with detailed descriptions of all the clothes worn and banners displayed, and lists of all the noblemen in attendance. Together, crime, pageant, wonders and disaster reports accounted for around a quarter of the total of surviving single subject pamphlets between 1513 and 1640.[13]

---

11 T. Watt, 'Publisher, Pedlar, Pot-Poet: The Changing Character of the Broadside Trade, 1550–1640', in *Spreading the Word, the Distribution of Print 1550–1850*, ed. R. Myers and M. Harris (Winchester and Delaware, 1998); Watt, 131, 147, 149; R. W. Scribner, *For the Sake of Simple Folk: Popular Propaganda for the German Reformation* (Oxford, 1994/2000), 3, 6; *The Shirburn Ballads 1585–1616*, ed. A. Clark (Oxford, 1907).

12 R. C. Simmons, 'ABCs, Almanacs, Ballads, Chapbooks, Popular Piety and Textbooks', in Barnard, 510; Watt, 143; A. McShane Jones, '"The Gazet in Metre; Or the Rhiming Newsmonger": The English Broadside Ballad as Intelligencer, a New Narrative', in Koopmans, 136–8, 144, 146.

13 Watt, 264–6; S. Clark, *The Elizabethan Pamphleteers* (1983); A. Walsham, *Providence in Early Modern England* (Cambridge, 1999); P. Lake, 'Deeds Against Nature: Cheap Print, Protestantism and Murder in Early Seventeenth-Century England', in *Culture and Politics*, ed. Sharpe and Lake, 258–62; Lake and Questier, *Antichrist's Lewd Hat*, 3–4, 12–13, 123, 352, 367; R. Streckfus, 'News before Newspapers', *Journalism and Mass Communication Quarterly*, 75:1 (1998), 88.

Printed pamphlets of news, sermons and polemic tracts could be hawked through the streets of London, or taken out into the country by carriers for sale, or enclosed with a letter and circulated among friends. The length of pamphlets varied up to about 50,000 words and these were potentially of more interest to the better educated, as they were more difficult to read and to understand than broadsides, particularly if they were in a roman type-face rather than blackletter print which the least literate found easier to read. They could also be more expensive, at perhaps two or three pence a copy rather than one penny. Print runs might be smaller, three hundred to five hundred copies rather than a thousand or two thousand copies, more typical of a ballad. Lake and Questier have suggested, however, that the more popular 'providentialised news pamphlets' could have had print runs of more than 1500. They explored their relationship with the market for theatre and sermons and showed how the stories moved from one genre to another, using similar material and appealing to the same broad audiences, competing with one another for a share of the limited expendable income available to the bulk of their audiences.[14]

Many tracts were published at the instigation of interested parties. The Crown and others, such as the East India Company, would publicise partic-ular events with the motive for publication often stated in the text. Offi-cial publications would usually come from the presses of the king's printer, including texts of state papers and treaties with foreign powers. Royal speeches, delivered in Parliament, were released to the press. Increasingly, James's decisions were justified in print; for example, he explained his deci-sion to execute Raleigh in 1618, though care was taken to emphasise that there was no obligation to give any account.[15]

Contemporary material from the Continent reached London, along with a wide range of books both in their original languages and in translation. Texts of foreign treaties, tracts apparently printed as pleas for assistance by distressed allies, reports of embassies and state occasions also appeared. Although generally favouring the Protestant cause, most translations of material originally published in other countries can be regarded as having been published in London primarily for commercial benefit. In the absence of evidence to suggest there was politically motivated financial support we must assume that availability and saleability were the chief considerations of their publishers and that they found the trade both convenient and prof-itable since such large numbers of proclamations, manifestos, edicts, narra-

[14] Lake and Questier, *Antichrist's Lewd Hat*, 14 fn. 19, 336, 359, 360–1, 377–8, 483, 502–3, 714.
[15] K. F. Pantzer, 'Printing the English Statutes, 1484–1640: Some Historical Implications', in K. E. Carpenter, *Books and Society in History* (1983), 69–99; Sharpe, *Image Wars*, 17–50; D. Zaret, *Origins of Democratic Culture: Printing, Petitions, and the Public Sphere in Early-modern England* (Princeton, NJ, 2000), 47–9, 53–5, 67; C. S. Clegg, *Press Censorship in Caroline England* (Cambridge, 2008), 15–16.

tives and polemical treatises translated from French and Dutch sources have survived. Together with reports of wars, sea battles, exploration and travel, they account for almost half of surviving Tudor and early Stuart pamphlets.[16]

Printed news of foreign events available in Elizabeth's reign, included items from Ireland, the Netherlands, France, Vienna, Hungary, Lithuania, Turkey and Spain, and there was a continuous interest in military news, including wars with the Turks, English involvement in the Netherlands 1566–1604 and the civil wars in France 1589–93. England's entry into war with Spain in 1585 was an additional spur to news production. Military news was communicated through all of the media, and the reporting of rituals such as hanging ensigns and celebrating victories (through discharges of cannons, ringing bells and thanksgiving) provided a range of familiar symbolic activities that gave credibility to news.[17]

John Wolfe stands out as a printer and publisher who, towards the end of the sixteenth century, took the foreign news trade to a different level. Wolfe had travelled and worked abroad. He maintained contacts in Italy and France and had connections with Gabriel Harvey that gave him access to Dutch news. He was a prolific printer and two-thirds of his publications were news translations. From 1594 he was appointed printer to the City of London. The English Crown's concerns about internal division in France after the assassination of Henry III and English intervention in the wars between the Netherlands, France and Spain provided opportunities to work in co-operation with Burghley and Walsingham to print news of events, particularly in France. Wolfe's work gave English readers what they were most likely to want, including news of Henry IV being supported by English soldiers, the villainy of the Guises, the Spanish threat, and flattery of the English and their queen, but included nothing of Leicester's unsuccessful Dutch expedition or the conversion of Henry IV. In true entrepreneurial spirit, if Catholic material was sufficiently interesting, it was published. The frequency and volume of his foreign news publications in the 1580s and 1590s do not however qualify him to be counted as the publisher of the first English newspapers. He did not achieve periodicity and his pamphlets and tracts lacked the principal distinguishing characteristic of corantos and newsbooks, variety of content.[18]

Occasionally, newsbooks appeared with a more varied content consisting of summaries, or extracts, from letters from a variety of sources. In 1595,

---

[16] Sharpe, *Reading*, 311–15; Streckfus, 'News', 88.

[17] N. Mears, *Queenship and Political Discourse in the Elizabethan Realms* (Cambridge, 2005), 149–52, 155–6; Streckfus, 'News', 85; Randall, *Credibility*, 8, 10, 13, 24–8.

[18] L. F. Parmelee, 'Printers, Patrons, Readers and Spies: Importation of French Propaganda in Late Elizabethan England', *Sixteenth Century Journal*, 25 (1994), 855, 858–60, 869; C. C. Huffman, *Elizabethan Impression: John Wolfe and his Press* (New York, 1940), Ch. 3; D. B. Woodfield, *Surreptitious Printing in England 1550–1640* (New York, 1973), 6–7; Levy, 17–18, 20, 23–4, 27, 31.

Newes from Rome, Venice, and Vienna, touching the … proceedings of the Turkes against … Austria, appeared in London published by Thomas Gosson, with a picture of a soldier on horseback at the front and subtitles throughout the text indicating the source of a variety of reports. It is interesting, not only because it so closely foreshadows the newsbooks that were to appear in the 1620s, but also because of its Catholic origin. Similarly, in 1597, *Newes from … Spaine, Antwerpe, Collin, Venice …* was printed by Valentine Sims. *A Relation of all matters passed … since March last to the present 1614* was published in London that year and translated from *Mercurius Gallobelgicus* from Cologne.[19] None, however, provided any sustained periodical reporting of news.

For regular and consistent coverage of events, the well-established way of transmitting news and views was by correspondence. Writing newsletters was a flourishing activity. The news and gossip exchanged by John Chamberlain and Dudley Carlton is probably the best-known example and remains a familiar historical resource.[20] Some letters were simply from one friend or relative to another and included news from time to time but many regularly corresponded with friends in distant parts for the sake of the news they could obtain. In reply, they sent news they had from other sources, such as merchants and political figures. Some had formal arrangements: with a continuing responsibility came a need to build contacts and check reliability.

In addition, the separates business involved the reproduction and distribution of political documents, state papers, polemical tracts and reports of parliamentary proceedings in manuscript copies in such large quantities that many have survived. Similarly, some letters may have had several hundred copies in circulation. Sabrina Baron suggests this medium had a capacity to generate two to five hundred copies of a letter and that writers could provide a weekly service for a cost of about £5 a year. It was a profitable business that continued to thrive long after the advent of printed news, as did the established practice of correspondence between gentlemen. Writers could include material of interest to those in power or near to circles of power but for which there was not sufficient demand to justify printing. A large body of anti-court material was given wide circulation during the early Stuart period for commercial reasons with many accounts appearing twice, first as separates then in compilations. Harold Love identified a further type of scribal publication, where a text continued to multiply until interest in it failed: the 'process of multiplication would be driven by cultural energies quite as powerful as those which sustained the printed text'. The motive could be ideological or to trade one manuscript for another. User publi-

19 *Newes from Rome* (1595), STC21294; *Newes from divers countries* (1597), STC18504.5; *A Relation of all matters* (1614), STC20862.
20 E. Thomson, *The Chamberlain Letters* (1965); *Chamberlain.*

cation rested on agreement between the copier and recipient and copies travelled through networks based on social groupings and common interests. A 'scribal community' could include groups from the Court, officials, the aristocracy, gentry, merchants, members of professions such as the law, military, church and navy. The Elizabethan Court acted as a hub for news connected to networks around ambassadors, with St Paul's acting as another centre for news and other networks in Lombard Street. From these, oral news, pamphlets and broadsides spread news as far as Norfolk, Cornwall, Shrewsbury, Wales and Ireland through networks of correspondents, neighbours, friends, parish ministers, merchants, booksellers and pedlars.[21]

These communities were also important for the circulation of printed news and for the dissemination of news from England to the rest of Europe. Their members shared the characteristics of political interest, literacy and a determination to keep abreast of the news through the exchange of information and they used manuscript and print in a complementary manner, transcribing and forwarding printed material with letters. Many letters of news circulated every year, ranging from the occasional and casual to letters written by witnesses of events in response to requests for an account of what they had seen. As networks spread out and interconnected across Europe, recipients could give letters a wide local distribution among family and friends. These letters were grist for compilations that became the raw material of printed news. Some went directly into the hands of printers who, if they foresaw sufficient public interest (or had space to fill), would use them to update their latest publication or to trade with those in other cities.

Gradually, as more people were brought into discussion about contemporary events, the availability of print increased along with a growth in manuscripts and public performances in the form of plays, sermons and executions. Was most of this gossip, or did at least some of it meet a modern definition of news by addressing political events in ways that led to public discourse? Was the growth, particularly of pamphlets and correspondence among the gentry, evidence of the development of public debate?

Mears has suggested that during Elizabeth I's reign all classes of society were involved in news communication and public debate but that this discourse was haphazard and multi-centred, taking many forms and addressed issues of religion, gender and nationalism. Questier and Lake showed how the Edmund Campion affair engaged all the media of the time, including the press, correspondence and the pulpit, and introduced wider European interests in the re-catholicisation of England. We can also see manuscripts and pamphlets being used around a number of other significant political

---

[21] Love, 4, 9–10, 12–13, 37, 45–6, 73, 83, 180–3; J. Scott-Warren, 'Reconstructing Manuscript Networks: The Textual Transactions of Sir Stephen Powle', in *Communities in Early Modern England*, ed. A. Shepard and P. Withington (Manchester, 2000), 27–8, 31, 33; S. A. Baron, 'The Guises of Dissemination in Early Seventeenth-century England', in DandB, 51–2; Mears, *Queenship*, 108–09, 113–5, 158, 168–70, 175–6.

issues debated in Elizabethan England. The earl of Essex became an expert in the circulation of manuscripts, while the Marprelate tracts used print to attack the corruption of bishops, though both backfired when the Crown countered through similar methods. James I and Robert Cecil similarly appealed to a public audience. However, much of the material in circulation at these times was partisan publication. What could be said, and to whom, remained critically dependent on shifting circumstances. Often inspired by members of the Privy Council in circumstances that allowed the 'maintenance of plausible deniability', it was seeking to promote arguments and persuade with a heady mix of propaganda, lies and half truths.[22]

Government aimed to address those who were most likely to be involved in decision-making or through Parliament, but people below that level were exposed to discussion. Freemen and the middling sort were interested and, by the 1580s and 1590s, they were being regarded as people with an opinion that it was useful to address. In the exposure of court 'in-fighting' to wider audience, its image and that of its councillors was tarnished. In particular, the publication of *The Treatise of Treason* in 1572 making the case for Mary Stuart as heir to the throne depicted Cecil and Bacon as conspiring to deceive the queen. John Stubbes's *Discoverie of the Gaping Gulf* in 1579, written as part of the opposition to the Anjou match, pointed to councillors it claimed were threatening to destroy English Protestantism and urged people to alert the queen to danger. As confidence in her councillors deteriorated, public duty came to be regarded increasingly to be about speaking out to protect the common weal while, under James, the Overbury scandal generated salacious stories that led to a widespread public perception of corruption at Court, and subsequently fuelled opposition to Buckingham and the policies with which he became associated.[23]

Interest in Bohemia

The treatment by the press of news of the marriage of Frederick V, Elector Palatine, to Princess Elizabeth and of the subsequent involvement of Frederick in Bohemia, testifies to the interest of readers and the readiness of

[22] Ibid., 7, 158–68, 182, 215–16; P. Lake and M. Questier, 'Puritans, Papists and the "Public Sphere" in Early Modern England: The Edmund Campion Affair in Context', *The Journal of Modern History*, 72:3 (2000), 590–6, 625–7; P. Hammer, 'The Smiling Crocodile: The Earl of Essex and Late Elizabethan "Popularity"', 95,99, 102–3, 106–7; and P. Lake, 'The Politics of "Popularity" and the Public Sphere: The "Monarchical Republic" of Elizabeth I Defends Itself', in *The Politics*, ed. Lake and Pincus, 62, 65, 74, 78, 80–87.

[23] Ibid., 58–60, 68–70, 87; P. Lake and S. Pincus, 'Rethinking the Public Sphere in Early Modern England', *JBS*, 45:1 (2006), 273–4, 276–9, 286, 291; Cust, 'The "Public Man"', 116, 126–7, 132, 135–7; Sharpe, *Image Wars*, 127–9; A. Bellany, *The Politics of Court Scandal: News Culture and the Overbury Affair, 1603–1660* (Cambridge, 2002).

London publishers to respond. The marriage was celebrated in London with at least sixteen different pamphlets, including *A full declaration of the faith and ceremonies professed in the dominions for Fredricke, Elector Palatinate,* and many poems and printed sermons, including *Heavens Blessing, And Earth's Ioy,* which described the official celebrations and fireworks attending the marriage, and *A Marriage Triumph, Of the Most Auspicatious Marriage* which praised Fredrick as 'the Protestants protector'. This was the first English royal marriage to be celebrated in nearly 60 years. There was excitement and hope too that, as a Protestant match, it would result in a secure Protestant succession.[24] Political comment focused on James's intentions, interpreting the match as a sign of true anti-Spanish and anti-Roman Catholic sympathies. Other titles captured the emotional tone of the celebrations, such as *The Magnificent, princely and most royall entertainments* and *The Marriage of two great princes,* and Ralph Mabbe published a sermon by George Webbe, *The Bride Royall, or The Spirituall Marriage* which stressed the Protestant nature of the alliance. Two years later a translation of a sermon published at the celebration of Frederick's majority described him as 'most Christian', and the translator praised James for making such a good match for his daughter. In 1614, the play *Hector of Germanie,* that symbolically expressed hopes for Frederick to take an active militant lead in Protestant expansionism, generated sufficient interest in London to warrant a second performance, transferring from the Curtain to a larger playhouse.[25]

The Bohemian Revolt and Frederick's decision to accept the Crown triggered a Europe wide increase in newsprint. The first material in English came from the Bohemian rebels who renounced the election of Ferdinand and infamously defenestrated two of his councillors and a secretary. Their propaganda was first published to convince German opinion. It stressed legal justifications for the revolt, arguing that it was illegal for Ferdinand

---

[24] W. Cobbett, *Parliamentary History of England,* 1 (1806), col. 1151.

[25] P. Burke, *Popular Culture in Early Modern Europe* (Cambridge, 1978), 262–5; Schumacher, 13–17; *A full declaration* (1614), STC19130; *A Faithfull admonition of the Palgraves churches* (1614), STC19129; *The Marriage of Prince Fredericke* (1613), STC11359; *The Magnificent, princely* (1613), STC11357; *The Marriage of two great princes,* Wright (1613), STC11358; J. Aretius, *Primula veri spanegerics,...Palatinum* (1613), STC736; A. Arelius, *In nuptus illustrissimus principis Frederici V* (1613), STC 960; G. M. Franchis, *De auspicatissimis nuptiis* (1613), STC11308, and *A Marriage Triumph,* (1613), STC11309; T. Heywood, *A Marriage Triumph, Solemisized* (1613), STC13355; A. Nixon, *Great Brittaines generall joyes* (1613), STC18587; H. Peacham, *The period of mourning...Together with nuptial hymnes* (1613), STC19513; A. Taylor, *Epithalamium upon the all-desired nuptials* (1613), STC23722; J. Taylor, *Heavens Blessing, And Earth's Ioy,* (1613), STC23763; G. Wither, *Epithalima: or nuptuall poems* (1612/13), STC25901; *Heavens Ioy* (1616), STC13019; H. Werner, 'The Hector of Germainie, or The Palsgrave, Prime Elector* and Anglo-German Relations of Early Stuart England: The View from the Popular Stage', in *The Stuart Court and Europe: Essays in Politics and Political Culture,* ed. M. Smuts (Cambridge, 1996), 118–24.

to control Bohemia while their king, Matthias, was alive; that Ferdinand violated the conditions of his election through attacking Protestant subjects in Bohemia, and that his election had been attained by force under illegal circumstances. This material began to reach London in 1619, after Matthias died and the Bohemian Estates formally renounced their earlier election of Ferdinand, bringing Frederick into the picture. Much was first written in German and Latin then translated into English and printed by George Waters of Dordrecht, whose publications also include tracts written or translated by John Harrison, an English administrator who worked for Elizabeth. Other material was published in English, possibly in Middelburg, Amsterdam and the Hague in 1620.[26] There was little attempt to explain German institutions or clarify arguments for the benefit of an English readership. Booksellers in London must have believed there were enough sufficiently well educated readers to buy these pamphlets who could appreciate the arguments as they stood. It was a cautious beginning for the London publishers, who could not, at first, have known how the Crown might respond.

The Golden Bull, setting out the legal provisions relating to the succession of Princes Electors, was translated into English and published in London in 1619 by Nathaniel Newbury. This was a safe choice: there could hardly have been any political objection to the publication of a historic legal document to which both the emperor and the Bohemian Estates could appeal for justification of their position.[27] News of the new election was registered for publication with the Stationers' Company in 1619 and Ralph Rounthwaite published *Newes From Bohemia. An Apologie*, which was a direct translation of an official statement in which the Bohemian Estates claimed they were defending themselves against subjection by the Church of Rome. Again, this was an official public document. By early 1620 Frederick had accepted the Crown and moved with Elizabeth to Prague. John Taylor's report of his visit to Bohemia was published in response to what he graphically described as continual requests for information about Bohemia and the fighting that had begun there, '[I] cannot passe the streets but I am continually stayed by one or the other, to know what newes, so that sometimes I am foure houres before I can go the length of two paire of butts.'[28]

---

[26] Schumacher, 23–6, 38–9; Shaaber, 83–5; *The Most Illustrious Prince* (Dort, 1619), STC11360; *The reasons which compelled the states of Bohemia* (Dort, 1619), STC 3212; *Declaration des causes* (London?, 1619), STC11350.7; *Bohemiae regnum electivum. That is a plaine relation of the proceeding* (1620), STC3206; *Bohemica jura defensa. The Bohemian lawes or rights defended* (London?, 1620), STC3205; *A briefe description of the reasons* (the 'Hayf' probably London, 1621?), STC11353.

[27] *The Golden Bull* (1619), STC13611.

[28] Arber, vol. 3, 656; *Newes from Bohemia* (1619), STC3211; also *Newes from Bohemia, a true relation of the warres* (1619), STC3211.5; *The Last Newes from Bohemia*, (1620), STC3208; *Travels ... Prague* (1620), A2–4.

Early reports of military encounters were encouraging and optimistic. Pamphlets and ballads called for recruits to go to Bohemia to join the Protestant forces. Others reflect the enthusiastic celebration of Frederick's decision and hopes of a strong Protestant alliance.

> The German States, and Netherlands,
> Have mustered up their martiall bands;
> The Denmarke king doth close combine,
> His forces to the Palatine.

This verse openly called for English aid.

> They looke for Ayde from Brittaine, Horse and Foote,
> With unbeleeved sommes of Golde to boote ...
> When they heare Religion is the Cause,
> They flocke amaine without stopping or pause.

John Taylor published a poem calling Englishmen to serve in Bohemia. Others listed Frederick's supposed allies. Yet these attempts to inspire enthusiastic hordes to rush forward and enlist seem to have fallen on deaf ears. Sir Horace Vere's effort to raise four thousand men was cut back to two thousand, and even then he found it difficult. He sent scouts out into the countryside and was met with what Chamberlain described as 'sharking and shearing, and such a deal of discontent'.[29]

By the summer of 1620 a clearer situation was emerging and James's position, as would-be peacemaker and international statesman, was beginning to show signs of cracks, especially once rumours reached London that Spinola was moving out of the Netherlands towards the Palatinate. Frederick published two tracts giving his motives for accepting the Bohemian Crown that were printed in English in Germany. Others made more emotional appeals, accusing Ferdinand's government of spoiling Protestant churches, kidnapping, murder and rape, while Ferdinand was criticised for being a Jesuit, having been educated at a Jesuit college, and having Jesuit advisers. Meanwhile, London publishers became bolder behind the shelter of false imprints. A tract called *A Plaine Demonstration of the Unlawful Succession*, with a 1620 Hague imprint, argued that Ferdinand had no lawful succession whatever since he was the product of an incestuous relationship. This was easily detected as a London publication: its only references were to English sources. It was traced to a publisher who was subsequently to become centrally involved in the regular publication of foreign news:

---

[29] *A most true relation* (Dort? London?, 1620), STC3210; *Gallants*, quoted in Schumacher, 80–1; J. Taylor *An English-man's Love to Bohemia* (Dort, 1620) STC23751; *The Late Good Successe*, STC3209/11356; and *Letter written by a French Gent*, STC10812, quoted in Thomson, *Chamberlain Letters* (1965), 355.

Nathaniel Butter was arrested. The printer, William Stansby, whose press was closed down for this initiative, was also later to associate himself with more regular publications. Secretary Calvert commented that the emerging interest in forbidden books and transcriptions was because sales were good but his particular concern was the continued reprinting of *Vox Populi* and its criticism of the relationship with Spain. No decision to control the press was made until later that year.[30]

In July the Spanish army set out for the Rhine and the Elector of Bavaria's army, led by Tilly, crossed the Austrian border. Sir Horace Vere set out via the Netherlands with English forces for the Rhine. Conway and Western were dispatched to assert the English diplomatic interest but it was only after Spinola attacked the Palatinate at the end of August that it became clear to James that a stronger political line was necessary. In October the first steps were taken towards calling Parliament to ask for funds. Writs were issued in November, just days before the fateful Battle of White Mountain.[31] With the most educated, literate and influential of the population about to assemble in London for Parliament and with subsidies to support a war in the Palatinate firmly on the agenda, the appetite for news was growing stronger. A few of the most interested publishers in London, through their contacts with the book trade in Amsterdam, Cologne and Frankfurt, in particular, already knew how to set about meeting this demand.

Conclusions

News circulated in many forms, reaching beyond London into rural areas and penetrating all levels of society. Literacy and economic growth were making print more accessible to more people, but oral, manuscript and printed communications were used in complementary and mutually rein-forcing ways as information flowed via carriers and through networks of merchants, neighbours, friends and families, from one mode to another and back, catering for readers and listeners alike. As more people were drawn into pubic discussion there were changes in the political climate, and criti-cism could become more intense, particularly with a growing distrust of court advisers. However, public debate remained patchy, somewhat haphazard, partisan and associated with specific issues.

Clear themes included court celebrations as well as scandals. Wars and

[30] *The Declaration and information of the King of Bohemia* (1620), STC11350; *A declaration of the causes* (Middleburg probably London?, 1620), STC11351; *Plaine Demonstration*, (1620), STC10814; *CSPD 1619–23*, 324; W. W. Greg, *A Companion to Arber* (Oxford, 1967), 61, 66, 209; L. Hanson, 'English Newsbooks, 1620–41', *The Library*, 4:18 (1937–8), 364.
[31] Wedgwood, 114, 121–2; P. H. Wilson, *Europe's Tragedy: A History of the Thirty Years' War* (2009), 295–8.

military activity, threats to domestic security and religion in Europe attracted widespread interest under Elizabeth. The marriage of Princess Elizabeth and Frederick focused attention on Frederick's role as a potentially active Protestant leader in Europe, and the London trade's connections within Europe enabled stationers to respond to interest in the Bohemian crisis, initially circulating the polemic and official material published abroad in English, German and Latin to address a well educated readership. In 1620, as Parliament assembled, the latest developments in this religious dispute and dynastic threat were of vital concern, but the strength of support for the defence of the Bohemian Crown was untested. There was every indication that news of the conflict would sell well in London, but it was less clear what would be acceptable in print and the question of how far James and Parliament would be willing to fund military action was yet to be explored.

2

The Developing European News Trade: Methods and Content

By the early seventeenth century, news was collected and exchanged in Europe through networks communicating across the Continent. Knowing how this happened, and why, helps us to see the appearance of periodical news in London in the winter of 1620/1 (and how the defeat at White Mountain was reported) in context and to understand the scope and nature of the news coverage, and the inherent limitations of the content available. This chapter explores the logistics of the international news trade to establish a baseline description of the material that the London trade received to inform discussion about the timeliness, extent, quality and accuracy of the information that reached readers and shed light on questions about whether networks were partisan and engaged in propaganda, constrained by government controls or influenced by patronage. This understanding, in turn, provides a context for addressing some underlying questions about the development of political awareness, opinion and the beginnings of an informed and critical public sphere. The news press became active in progressively more cities as the Thirty Years War continued, and more soldiers and embassies departed from Britain to the Continent, allowing the London trade to diversify its sources as the European news trade evolved.

England was part of a Europe-wide news trade community both economically and politically. It played its part fully, transmitting and receiving news through a diaspora that included printers, agents and correspondents. There are now more than 50,000 known copies of pre-1700 German printed periodical news publications in addition to known Dutch corantos, the work of the French presses in the 1630s and perhaps a further two thousand periodical news issues from the Habsburg Netherlands. This growing body of material allows us to see the role of London in the context of how news was gathered and how the industry worked as an interconnected whole.[1]

---

[1] DandB, 7–8; S. Fish, *Is there a Text in this Class? The Authority of Interpretive Communities* (Cambridge. MA, 1980); K. Sharpe, *Reading Revolutions; The Politics of Reading in Early Modern England* (New Haven, CT and London, 2000), 37, 59–60; J. Scott, *England's Troubles: Seventeenth-Century England's Political Instability in a European Context* (Cambridge, 2000), 4, 15; Ries, 170–232; F. Dahl, *Amsterdam – Earliest Newspaper Centre*

Print was used increasingly during the sixteenth century to present information, persuade, reinforce allegiance and influence opinion. In the United Provinces and France public debate developed rapidly with the state playing a central role. During the Reformation, especially in Germany, images became a speciality of Protestant propaganda. By the seventeenth century, Germany experienced a flood of leaflets and pamphlets that reached a climax with the Swedish invasion in the 1630s.[2] Meanwhile, from the fourteenth century onwards across Europe, merchants' factors, private intelligencers and diplomatic agents wrote reports on recent events. This activity grew alongside printing. Business interests of trade and belief systems that stressed universalising principles were already strongly established by the seventeenth century. Formal and informal information networks linked all courts and cities. Once the Thirty Years War started merchants also needed to know the whereabouts and activities of military forces, while broader confessional interests in the progress of the war stimulated demand for news from a wider readership.

International trade, diplomacy and financial interests depended for their success on the exchange of information. Jürgen Habermas has been influential in developing a theory of the links between knowledge and power based on a model or ideal of a 'public sphere' or 'spheres' in society throughout Europe, characterised by communicative forums, arenas and meeting places where people discussed and debated matters of public interest. This sphere consisted of the political realm, the world of letters, clubs and the press, and the culture of products. It included merchants, traders, officials, academics and scribes and was pluralistic, engaged in a process of rational consensus formation through public discourse (later called by Habermas 'communicative action'). The theory recognised that early capitalism brought about a new social order based on trade fairs and long distance trade routes. The traffic in news developed alongside the traffic in commodities because merchants required ever more frequent and exact information about distant events. Merchants organised the first mail routes and trading cities became centres for news. News became regular like the trade in commodities itself, with newsletters becoming weekly reports. The German 'Fuggerzeitungen' were typical. These sixteenth-century handwritten newsletters, for use in the Court and within their firm, relied upon the great trading centres as the most productive sources of news. They covered events reported from Antwerp, Middelburg, Hamburg, Frankfurt, Cologne, Venice, Rome, Paris and Constantinople. In the sixteenth century printers in Augsburg and

of Western Europe (The Hague, 1939); F. Dahl, Dutch Corantos 1618–1650, A Bibliography and an Introductory Essay on Seventeenth-century Stop Press News (The Hague, 1946); Arblaster, 4.

2 P. Lake and S. Pincus, 'Rethinking the Public Sphere in Early Modern England', JBS, 45:1 (2006), 285–6, 291–2; R. W. Scribner, For the Sake of Simple Folk: Popular Propaganda for the German Reformation (Oxford, 1994/2000).

Strasburg began to make them public, adding them to the market in broadsheets that spread news of wars, earthquakes and decrees. By the turn of the century there were semi-regular news sheets and pamphlets being published in many European cities covering Imperial Diets, wars, harvests, taxes, fleet news, the transport of gold and silver and reports on foreign trade. The reports had thus themselves become a commodity. The names of this correspondence varied across Europe. In Venice writers of newsletters were called 'scittori d'avisi', in Rome they were 'gzettani', and in Paris, 'nouvellistes'. In London they were called 'correspondents' and 'intelligencers', while in Germany they were 'Zeitunger' or 'Nouvellistes'. Most of these terms were shortly to provide the names for printed new publications.[3]

The Habermasian account pointed to 'a broad strata of people participating as consumers of mercantile policy'. It underlined the commercial and functional nature of information exchanged across Europe. The sources of information circulated were largely free of confessional or political pleading since the primary objective of participants was to exchange the most accurate information to allow trading, transport of goods and the circulation of letters of exchange. The commercial and utilitarian nature of the newsletters on which published news was based is evident from any publication. Week in, week out, they monitored and reported conditions of roads and travel, the prevalence of bandits (or, at sea, pirates and privateers), the impact of floods, famines, new taxes and diseases, as well as the whereabouts and movements of courts and ambassadors. All of this constituted vital information for those planning to transport commodities, open up new markets or give financial backing to states or new enterprises.

The cultural neutrality of Habermas's model means that his explanation does not, however, fully account for the transition of letters into print for sale to a general reading public, or explain why the transition began primarily in the German, Dutch and English speaking regions of Europe. For this it is necessary to consider the significance of the role of Protestantism, with its emphasis on the application of conscience and opinion in self-reflection. What we now term 'public opinion' was centre stage in many of the key political events in seventeenth-century England. David Zaret has argued that printing shaped new modes of thought based on its appeals to public reason and that religion, science and printing all had roles in giving public opinion authority. He and Kevin Sharpe have pushed back the idea of appeals to public opinion to the reign of James I but Zaret has conceded that this earlier public discourse did not reach the same level of rationality or universality as in the Habermasian liberal model. Instead, the

[3] J. Habermas, *The Structural Transformation of the Public Sphere: An Inquiry into a Category of Bourgeois Society*, trans. T. Burger (Cambridge, MA, 1989), 14–26, 30; C. Calhoun, ed., *Habermas and the Public Sphere* (Cambridge, MA and London, 1992), 6; V. Von Klarwill, The Fugger Newsletters 1568–1606 (1926); H. Langer, *The Thirty Years' War* (Poole, 1978), 235–7.

English revolution in the 1640s was the key turning point.[4] While many historians can accord with the argument that the 1640s marked a watershed for England, with much printing politically and religiously motivated and extensive evidence of public engagement in political debate, David Norbrook has pointed to the significant expansion in public political discussion in England from the 1620s onwards. Like Zaret, Norbrook linked this with strong religious motivations behind the emergence of the public sphere where 'the English monarchy could not be trusted to resist the process [of re-catholicisation] but was on the contrary likely to be complicit in it'. The belief systems of Europe encouraged a community of interest that transcended national boundaries. Churchmen on both sides of the confessional divide travelled and shared ideas. The Synod of Dort addressed issues of concern for Protestants across Europe and the Counter-Reformation made Protestants defensive and fearful.[5]

Thomas Schroder has identified the driver behind the growth of the news industry in seventeenth-century Germany as a thirst for knowledge. The invention of new mechanisms for the diffusion of information provided the basis on which a new public sphere could then be constructed. This is what Habermas called the 'architecture', or a foundation course, for the subsequent development of more self-reflective elements that characterised the fully formed liberal political public sphere. There was a growing commodification of politics as printers seized commercial opportunities. Smaller German courts and Dutch municipalities supported the development of printed news as a supplement to existing systems of information that could also be influenced through patronage and granting privileges for a monopoly in a city. The threat to Protestantism that grew with the victory of the emperor at White Mountain and subsequent Habsburg victories created an intense interest in European news beyond the merchant and ruling classes. Thus, the war itself was a stimulus for news publication. As Scott explained, 'The crisis of 1618–48 threw not only the whole of religiously mixed, half-reformed central and western Europe into conflict, but Britain too, because

---

[4] P. Johnson, *Habermas: Rescuing the Public Sphere* (London and New York, 2006), 15; Calhoun, *Habermas*, 41; P. Lake and S. Pincus, ed., *The Politics of the Public Sphere in Early Modern England* (Manchester, 2007), 18–22; D. Zaret, 'Religion, Science and Printing in the Public Spheres in Seventeenth-century England', in *Habermas*, ed. Calhoun, 214–16, 223–6; D. Zaret, *Origins of Democratic Culture: Printing, Petitions, and the Public Sphere in Early-modern England* (Princeton, NJ, 2000), 165–84; K. Sharpe, *Image Wars; Promoting Kings and Commonwealths in England, 1603–1660* (New Haven, CT and London, 2010), 17–8, 35, 38, 122, 124–33.

[5] S. Achinstein, *Milton and the Revolutionary Reader* (Princeton, 1994). J. Raymond, 'The Newspaper, Public Opinion, and the Public Sphere in the Seventeenth Century', in *News, Newspapers, and Society in Early Modern Britain*, ed. J. Raymond (London and Portland, OR, 1999), 117, 128; D. Norbrook, 'Areopagitica, The Early Modern Public Sphere', in *The Administration of Aesthetics: Censorship, Political Criticism and the Public Sphere*, ed. R. Burt, 5–7 (Minneapolis, MN and London, 1994).

Britain was part of religiously mixed, half reformed central and western Europe too', sharing neighbours' concerns for the survival of Protestantism.[6]

News of military activity was inherently interesting. Ambassadorial visits became more frequent and the discussion and anxiety around them became more intense. The number of ambassadors sent, even by the Stuarts during the 1620s and 1630s, was impressive and interest in the prospect of a marriage between Charles and the Spanish infanta excited public interest across Europe. As conflict widened, soldiers were recruited from across Europe. War news supported recruitment, increased travel by soldiers and left families at home seeking news. Merchants needed to know where forces were being levied, their locations, provisioning and movements back and forth. Their reports also covered skirmishes, battles and clashes between soldiers and the local population. This miscellany of information was recorded anonymously by merchants' factors and postal agents in a largely neutral, factual and functional manner. Periodical publication met demand for the most current news possible. The main drawback was that reports were assembled from all directions, written by people from all confessional backgrounds in a level of detail that could be bewildering for general readers anxious about the preservation of Protestantism across the Continent.

News networks

The means of communication, using hand written letters carried on foot and horse from town to town, allowed networks of individuals with common interests to communicate. The press could pick up some of these exchanges and disseminate these further in print. This was an informal process not so dissimilar to that developed at the start of the twenty-first century through the internet and social media. An examination of the trade and diplomatic networks that had developed by the seventeenth century shows that the informality and diffuse nature of these networks gave them resilience and an ability to stay relevant to readers.

Paul Arblaster described the 'interlocking news writing networks' as flexible, able to adapt to new institutions and events, and operating well beyond the control of any single government. He identified a news community functioning across Europe and extending beyond, throughout the mercantile networks, for example, in the East and West Indies and Constantinople. Focusing particularly on Catholic writers, he illustrated the network: Roman news writers provided papal court news, news from south Italy and the diplomacy of Catholic powers. This was supported by Jesuit correspondents

6 T. Schroder, 'The Origins of the German Press', 123, 134–7, and O. Lankhorst, 'Newspapers in the Netherlands in the Seventeenth Century', 153–5, both in DandB; T. Blanning, *The Culture of Power and the Power of Culture: Old Regime Europe 1660– 1789* (Oxford, 2002), 158; Scott, *England's Troubles*, 28.

in Vienna and Brussels. Verstegan, a Catholic refugee from England living and writing in Antwerp 1617–33, supplemented his news from the Jesuits with that from a consortium of English Catholic cloth merchants who had a clandestine trade in English Catholic books. Originally called Richard Rowlande, he had operated a secret press in Smithfield in 1581–2, fled to Paris on discovery, then settled in Antwerp where he acted as an Anglo-Catholic agent, spy, intelligencer, author and translator. He had contacts with the Portuguese merchant community and his networks connected with others, including the Protestant news service of Johann van den Birghden that was based at the Frankfurt post office until he was dismissed as Imperial Postmaster for his anti-Habsburg stance.[7]

News networks evolved and interacted organically. They fed off what was available and reacted to new stimulus, ensuring that readers were well provided with coverage of major events. They could easily extend to bring news from a new venue when events there became newsworthy. They supported one another, passing on whatever they received so that news of events rapidly reached others. A news publisher could build up the quality and variety of a publication by subscribing to these networks. Thus, Abraham Verhoeven, publisher of *Nieuwe Tijdinghen* in Antwerp, took newsletters from Cologne and Paris in 1620 then switched from Paris to Calais in 1622 and assembled regular reports from at least seven cities plus the army of Flanders, while Johann Rudolf in Zurich was assembling news from eleven main centres. By contrast, Jan Adrienssen simply reprinted Broer Jansz's Amsterdam coranto, only rarely adding material from another source. However, as Arblaster observes, a closer look at sources for any of these publishers shows how broadly similar subscription strategies were – using Rome, Venice, Vienna, Prague, Cologne, Amsterdam, The Hague and adding Lyons, Leipzig, Breslau, Bremen and Brussels less often. The result was a 'degree of sameness'.[8] London publishers tapped into these networks by subscribing to publications in Amsterdam then broadening their reach to German and Antwerp sources. In this way they replicated the pattern of subscription adopted by others.

Though correspondents were normally found in higher social positions, this was not generally the correspondence of those with 'an inside track' on diplomacy or military strategy. They provided more reasonably priced, less exclusive news than those with the best contacts. News networks primarily

---

[7] P. Arblaster, 'London, Antwerp and Amsterdam: Journalistic Relations in the First Half of the Seventeenth Century', in *The Bookshop of the World: The Role of the Low Countries in the Book-trade 1473–1941*, ed. L. Hellinga, A. Duke, J. Harskamp and T. Hermans (Houten, The Netherlands, 1999), 147–8; L. Rostenberg, *The Minority Press and the English Crown* (New York, 1971), 22–3, 32–3, 38, 139–40, 165, 182–4; Arblaster, 54–6, 75–80, 82, 85.
[8] Ibid., 6, 77–82, 84.

had access to news that was already public in their locality, whether through letters, proclamations, or conversations with those closer to events. Through these a large amount of generally reliable information was available. Amsterdam functioned as a market for information where merchants' families corresponded and people from many places passed through. Merchants met at the Bourse and on the bridge over the Damrak to exchange news. From the 1590s Henrik van Bilderbeke supplied the States General, The Hague, and city magistrates with news assembled from Rome, Venice and Milan which in turn gathered news from Turkey, France, Spain and Italy. Foreign powers also participated. Nearly thirteen hundred copies of chiefly Amsterdam newspapers for 1618–65 have been found enclosed in letters sent by Swedish agents to Stockholm.[9]

London similarly functioned as a news hub. John Earle's *Micro-Cosmographie* described the way St Paul's Walk in London acted as a point of news exchange, while Richard Brathwaite's description of a 'corranto-coiner' shows that news was also gathered in St Paul's (in the winter) and Moorfields (in the summer).[10] People from all walks of life would congregate there to hear and exchange news. Newsletter writers such as Chamberlain and Pory would visit regularly to pick up news as well as relying on what they purchased and personal contacts. John Pory and Joseph Mead supplemented domestic news by making extensive use of the printed news from Europe in the services they supplied to customers outside London. James Howell's correspondence illustrates his method. In March 1622, he wrote to Mr William Martin in Brussels and promised to correspond with Mr Altham and buy letters. In return, he received German letters from William Martin that were 'so neatly couch'd and curiously knit together that [they] might serve for a pattern for the best Intelligencer'. News dissemination was iterative and reciprocal. Readers were writers who were seldom eyewitnesses. News radiated back from London to the Continent. Paul Arblaster found that between 1620 and 1629 Abraham Verhoeven was able to include 361 reports from England of which less than forty percent reached him directly from England. The remainder circulated through news networks and reached his publication second or third hand: twenty-two percent arrived in

[9] C. Lesger, *The Rise of the Amsterdam Market and Information Exchange: Merchants, Commercial Expansion and Change in the Spatial Economy of the Low Countries c 1550–1630*, trans. J. C. Grayson (Aldershot and Burlington, VT, 2006), 215–25, 235.
[10] J. Earle, *Micro-Cosmographie. Or, A Peece of the World Discovered: In Essayes and Characters* (1628), sigs. I11-K, quoted in Raymond, 'The Newspaper', 114–5; R. Brathwaite, *Whimzies: or a new cast of characters* (1631), quoted in *The Times Tercentenary Handlist of English and Welsh Newspapers, Magazines and Reviews*, 9–10; R. Cust in 'News and Politics in Early Seventeenth-Century England', *PandP*, 112 (1986), 70.

Antwerp via France, twelve percent from the United Provinces and eleven percent came from Spain and Italy.[11]

Networks can be identified by mapping news sources from any major centres. The cities that acted consistently as news hubs were Vienna, Prague, Cologne, Rome, Venice, Paris, Amsterdam and Hamburg. In addition, Madrid, Danzig, Calais, Breslau, Brussels, Antwerp, Milan, London and Augsburg are frequently cited. Less frequently we see Mainz, Genoa and Constantinople, plus others, including Lyons and Rouen. We can observe extensive networks in Germany, Austria and Bohemia reflecting interest in the war but also the engagement of major cities in Italy, Spain, the United Provinces, Habsburg Netherlands, Poland and England. Not all the news was print based: Venice, Genoa, Florence, Milan, Naples, Bologna, Rome and Turin had their first locally printed news between 1639 and 1645. Spain was also fully part of the news market but the newsletters they sent focused on domestic events. Seville produced several printed news pamphlets containing news for a range of European cities sporadically from 1618 onwards and Madrid had a quarterly news publication from 1621. Portugal began printing its own news in Lisbon in 1640s.[12]

Printing made the work of the news community more visible as an international activity and revealed to a wider audience how much this community shared a similar perspective on what mattered.

Postal system

The postal system was key to this trade. London readers were told that corantos published in other countries were 'publiquely brought over by the posts', while many German publications referred to the posts in their titles. The Frankfurt news periodical was variously headed, *Univergreiffliche Postzeit(t)ingen*, *Ordentliche Wochentliche Post-Zeitungen* or *Ordentliche Wochentliche Postzeitungen*. The Hamburg news of the late 1630s and early 1640s was simply entitled *Post Zeitung*, and the Cologne *Raporten* from 1625 to 1636 was called *Wochentliche Postzeittungen*.[13]

---

[11] *Pory*, 56–8; J. Howell, *Epistolae … Familiar Letters*, Sec 2 (1645), 47–8, Wing3071; J. Morrill, *Revolt in the Provinces, The People of England and the Tragedies of War 1630–48* (London and New York, revised 1999), 36; D. Randall, *Credibility in Elizabethan and Early Stuart Military News* (2008), 15, 17; Arblaster, 79.

[12] Ibid., 108; M. Infelise, 'The War, the News and the Curious: Military Gazettes in Italy', and H. Ettinghausen, 'Politics and the Press in Spain', 202, both in DandB; H. Ettinghausen, 'The News in Spain: Relacions de sucesos in the Reigns of Philip III and IV', *ESR*, 14:1 (1984), 11–14.

[13] (13 December 1623), 1, STC18507.136; E. Bogel and E. Bluhm, *Die Deutschen Zeitungen des 17 Jahrhunderten*, vol. 1 (Bremen, 1971), 10, 23, 41.

Established in 1489 under Johann von Taxis, the Imperial post of the Holy Roman Empire spread from Augsburg into other European countries and opened up to use by the general public in the sixteenth century. The office was hereditary and protected the routes and its couriers, even in times of war and even in an enemy's country. The routes were well known and the roads were in generally poor condition, except in Spain and Italy where they were paved. This meant that winter travel was particularly difficult, especially in Germany. Couriers provided a slower service (by foot, wagon or boat) and other travellers opted for sea routes in preference when they could. Links around the Mediterranean and up the western coast of Europe were easier to negotiate than routes across the inland of central Europe.[14]

Brussels became a headquarters of the postal service. From 1518 the schedules remained broadly similar for well over a century. For Brussels to Paris journeys were thirty-six hours in summer, forty-four in winter, to Rome ten days in summer, twelve days in winter.[15] Times were tightly scheduled and involved using relay stations, riding post horses and sleeping and eating at posting inns. Difficulties, such as adverse weather, disease, or hostilities, could slow journeys down considerably. Travel by road was vulnerable to disruption during war. A newsbook of 18 July 1623 reported that, 'The Imperiall and ordinary post of Vienna having twice together about the middle of June failed to come that way, from whence we received our intelligence'.[16] An issue of December 1623 explained,

> from Cullen [Cologne] is written to the marchant by way of advice not to travell such and such ways either to Strasbourgh or Franckford, by reason the passages are dangerous and that the campe being broken up before Lipstat, many of the souldiers ... doe not only intercept the markets, but robbe all passengers.

When the post from Leipzig was late in the winter of 1640/1 the Nuremburg correspondent immediately assumed that General Bannier had arrived with troops.[17] Merchant and pilgrim routes could be varied in response to a warning but the post took the most direct routes and stuck to these. At times posts became almost impossible to maintain. In the winter of 1631/2 Prague was cut off by road. A report, dated 25 December begins, 'I would have written unto you, but that I know no letters could passe. Now understanding the posts are againe established, ... I will ... write unto you every week.'[18]

---

[14] E. J. B. Allen, *Post and Courier Service in the Diplomacy of Early Modern Europe* (The Hague, 1972); H. G. R. Reade, *Sidelights on the Thirty Years' War* (1924), 89; C. H. Scheele, *A Short History of the Mail Service* (Washington, DC, 1870).

[15] Ibid., 24–5.

[16] (18 July 1623), STC18507.119.

[17] (2 December 1623), 11, STC18507.135; (11 January 1641), 436, STC18507.343.

[18] (8 February 1632), 11, STC18507.240.

Antwerp's trading kept going through times of conflict. In the 1620s it supported a flourishing trade in furniture, paintings, books and lace. It handled English wool and German ticking, soaps, diamonds and wine, and provided international messenger services between central and Atlantic Europe, and Catholic and Protestant lands, with daily services to Brussels and weekly services to Paris, Italy and Dunkirk. These, in turn, ran services by sea to London via Dover and to Lisbon, Seville and the ports of Spain. Its merchant carriers competed with the Imperial post under licence from the city carrying packets to Paris, London and Calais, Dordrecht, Emden, Rotterdam, Hamburg, Amsterdam, Delft, The Hague, Middelburg and Liege. Almost all post from England to the Continent passed through Antwerp. Whenever the post from Antwerp failed, as correspondents like Pory and Mead were well aware, England received no news.[19]

England's supply of news was vulnerable to disruption by the weather and by Dunkirkers stopping shipping in the Channel. From a newsbook from the end of November 1625, we learn that through,

> the adversitie of the winds wee were frustrate a long time for our intelligence, neither were the winds onely opposite to our appetites, but wee were hindered by another unfortunate distaster, for a Pinke, of which one Blastoule of Flushing a duchman was owner, in the which, the Post from Holland was a passenger, and was unhappily surprised and taken by the Dunkerkes all the men in it being capivated and carried to Oastend.

In this case, they found an alternative, 'by the means of the land passengers we have purchased the possession of them, for there was a Post which passed through Flaunders into France, and so from Calice [Calais] sayled to this our soyle, by whom we haue this intelligence'. Another time, they were less fortunate: Mead wrote to Stuteville on 8 April 1626, 'Of foreign news we hear nothing. The Dunkirkers stop all.'[20]

Taking their lead from Folke Dahl, bibliographers and historians writing on early English news publication have focused on the fact that copy for London publications can often be matched with those from Amsterdam. Antwerp's role in the development of methods of production, control and censorship in England is less appreciated. In the early 1620s the ready availability of the news from the official licensed news publisher of the Spanish Netherlands, Abraham Verhoeven, provided an alternative to news from Amsterdam. London publishers used news from both sides of the confes-

---

[19] Arblaster, 18–26; P. Arblaster, 'Posts, Newsletters, Newspapers: England in a European System of Communications', in News Networks, ed. Raymond, 21–2; Pory, Pory to Scudamore, 13 October 1632; Mead to Stuteville, 10 December 1625, Harl. MS 389, fo. 512.
[20] (November 1625), 1, 2–37, STC18507.353; Harl. MS 390, fo. 40; 15 April 1625, Harl. MS 389, fo. 42.

sional divide in the Low Countries until 1632, when the Dutch Stadholder, Frederick Henry, invaded the Spanish Netherlands and seized the fortresses of Venloo, Roermond and Maastricht, breaking the only link between Brussels and the west of Germany, and cutting the main roads from Antwerp and Brussels. Posts were re-routed via Luxemburg and Alsace. Antwerp lost its dominance and its news, while a royal ban in England eliminated weekly publication of news in London for six years.[21]

An inspection of the datelines of English corantos and newsbooks shows that news travelled across Europe to the Low Countries and England in a broadly north-westerly direction and that the source locations identified in them reflect exactly those found in publications in the Low Countries at that time. The oldest news came from the central and eastern Habsburg lands and from Italy and Constantinople. German news came next. The freshest news was usually Dutch, though news from northern France, the Spanish Netherlands and Westphalia, when it was available, was seldom more than a few days older and was often added at the end. News from places north of the Netherlands, such as Denmark and Sweden appeared less frequently, and via a variety of routes, but the activities of Danish and Swedish troops in Germany were eagerly reported.[22]

Each town received news from the others. Many of the German titles catalogued the places covered. For example, the Strasburg publication from 1622 to 1624 had the long title, *Relation Aller Furnemen und Gedenckwurdingen Historien/ so sich hin und wider in Hoch: und Nider Teutschland/ auch in Franckreich/ Italien/ Schott: und Engelland/ Hispanien/ Hungarn/ Oesterreich/ Mahren/ Boheimb/ Ober und Niderlaussnitz/ Schlesien/ Polen/ Siebenburgen/ Wallachey/ Moldaw/ Turckey etc....* The Wolfenbuttel title of the same period listed *Deutsch: und Welscheland/ Spannien/ Neiderlandt/ Engellandt/ Frankreich/ Ungarn/ Osterreich/ Schweden/ Polen/ Schlesien/ item Rohm Venedig/ Wien/ Antorff/ Amsterdam/ Colln/ Franckfort/ Praag/ und Lintz, etc. So von Nurmberg.*[23]

The start of printed periodical news in English and dateline evidence

News printing began primarily as a German and Protestant phenomenon with at least thirty-four newspapers before 1700. The oldest remaining periodicals were the Strasburg *Relation* from 1605 (which was Protestant even though Strasburg became a recatholicised Imperial city) and the Wolfenbuttel *Aviso*, from 1609. Others followed, including *Wochentliche Zeitung*, printed in Hamburg from 1618 by Paule Lange and edited by Johann Meyer,

[21] Arblaster, 110; P. Arblaster, 'Policy and Publishing in the Habsburg Netherlands, 1585–1690', 185, in DandB; Arblaster, 'London', 148–9.
[22] Scheele, *A Short History*, 23–5.
[23] Bogel and Bluhm, *Die Deutschen*, 1, 4, 53, 65; Langer, *The Thirty Years' War*, 235.

a licensed carrier and professional news writer. This adopted a cautiously Protestant tone, though his sources included Antwerp. *Wochentliche Zeitung* in Frankfurt, from 1615, and *Avisen aus Berlin* in Brandenburg, from 1617, were published by the postmasters Johann van den Birghden and Christoph Frischmann respectively. German newsbooks reported mostly German news with some news from Italy and France, while those from the Low Countries and Cologne also covered England and Spain. Some Danish news was also covered, reaching Amsterdam directly from its Baltic trade and Germany via Hamburg.[24]

Despite the political pamphleteering campaigns of 1614–17, which showed that France possessed a broadly accessible sphere of public, politically orientated communications, France relied on Jansz's corantos from 1618 and regular news publication only began in France in 1631 with a coranto called *Nouvelles ordinaries des divers endroits*. This was published in Paris by Jean Martin, Louis Vondosme and Francois Pommeria and was based on the correspondence of a German, Louis Epstein. It was quickly supplanted by Theophraste Renaudot's *Gazette*, which was supported by Richlieu and given a monopoly. From 1634 Renaudot also published editions of his *Gazette* in Lyon, Rouen and Orleans.[25]

The earliest Dutch series began in Amsterdam sometime before June 1618, entitled, *Corante uyt Italien, Duytslandt, &c* and printed by George Veseler. By 28 August 1620 Caspar Van Hilten had taken over. His son, Jan Van Hilten, succeeded him. Broer Jansz began a second and similar series, *Tydinghen*, some time before February 1619. They supported Frederick and the Protestant cause in Bohemia with accounts of how the stand against the Catholic enemy was developing.[26] Jan Jansen published news in Arnhem from 1621 for a more local market and Jan Adrienssen reprinted Broer Jansz's Amsterdam coranto for the Delft market from 1623. Broer Jansz exported copy to Cologne to be translated and published as *Wochentliche Niderlandische Postei-tungen*. Much to the consternation of the States General, concerned with preventing problems with other states through the export of printed work abroad, by the early 1620s Amsterdam also published news in French and English. All of these were Calvinist and Orangist. Abraham Verhoeven's *Nieuwe Tijdinghen*, which began in Antwerp in 1620,

[24] J. D. Popkin, 'New Perspectives in Early Modern European Press', in Koopmans, 12; Schroder, 'The Origins', 123–5; Arblaster, 82–8.

[25] J. Sawyer, *Printed Poison: Pamphlet Propaganda, Faction Politics and the Public Sphere in Seventeenth-Century France* (Berkeley, CA and Oxford, 1990), 7–10, 133–4; H. S. Solomon, *Public Welfare, Science and Propaganda in Seventeenth-Century France: The Innovations of Theophraste Renaudot* (Princeton, NJ, 1972), 105, 107, 112–9; J-P, Vittu, 'Instruments of Political Information in France', 166–7, in DandB.

[26] Dahl, 'Amsterdam–Earliest'; F. Dahl, 'Amsterdam – the Cradle of English Newspapers', *The Library*, 5:4 (1949), 169; G. Leth, 'A Protestant Public Sphere: The Early European Newspaper Press', in *Annual* (1993), 75–7.

was inspired by the pro-Spinola faction and aimed to encourage support for the army of Flanders. It was published for the loyalist Spanish Habsburg market.[27]

The Dutch began exporting English translations of corantos in 1620. The earliest known issue, dated 2 December 1620, appeared on the London market at a crucial time, just after writs for Parliament had been issued and news of a decisive defeat of Frederick at White Mountain was breaking. The coranto, a single, two-column sheet, just like the Dutch corantos of this period, begins *The New Tydings out of Italie are not yet com*, implying an expectation of news that suggests it may not have been the first English coranto, though its abrupt beginning may simply mean it was translated but not edited. It contains news from Vienna, Prague, Cologne, and the Upper Palatinate. News from Cologne, dated 21 November, reports, 'Heere is tydings, that between the King of Bohemia & the Emperours folke hath beene a great Battel about Prage, but because there is different writing & speaking there uppon, so cannot for this time any certainety thereof be written.' Later reports from Bohemia, dated 12 November, confirmed there had been a major battle and that Frederick had withdrawn. There was nothing definite because 'all the passages are so beset & dangerous to travaile … Spoyling and killing is done dayly uppon all wayes'. The second surviving coranto is dated 23 December 1620. It included, from Vienna, 28 November, 'the victorious houlding of the field by Prague' (as confirmed by the Sunday posts) with the emperor himself in the procession.[28]

The third surviving issue of this series, dated 4 January 1621, provided a wide sweep of European news, foreshadowing events at Rochelle, discussing whether the Swiss cantons would ally with the French against Spain and reporting Bethlem Gabor's negotiations for reinforcements. From Poland, there was news on skirmishes with the Turks and, from Frankfurt, news of Spinola's activities on the Rhine. Defeat was confirmed from Prague with reports of the damage done by soldiers in the city where there was now sickness and disease and people were fleeing. The coranto expressed the hope that the emperor would call the Parliament in Bohemia and reported that Mansfeld and Gabor were reassembling forces in Moravia and Silesia.[29]

The reports were simply translations of news as received and sold in Amsterdam. No steps were taken to make them comprehensible to an English readership in London. They provided information without interpretation. Subsequent issues expressed optimism that there would be an alliance between Denmark, Sweden, the princes of the Union and Bethlem

---

[27] S. Groenveld, 'The Mecca of Authors? States Assemblies in the Seventeenth-Century Dutch Republic', in *Too Mighty to be Free: Censorship and the Press in Britain and the Netherlands*, ed. A. C. Duke and C. A. Tamse (Zutphen, 1987), 63–86; Arblaster, 85–7; Lankhorst, 'Newspapers', 151–2.

[28] (2 December 1620), STC18507.1; (23 December 1620), STC18507.2; Plate, p. 46.

[29] (4 January 1621), STC18507.3.

Corrant out of Italy, Germany, &c.

From Venice, the 27. of November, 1620.

Letters from Roome are not yet com/ because of great stormes and highe waters.

At Genua are expected 2000 souldiers / the which should be sent to the River Ponente: because it is understoode that the Duke of Savoy doth Arme himselfe againe / by the which are 3000 Frenche-men com from Dauphine.

Wee heere from Milanen / that there is lodging made for many 1000. souldiers: And the two Rivers Bormio and Canaro were risen up so highe / that they have not only caried away the Lands and Trees/ but also many 100 houses/ People/ Cattle/ with other goods / and done great harmes.

From Lublin in Polen, the 26 of November.

This day is a Post arived heere from the Lomberg/ brings certaine newes / that the Polish Camp is overthrowen / and disparced / and the greate Chancelor / with many Chiefe Officers/ and other People are taken prisoners / and the Lord Farens-Beck/ and others / are slaine in the Battle. The Carters are com under Lomberg in 4 Companies / set on fire/ and spoyle all with in a mile round aboute : begin to pich a Camp 3. Miles from the Lomberg / those 60. Waggens with Women and Children (there under were Chief persons of the Gentelitie) which would have tooke their flight this wayes are taken prisoners/ and caried away. A Chief Carter/ which is taken prisoner / hath revealed that they had comision of the Turke/ to pitch a Cap by Lobarg/ & there to expect the coming of the Turk/ which hath concluded to take his way towards Crakow/ and there to holde his Winter-Camp. In the meane while resort together againe about 10000 Cosacks/ and many Gentlemen heere about/ but they will not goe forwards except that the King of Polen in his owne person doth goe with them.

From Leypsich, the 30. of November.

The Duke Electo of Saxens Souldiers have taken in againe 2. places in Nether-Lausnitz / and gotten great spoyle/ the which those of Bohemia had brought thither/ to flie away / it is said/ that they will also set upon the Cittie Gorlitz.

At Prage hath the Duke of Beyeren / before his departure/ taken an inventarie of all things/ also Copied the Letters in the Secretarie/ sealed them to/ and sent them the Emperour to Weenen/ had also given command / that the Cittizens should not be ronged : In the meane while durst no man in Prage give advise.

Letters out of Breslaw mention/ that the King and Queene/ with 2. Dukes of Weymar/ Earle of Slick/ Dollar/ Solms/ and other Lords/ were arived there/ with 300 Waggens with bagage/ also there followed him 18. Cornets of Horssemen/ and very many footemen/ so that the speech goeth that the cause should be taken in hand againe. In the meane while runne the Posts toe and fro / to take advise of other kings and Potentates.

From Elboghen in Bohemia, the 1. of December.

Although Crerherie / ill Gouvernment of the Souldiers / also that the Bohemians have not assisted the King of Bohemia with on accord/ and more other matters / are judged to be the movall causes of the losse of Prage / with the appendixes : yet is the chiefe causuall cause accounted to bee an Indignation of God over the perticuler rulers therof/ for sinne/ for now those Lords and Gentility / which formerly in high degree did use great Tyranny over their subiects the same are now dispised of them/ for in the Cities they are not suffered/ neither dare they com by their Subiects / of whom they are slaine.

And in the Satser Craits are gathered together som certaine 1000. of Contrymen more/ they think to defend themselves by force / if they had but a Gouvernour : and that the King/ who having the chiefe Priveledges and Iuwels with him / gathering his forces againe very strongly / hath advertised them that hence forth they should be free: therefore will they assemble many 1000. unto them.

And although som Counties in Bohemia have given themselves under the Emperours Comisioner van Walsteen/ som being constrained there unto by force/ others through threatning. as som few dayes agone are arived heere the Emperours Comisioners / and have propounded / that this Cittie and Countie should com to the Cittie Laun and give themselves under subiection / if not/ they would persecute us with fire and sword: but they have gotten but a slight answer. We hope to defed our selves better then the other Bohemish Counties have done.

In the meane while is Taus/ Mies/ Cacha/ and other Citties/ strongly beset with the Emperous or Beyers Garison. The said Comisioners have enterprised to establish Mas-priests in certaine places / thereupon the Subiects are very disquieted/ and grieved/ therefore the Garisons are in great danger. The Governour of Taus hath perswaded the Lord of Illa (who is Evangelist) from such a Reformation / exorting him not to Reforme the foresaid Comision of the Emperour/ but to punnish the disobediente calling to minde the issue of the like former Compulsions. The warres will first rightly begin against the Spring: And there might arise a general tumult: for there hath beene an uproer in the oulde Cittie of Prage against the Sedition of the Souldiers/ what the issue will bee / time can reveale.

From VVeenen, the 28. of November.

Concerning the victorious houlding of the field by Praghe / and the obtayning of the same (as is confirmed by Sundry Postes) is held a stately Profession/ by the which the Emperour himself was present : the Cardinale of Biedenrichsten made a Sermon of thankes-giving / after which all the ornance upon the Walles were shot at 3 severall times/ in like manner discharged all the Muskets.

The Moravians which weere guarnished in these Lands / doe flye from the same / and doe dayly more/ and more/ retire towardes they

Plate 1. The front page of the second known surviving single-sheet coranto in English (Amsterdam, 23 December 1620) shows the brief reports under city datelines, as the news of events in Bohemia unfolded. Much of the source material used by the London press in subsequent years came from reports of this nature.

Gabor. They reported that Brunswick and Luneburg were arming and that the king of Denmark was sending his army to the Palatinate.[30] In creating a more optimistic impression than was warranted they were mirroring the hopes of Protestants across Europe. Their structure was typical of contemporary European news publications. The news content was varied and in short bulletins. There were no headlines indicating the content of a report as we expect today. Instead, the common practice was to marshal news under a 'dateline' indicating the city and date of each report.

At first sight, datelines appear to offer a useful resource for modern historians who could analyse the data to determine which publications relied on which sources and how long it took to get the reports and print them. However, Paul Ries's dateline study of news reports reaching Copenhagen and Hamburg in the seventeenth century quickly revealed difficulties. You cannot always tell whether a report is using Old or New Style dating nor readily work out the difference between dates of writing and printing. He concluded that you cannot, therefore, really determine the efficiency of the industry from analysis of dateline and publication dates since these give only a general idea of the time it took news to travel (for example, two to thirteen days from Amsterdam to Hamburg, and two to eighteen from Vienna to Copenhagen).[31]

From the datelines, however, Ries identified a range of methods used by publishers to assemble their issues. The most obvious was to rely on the regular supply of news from permanent correspondents across the breadth of the postal network. This allowed the publication to cover the whole of Europe evenly. *Nordisher Mercurius*, published by Georg Greflinger in 1669, represented to Ries 'the newspaper industry at the peak of its development and in its true international context'. It included news assembled locally, but from a wide variety of places, translated in Hamburg into German from French, Italian, English, Spanish and Scandinavian. By contrast, a Copenhagen publication printed by Henrik Gode was an amalgamated edition of three Hamburg publications.[32]

Datelines generally signify the city where the news went into print. Arblaster found that Verhoeven relied on about twelve cities for *Nieuwe Tijdinghen*, but each of these were at the centre of their own networks, making it important to distinguish between the place of origin of a report and the place where the events took place. Rome datelines would cover events in Rome and often Naples. A Venice dateline would usually contain little about Venice itself, but would cover events in Milan, Rome and Constantinople. A letter from Venice published in Antwerp in 1624, for example, related news from Milan about the preparation of Spanish harbours and news from

---

[30] (21 January 1621), STC 18507.4; (31 March 1621), STC 18507.5.
[31] Ries, 184–5, 190, 200; Plates, pp. 46, 132 and 244.
[32] Ries, 190–228.

Livorno that English and Dutch mariners had brought news from Gibraltar about the Algerian coursairs. This was printed in Antwerp adding an additional layer of transmission. From there it might also appear in London or elsewhere, still bearing the same dateline. So datelines demonstrate something of the networks operating but are a poor substitute for a study of postal schedules combined with the content of reports.[33]

The datelines for news published in London in the 1620s show that it took the best part of a month for news to travel from central Europe (Vienna and Prague), being printed in at least one Dutch coranto or German aviso en route. It took more or less than a month from Rome, depending on the season and the weather, whereas from Amsterdam, it took only a matter of days to get news onto the streets in London. Many early imports to England relied primarily on the collection of international news in Cologne. They often indicated the end with a ruling then added news from Amsterdam or snippets of news obtained in Amsterdam from other places. For example, in the English issue of 9 August 1621, news from Brussels, Rochelle and Venice follows the ruling after the news compiled in Cologne and, in the issue of 6 September, news from France, Sweden, Denmark, Arnhem and Utrecht is added.[34]

Evidence of news being printed in London that was updated in Amsterdam is abundant. The issue of 13 October 1631 had an Amsterdam dateline of 25 September and under this a report that the Dutch had burnt five Spanish ships off Brazil, a report on the arrival of the fleet from Russia, and finally an item beginning, 'We have lately received tydings of a sore and pitifull mischance happened in the City of Prague where divers, great and costly houses, were consumed by fire.' A newsbook dated 17 August 1627 ends with news from Groll, Wessel and finally Amsterdam. This Amsterdam dateline of 31 July covered news from Antwerp that the Spanish troops were on the move. A dateline of 10 August introduced the statement, 'We received the Newes at this instant, that the Prince of Orange hath taken the Towne. But we cannot learne as yet upon what conditions.' The last dateline, from Amsterdam, confirmed this. The issue was being updated in Amsterdam with news from Antwerp, probably even as it rolled off the press. It then travelled back through Antwerp to London.[35]

The process in any German city was just the same. The 3 October 1632 issue also contained a dateline showing the same process at an earlier stage. Under a Frankfurt, 16 September, heading was news from Nuremburg about the king of Sweden's march, leaving behind eight thousand men and the oxen, and from Vienna confirming Archduke Leopold was dead. A newsbook dated 27 September 1622 has two datelines from Cologne. The first,

[33] Arblaster, 67, 79–82.
[34] (9 August 1621), verso, STC18507.13–15.
[35] (13 October 1631), 13, STC18507.226; (17 August 1627), 13–14, STC18507.187.

dated 3 September, has news from a private letter from Vienna and news from Marseilles. The second, dated 20 September, has news from Rome, Constantinople and Flanders.[36] This process of news collection was itself a matter of interest to English readers and was explained to them in London.

The relationship between Cologne and Amsterdam was particularly complex since news collection and distribution was an iterative process and Cologne collected news from Amsterdam and London as well as supplying news to them. This factor has implications for our understanding of how the news trade started in London, since London publishers obtained printed copy direct from Cologne as well as Amsterdam. The majority of the main texts of the earliest English language corantos end with news from Cologne. If the Dutch were simply printing a translation of a German coranto, the last dateline was German: for example, the last datelines in the issues of 2 December and 23 December 1620 were Cologne 24 November, 'letters out of Newenburghe of the 20 of this present' and Cologne 12 December relaying Prague news. It is not possible to tell from this whether a translator was working on a German or a Dutch original or, indeed, in the absence of further evidence from these cities where the news was translated into English.[37]

Internal evidence illustrates the way in which news travelled back and forth. For example, towards the end of a June 1621 issue, under a Cologne dateline there is a report from Amsterdam, 'Upon Thursday evening the 3. of June about evening, the King of Bohemia . . . and a great trayne came to Amstelredam and were honourably received.' After Spanish news (which could have been added in the United Provinces or in Cologne) there followed another account, 'The King and Queene of Bohemia have arrived here the last weeke on Tuesday about 5 of the clocke ... and stayed ... then they came to our Church, both hee and shee & her eldest sonne: Master Paget preached.' This last item does not give any provenance but we can safely say it was from Amsterdam since John Paget had been Presbyterian minister there since 1607. As the message was of special interest to English readers it could have been added by whoever sent it to England, but is more likely to be directly from what was a poorly edited Dutch original that was a translation of a Cologne publication.[38]

Wherever you look in the chains of printers and correspondents you see the industry in the early seventeenth century functioned by bundling up and editing whatever was available at the time, then adding any fresh news reports received locally. This picture is consistent with Dahl's finding from his study of London newsbooks from 1622 onwards that sixty to seventy percent of English newsbook contents originated in the Netherlands. The

[36] (3 October 1632), last page, STC18507.273; (27 September 1622), STC18507.80.
[37] (2 December 1620), verso, STC18507.1; (23 December 1620), verso, STC18507.2, Appendix 1.
[38] (13 June 1621), STC18507.8; Appendix 1.

London news printing industry was, therefore, similar to Copenhagen's when Gode's publication began later in the century. The result was that there was little clear difference between the bulk of the news being covered by Catholic and Protestant papers. The news was largely the same wherever it was published. This was true of the publications of Broer Jansz, the staunch Calvinist, even though he had sources in Denmark that were not shared by others and for Abraham Verhoeven's *Nieuwe Tijdinghen*, notwithstanding his Habsburg loyalist affiliations and access to material from the army of Flanders. Van Hilten also had access to some independently collected reports through Abraham Casteleyn in Harleem, but Casteleyn in turn was relying on reports from the most important towns in Europe and, consequently, the same networks.[39]

There were no dedicated reporters with a 'house' policy. Contributors to the news networks were associated through interconnecting and interdependent chains, some of which, like the Papal network, had distinctive political ideologies and religious affiliations. Others had purely financial and mercantile interests. Correspondents and postmasters could be Catholic if the city was Catholic, or maybe unwilling converts if the city was in the process of re-catholicisation. They were more likely to be Lutheran or Calvinist in the north and west. They earned their place in the networks by keeping their ears open and having the right contacts: they kept these contacts by being reliable sources of information. This was, as Schroder has labelled it, 'predominantly fact-orientated event coverage' and, while there was no clear separation between information and judgement, and contradictions and mistakes in numerical data were frequent, the informative function dominated. Commentary was often non-partisan, for example, criticising behaviour that endangered peace or a reproduction of comments from those closest to the events.[40] All relied primarily on the copy they received and shared an essentially similar view of what was of interest. This 'sameness' is an important factor that underlies the story of the early news trade and must temper all consideration of the quality, accuracy and political or religious affiliation of the news reported.

News content

To understand the nature and quality of the news arriving in England it is necessary to probe beyond datelines and examine the material itself.

London newsbooks made no mystery of their sources, stating that they included,

---

[39] F. Dahl, 'Amsterdam – the Cradle', 171–3; Dahl, *Dutch Corantos*, 18, 22–6; Ries, 229; Arblaster, 6, 57, 84–5, 102–06.
[40] See quotation, 4 October 1622, p. 139; Schroder, 'The Origins', 126–7, 141.

what is extracted out of true and credible Originals; that is to say, either Letters of justifiable information, or Corantos published in other Countries in the same manner, as we here accustome; ... or privately sent to such friends and Gentlemen as do correspond with understanding men in forraigne parts.[41]

To establish a baseline of the material that the London news trade was working with, we need examples of issues where there was no London editing.

An issue produced hastily in London on 11 September 1624 without editing shortly after the untimely death of the editor, Thomas Gainsford, had three separate sources of Protestant material. It included a report from Cologne about the movement of Tilly's troops and hope for a Protestant union: 'It is held for certaine and true, that the aforesaid union ... is now firmly made: and that there is such a unity, ... they are resolved & meane to unsit the house of Austria, Burgundy, & the King of Spaine.' On the siege of Breda by Spinola was the assurance that, 'they shall be answered as at Bergen, for the valianest and best Souldiers and Officers lye therein. As also above a 1000 Voluntaries, as well French as English, most persons of qualitie, who with the Souldiers will bravely bestur themselves.... In the meantime the Spaniards make great outrage.' A new title, 'A Continuation of the weekle Newes word for word out of the Coranto printed by Broer Janson Currantier to the Prince of Orange, and for the Leaguer 1624' provided a fresh start, followed by 'The Coppie of a letter written from the Hage, to his friend in London, concerning the present affaires of the Low-Countries.' It concerned West Indian ships and the seige of Breda, telling us that 'in the towne are many brave English, Scots, and French Commanders, as resolute and expert Souldiers'.[42]

By contrast, the newsbook published on 29 August 1623 had the words 'Ital Gazet. Nu. prio' next to the number and gives the sources as Antwerp and 'Brought by the Venetian Courantier':

Whereas hitherto I have published ... letters both written and printed in the Dutch Tongue ... I have now lighted upon other Letters, and other Authors, some in Latine, some in Spanish, and most in Italian from whence I have extracted the whole occurences of last Moneth.[43]

Editorial work and the way this was presented to readers are covered more fully in Chapters 5 and 6. In practice, material from Dutch and German Protestant sources predominated. Where Catholic material was used a disclaimer was often made.

---

[41] (13 December 1623), 1, STC18507.136.
[42] (11 September 1624), 5, 6, 7, 9, 18, 19, STC18507.151.
[43] (29 August 1623), title page and 1, STC18507.124.

The series that began in London in December 1638 consisted of unedited translations of European publications. By this time printed news was appearing in more European cities and it became the practice to publish three, and sometimes four (if there was additional miscellaneous material available), separate numbers on the same (or almost the same) day. Each number consisted of four, slightly larger pages and the title page was replaced by a short caption in most cases only stating which continental publication was translated. The tenth, eleventh and thirteen series (up to the twentieth issue) consequently provide a record of the news sources being used in London for sixteen months from the beginning of 1639 until 23 April 1640. For example, on 1 January 1639 four were published. Number six was *From Norimberg. Ordinary avisoes from severall places*; number seven was the *Ordinary weekly currantoes from Frankford*; eight, the *Ordinary weekly currantoes from Holland*; and nine contained *The articles and other circumstances and particulars of the taking of Brisack by the Duke of Weymar.* Subsequent titles show that the publishers were in receipt of a regular supply of publications from Holland, Frankfurt and Nuremburg.[44] London publishers used Amsterdam material extensively, but they did not rely on the Dutch and their sources had expanded.

Full texts of official papers were often valuable copy in their own right and published separately. Also, if a monarch wanted a full text published they would use their own printers, but official papers were used in news periodicals whenever an opportunity arose, often reaching them second hand. Single sheet corantos were most likely to include a short summary because little space was available. Newsbooks, such as the issue of 8 April 1641 quoted official text from Spain verbatim. The 14 March 1631 issue included the French king's letter to the Court Parlement of Normandy about the 'restraint of the Queene Mother, and other of the Nobility of France'. This included a picture, an imprint, and the text in both English and French.[45] Proclamations and official publications of treaties, surrenders and edicts had a formal style. They were not written for the benefit of English readers. Nevertheless, if the London newsbook publishers were the first to get hold of a copy, they were reproduced in English newsbooks even when they made reference to events, formalities and places which would seem unlikely to interest the English market. Readers were accustomed to reading official publications from the king's printer, so the genre would not have been unfamiliar.

The issue of 5 May 1629 *Newes of Certaine commands lately given by the French King* is an example, based on avisos from Germany with the Articles of Peace offered by the king of Denmark to the emperor at Lubeck following his defeat by Wallenstein at Wolgast in September 1628. It has the official

---

[44] (1 January 1639), STC18507.278, 279, 280, 281.
[45] (8 April 1641), 133, N&S, 64.409; (14 March 1631), 7, 11, STC18507.209.

response from the emperor and Denmark's answer, saying that there was no hope of peace on terms like that, and the emperor obviously had no real intention of peace. The emperor's response was included and ended, 'This is the last answer giuen by the Imperialists, which came into my hands with a Letter of the 1. of Aprill' saying that the Danes are getting impatient with these negotiations and are going home. Most of the Imperial army was heading to Prussia to help the Poles against the Swedes. Later in the same issue the proposed articles of the Lubeck peace are provided in full. [46]

The same issue included a 'Copie of an horrible and fearefull Oath, which by the Emperour is forced upon the Protestants in Bohemia and the Palatinate, either to take it or forsake their Country'. This oath, part of the process of restoring Roman Catholicism in the wake of the Edict of Restitution, is an official document which, when published by Protestants, became ready-made anti-Catholic propaganda. A number of extracts of letters came from Protestant sympathisers, even in strongly held Catholic cities. News dated 16 March (probably from Breslau) about the Polish defeat by the Swedes first mentioned the 'Romanists' attempting conversions, in this case, in Silesia. Then it tells us that the Imperialists had attempted to billet twelve companies of foot in the territory of the duke of Brieg. He had refused and complained to Vienna, 'Wherof it is thought the Emperour with his Jesuiticall Councell will make as much account as of all other complaints the Protestants bring before him'. From Vienna, on 19 March, comes news of the proclamation demanding that all merchants, tradesmen and strangers must profess to the Catholic faith by Easter. Information on fines and expulsions is provided with a conclusion, 'So that it appeares, that those poore Protestants whethersoever they flye are still persecuted'. Of course, we do not know where along the chain of correspondents, or by whom, this comment was added but we can see that English readers had access to a window that opened, albeit spasmodically and inconsistently, with a view that penetrated deep into the diplomatic, confessional and military developments of the war and Counter-Reformation.[47]

Courtly and diplomatic news, including the progress of embassies, updates on synods and trials, disputed successions and protracted marriage negotiations provided a substantial proportion of the news. Since the policies of rulers and the diplomatic correspondence were not available there were frequent references in reports to audiences, visits and letters arriving or being sent without information about their content, though sometimes with guesses at the political intentions. There was always something happening in public court life to be relayed and lifestyle news from courts was helpful to merchants, bankers and civic delegations. Reports of events such as births, weddings, deaths, coronations and elections were also covered, but as with

---

[46] (5 May 1629), 1–10, STC18507.200.
[47] Ibid., 11–14.

proclamations, they were generally reported more effectively and fully in single-issue pamphlets. Judicial proceedings and pronouncements were of little interest unless they dealt with matters of state, the protection of trade routes, taxes, grievances or religious persecutions or restitutions, though again, public events and executions were reported.

When the writer could be vouched for, private letters were regarded as a good source of information. Some arrived as a result of an agreement with a publisher. Others arrived in the packs of merchants and private travellers journeying along the main trade routes. For example, in a newsbook of 12 March 1624, under a dateline for Amsterdam, 3 March, is the statement, 'I have a letter from Amsterdam, which was enclosed in another Merchants Letter, and was thus written to a friend in Tems – Street'. Under Brussels, 5 March, is the statement, 'I have three severall letters from Brussels. A soldiers, a townesmans, or burger of Brussels and marchants factor, of London … I will truely set you downe their owne words.'[48] A newsbook of 20 October 1624 contained 'A letter written from a commander of the Prince of Oranges leager, dated 7 of October 1624 Relating and confirming the truth of the late danger of Prince of Orange', and also carried 'A particular concerning the newes of France, related to us the 11 of October', demonstrating that the publishers were so keen to diversify their sources that they even included an oral account from a traveller arriving in London.[49]

News from soldiers' letters could be added at any point in the network, including in London. Whenever there was military action, soldiers would write home or sell their stories. In 1622 James allowed a regiment of two thousand volunteers under Sir Horace Vere to put out from Gravesend for the Low Countries. Thus, in 1622, the newsbooks were able to report in great detail on the activities of Mansfeld and the Battle of Fleurus.[50] Doctor Wells, Horace Vere's physician, is identified as having sent a letter in June 1622.[51] Also in June 1622, Bourne and Archer published *The True Copies of Two Especiall Letters verbatim sent from the Palatinate by Sir F. N.* Sir F. N. is described as 'a commander of the Prince of Oranges leager'. He was evidently a hero in London, and probably The Hague too, because he enjoyed considerable notoriety due to his eccentricities. John Bartlet explained in his publication on 21 June 1622 that, 'these Letters are Printed without the privitie of those that sent them, but I suppose that they will not take it offencively, that all such as are well-wishers to the cause of the Palatinate, should bee made acquainted'.[52] Many letters were probably written without any intention of publication and anonymity also protected the identity of the recipient of the letter who handed it to a publisher.

48 (12 March 1624), 15, 20, STC18507.144.
49 (20 October 1624), 21, 8, STC18507.155.
50 (25 September 1622), 3, 12, STC18507.79; (30 October 1622), 15–17, STC18507.85.
51 *A True and Ample Relation* (14 June 1622), 1–2, STC25233.
52 (21 June 1622), STC18507.55; *Coppies of letters* (21 June 1622), 1, STC18507.56A.

By the early 1630s, many men from England and Scotland were serving in Germany, so reports of military action were readily available. On 16 October 1632 there was a diary-like account of the siege and fall of Maastricht, 'Written by a gentleman of qualitie; and an actor in most of the proceedings', followed by a list of the English Scots, French, Walloons and Dutch killed during the siege, as well as reports of spectacular success for the Swedes from the Swedish camp and the Allied Saxon army. Often accounts from the camps, with interesting first-hand experiences, appear genuine because of the detail they contain. A report concerning the crossing of the River Lech by the king's army described the weather and geography of the area very carefully, but provided a very patchy account of the ensuing encounter with Tilly. This reflected the limited perspective we might expect of someone involved in the action rather than at the front to observe and report. In the same issue there were letters from civilians in the cities affected by the military advance. One from Augsburg reported that the Swedes have begun to arrive and that the leaders of the city are leaving. Two more companies of Bavarian soldiers have been sent to strengthen the city, 'but we can easily perceive that they have no courage to fight'. From Augsburg a week later, we are told that Tilly and the Swedes are nearby and Altringer has been to the city to order fortifications, 'But I cannot see how this citie shall long hold out.'[53]

'A Coppy of a Letter written from the Army of his Majestie of Sweden', included in the 28 April 1632 issue, combines some of the best features of letters 'from the front'. It locates the Swedish army, two leagues from Tilly and recounts an incident where the king of Sweden went incognito over to Tilly's base and, unrecognised, addressed an Imperial soldier. The king began by asking, 'Good morrow Monsieur, where is olde Tilly' and was answered, 'Good morrow to you, Tilly is at Rain in his quarter. Comradee where is the King.' Gustavus Adolphus replied, 'Hee is now in his Quarter, what else doe you else desire to know of him?' The sentinel then asked, 'Doth the King give quarter?' He was answered, 'Yes, I assure you; come but over to us. You shall have good quarter.' The soldier's letter continues with matters of interest to him, commenting about the booty they have taken, 'but we cannot sell them, for they will yeeld us but little money or none at all, a good faire Horse may be bought for foure Rixdollers, a Cow for ... Mony is that which is here lookt after'. This version of the encounter of Tilly with the king of Sweden is not quite the same as that related by Wedgwood, but no doubt many versions were circulating by the time the story had spread around the camp and found its way into soldiers' letters.[54]

---

[53] (16 October 1632), STC18507.276; see also (26 June 1632), 8, STC18507.254; (23 June 1632), 8, 10, STC18507.256.
[54] (28 April 1632), 5–6, 10, STC18507.248; Wedgwood, 315.

In the late 1630s, in addition to publishing the regular issues from Frank-furt, Nuremberg and the Netherlands, Butter and Bourne published news of the Swedish Marshal, Johan Bannier's victory against the Saxons at Chem-nitz in *A True and Particular Relation of the Battell fought neare Kemnitz*. News of the skirmishes off Dunkirk, the arrival of any merchant fleet, at the ports, and the activities of the Prince of Orange from The Hague were usually provided by the Dutch. In June 1639, the taking of thirteen 'Zealand Pinks and Boyers' sailing from Gravesend to Vlissingen and carrying two hundred passengers by Dunkirkers was reported. On 27 March 1640 Butter published *A True Narration of the late sea fight betwixt 15 men of warre of Dunkerke and one . . . of Sealand.*[55] Military news included battles, raids, skirmishes, block-ages and sieges, also recruitments and levies, supplies, billeting and contri-butions for troops. Information about ill discipline among forces, outrages, sackings and the punishment of soldiers were all reported. Throughout the period the constant and confusing reports of movements of troops were recorded in detail and were of vital concern to merchants, traders and trav-ellers.

In April 1640 we can see how rapidly news travelled in every direction when troops were on the move. Bannier's march south towards Erfurd, east of Frankfurt, was reported by civilians in Prague and Erfurd, Mastricht and Hamburg, while reports of letters from Bannier to governors in the United Provinces about provisions and progress led to speculation about his plans. In June, reports from Italy to Germany recorded plundering and arson in Piedmont at the hands of French troops and the Spanish troops gathering to retaliate. In the same issue we learn the Imperial army was advancing and taking Dresden and neighbouring castles and expecting to be joined by the duke of Bavaria, while a report from Erfurd stated that the Swedes had defeated both the Croat and Imperial troops. Many writers had only rumours, yet these were sufficiently consistent to alert merchants of the locations of trouble-spots and inform English readers of the extent of the warfare and distress in many regions.[56]

The issue of 11 January 1641 similarly gives a clear impression of the anxiety of people in areas affected by military activity. Letters from city to city crossed with one another and displayed the confusion of reporting when several armies were advancing. In February, news of Swedish advance towards Regensburg, where the Imperial Diet was in session, was reported with surprise from Nuremburg. The wealthy took what they could and fled. Some arrived in Nuremburg as Piccolomini's forces departed from the city, newly equipped with 'money, shirts, cloathes, stockings and boots ... having

---

[55] (between 22 and 27 May 1639), STC18507.308; (21 June 1639), 348, STC18507.313; (27 March 1640), STC18507.328.
[56] (23 April 1640), 7–12, STC18507.337; (6 June 1640), 113–14, 118–19, 120–3, STC18507.338.

done great mischiefe amongst the inhabitants'. Reports from Cologne told of the arrival in Vienna of people fleeing from Hungary as Turks invaded. Despite poor editing, disorganisation and repetition, we get an impressive account of the locations of armies, the levying and organisation across Europe in preparation for summer campaigns.[57]

The arrival of a silver fleet was also an important event and the dangers of pirates, whether off the northern shores or in the Mediterranean, was a continuing theme through the period. From Rome in the summer of 1639 it was reported that the French had taken a Spanish ship with cloth worth 20,000 crowns and the Neapolitans had taken two Turkish ships, while the Florentines captured an Algerian ship with thirty-two pieces of ordnance and liberated three hundred Christian slaves. News from Milan in January 1641 reported from an English ship arriving in Genoa of fighting between the Catalonians and the Castilians. News of far distant lands reached newsprint when fleets returned. Naval war between Venice and the Ottomans was reported extensively in the 1640s.[58]

Fleet and diplomatic connections meant that letters from the Mediterranean could reach London fairly directly, retaining interesting and seemingly authentic detail. One from Galatia concerned Turkish discipline problems because women were 'very rare and deare in these parts'. So the Turks had brought in women from the area to sell to the citizens and soldiers 'who marry the same and sometimes proves very profitable'. It continues,

> Those who doe lesse sympathize with the miseries and afflictions of other men, than I doe, would take great pleasure to behold these Creatures, the next Moneth of October, for that is a time when they return from hunting, for in the last captivity you might have seen those poore and silly women and Wenches led captively in triumphe, in 24 Barques, accompanyed with 28 Gallies of Ottomon.

The following year, readers learned from Constantinople about 'Testerdar' being taken captive and executed and his body being displayed on a tree near where the Janissary Aga was hanged. We are told that the punishment pleased the people, but nothing more about the attempt on the throne.[59]

[57] (11 January 1641), STC18507.343; (11 February 1641), 3, 5, STC18507.345; (8 April 1641), 134–8, 239, N&S64.409; Wedgwood, 436–46.
[58] (21 June 1639), 338, STC18507.312; (11 January 1641), 420, STC18507.343; (11 February 1641), 14, STC18507.345; *Moderate Intelligencer* (3–9 September 1646), 641–2, N&S419.079, E.353(18); (21–8 January 1647), 874, N&S419.099, E.372(15); (11–18 March 1647), 966, N&S419.105, E.381(3*).
[59] (13 October 1631), 1, STC18507.226; (6 June 1632), 5, STC18507.254.

News quality

The more cities a report passed through, the more it could be summarised, and vivid or significant detail lost in the selection of material.[60] Reports from the Continent could go through this process several times at the hands of editors in different cites, with varying skills, before arriving in London. They were also translated, sometimes more than once en route.

As we have already seen, material was often so abbreviated that it is difficult to determine where a report was put together, or whether a 'we' or 'I' referred to a writer or to an editor on the Continent. A further frustrating feature throughout the period was that publishers could not secure a continuous supply of letters from one particular source (or subjected to one consistent editorial process), yet the writers, of course, assumed that their recipient had received earlier letters and knew the context. This gave publications a peculiar and distinctive characteristic of discontinuity despite frequency. This must have been a serious obstacle to comprehension and is still worse for historians who have to follow through issues in different archives and allow for the fact that many issues, particularly in periods of low sales with small print runs, have not survived. But possibly our reading experience today is not that dissimilar from a seventeenth-century reader's in a provincial town, reliant on carriers and without a subscription to guarantee continuous supply. Survival rates are adequate to show that stories that began part way through were common. Letters were taken singly from a series of correspondence, or from one issue in a series from another town. Typical of these is a story from Rome which began the issue of 6 June 1632, 'When the Cardinall of Strigonia understood hee should not be admitted to have audience of the Pope as Imperiall Ambassador, he did desire, that he might be heard by what title soever.'[61]

The passive system of news collection inevitably meant publishers could have no real reassurance about the quality of material. They could rely on the status of the writer, if they knew it, as some kind of assurance as to the veracity of a report. Mostly, however, they could have had no idea of the source of a letter. Any assurance as to the reliability of the reports came from the fact that the whole functioning of news networks was mutually reinforcing. Ultimately, no one would be interested in repeating or exchanging news with an unreliable source.

Major events triggered many reports. Reports of battles and sieges often continued to appear for weeks after events. Details of the numbers involved, of deaths and injuries and even of the outcome could vary, be modified and amended. Rumours could spread rapidly and this phenomenon, prob-

---

[60] Raymond, 142–4, illustrates the process, using an army letter in a newsbook in the English Civil War.
[61] (6 June 1632), 1, STC18507.254.

ably more than any other, tended to undermine the credibility of the news trade, particularly when the conflicting, confirming and qualifying reports also revealed the affiliations of writers from the way the behaviour of military leaders was alternately praised or criticised. A single publication could contain several contradictory reports of the same event. Archer's newsbook of 7 August 1628 gave differing accounts, even on the same page; that Stralsund had fallen, and that this news was false. Yet the writers appear to have done their best to establish the facts: a letter from Gustrow, in Mecklenburg, reported,

> That I have not written any newes within that space of eight dayes, hath beene by reason that the tidings which came did varie, and differ much from one another: But now wee have learned by a man of qualitie, who is lately, come from Stralesont how that ours of the 26 of June, gave a fierce assault to the said Citie, and continued it till the 28 of the same, but lost about 5000 and they of Stralesont, about 800 ... the King of Denmark has now sent in troops, the Swedes have sent troops to Pomerania to make a diversion, to cross the Imperialists in their designes ... The Imperialists have lately offered to make an agreement.

Similarly, in an issue of 17 October 1627, a correspondent added, 'this last weeke we have here no certaine newes to relate, all reports being so uncertaine: But for the rumors that here I shall relate, hoping they will prove true.' These rumours concern the number of soldiers in Wallenstein's army and the possibility that he may have been killed.[62]

However, the range and number of reports also provided the media with some quality assurance. It meant that 'the truth' would eventually emerge and this was ultimately beyond the control of the government, editor or publisher, though there was some scope to influence the content of a publication through selection and presentation. Abraham Verhoeven, working in Antwerp in the 1620s with the protection of a monopoly, had time to prepare his *Niewe Tijdinghen* without fear of competition from rival publications rendering his news stale. He demonstrated what could be done to transform what was essentially a 'rag bag' of reports into a more consistent account. Verhoeven was, in Arblaster's words, an 'outspokenly loyalist publisher' who 'hero worshipped Bucquoy and Spinola', and his publication was intended to appeal to the loyalist readership that subscribed to support the Habsburg Netherlands troops in Bohemia and the Palatinate and to win over those in Brussels who had voted against taxes to support the war effort.[63]

---

[62] (7 August 1628), 7, STC18507.357; (17 October 1628), 12, STC18507.191.
[63] Arblaster, 39, 41–2, 48. Verhoeven's publication process also had a delay of two days while issues were checked by a cathedral canon, 87.

Verhoeven invented the idea of a title to summarise the events covered in the issue, introduced illustrations and adopted an eight-page booklet format. Editorials emphasised the good news of Catholic military successes and he used the headlines and woodcuts to talk up any news that enhanced the reputation of the monarchy. His reports stressed the good organisation of the army of Flanders and its successes. The military affairs of enemies could not be disregarded entirely but news of Spanish defeats and disasters appeared more slowly, delayed in the hope that better news might arrive, and were under-reported. Similarly, Dutch fleet successes were not as prominent as news of Spanish fleet arrivals. Verhoeven, for example, reported the investiture of the duke of Bavaria but omitted the absence of the Spanish ambassador. He covered the progress of the Spanish Match but did not report the jubilation in England when the prince returned without a bride. Instead, he invited readers to rejoice because Charles was safely home and the infanta would follow in the spring. If all else failed Verhoeven handled both doubt about his sources and reluctance to accept the veracity of reports by adopting what Arblaster has termed 'a rhetoric of truth telling', with the frequent use of expressions such as 'whether it is true time will tell', or 'it is rumoured'. These allowed the publisher to avoid taking responsibility for the content of reports and disassociated him especially from those reports least likely to be palatable to readers. Despite this, Arblaster found that 'a careful reading of the inside pages shows that a range of stories were carried which put the Habsburg and Catholic forces in a bad light'. Overall, even the *Niewe Tijdinghen*, despite its surface appearance of Catholicism, was carrying essentially the same mixed content, supplied in the same way, through the same subscription networks found in all the printed news at this time.[64]

In Amsterdam, by contrast, news was produced in a competitive and less controlled market. Publishers were consequently on the lookout for fresh and more reliable sources. Dahl demonstrates this with a quotation from Abraham Casteleyn, a Haarlem printer:

> The falseness of the corantos ... has forced me to write for special news from the most important towns in Europe.... The late Mr Jan Van Hilten asked me, when he saw this news at my house, to put them or something from them at his service every week, a thing which I did now and again and which made his corantos better than those of the others.[65]

News could appear in print in Amsterdam as much as two weeks earlier than it appeared in Antwerp. This gave little time for editorial niceties such as headlines and editorials or for the luxury of withholding unpalatable

---

[64] Arblaster, 57, 66–9, 103, 105.
[65] Dahl, *Dutch Corantos*, 18–23; Dahl, 'Amsterdam – the Cradle', 173.

news in the hope that subsequent reports would be more acceptable to their Calvinist readers. Faster, cheaper production did not result in a significantly different range of news but meant that there was no time to wait for news to be confirmed by further reports. As a result, more mistakes were made. For example, Broer Jansz printed news of a wedding between Prince Charles and the infanta in Madrid before he returned to London unwed. Similarly, in Germany, there was often less checking than in Antwerp.[66]

Conclusion

From 1620 onwards London was in regular receipt of rich and varied reports covering diplomatic, military and mercantile news from across Europe and sometimes also news from as far away as Turkey, Russia and the East and West Indies. The material was primarily from newsletters covering events that were publicly known in the cities they came from and had been published at least once before it reached England. German and Dutch publications were the main sources. In addition, publishers had access to letters and sometimes to official publications of proclamations and treaties. None of these were 'impartial' if what is meant is that the professionalism of writers, postmasters and publishers resulted in a purely factual coverage of military and diplomatic events, uncoloured by religious or other affiliations. However, the purpose of most correspondence was to exchange information rather than to persuade. Writers of all affiliations participated and did so in a sufficiently business-like way to make them all equal as the passive recipients of reports and correspondence in exchange for the best information that they could offer in return. They could not check facts. Yet these writers were regularly relied upon in the same way that they relied upon others, so if they failed to provide valid and frequent reports they would not have been able to maintain their position within their networks.

Governments had a role granting privileges or inspecting copies, and from time to time they intervened; for example, Johann von den Birghden was dismissed as postmaster in Frankfurt. However, the international, informal and flexible nature of the networks meant they were largely beyond the control of governments. This does not mean that the public sphere was 'non-instrumental' in the pure sense used by Habermas. It could be deployed to some degree to serve the interests of a particular group or achieve a particular political or confessional effect. Abraham Verhoeven's Antwerp publication encouraged support for the army of Flanders, and Theophraste Renaudot's *Gazette* in Paris provided a mouthpiece for Richlieu. The Protestant publishers of Germany, the United Provinces and England were responding to the threat of the Counter-Reformation by printing reports

---

[66] Arblaster, 86–7.

and, thereby, making a commercial venture out of a market created by the fears of their readers. There were, however, limitations on the extent to which news could be manipulated and these resulted in the publication of very similar content in all the participating cities. News publishers were in the hands of their suppliers and at the mercy of the weather. They were not in a position to withhold indefinitely news of events that were unpalatable to them, since it could reach readers via other routes. They could not check the material they received, though the repetition of the same news from different places provided some assurance of accuracy. As the London editor in 1624 put this, 'for the truth I referre you to the Discourse, not that any of these be untrue, concerning the substance; but that they vary in some circumstances and names and places'.[67] The editor in any city had limited autonomy to decide to repeat good news by using many reports of the same event or possibly to hold back certain news for a while until the truth was inescapable. Only the most innovative, such as Verhoeven, would write a covering introduction tailored to a particular readership. Mostly they used whatever they received.

Reports were neither as timely nor as reliable as we have come to expect, but they were sufficiently well regarded to keep the trade flourishing and growing, taking in progressively more cities as the war continued. All participated in exchanging, trading or reading the news because they were part of the conflict, whether directly or by proxy when their sons enlisted or their leaders paid contributions from funds levied locally, through diplomatic negotiations, trade and mercantile interests or shared religious and dynastic concerns. The sources of information available were diverse, and production and dissemination in England allowed readers to develop and polish their critical faculties, form their own views or apply their beliefs and prejudices to interpret according to their own worldview.

[67] (12 March 1624), 9, STC18507.144.

3

English Corantos and Periodical Newsbooks 1620–2: A Publishing Initiative

Publishers were central to the development of the London foreign news trade. They imported material, took political and commercial risks and challenged mechanisms for controlling and directing their trade. The emergence of formalised periodical reporting, with the introduction of weekly supply arrangements, issue numbering, and collaboration between publishers and with the authorities, took place over a period of two years from the reporting of the Battle of White Mountain. Events in this period and the provenance of publications (especially in 1621) have been disputed by historians and bibliographers. Reviewing the evidence in the light of recent historiography on censorship, the role of the Stationers' Company and James's attitude to the press, helps us to understand the publishers' role and to appreciate the scale of innovation and change.

The term 'stationer' was used throughout this period to encompass printers, publishers and booksellers. Most stationers kept shops and issued works in their own names or concentrated on selling but did not print.[1] By 1614, journeymen complained of the ascendancy of these entrepreneurs within the trade: 'the Stationer hath all the profit both by Printing and Bookselling'. George Wither commented 'the Bookeseller hath not onely made the Printer, the Binder and the Claspmaker a Slave to him: but hath brought Authors, yea the whole Commonwealth … [to] labour for his profit, at his owne price'.[2]

Successful newspaper production required the development of publishing skills ranging from international networking, to commissioning translations, handling the authorities and organising subscriptions, sales and distribution. Contemporary commentators were aware of the central role of the London news publishers and these publishers themselves first used the word: 'publish' meant to 'make public' and came to be most closely associated with the sale,

---

[1] S. H. Steinberg, *500 Years of Printing* (1974), 182; F. Dahl, *Amsterdam – the Earliest Newspaper Centre of Western Europe* (The Hague, 1939), 184; W. G. Hellinge, in *Copy and Print in the Netherlands* (Amsterdam, 1962); McKenzie, 57–60.
[2] Plant, 66; quoted in F. A. Mumby, *Publishing and Bookselling*, 1 (1974), 94.

distribution and dissemination of news.[3] Publishers also had a crucial role in taking risks, initiating the domestic production of corantos and shaping their evolution into newsbooks for the English market.

One of the first challenges was handling the authorities and there are a variety of views amongst historians about both the nature and extent of government control that the publishers encountered.[4] Frederick Siebert established a view that censorship was a significant and effective force in the early Stuart period, arguing that,

> Within a short space of time all the devices of the Crown for the control of printing were employed in regulating the first newspapers – royal proclamations, prosecution by the Councils, the licensing system, the machinery of the Stationers Company and finally the power of the Crown to grant privileges of monopoly.

This view is now widely questioned. As we have seen, the traffic in news was increasing under James, suggesting that he was more generous than his predecessors in allowing news, or that censorship was largely ineffective because of a combination of reluctance to take action and weaknesses in the institutions and mechanisms available. Pauline Croft has observed inaction despite the virulence of attacks on Cecil earlier in James I's reign. She concluded that only in times of acute tension threatening political stability that the government would consider punitive steps.[5]

Sheila Lambert has done most to counter 'the idea that an all-pervasive censorship, which successfully prevented all expression of unorthodox opinions, was intended by the autocratic and repressive governments of James I and Charles I'. She has suggested that the notion of strict state control was a useful concept, capable of excusing a multitude of early printing 'sins', including poor copy. 'It is only natural that historians of the newspaper press, believing that "the battles for a free Press are a part of the march of democracy", should seek to emphasise the extent to which the journalistic

---

[3] (16 July 1630), 14, STC18507.205; Dahl. 168; Add MS 69,911, fo. 87; L. Rostenberg, 'Nathaniel Butter and Nicholas Bourne, First Masters of the Staple', *The Library*, 5:12 (1957); L. Rostenberg, *Literary, Political, Scientific, Religious and Legal Publishing, Printing and Bookselling in England*, 1 (New York, 1965), 75–93; G. Mandelbrote, 'From the Warehouse to the Counting-house: Booksellers and Bookshops in Late Seventeenth-century London', in *Genius for Letters*, ed. R. Myers and M. Harris (Winchester and New Castle, DE, 1995), 77.

[4] C. Hill, 'Censorship and English Literature', in *The Collected Essays of Christopher Hill*, 1 (Brighton, 1985); Lambert, 1–32; C. S. Clegg, *Press Censorship in Jacobean England* (Cambridge, 2001).

[5] Siebert, 151; K. Sharpe, 'A Commonwealth of Meanings, Languages, Analogues, Ideas and Politics', in *Politics and Ideas in Early Stuart England* (London and New York, 1989), 9; P Croft, 'Libels, Popular Literacy and Public Opinion in Early Modern England', *Historical Research*, 68 (1995), 276; Levy, 13, 27–8.

profession has triumphed over great odds.' She has depicted James's procla-mations between December 1620 and 8 March 1624 as intended to assure the Spanish Ambassador that the State was doing its best ... to give him proper protection' while responding to concerns expressed by the Stationers' Company over overseas piracy of books for which there were domestic patents.[6]

Post-revisionist accounts range from Thomas Cogswell's *The Blessed Revolution*, suggesting that censorship was effective, to Cyndia Clegg's *Press Censorship in Jacobean England*, emphasising the multiplicity of players in the 'enormously complicated' political print world of Jacobean England. Censorship operated mainly in times of crisis, suppressing works infre-quently and only temporarily, often in response to the concerns of political allies. Foreign ambassadors and court members influenced James, validating the frequent speculations of contemporary commentators who pointed at the role of Spanish ambassadors. In this account censorship was a complex cultural negotiation 'made to serve multiple cultural ends'. The ecclesiastical hierarchy, on whom the Crown would normally rely, was, however, inactive in tackling foreign news while the press itself was amassing authority and power of its own.[7]

The story of the inception of the periodical news trade in London fits well with Clegg's analysis. In the first two years London publishers took advantage of the availability of periodical news and the surge in interest. Compromise and innovation resulted in establishing parameters within which this new trade could operate and gave the publishers public and offi-cial recognition.

Coranto publication

Though the earliest corantos in English were produced in Amsterdam, production was soon taken up in London, but bibliographers have disputed the way in which these transitions occurred and the reasons why.

On 29 November 1620, the Dorchester merchant William Whiteway recorded in his diary that 'newes came to the towne that the King of Bohemia was overthrown by Count Bucquoy and fled with the queen into Silesia'. This news was already spreading across England when the first surviving corantos in English reported the defeat at White Mountain. How and why did these reports reach London? They gave the seller's name and address as Peter de Keere in Calverstreet, Amsterdam, which suggests they were printed initially for sale to Amsterdam's local immigrant English speaking population. De Keere seized the marketing opportunity in the wake of Impe-

---

6 Lambert, 1–2, 20–3.
7 Cogswell; Clegg, *Jacobean England*, 14, 15, 18, 19.

rial troops' advance on Prague. He was an illustrator of newsprints and a map engraver whose Calvinist family had fled to London from Ghent when he was 11 years old. He was related by marriage to the coranto publisher, Jan Jansson. He had worked for John Nordon and maintained close associations with London stationers. He provided engravings for John Speed's 1627 atlas of Great Britain that was published by George Humble who traded at the sign of the White Horse in Pope's Head Alley. With these contacts he was well placed to start sending printed news to London, probably to Thomas Archer whose bookshop was in the same alley.[8]

Initially, de Keere's name and address would have given authenticity to the product. It was probably familiar to customers who attended the Dutch Church in Austin Friars near Pope's Head Alley, as well as to local stationers. Once the series was established in London his name on copies would have been less important. The removal of English news from the series, then the omission of his name from the imprint from 9 April 1621 suggests a gradual transition of their main market from the Netherlands to London as interest in the international crisis grew.[9]

This series was to continue through the spring and summer of 1621, covering news that provided a backdrop to parliamentary discussion. After MPs had been summoned, James issued a proclamation against 'Lavish and Licentious speech of matters of State' on 24 December 1620 which referred to the growth of 'Intercourse with foreign nations' and cautioned everyone 'from the highest to the lowest, to take heede, how they intermeddle by Penne, or Speech, with causes of State, and secrets of Empire, either at home, or abroad', threatening punishment for offenders.[10] Announced before copies of the second surviving coranto reached the streets of London, the proclamation provides no evidence to suggest that the Crown was singling out corantos. James's aim was to avoid war. Unwilling to support his son-in-law's succession to the crown of Bohemia, yet concerned to protect the Palatinate from Spinola, James was faced with a dilemma which he meant to address in Parliament. His proclamation was directed against all forms of public discussion of foreign affairs and was supported by an order to the bishop of London to summon the clergy 'to charge them from the King not to meddle in sermons with the Spanish match or any other matters of state'.[11]

Historians have disputed the interpretation of this proclamation. It said nothing about printing. Francis Bacon wrote to Buckingham on

[8] Frearson, 236; Appendix 1, STC18507.1–7; R. A. Skelton, 'Pieter Van Den Keere', *The Library*, 5:5 (1950); G. Leth, 'A Protestant Public Sphere: The Early European Newspaper Press', in *Annual* (1993), 71–2.
[9] F. Dahl, 'Amsterdam – the Cradle of English Newspapers', *The Library*, 5:4 (1949), 169.
[10] Quoted in full in *Proclamations*, 1, 208, 218.
[11] Clegg, *Jacobean England*, 84, 185–6.

16 November 1620 expressing concern about the level of talk about foreign affairs and he drafted the December proclamation as part of the preparations for Parliament. Foreign affairs were being debated at every level. In the press, pulpit and tavern, 1588 was being relived, and the Bohemian events were being debated. Pictures of the *Double Deliverance* from the Spanish Armada and Gunpowder Plot were in circulation in London. The proclamation also followed close on the heels of the appearance of *Vox Populi* by Thomas Scott, a puritan cleric. This exposed Spanish influences on English policies at home and abroad through a fictional dialogue between Spanish ministers and Count Gondomar. *Vox Populi* ran to seven editions in its first year with many manuscript copies also in circulation. Its production coincided with the arrival of Gondomar for his second term as Spanish ambassador in England and so angered him that he complained to James. When news of the White Mountain disaster arrived, London became so angry that Gondomar was jeered and his litter attacked in the street. The proclamation consequently appeared at a time when the whole country was at fever pitch with anxiety over events in Bohemia and the Palatinate.[12]

This was a new situation for James. The decision to call Parliament made the question of what was being reported more sensitive. He regarded foreign policy as a matter for his own deliberation but he needed Parliament's support to raise money and this dependence made the already unclear distinctions between domestic and foreign affairs, acceptable comment and unacceptable criticism, open to question. When Parliament assembled it was in a radical mood and immediately questioned the king's motives in making the proclamation. Calvert explained that it was 'intended against such as make ordinary table talk of state matters in taverns and alehouses, and not against parliament men'.[13]

It would have been easy enough, even at the time, to be less than completely clear about what James intended by this proclamation. Subsequent events, including the examination of Floyd by the House of Commons for disrespectful speech about Frederick and Elizabeth, and the arrests of the earl of Oxford and Edwin Sandys for inappropriate speech, not to mention the anti-Spanish sermons inspired by the conflict, demonstrated the need to cool passions while administrative action showed that James was concerned about the impact of imported material in encouraging public discussion.[14]

---

[12] F. Bacon, *Works*, ed. J. Spedding, 7 (1874), 14, 150–1; Proclamations (December 1620 and July 1621), quoted in *Proclamations*, 208, 218; D. Colclough, *Freedom of Speech in Early Stuart England* (Cambridge, 2005), 104–05; R. Zaller, *The Parliament of 1621* (Berkeley, CA, 1971), 27–8; H. Pierce, *Unseemly Pictures: Graphic Satire and Politics in Early Modern England* ((New Haven, CT and London, 2008), 36–41; J. O. Halliwell, ed., *The Autobiography and correspondence of Sir Simonds D'Ewes*, 1 (1845), 159–60, 187.
[13] Ibid., *The Parliament*, 38.
[14] Ibid., 104–09; Clegg, *Jacobean England*, 263, fn. 103; Chamberlain to Carleton, 22 December 1622, *Chamberlain*, 2:331.

Anna Simoni's *Catalogue of Books from the Low Countries 1601–1621* shows 367 news pamphlets from the Low Countries now in the British Library. Puritan refugees were smuggling works to England and harbouring Thomas Scott who had left England because of the outstanding success of *Vox Populi*. Catholic sympathisers in Antwerp, where Richard Verstegan, another English refugee, became one of the earliest identifiable European news journalists, were also making foreign news more readily available in England.[15] Government turned its attention to the ports: on 21 December 1621, Lord Zouch, Warden of the Cinque Ports, and Mayor of Dover confiscated 108 'dangerous books' being imported from France. Much of the port control activity focused on Catholic publications since James was criticised in Parliament in 1621 for allowing the increase in French and Spanish ambassadorial personnel, their attendance at Catholic masses and for their importation of Catholic books.[16] However, import control was always problematic and, like the proclamation of December 1620, activity at the ports appears to have had little effect.

James appealed to the Dutch Government and on 16 January 1621 the States General issued a proclamation stating that there had been secret and public printing in 'Latin, French, English, Scottish and various other languages, both on ecclesiastical and political matters, touching persons and governments of Kings, Princes, friends and allies'. The Dutch were therefore forbidden,

> to send the same to other countries and realms and particularly not to send some twelve scandalous writings and pamphlets concerning other Kings and potentates, friends and allies, touching their political or ecclesiastical governments, and especially none against the King of Great Britain and his principal ministers, spiritual and temporal.

We do not know which publications had caused particular offence.[17] The emphasis was on pamphlets and tracts and, again, there was no noticeable impact on the publication of corantos in English. It seems that neither de Keere nor Veseler had any concerns about political impropriety. Even when de Keere's name and address disappeared from the imprint in the spring, issues continued to identify Veseler as the printer, making production easy to trace.

[15] A. Simoni' (1999); L. B. Wright, 'Propaganda Against James I's "Appeasement of Spain"', *HLQ*, 6 (February 1943), 2; P. Arblaster, *Antwerp and the World: Richard Verstigan and the International Culture of Catholic Reformation* (Leuven, 2004).

[16] Frearson, 241; L. Rostenberg, *The Minority Press and the English Crown* (New York, 1971), 144, 78–80, 119–20, 166.

[17] *Groot Placet Boeck*, 1 (1658) 409, 441, quoted in the *Tercentenary Handlist of English and Welsh Newspapers, Magazines, and Revues* (Times, 1920), 9.

Having found the authorities either less interested in their small digests of news than in the more political fare of the polemicists, or unable to do anything effective to stop them, de Keere might have continued to export copies to England as Broer Jansz did to France. However, this approach had limitations. Shipping costs would have been high for such a low value product and the larger the shipments became the greater the chances of them being intercepted on the docks. Importing would only work long term with a stable, moderate demand from a clientele who could afford to pay for a special service via a subscription list like those used for manuscript news. But with the assembly of Parliament and MPs arriving in London with support for Frederick and Elizabeth on their minds, demand for news was running high. Stationers in London could not have remained content for long with a sales role, still less with the prospect of missing sales if shipments proved too small. Publication in London would have been cheaper and Londoners were better placed to exploit marketing opportunities.

Mead provides evidence that supply did not keep up with demand. His correspondence begins with news of the White Mountain defeat which he got from a letter from 'an English gentleman there'. Then Mead relied primarily on transcripts of corantos through the spring of 1621 but commented on the scarcity of supply on 9 February and again in April when he referred to 'a later Courrante ... I have seen it but could not be the owner of any of them'. Even after he began to pass on printed corantos in April over half of his foreign news continued to be transmitted in transcripts.[18]

To switch production to London, publishers needed a deal with traders in Amsterdam for a regular supply of copy and, if printing were to take place weekly in the City under the noses of the wardens of the Company, crown officials and Ecclesiastical Commissioners, they would need some assurance that this would be acceptable. The prospects cannot have looked promising in the spring of 1621, so the first approach was simply to avoid dealing with this altogether through sporadic illicit publication. At first sight it would appear that the main competition to de Keere came from a second series from Amsterdam. There are fifteen surviving issues of English corantos with Amsterdam or other Dutch imprints, dated from 9 April to 10 August, of questionable authenticity. A letter from John Chamberlain to Dudley Carleton, 10 August 1621, tells us that presses in London printed 'every weeke, at least, corantos with all manner of, newes and as strange stuffe as any we have from Amsterdam', and a typographical analysis by Hanson shows the trade was very quickly picked up in London, probably by Thomas Archer using false imprints with at least some of the issues coming from the press of Edward Allde.[19] Despite this, and considerable bibliographical

---

[18] Harl. MS 389 fo. 1, 11, 61.
[19] Appendix 1; *Chamberlain*, 2:396; L. Hanson, 'English Newsbooks, 1620–41'. *The Library*, 4:18 (1937–8), 356–64; Dahl, 42.

research, the evidence of the earliest London publication of corantos remains confused and confusing, complicated by the uneven pattern of the survival of issues. What is clear, however, is that the initiative rested entirely with enthusiastic publishers who deliberately obscured the origins of early issues.

Thomas Archer was probably the first to take the plunge into London publication and the authorities caught up with him quite quickly. Joseph Mead, on 22 September 1621, told Sir Martin Stuteville that 'my Corran-toer, Archer was layd by the heales for making or adding to Corrantoes'. Further information about Archer's activities as a supplier of news to Mead can be found in Mead's papers. There are eight transcripts of corantos in this correspondence, plus two references to other printed corantos during 1621 that Mead copied from and for which there are no other records and there are many other foreign news reports. The papers also include nine of the earliest surviving corantos: eight of them among those identified as having false imprints. Since Mead said specifically on occasions that he was relying on printed copies, it seems reasonable to conclude that when he did not specify his material arrived in manuscript form. He also referred to drawing on at least two sources, one of which was Dutch and more 'continual'.[20] This suggests that first there was a scribal effort to supplement the supply of printed corantos and this continued after Archer began to publish in London. The second stage was illicit printing. When Mead said he was getting corantos from Archer he probably was, which is why the ones he received were mostly those with false imprints.

Archer's involvement is best understood by looking at the way he traded. He was apprenticed to Cuthbert Burby, a bookseller in Cornhill near the Exchange, and had little opportunity to learn to print. He became a freeman in January 1603 and began publication that year with Henry Timberlake's *True and strange discourse ... of two English pilgrimes*. In his early years he occupied a series of premises, a little shop by the Royal Exchange, the Long Shop under St Mildred's Church in 1604, and Popes Head Palace near the Royal Exchange in 1607. Then he moved to Pope's Head Alley, by the Sign of the Horse-Shoe, where he dealt in plays, jest-books and popular litera-ture. He was brought before the Court of the Stationers' Company and fined in August 1619 for 'Bynding Fran. Williams(on) at a scriveno(rs) and for keeping him Contrary to order'. In 1617 both he and Nathaniel Newbery, another stationer who was later to join the news syndicate, went into the news trade. News became Archer's major interest. We do not know how much of this was scribal.[21]

John Dunton's career, though later in the seventeenth century, shows how a bookseller with little capital worked with cheap publications. Once he had a publication, he traded with other booksellers to get a variety of pamphlets

---

[20] Appendix 2; Harl. MS 389 fo. 122; Levy, 34; Harl. MS 389 fo. 11.
[21] Jackson, Fine Book, 112; Shaaber, 289; Rostenburg, 'Nathaniel Butter', 28.

and to assemble stock with the minimum financial outlay. Dunton did not expect to pay much for material: when asked by a writer for more money, Dunton was indignant, saying that they wanted to become 'half-booksellers' and there would be no profit. He would also publish without an author's consent.[22] Archer, like Dunton, had to build up capital gradually, concentrating upon cheaper works where the outlay would be low.

In the seventeenth century most publishers needed to seek work actively, especially to specialise in news from abroad. Venturing into the European market meant entering into a world of letter writing to secure a steady supply of copy. Archer may well have approached de Keere or Veseler to change the arrangements. We have no evidence that he did, other than the fact that de Keere dropped his name from the English imports on 9 April; the day the first surviving London issue appeared, suggesting that de Keere and Veseler may have been aware of the decision to begin to print in London. However, Veseler decided to continue to export in any case.[23] Without an agreement Archer published what came to hand so that the issues with false imprints came from a variety of sources.

Archer was venturing into a market where he had reason to expect that, despite the very considerable interest in European affairs at the time, he might not attract too much unwelcome official attention. The accounts of events of distant and unfamiliar places, sometimes with conflicting reports of a single event generated by the confusion of warfare, were not aimed for popular consumption by the ignorant. Only a discerning reader was likely to get very much intelligible information from them. Dutch imports had tested the market, giving him the expectation of a good trade, particularly among discreet newsletter correspondents. The Dutch also inadvertently gave him the opportunity to shelter behind the names of respected Amsterdam tradesmen who were openly associating themselves with the trade. It may at first have seemed a relatively simple matter, and a good marketing ploy, to take advantage of their imprints.[24]

Mead's letter of 22 September 1621 shows he believed the trade was officially sanctioned, but his assumption has no basis in the records of the Stationers Company and it is not clear why Mead thought this if the only corantos in London at this stage had a Dutch imprint, authentic or false. To Mead the term 'Corrantoer' may have meant seller or transcriber of corantos. Honest translation, rather than the question of whether they could be lawfully sold, seems to have been the key issue for him. Morison has suggested that Archer was probably punished for doing literally as Mead said, 'adding to his corantos' by making use of the blank space at the end of the coranto to add items of more local news, but there is nothing to support

[22] Printed for S. Malthus (1705); S. Parks, *John Dunton and the English Book Trade* (1976); G. Wither, *Schollers Purgatory* (1625) quoted in Arber, vol. 4, 14–19.
[23] Appendix 1.
[24] S. Lambert, 'Coranto Printing in England', *JNandPH*, 8 (1992), 7.

this.[25] The frequency of the news service may have convinced Mead that the business was legitimate or it could not continue. By the same token, however, it could only have been a matter of time before the Stationers' Company would trace their source to Archer and seek fees for entering issues in their register.

Archer was fined in July 1621 for publishing unlicensed books. The Fine Book of the Company states, 'It is ordered that Tho Archer for causing to be printed certain books unlicensed and unentered shall pay for a fine ... xls'. In August they took further action: Archer was imprisoned just as Mead reported but for the publication of a foreign news pamphlet with a false imprint from the press of Edward Allde, ostensibly printed at the Hague by Arnold Meuris.

> It is ordered that Mr Alldee and Thomas Archer shal be comitted to prison, upon Mr Secretaries Calverts Comands for printing a book called, A briefe declaracon of Ban made against the King of Bohemia as being the Electo(r) Palatine Dated 22 Janurij last of noe value or worth, and therefore not to be respected. It is alsoe ordered, that the barres of his presses shal be taken downe.[26]

Edward Allde was a printer who took risks: he had earlier antagonised the authorities by printing Catholic publications, an illicit edition of *Basilicon Doron* and using a fictitious imprint. He and Archer seem to have been collaborating on a number of works. The Court Book entry for Edward Allde's release from prison, dated 8 October 1621, shows he was questioned about printing several unlicensed works, not just the one specified in the entry for 13 August,

> Whereas Mr Alldee, hath latlie Imprinted diverse bookes without lycense or entrance, and being called into question for the same, hath used verie unfitting wordes and scandalous speeches.... It is therefore this daie ordered that he shall not ... attend anie more as a liveries man untill he shall submitt himselfe to this table.

Archer appears to have remained in prison throughout the winter. His name did not reappear in the Stationers' books until the following May when he was reminded of his outstanding debt to the Company for the fine for unlicensed publications. It took Allde rather longer to 'submitt himself' to the table. In July 1623 he fully apologised for 'printing certaine Currante and other bookes w[ith]out lycense or Entrance', for careless work, and for disorderly behaviour.[27]

---

[25] S. Morison, *The Origins of the Newspaper* (1954), 20, 24.

[26] Jackson, Fine Book, 466, 9 July 1621; Lambert, 'Coranto Printing', 8; Jackson, Court Book, 137.

[27] Ibid., 138, 146, 156; Rostenberg, *Minority Press*, 59–60; R. B. McKerrow, 'Edward Allde as a Typical Trade Printer', *The Library*, 4:10 (1929), 123–4, 133–5, 139.

The Crown's sensitivity and action by the Stationers' Company against Archer and Allde must be seen in the context of the growing crisis in Europe and a confused domestic response. James's failure to show sufficient public sympathy for the fate of Elizabeth and the Protestant cause put him onto a collision course with public opinion, and Parliament proved more difficult to direct than anticipated. As a result, an enterprise that may have seemed low risk in the winter of 1620/1 grew more hazardous. James reissued his proclamation against 'Lavish and Licentious speech on matters of State' in July 1621, at the height of a summer full of news and rumour. This reissue followed the investigation of a book called *Withers Mottos*. The Company, the Crown and the High Commission collaborated: the prosecution of Nicholas Oakes for his part in *Withers Mottos* was brought before the Archbishop of Canterbury on 10 July by the Stationers' Company and the hearing of evidence ran through to 12 July. A fine was then registered in the Stationers' Company Fine Book on 23 August 1621.[28]

The July proclamation may be interpreted as part of a more general effort to contain controversial printing during the summer recess. Clegg describes 1621 as the 'high-water mark' in government efforts to contain criticism of James's foreign policy. Parliament adjourned at the beginning of June with a promise of subsidies if peace could not be restored by treaty but it voted no more cash and Digby's mission to Vienna to negotiate for the restitution of the Palatinate was met coldly. There was no resolution in sight.[29]

Corantos were, by this time, reflecting increasingly unrealistic hopes of a Protestant alliance for the recovery of the Palatinate. According to them, this was to include Bohemia, Denmark, Sweden, Lower Saxony and the United Provinces, despite the Treaty of Mainz in April, in which the Evangelical Union had agreed to withdraw their troops from the Palatinate and effectively disbanded. They were even more out of step with the diplomatic situation when they criticised Spain. A coranto with an 'Altmore' imprint of 29 July 1621 included the text of a letter from Mansfeld to Bethlem Gabor referring to 'the tyrannie of the Pope and crueltie of the Spanish yoke'; while an issue of 9 August, with a 'Joris Veseler' imprint, included a report from Frankfurt of Spanish garrisons that were not allowing farmers to work their land without paying large levies. Crops were being spoiled and people running away. The reports were counterbalanced over the summer by the honest reporting of the damage and sacking done by Mansfeld's forces. But criticism of Spain was a particularly sensitive issue. James's hopes of settlement for the Palatinate rested on negotiations supported by Spain: a general cease-fire and subsequent six-week extensions were negotiated by James through Madrid.[30]

---

[28] SPDom. 14, fo. 122, art.18, 12 July 1621; Jackson, Fine Book, 46.
[29] Clegg, *Jacobean England*, 194; Zaller, *The Parliament*, 137, 143.
[30] Appendix 1 (29 July 1621), verso, STC18507.26; (9 August 1621), verso, STC18507.13; (9 July 1621), verso, STC18507.23; Zaller, *The Parliament*, 142.

Yet the coranto trade did not stop. Mead's letter of 22 September 1621, reporting Archer's arrest added: 'now there is another that hath got license to print ... and sell them, honestly translated out of the Dutch'.[31] The first surviving coranto with a London imprint stated, 'London Printed for N B September 24th 1621 Out of the Hie Dutch Coppy printed at Frankford'. Seven issues from this series have survived, with the last dated 22 October 1621. They refer to 'N B' as the publisher. This was either Nathaniel Browne, a London bookseller at St Paul's, who published foreign news pamphlets from 1617, or Nathaniel Butter or Nicholas Bourne both of whom were subsequently involved with foreign news for many years. It was probably Butter. John Nichols, in *Literary Anecdotes*, also lists a 'Courant, or Weekly Newes from Foreign Parts' in blackletter, 'out of the High Dutch, printed for Nath. Butter' dated October 1621, which may have been a slightly different version of the issue of 9 October.[32] These corantos appear to follow on directly from the last surviving issue of the Veseler series, dated 18 September 1621 but we do not know if Butter came to an agreement with Veseler, possibly as part of a rationalisation once Van Hilten took over management in Amsterdam. Again, it could be the chance survival of copies that suggests succession. Butter's first publication claimed to be a translation of a German original, not Dutch.

However, this venture was even more short-lived than Archer's. As Parliament resumed its debate on the Palatinate, soon after the date of the last surviving 'N B' coranto, Butter was called before the Court of the Company of Stationers. There is nothing to throw light upon the Mead's statement, that 'another hath got license to print them'. We do not know whether a licence was granted, only that these issues were not registered with the Stationers' Company. Butter may have thought this unnecessary or, like Mead, he may have believed he had been given a privilege that exempted him from Company registration. Alternatively, as these were only single sheets, he may have thought them too ephemeral to warrant registration. Historians can be forgiven for finding it difficult to know what was considered permissible when contemporaries could not assess the situation correctly. Whatever discussions Butter had with either the Stationers' Company or court officials before deciding to put his initials to the September 1621 series, he must have thought he was safe enough. He was mistaken.

Nathaniel Butter was already an experienced publisher of news. He is the best known of those involved in this early news trade and by the time he died in 1664 he had a total of 60 years experience as a stationer. Butter was born into the trade. His father, Thomas, was a bookseller with premises at St

---

[31] Harl. MS 389 fo. 122.
[32] (24 September 1621), STC18507.29; (22 October 1621), STC18507.35; (9 October 1621), STC18507.33; Dahl, 51, 53–4, quotes Nichols, 4 (1812), 38.

Austin's Gate, St Paul's Churchyard, who appears to have confined his business largely to distribution and had few publications. At his death his widow continued the business. She married another stationer, John Newbery, but continued to conduct her own business. Nathaniel served his apprenticeship under her and his stepfather. He was made a freeman on 20 February 1604. As with Archer, there was little opportunity to become a printer. He may have inherited a little working capital from his mother, but there appears to have been no question of financial enterprise on a large scale.

Butter set up a shop at the Pied Bull near St Austin's Gate. His first registered publication appeared on 4 December 1604 and was entitled, *The Life and Death of Cavaliero Dick Boyer*. His interest spread to other types of work at the popular end of the market – sermons, tracts and pamphlets. In 1605, he published *Sir Thomas Smithes Voiage and Entertainment in Rushia*. Between 1607 and 1611 he published a report on the 1605 expedition to Guiana and a report from Norwich assizes, *The Originall Ground of the present Warres of Sweden*, and *Newes from Spain*. He also took an interest in some better quality works, including Chapman's translation of the *Iliad*, Dekker's *Belman of London* and Shakespeare's *King Lear*.[33]

As early as 1611 he had trade contacts abroad. George Waters, at Dordrecht, printed an edition of the school primer for him and he began to sell his publications at the Frankfurt Book Fair, where for many years, numerous religious tracts and news pamphlets of his were recorded in the English catalogues. By 1614 he was well established and able to lend £36 15/- to Ralphe Mabbe a bookseller in London, who was later to become a competitor in foreign news. In 1616, he invested £50 in the stock of the Stationers' Company. By 1622 he had trained four apprentices and published some two hundred books nearly half of which may be regarded as news tracts, including sensational news of murderers, travel stories, accounts of the Irish rebellions and foreign news. Rostenberg claims that he was able to 'scent the literary trends of the day and anticipate the changing tastes of the morrow'.[34] But he also had brushes with the authorities. He lost his share in the English Stock when it was concluded that the primers printed in Dordrecht were pirated. On 3 April 1620 he was fined for keeping an unbound apprentice. Then he was imprisoned, and William Stansby fined, for printing *A Plaine Demonstration of the unlawful succession*. These penalties presented Butter with serious financial problems. He petitioned Sir George Calvert for release, asking for his freedom because his wife was pregnant. They had three small children and no income other than his business:

> To the honorable Sr George (Calvert) …
> The humble Peticon of Nathaniell Butter.
> Humbly shewinge that whereas your poore Suppliant hath byn Comytted by my

---

[33] ODNB, Butter.
[34] Rostenberg, *Literary*, 77–8; Rostenberg, 'Nathaniel', 24.

lords grace of Canterbury the space of 28 daies being since brought before your honour and examyned about the printing of a booke Concernynge the Emperor wherein he hath answered truly and freely and for which he doth humbly acknowledge his fault, being Comytted to a Messenger he knoweth nott howe to obtayne his libertie haveing a poore wief greatt with Childe and three small Children, and is like to be undone, without your honours Consideration.

Wherefore he humbly desiereth your honours Comiseraction in grauntinge his libertie uppon good and sufficient bayle[35]

He was released before 8 April 1621 when he was once again making entries in the register of the Stationers' Company for publications. Then, like Archer later in 1621, he was in trouble again, this time for 'printing certayne lets from the Pope to the ffrench King w(th)out entrance'. The work was *A Letter to the French King Louis xiii*. His name appears in the Fine Book again, in March 1622, this time for *David's Straight; a sermon*, printed by Eld for Butter that year, without entrance in the register. Then, on 11 May 1622, again like Archer, he reappeared before the Stationers' Court seeking to settle matters.[36]

An intriguing postscript to this early stage in the history of the periodical news trade comes from a letter from John Chamberlain on 16 February 1622. It refers to the news press having been running in London for two years:

The uncertainty likewise and the variety of reports is such that we know not what to believe of that done under our nose; and what gives out today for certain is to-morrow contradicted. For, since two years that forge, or mint, was set up at Amsterdam we have never left off coining, so apish are we in imitation of what is worst.

This confirms Chamberlain's earlier assertion that the corantos were being published in London, but brings their first appearance forward, suggesting that they had been printed in London from February 1620 rather than for five months from the commencement of the 'N B' series in September 1621. Of course, Chamberlain's reference need not be interpreted as referring exclusively to corantos, since, from 1619 onwards, the presses had been busily turning out proclamations, justifications and news pamphlets related to the Bohemian Revolt. However, the characteristics he described, variety of reports, apish imitation and news being given out one day, then corrected another, leaves little doubt that he had corantos in mind.

If corantos appeared in London before the first surviving one from December 1620, numbers were probably low. There was little reason to keep them until reports of the defeat of Frederick at White Mountain began

---

[35] SPDom., 14 (James), 4 fo. 130 (in the papers for 1623); Lambert, 'Coranto Printing', 8.

[36] Jackson, Court Book, 139 and Fine Book, 467; Jackson, Court Book, 145.

to appear and Parliament was called, bringing this news to the top of the political agenda. Thomas Archer appears to have been the first to develop the trade in London. His decision to shelter behind false imprints seems to have been astute since he found himself in prison within a matter of months, albeit in connection with another work bearing a false imprint. By the autumn of 1621, with the appearance of the 'N B' series, we see the first sign of an attempt to adopt a more established approach backed by a supply arrangement, though this too stopped abruptly. The arrests of Archer and Butter in 1621, both officially for reasons unconnected with their involvement in the coranto trade did not mean that there was no connection; only that the authorities preferred to take action on familiar grounds.

As imported ephemera, corantos were difficult to pick up through searches at the ports and they were a new type of publication, easily produced and quickly dispersed. It was seldom thought necessary to license single sheets such as broadside ballads or to enter them in the registers. Given the short shelf life of corantos, there was no advantage in registering ownership.[37] Without a specific ban against them, the Company's jurisdiction in this field was probably unclear, but it was no doubt a matter of concern to the officials of the Company by the summer of 1621 that corantos were being regularly produced in London, under false imprints. It made sense for them to obstruct publication by the simple expedient of attacking those thought to be involved on other grounds. The Company's first response was, it seems, to decide to require licensing and a fee. But their authority was by no means fully established. Butter went ahead in September and October with his series without entering them and without making any attempt to hide his identity.

It took time, but the corantos were stopped towards the end of 1621. Does this mean that Lambert's challenge to the Whig account is unhelpful and we must revert to the idea that censorship was a significant and effective force in the early Stuart period? Siebert created the impression that the king, faced with a new type of threat to absolute monarchy, set out systematically to use every means available to him to suppress corantos, then brought them within his direct control. But, while government tried to use most of the powers available to stem the flow of foreign publications, James's approach was far from draconian and, as Lambert has successfully demonstrated, any analysis must acknowledge the independence and very different interests at play in the Stationers' Company.[38] The Company and the Crown collaborated. It took up to two years to stop the corantos and it was the Stationers' Company, not the Crown, acting directly that achieved

---

[37] D. F. McKenzie, 'Printing and Publishing 1557–1700: Constraints on the London Book Trades', in Barnard, 565; A. McShane Jones, 'The Gazet in Metre; Or the Rhiming Newsmonger' The English Broadside Ballad as Intelligencer, a New Narrative', in Koopmans, 139.
[38] Licensing for trade regulation and revenues, Clegg, Jacobean England, 178, 180, 246.

this. However, we cannot simply write off the experience of 1620–1 as a demonstration of ineffective government either. James had at his disposal a variety of means of exercising control, directly and indirectly, that worked.

The emergence of a new approach from October 1621 to May 1622

The story did not end there. There was a keen public interest and a good deal to report, with the conquest of Bohemia and the invasion of the Palatinate. From July to October 1621 alone, twenty-two extant corantos were published, at least one a week. Import control had failed to stem the flow of print. It was time for a more negotiated approach in London.

Reflecting contemporary interest, Sir Simonds D'Ewes looked back on his diary from the winter of 1620/1 to 1622 that was full of the most sad and calamitous news of the flight of Frederick and Elizabeth.[39] Royal proclamations, the correspondence of Mead and the comments of John Chamberlain all point to the desire for news. But how effective were corantos in responding to this demand? Were they the right vehicle for the London market?

Their short format meant they were terse and often difficult to interpret without some prior knowledge of who was who and what was where. Records of readers come from the diaries and correspondence of social elites. They did not give corantos (or their successors, the newsbooks) much of a recommendation. It is not surprising that contemporaries with more direct sources of information from the Continent found the news stale. Yet complaints about the slowness and inaccuracy of the printed news may have been fed by a snobbish feeling that private sources of information had to be superior. Only a real expert in the news business used to direct reports, like Joseph Mead, could complain on 2 June 1627 that the only available news 'is from the corranto & that so ancient as it concerns nothing done since May began'. Even so, Mead continued to get corantos regularly and forward or describe them or send transcripts. So, they had a role, filling in gaps in news left by the coverage of correspondents and, given the criticism whenever there was delay, we can take it that they were valued for reasonable speed.[40]

Despite evidence that social elites, people of influence in their counties and in Parliament, continued both to read and to criticise printed foreign news, twentieth-century historians decried the significance of the arrival of corantos in England and most accepted that censorship was effective. Zagorin and Cust accepted that domestic news was banned throughout the period and Zagorin saw the corantos and newsbooks as 'dry', acknowledging simultaneously considerable public interest, which made it impossible for

---

[39] *Autobiography D'Ewes*, vol. 1, 151–5, 162, 221.
[40] Schumacher, 62–3; Dahl, 152.

the government to stifle them. Cogswell has described them as 'heavily censored and bland' and contrasted them with scribal texts that avoided censorship. Not unreasonably, he suggested that tracking down anonymous poets was much more difficult than tracing a printing press.[41] However, we cannot assume corantos went unread or that they had little impact. It would also be a mistake to assume that censorship had any role in shaping them. The initial impact of official interventions was only to stem their appearance in London temporarily. This did not affect their content. In all the cases where it has been possible to match English corantos with their continental counterpart the text has been practically identical. We need to re-evaluate the evidence.

Joseph Mead was part of a network of correspondents in England and exactly the kind of customer for whom the corantos were most suited. He had the time, patience and interest to follow issues regularly and carefully, comparing reports and dates, and drawing his own conclusions. His corre-spondence with Sir Martin Stuteville shows he was a good customer, with evidence of a great deal more coranto activity in England than we might guess from the sparse survival rate of printed issues. Even by early February 1621 it reveals an expectation of regular news. By June, a hitch in supply was remarkable, he wrote, 'The last Saturday failed almost wholly of foreign news; the winds I suppose have been these three weeks opposite', then the next week, 'Corrantoes, I know not what is become of them'.[42] By early summer 1621, there were four or more corantos a month in circulation. He compared sources and annotated the contents of a London letter dated 18 May 1621 with comments such as, 'The Corranto says that it was' and 'The Corranto (from Vienna) says'. At the end he added, 'More out of the Corranto Amsterdam May 24 styl nov.1621'. Mead distinguished carefully the sources he used, identifying those from Amsterdam separately from those from Cologne. For example, 'Cullen Feb 12 and 19 1620/21 sn' and 'Cullen Aprill 29 Amsterdam May 1 styl novo'. He recognised, more clearly than we can now, two distinct series in circulation, explaining his source as 'a friend of mine one of the clergie in the Cittie whom I had ... begun to imploy for the getting of the Cullen Coranto' and his preference for the Cologne news 'as being though not so continuall yet better then those of the Hague'.[43]

When Butter began coranto publication in September 1621, he too distinguished carefully between Dutch and German sources. We have four surviving issues from the High Dutch dated 24 September, 2, 9, and 22 October, the first of which specifies its source as Frankfurt. Issues of 30

[41] P. Zagorin, The Court and Country (1969), 107; R. Cust, 'News and Politics in Early Seventeenth-Century England', PandP, 112 (1986), 62; K. Thomas in The Written Word: Literacy in Transition, ed. G. Baumann (Oxford, 1986), 97–122; T. Cogswell, 'Underground Verse and the Transformation of Early Stuart Political Culture', in Amussen, 278.
[42] Cust, 63, 70–1; Harl. MS 389, fo. 11, fo. 100.
[43] Harl. MS 389, fo. 74, 75, 16, 32, 63, 11; Appendix 2.

September and 6 and 11 October are identified as Dutch. Butter was making a serious attempt to present the public with clearly authenticated translations and appears to have had supply networks in place.[44]

The next step was the emergence of the newsbook format in preference to the single sheet coranto. This gave scope to break away from the summary and terse reports of the Dutch corantos. The change also made sense in the context of the registration of publications by the Stationers' Company and facilitated the inspection of issues by 'Mr Cottington', the appointed licenser.

Entries for two newsbooks with licences from 'Master Cottington' appear in the register of the Company for 23 October and 6 November 1621. One was for a newsbook, like a pamphlet but with a variety of reports providing news from many different places. It was entitled *The Certaine and True Newes, from all Parts of Germany and Poland*, and was printed for Bartholomew Downes and William Lee, his apprentice.[45] The other, *Newes from Poland*, was a more traditional pamphlet, but with an English diplomatic agenda. It told of Sir Thomas Glover's embassy in Constantinople, and audience of the English ambassador, Sir Arthur Ashton in May 1621. It explained why Osman had to have his brothers killed when he took over and how Turks fight abroad to keep peace at home, thus posing an ongoing threat to Europe. It continued with a history of Poland, explaining Polish/Turkish conflict and the Polish search for assistance, including from King James.[46]

The licensing of these newsbooks suggests that negotiations had been going on behind the scenes to accommodate these news publications within the existing machinery of press control. The decision to bring news publication into the more familiar newsbook format corresponded with a decision to allow publication in London. Approved publication had many potential advantages. Work would be provided for London printers and journeymen, probably at a better price than for the double column pages of corantos.[47] Entry in the registers of the Company would ensure that it had some control plus a registration fee for every issue. At the same, time arrangements could be made to give the Crown a more effective role in monitoring the content.

The system for these arrangements was that originally established in 1586 by the Star Chamber Decree. It required all books to be licensed by an ecclesiastical or a state official, as well as being entered in the registers of the Stationers' Company before going to press. The arrangements empowered wardens of the Company to search for unlicensed publications and punish members of the Company who failed to meet requirements. Implementation depended on the interests of senior members of the Company

44 STC18507.29–35.
45 Arber, vol. 4, 22, 23; (after 29 October 1621), STC18507.35C.
46 (after 4 October 1621), STC18507.35A.
47 D. Bidwell, 'French Paper in English Books', in Barnard, 588.

and, as Lambert has successfully argued, these tended to be commercial and financial: there is little doubt that the wardens saw the system as a means of gathering revenue.

The interests of the state in controlling publications were usually addressed through ecclesiastical licensers who were readily available in the London area and London publishers actively sought a licenser when copyright was a concern. They could then register the work with the Stationers' Company. Frearson shows that four of the newsbook publishers – Bourne, Butter, Archer and Sheffard – sought the services of thirteen different ecclesiastical licensers between 1600 and 1620 on specific works. However, given the ephemeral nature of the news reports from Europe, this was not a primary concern and no one was seeking ecclesiastical licences.[48] The High Commission was usually an important vehicle for controlling the press, yet it seemed less interested in doing this under Archbishop Abbot. His sympathies lay in areas of foreign affairs that the king wished to silence, so its role in 1621 was less effective than it might have been. Abbot was strongly aligned with the English Protestants who advocated war in Bohemia. In the spring of 1621, he had openly criticised James's foreign policy and was confined to Lambeth Palace.[49] So, instead of licensing under the supervision of the High Commission, James turned to a state official.

State officials were appointed only at times of heightened political tension. In accordance with new arrangements established from October 1621 until March 1624 'Master Cottington' was appointed to the task of licensing these newsbooks. In this period he licensed more than seventy individual issues and little else: this was clearly a special arrangement. These periodicals provided a mass of detail of military campaigns and fortunes of the Protestant cause in Bohemia and the Palatinate while James was attempting to negotiate, particularly with Spain. Given the sensitivity of James's relationship with the Spanish ambassador, it would seem reasonable that he would have decided that newsbooks could be licensed by someone who knew about European politics and was sympathetic to Spanish interests at Court. Siebert assumed that Francis Cottington, clerk of the Privy Council and Secretary of State to Prince Charles, was the 'Mr Cottington' appointed to license the newsbooks even though Sir George Calvert remained Secretary of State with overall responsibility for the licensing of political works until 1625.[50] Cottington had spent many years as an English agent in Spain and had mediated for James over Bohemia. He supported the Spanish party and became so closely associated with the Spanish marriage

---

[48] Frearson, 250.
[49] Clegg, *Jacobean England*, 189–96; C. S. Clegg, *Press Censorship in Caroline England* (Cambridge, 2008), 32–7, 39–40, 144; K. Fincham, *Prelate as Pastor* (Oxford, 1990), 50–1, 226; K. Fincham, 'Prelacy and Politics: Archbishop Abbot's Defence of Protestant Orthodoxy', *Historical Research*, 61 (1988), 36–69, 52.
[50] Siebert, *Freedom*, 153.

plans that, on their failure, he was temporarily deprived of his office. He converted to the Catholic faith in 1623 but renounced it on return to England, adopting it again later in life.[51] His close links with Spain and his leaning towards Catholicism would have satisfied any opposition from the influential Spanish faction who, by this time, had experience of Abraham Verhoeven's successfully state-controlled pro-Spanish news publication in Antwerp.

These arrangements indicate a pragmatic approach, caution and an eye to diplomatic relations. However, the identity of Cottington, as the licenser, has never been proved. He is referred to throughout in the register of the Stationer's Company as 'Mr. Cottington', without first name or initials. Greg suggested the licenser was George Cottington, licenser in 1623 of Thomas Heywood's *Ovid's Art of Love*, but otherwise completely unknown, a choice which, if true, would suggest that these publications were considered far less important. Frearson considered the unknown George an unlikely candidate since a classical translation bears no relation to the news and George appears to have been neither an ecclesiastical licenser nor a state official. Also he could see no reason why James would have chosen someone unknown when Francis had excellent credentials for this job. In addition, Frearson pointed to an intriguing reference to Francis Cottington in the State Papers dated 3 February 1623 in a document in Edward Conway's letter book, which seems to refer to books being authorised for printing: 'Sir Francis Cottington. Sendinge him two Bookes signed for the Prince.'[52]

There was just one problem; from October 1621, at the time of the appointment of the licenser, to October 1622 Sir Francis Cottington was not in England but in Spain. While he may have been appointed with every expectation of an early return, the fact remains that more than forty newsbooks were licensed in his absence. This leaves us with the option of speculating that someone in his service was granting licences on his behalf. Maybe this was George, Francis Cottington's cousin, who was later to serve in the Rochelle expedition? There is no evidence to confirm this.[53] The only thing that we can be sure about is that entries in the register at this time mark official acceptance that a periodical coverage of the continental war need not be such a problem, providing there was adequate control and each issue was scrutinised by someone with an appropriate understanding of the subject matter and of the government line.

Unfortunately, initially at least, this did not work either. The crucial role of the publisher in securing a regular supply of copy had not been suffi-

---

[51] *ODNB*, Cottington.
[52] W. W. Greg, *Licensers for the Press* (Oxford, 1962); Clegg, *Jacobean England*, 181; M. C. Frearson, 'London Corantos in the 1620s', in *Annual* (1993), 11–3; Frearson, 251–5; SPDom, 14, 214 fo.106.
[53] M. Havran, *Caroline Courtier: The Life of Lord Cottington* (Basingstoke and London, 1973), 51, 65–8, 126.

ciently recognised, and it was soon apparent that Downes and Lee did not have the right connections overseas, so others ventured into the market. The appearance that winter of a report of peace between the Turks and Poland in *Newes from Turkie and Poland* and *Newes from the Palatinate*, with Hague imprints though they came from the press of Edward Allde early in 1622 must have been particularly worrying: these publications demonstrated that having an agreement with Downes and Lee would not stem the tide of unlicensed works with false imprints.[54]

Two publications appeared in the spring of 1622 that criticised news appearing in London. *Good Newes for the King of Bohemia?* claimed to have been written, 'Because I see, that the generall Currantos coming weekely over, have rather stifled their owne credits then given satisfaction ... yet men throng as fast to heare Newes'. It contained few dates or facts, only a story of the duke of Brunswick getting money from the Jesuits. *More Nevves from the Palatinate and more comfort to every true Christian* had no imprint. It included criticism of the English Parliament for failing to vote adequate war subsidies. The writer hoped that 100,000 soldiers would fill the fields in the summer though this might 'seeme ridiculous to Polliticians, who presently demand after the money to pay them'. He added, 'I make no question of a recovery in the Palatinate', even though Protestant armies 'which pretend defense of the King of Bohemia's cause are either most of them Papist, or of no Religion and yet forrage, and spoyle ... though the Papists maintaine their absurd opinions, yet shall they be made instruments of Gods glory'.[55]

Neither of these was a simple translation of digests of news. The second was the work of someone from England, reading and reflecting upon news from Westminster, as well as abroad, who understood the pressures upon London publishers. Its appearance was a challenge to the authorities. Its combination of optimism while acknowledging uncomfortable facts (about the mercenary Protestant armies that took men irrespective of their faith and were obliged to live off the land through plunder) was not a particularly uncommon feature of war reports, but the fact that this newsbook was openly addressed to an English readership who supported the Palatine cause was a step beyond the largely neutral and factual summary reports of corantos.

A further compromise was needed that took into account the interests of publishers with reliable business contacts abroad if licensing was to work. Only these men could maintain supply and enter into agreements with the Stationers' Company and the Crown that could be sustained. Doing business with Butter and Archer may have seemed like a climb down to the Crown and was perhaps even more unpalatable to the Stationers' Company given

---

54 (1622), STC18507.36; (March 1622), STC18507.37.
55 (17 April 1622), STC18507.40; (late March, 1622), title page, 5, 16, STC18507.38.

the extent to which the two flouted controls. Other options were considered: among the State Papers for this period there is a statement possibly in Thomas Wilson's hand explaining that the *Mercurius Gallobelgicus* was sold in Germany and that such avisos were also sold in France, Italy and Spain. It claimed that many towns all over Europe reprove England because it did not receive weekly news and presented a strong and enlightened case for the publication of periodical news in England, explaining that, 'In all these places ... and Provinces the ploughman and artisan can talk of these matters and make ... benefit'. It showed how publication would provide a useful instrument for the political and religious instruction of the vulgar and asked that he and Mr Pory be given a patent to be 'overseers of all bookes of humanly which shalle be printed' and leave to 'print the Gazetts or weekly occurrents which we shall gett from other parts'.[56]

John Pory, a well-connected graduate of Cambridge University (BA, 1592 and MA, 1595) and Oxford (MA, 1610), who had represented Bridgewater in Somerset as a Member of Parliament for six years and travelled in Europe as well as North America, was fluent in French and Italian with some Spanish. He had news contacts including Dudley Carleton, John Chamberlain, Thomas Locke, Lord Brooke, Sir Robert Cotton and Henry Wotton and was already skilled in the collection and dissemination of news. On return from Virginia in 1624 he settled in London and corresponded as an intelligencer with Joseph Mead and later with Sir Thomas Puckering, and John Viscount Scudamore. He was in many ways an ideal candidate, but the application was unsuccessful. Possibly drafted earlier, before Pory set out for Virginia, then reviewed in 1621, it may have helped to persuade the king that controlled publication was not necessarily harmful. It fits well with Levy's arguments that portray this period as one of expanding political awareness due to James's relatively permissive approach. While Richard Cust's study of the news records of country gentlemen in the early 1620s revealed the extent to which these writings were dominated by those opposed to royal policy with 'very little evidence for the "Court" side of the story', the fact that licensing arrangements had already been set up by this stage shows that James was willing to go along with controlled publication. However, this is insufficient to suggest that he saw the need to put across his own point of view. Granting a monopoly to Pory, who was not a member of the Stationers' Company, was unlikely to have worked and would have been unnecessarily contentious, especially since the failure of the Cokayne project in 1616 made new monopolies politically sensitive. Pory needed a partnership with a publisher if he was going to get into this trade. James and

---

[56] *CSPD, 1619–23*, 330, No 113; SPDom. 14, fo. 124 (undated and unsigned); Lambert, 'Coranto Printing', 5; Levy, fn. 59, suggests it may have been earlier – 1619 or 1620.

the Stationers' Company needed a publisher on whom they could rely who was a member of the Company with contacts with European networks.[57]

When Butter and Archer returned to the scene on 11 May 1622, making amends before the Court of the Stationers' Company, the stage was set for a deal.[58] Archer, in partnership with Nicholas Bourne, took the next step, and began to register newsbooks and publish foreign news regularly and openly with the full co-operation of the Company, using the new arrangements for licensing by the Crown which had first appeared in the autumn when Downes and Lee published their first digest of news.

Official recognition

Licensed news publication did not eliminate competition and simplify control until the formation of a syndicate in October that year. This syndicate took responsibility for all periodic foreign news reporting.

The first entry to Thomas Archer and Nicholas Bourne in the register of the Company states, 'Entred for their Copie under the handes of Master Cottington and master knight warden, A Currant of generall newes Dated 14th of may last vjd'.[59] The periodic publication of the continental war news was now officially recognised in the hands of publishers who could maintain a regular output of similar digests. Their work took place within the existing systems for the regulation of the press while drawing upon the joint experiences of Archer and Bourne, a long time associate of Archer, but a very different character; a well respected and law abiding senior member of the Stationers' Company. It was an inspired compromise.

Bourne was the third of the publishers to join the periodic news trade and to stay seriously involved for many years. He was the son of Henry Bourne, a cordwainer. He was Archer's junior and succeeded him as an apprentice at Cuthbert Burby's shop in the Cornhill. Bourne inherited Burby's business and ventured into publication cautiously in association with others. Though he had nothing like the number of publications behind him that Butter could boast, he was successful. He acquired several titles through the assignment of widows of late colleagues including Elizabeth Burby, Elizabeth Oliffe of Long Lane and Katherine Rockitt of the Poultry. He worked alone or in partnership with Dawson, Newbery and Bellamy. Between 1608 and 1622 he trained three apprentices and published seventy-eight books and pamphlets. Of these, Leona Rostenberg estimates that half reflect an interest in news, including *Articles of a treatie of truce, made in Antwerp the 9 of April, 1609, A True relation of the travailes ... of William Davies ... under*

---

[57] *Pory*, 6, 9, 25, 33–6, 42–9, 51–9; Levy, 28, 34; Cust, 'News and Politics', 81.
[58] Jackson, *Court Book*, 146; Arber, vol. 4, 29.
[59] Arber, vol. 4, 30.

the Duke of Florence 1614 and a speech made by Dudley Carleton as English ambassador in the United Provinces in 1618.[60] Many of his other publications were religious.

His partnership with Archer was productive. They published *A Garland of triumph for the honour of the Duke of Brunswick and Lauenburg*, which was entered 16 May 1622. Their first weekly news appeared on 14 May 1622. It contained little of cheer – a report on the death and burial of Prince Ernst of Holstein, hunger riots in Naples, starvation in Prague, fighting in France against the Hugenots, and the breaking of sluices in Flanders.[61] This did not deter them even though, as the summer progressed, the fortunes of Frederick continued to falter. Over the following twenty weeks Bourne and Archer published twenty-one further extant newsbooks and entered five further newsbooks in the registers, of which no copies have survived.

Unfortunately for Bourne and Archer, they had no monopoly. As summer campaign news became abundant, others entered the market. The usual convention, that a publication became the patented property of whoever registered it, continued to apply on an issue-by-issue basis: the ramifications of periodicity had not yet been thought through. There was little benefit in protecting the copyright of a single issue that would be replaced by fresher news within days, but there was a commercial value in the right to produce a continuing series. Butter resumed news publication in June, working at first in partnership with William Sheffard, then mostly alone, while Sheffard published two issues with Nathaniel Newbery and four others with Bartholomew Downes. Cottington and the wardens accepted these in addition to Bourne and Archer's, granting licences and entering nine newsbooks to Butter, including one with Downes. Sheffard, Newberry and Downes, separately and in a variety of combinations, also registered eight newsbooks between June and October; John Bartlet, one.[62]

There was no fixed style or approach. Butter included in his publication of 4 July further reports of the murder of Osman and the coronation of his uncle. On 15 July, Bourne and Archer published a newsbook on the Turks, including an account of Mustapha's survival in prison before the coup, which it claims was brought about by God's providence to help 'the preservation of Christendom in these troublesome times'. This issue was more like the old news pamphlets dealing with a single topic. The writer even took the opportunity to be critical of corantos:

Where are your dreaming Gazettes, and Coranto's now, that talkt of such formidable preparation, and so many hundred thousand in an Army? ... I can but

---

[60] Rostenberg, 'The Debut', 83.

[61] Dahl, 60; (14 May 1622), STC18507.45, *A true relations*, Bourne and Archer (May 1622), STC18507.47 is reproduced in P. H. Wilson, *The Thirty Years' War: A Sourcebook* (2010), 86–90.

[62] Arber, vol. 4, 30–45.

wonder at the shamelesse reports of strange men, and weake Certificates by Corantes from Foraine parts, especially to have them Printed, to talke of so many Thousands slaine, the Prince kill'd, Sigismond defeated, and the whole Army put to flight.[63]

The criticism had some validity. Despite early optimism that there would be a recovery of Bohemia, this had become increasingly less likely. Since the Rhenish Palatinate had negotiated with Spinola in 1621, Strasburg, the Landgrave of Hesse-Cassel, Ansbach and Wurttemberg had all left the Evangelical Union. Yet writers persisted in their hope for an alliance. However, the fact that this criticism appeared in a publication from Bourne and Archer, the leading publishers of newsbooks at this point, indicates some confusion. Working hurriedly to get whatever copy they received out on the streets quickly, they were not vigilant or selective about what they used.

John Bartlet, a new comer to this trade, published a single letter pamphlet. In it, Wells, the physician to Sir Horace Vere, offered an unashamedly pro-Protestant account of what was happening in the Palatinate or, more accurately, he put what might be termed 'a brave face' on it. Wells claimed that he did not write with a desire for publication or to 'countermand such Pamphlets, as are rather framed out of conjecturall braynes then honest intelligence, but meerely to satisfie my friends', but if the account is given to the press, then 'culling out … the principall poynts … will be better'. He reported that since the king of Bohemia joined Mansfeld there had been many successful skirmishes. An admirer of Frederick, he assured readers that the king fought bravely and that 'there is a pleasure to behold Him, and a delight to converse with Him'. He claimed that the encounter between Archduke Leopold and Baden-Durlach at Wimfen in May resulted in equal losses on both sides, that the king took much of Leopold's baggage, powder and good furniture. The Marquis of Durlach, 'though he lost more ordnance, yet not halfe so many men: besides, that losse is doubled by so many troupes as are gone over to our side, and God be praised are most willing to serve his Majestie'. Yet the fact, unreported here, was that Baden was defeated and fled. Wells went on to describe the way Tilly had so far prevented the forces of Frederick and the duke of Brunswick from joining up, and depicted the retreat of Frederick to Manheim at the end of May, as resulting in equal losses on both sides and a lucky escape for Frederick. John Bartlet's next publication, *Coppies of letters sent from personages of accompt* so underplayed the subsequent Battle of Hochst that it claimed Brunswick had only lost baggage.[64]

---

[63] (4 July 1622), STC18507.60; (15 July 1622), 'The Printer to the Reader', STC18507.62.
[64] *A True and ample relation* (14 June 1622), 6, STC25233; (21 June 1622), 5, STC18507.56A.

Bartlet's publications were not typical. Rather, they are extreme examples from that summer of Protestant reporting. Newsbooks passed on reports exaggerating minor victories and discounting setbacks. Accurate descriptions of Mansfeld's victory at Mingolsheim on 17 April were reported in the newsbook of 27 May and Mansfeld's victory at Fleurus on 19 August in the issue of 14 September. Protestant victories not only sold copies but the earliest reports of a battle usually came from Dutch or German Protestant writers who had only heard the Protestant side of the story. So even though the English newsbooks cautiously labelled such reports as unconfirmed, readers were often disappointed as the fuller truth emerged.[65]

Despite the difficulties of rumour and disappointment that typified the summer, Butter expressed an intention of establishing a series of his own in a notice printed in his issue of 23 August 1622:

> If any Gentleman or other accustomed to buy the Weekly Relations of Newes, be desirous to continue the same, let them know that the Writer … hath published two former Newes, the one dated the second, the other the thirteenth of August, all of which doe carrie a like title … and have dependance one upon another: which manner of writing and printing, he doth purpose to continue weekly by Gods assistance from the best and most certaine Intelligence.[66]

He made a real effort to set his work apart by offering a coherent and readable issue for an English market, with the coat of arms of the king of Bohemia on the verso of the title page. However, his plans changed quickly.

In September, three publishers came together to form a syndicate. Then, in October, the first series of dated and numbered newsbooks began. The publishers' version of what precipitated this change was reported on 14 September:

> There was printed the 9. of this month a Relation or booke of newes, wherein were foisted in (without the Licensers knowledge) certaine fabulous passages namely that Count Mansfield shoud have in his Campe 5,000, women or whores, and some other newes not only false but also scandalous, to … Neighbours and friends, which may perchance give occasion some to thinke the weekly Currants are passed without any care or regard … (as formerly when things were done without order) but I will assure you the contrarie, and whatsoever is licensed is thoroughly examined and printed according to the high or low Dutch printed copies, or out of Letters of the best credit from beyond the Seas, and that whosoever hath or shall obtrude, or put anything more then hath beene judiciously

---

[65] Schumacher, 85, 62; D. Randall, *Credibility in Elizabethan and Early Stuart Military News* (2008), 109.
[66] (23 August 1622), 19, STC18507.72.

examined and approved, is liable to be severely punished: therefore expect no such bold attempt from any of us thereafter. Farewell.[67]

It became apparent that summer that the publishers needed to take greater responsibility for the content of their newsbooks. As we have seen, on 15 July, Bourne and Archer had included material that was probably unnoticed at the time of going to press. Mistakes were easily made since they were publishing so frequently. They were aiming to get their issues onto the streets before their competitors and they probably did not allow time to check carefully. This time the error was more serious: the criticisms related to Protestant forces in the Palatinate and had caused offence. Bourne and Archer were being accused of adding to the newsbook after 'Mr Cottington' had approved the text.[68] Despite the reference to being punished severely, no record has been found of this punishment. However, Butter and Sheffard issued two further newsbooks before either Archer or Bourne's names reappear. If they were imprisoned, it could only have been for about two weeks. In any event, when they resumed publication, they too were working in cooperation with Butter. Butter and Archer published the issue of 27 September 1622 and Butter and Bourne the issue of 4 October.[69]

The words 'expect no such bold attempt from any of us thereafter' did not come from Bourne and Archer themselves. They are less an admission of guilt and rather more like an attempt to point a finger but they appear to amount to a public statement of a shared commitment to responsibility on the part of all five who were now involved, that is Butter, Sheffard and Downes who put their names to the issue of 14 September, and Bourne and Archer who did not. An early sign that an agreement may have been reached is that from the 14 September none of the issues separately specifies the addresses of the shops where copies may be obtained, suggesting that all issues were available at all their premises. From then on, the names of Nicholas Bourne, Nathaniel Butter, Thomas Archer, William Sheffard and Bartholomew Downes appeared in imprints in a variety of combinations. These combinations did not always tally with the names given in the register for the same issue, suggesting that every one of them was responsible for every number, irrespective of the names given. This was further demonstrated in a ruling of the Stationers' Court in the following February. Nathaniel Newbery, who had not joined the syndicate, published *The Peace of France*. This edict then appeared in the syndicate's newsbook of the following day. Newbery responded by defending his copyright against the syndicate, taking the case to the Stationers' Court and winning. The Company's Fine Book shows the fine and order to pay compensation to

---

[67] (14 September 1622), 21, STC18507.77.
[68] (9 September 1622), STC18507.76; Arber, vol. 4, 42.
[69] (27 September 1622), STC18507.80; (4 October 1622), STC18507.81.

Newbury were directed at Butter even though Bourne and Archer had registered it and Downes and Archer's names were on the issue. That Butter was
penalised when his name was neither on this imprint nor in the register
suggests that all of them were potentially liable to pay compensation.[70]

On 15 October the syndicate began their first series of numbered and
dated newsbooks. Fifty numbers were published in the following fifty weeks.
Syndicate members also collaborate on publications that were not part of
the series. Thus, between them, this syndicate provided a significant service
of officially registered news. Bartholomew Downes dropped out after 28
January 1623 and Nathaniel Newbery joined the syndicate in their second
series.

So what had prompted this remarkable co-operative effort? Sir Francis
Cottington returned to England from Madrid in October 1622. News of his
imminent return to England precipitated first a drop in output in September
and then the formation of a syndicate in October.[71] The evidence of a
sudden sharpening of focus on effective licensing, taking place in the wake
of Sir Francis Cottington's return, completes the case for the argument that
he was the appointed licenser. He almost certainly sent some officials ahead
as he set out for England. They, enquiring into the work that had been done
in his name in his absence, found the situation unacceptable and started to
put things in order.

With so many rival publications, the task of checking issues was onerous.
Unacceptable content had crept in and stern action was needed. To avoid
competition, piracy and false imprints in the future it was vital that the
publishers worked together. Within a month a solution was found in the
form of a numbered series. This was a monopoly, and the Newbury case
effectively defined its parameters to include all digests of foreign news,
but exclude freestanding official documents registered by others. However,
it was not an official monopoly in the conventional sense, with an atten-
dant, overt implication of close co-operation with the Crown. Numbering
provided a guarantee of order and completeness to the new phenomenon of
a periodical publication. The agreement appears to have been annual and
to have provided for approximately one publication a week: though this
rate of production varied, fifty issues were subsequently produced in most
of the ensuing eight series. The number may reflect standard provisions of
a news network supply contract. Frequency of one issue a week was probably about as much as the licenser could be expected to handle without
making mistakes and missing unacceptable text. It also gave an average that
assumed reasonable intervals in the supply of news. As we have seen, supply
varied seasonally and in response to noteworthy events and weather in the

[70] *The 4 of November. The Peace of France* (4 November 1622), STC16841; (5 November
1622), STC18507.87; Jackson, *Fine Book*, 469. Jackson, *Court Book*, 154, names all five
members of the syndicate.
[71] Frearson, 256–7.

Channel, but the posts out of London were regular. So the syndicate would have aimed as far as possible for one issue a week to maintain effective distribution.

These new arrangements were publisher-focused and based on an agreement with a licenser operating on behalf of the Crown that was tailor-made to the needs of periodical publication. The Stationers' Company protected its interests: copies were to be registered and entry fees paid. The arrangements assisted the further evolution of the foreign newsbook trade in London, since cooperation in the syndicate allowed publishers to pool their resources and plan.

Conclusions

The publication of corantos in English began in Amsterdam, initially for the English speaking community there, but, through a rapid process of evolutionary changes, they were soon being imported to England. The number of copies in circulation was supplemented with transcripts and then with print (at first with false imprints). As soon as the trade gained official recognition the format was changed to quarto booklets. Finally, the formation of the syndicate ushered in transformation into a weekly, numbered and dated series of newsbooks. The evidence suggests that a great many more issues were available in earliest days than is generally recognised. Even so, it was the intensity of interest in the affairs of Frederick and Elizabeth, coupled with the decision to call Parliament, rather than the arrival of corantos in London as such, that first led to official concern and attempts to moderate discussion and speculation.

Censorship was not the all-powerful, effective machine described by Whig historians, but the mechanisms that existed could make life difficult for those who functioned on the margins. James's concern to orchestrate events leading to the opening of Parliament and to appease Spanish interests led him to explore these mechanisms, but he was also willing to accept a pragmatic way forward: the public could have news, so long as it was monitored with sensitivity. Revisionist and post-revisionist arguments about the importance of the trade are supported by this agreement. Publishers had to work within the system and no arrangements could be introduced and made to work without the Company of Stationers' full assent. All the interested publishers had to be part of an agreement and they had every incentive to collaborate. Periodical publication was evidently lucrative in 1621 and 1622, but impossible to sustain effectively on an illicit basis. The outcome could be depicted as a compromise with the publishers emerging as strong parties in the negotiations. However, the term 'negotiation' implies a degree of self-awareness and purpose that seems was absent from a process that was more one of trial and error until October 1622, when the need to get all the publishers together with collective responsibility was recognised.

4

Commercial Production and the Implications of Periodicity

As we have seen, London publishers drove forward a period of rapid innovation that established periodical news production at a time when demand was so high that they could scarcely keep up with it. They went on during the 1620s and 1630s to embed the trade within the print industry and through news dissemination networks. Understanding their role involves looking at their reasons for collaboration and at how these related to capital investment, output and distribution. Initially, considerable known demand for news must have bolstered their determination to overcome obstacles. However, sustaining the periodical trade involved a number of new challenges that made it speculative and risky. For this enterprise to work, news supply mechanisms needed to be secure, production needed to be speedy and one issue had to be moved out of the publishers' premises and sold before the next was available, usually within a week. These considerations created unique pressures in an industry where, hitherto, timeliness had not been a significant concern and where the means of supply and distribution needed to be adapted to the demands of regular news. Publishers selected the printers, supervised production and worked to expand sales through other booksellers, street vendors and carriers who took copies out beyond London. Understanding the constraints of the business can help us to assess the possible scale of production, while looking at costs, retail prices and wages helps us to assess how affordable newsbooks were and the potential for sales beyond the London market.

The publisher's role in production

The publishers' work involved business correspondence with contacts in Europe and England and careful accounting. As business records were destroyed in the Fire of London, often the closest evidence available is from the accounts and records of publishers in other cities, such as Paris. One consequence is that few historians have ventured into this area, though many have studied the printer's business from a technical production perspective. More recently historians have taken an interest in the mecha-

nisms of distribution, greatly expanding our understanding and appreciation of how potentially pervasive the print media had become by the early
seventeenth century. However, we know less about the commercial business
of financing and production, or about the logistics of the distribution of
the foreign news, and how publishers worked to maintain sales momentum
through ramping up the speed of turnover and establishing frequent and
reliable contacts with customers to encourage regular repeat purchases.[1]

The five men who formed the news syndicate in October 1622 appear to
have had little else in common. Butter was trading at the sign of the Pied
Bull, St Austin's Gate, at the south-east corner of St Paul's Church Yard
and was already established in news publication. Archer, at the sign of the
Horse Shoe at the Royal Exchange end of Pope's Head Alley, had rather
less publishing experience. Nicholas Bourne, though younger than Archer,
was better established in the trade. Like Archer, he had been apprenticed to
Cuthbert Burby and he traded at the south entrance to the Royal Exchange,
so he was a close working neighbour to Archer. Bartholomew Downes by
contrast, was a bookseller and binder. He appears to have had no news
supply contacts and did not work as a publisher except in this venture. His
house was to the west, near Fleet Bridge. All four were of much the same
generation, but William Sheffard was younger. He had traded from the
shop of his former master, Nathaniel Newbery, at the Star under St Peter's
Church in Cornhill and in Pope's Head Alley, but, by 1622, he had his
own shop at the south Lombard Street end of Pope's Head Alley. He was
also working with Nathaniel Newbery and subscribed to the Frankfurt Book
Fair in 1622. There was a location link with Archer and, like Butter, his
publications revealed a Protestant and a European trading interest, but after
he left the syndicate in 1624 he concentrated on religious books, rather
than news and ephemera. So, though these men would have known one
another, they did not share many similar interests. They were likely to have
the greatest mutual interest in sharing the financial burdens and their distribution contacts for news publication.

---

[1] P. Gaskell, A New Introduction to Bibliography (Oxford, 1972); C. Clair, A History of
European Printing (1970); S. H. Steinberg, Five Hundred Years of Printing (Harmondsworth
and Baltimore, MD, 1955); Plant; J. Harthan, The Illustrated Book (1981); McKenzie;
D. F. McKenzie, 'Printing and Publishing 1557–1700: Constraints on the London Book
Trades', in Barnard; M. Spufford, Small Books and Pleasant Histories: Popular Fiction and
its Readership in Seventeenth-century England (1981); Watt; T. Watt 'Publisher, Pedlar,
Pot-Poet: The Changing Character of the Broadside Trade, 1550–1640', in Spreading
the Word, ed. R. Myers and M. Harris (Winchester and New Castle, DE, 1990); 61–81;
M. C. Frearson, 'The Distribution and Readership of London Corantos in the 1620s', in
Serials and their Readers, ed. R. Myers and M. Harris (Winchester and New Castle, DE,
1993), 1–25; G. Mandelbrote, 'From the Warehouse to the Counting-house: Booksellers
and Bookshops in Late Seventeenth-century London', in Genius for Letters, ed. R. Myers
and M. Harris (Winchester and New Castle, DE, 1995), 49–84; A. Johns, The Nature of
the Book (Chicago, IL, 1998).

Capital was required for obtaining copy and preparing it for publication. As with other books and pamphlets, the costs of paper and wages had to be met before sales brought any return. Partnership in publication is as old as printing precisely because book production makes great demands on capital resources before any return is possible. Books tend to sell slowly, so the turn-over is likely to be slow and uncertain. There were many examples of groups of publishers working together to share both the outlay and the risk for this reason.[2] However, newsbooks had little in common with major publications of large volumes on good paper. They were quite short and on cheaper paper, and the publishers could potentially recoup and repeat much of their investment regularly, but the need to sell one issue before the next was available created its own pressures. Print runs needed to be short enough to reflect the sales and distribution that was achievable within a week (or less, if copy was abundant and production more frequent, such as in the early 1630s). Most of the key elements for successful publication of newsbooks, therefore, had little to do with having large capital sums tied up for a long time. Enough capital was needed to secure good deals on the Continent to ensure a reliable supply of material, but organisation and funding were needed to back a rapid turn around in London of the largest print runs that could be distributed before the next issue was on the streets.

Butter and Bourne had enough money in 1616 to be able to pay for livery shares in the English Stock, but by 1620 Bourne was borrowing money (and again in 1624). Butter too borrowed money before May 1622. He could not afford to pay back his debts so he forfeited his yeomanry share. In 1623, he was dismissed from his membership of the Stationers' Stock Company for having overdrawn his account. Archer too mortgaged his half share in yeomanry stock in September 1619 and was still in debt for unpaid fines in May 1622. So, even though the frequency of newsbook publication shows they were successful, Butter, Archer and Bourne went into debt early in the venture. Together with Downes and Sheffard, Archer and Butter took on more apprentices at this time. These four were providing the necessary extra labour for the venture. Whereas Bourne, the only one who ultimately came out of the venture successfully, took on more apprentices only in the 1630s. Bourne was the financier: he provided capital, taking out two more loans to support the syndicate.[3]

In total, Downes, Sheffard, Archer and Butter took on between six and eight additional young men to help cope with the news trade. To determine how typical this was of the trade, we must look to the Continent. A news-paper office in Germany in 1632 employed seven people. These included an editor/writer, couriers, newsboys and vendors. The parallel, however, ends

[2] H. S. Bennett, *English Book and Readers 1603 to 1640* (Cambridge, 1965), 224–5.
[3] L. Rostenberg, *Literary, Political, Scientific, Religious and Legal Publishing, Printing and Bookselling in England*, 1 (New York, 1965), 77; Frearson, 120–6.

here because the office also carried out its own printing and included an engraver, compositor and printer.[4]

This act of binding additional apprentices is more significant than it might at first appear, given that apprentices were not paid. Apprentices were a useful source of cheap labour, but they had to be accommodated, fed, clothed, trained and cared for in the event of sickness. They were bound for seven years, so this long-term commitment demonstrates that the publishers hoped for sustained good sales: they had a degree of confidence in the new market and also, possibly, believed that, with forces occupying Bohemia and the Palatine, the conflicts they were reporting would be difficult to resolve. Taking on these apprentices was a risk; they would have been a burden if the interest in foreign news or its supply waned. Apprentices were most likely to have handled the printed copies, moving them from the printers to their warehouse and book shops, counting out batches of copies and packing them for dispatch to other bookshops around London and to carriers and travelling salesmen and women heading for the provinces. Unless the distances were short, the newsbooks would have travelled in sheets, unbound and packed up in chests or barrels. This work was intensive and necessitated keeping careful records. The number of additional boys reflects an intention to provide a volume trade with a fast turn around, to catch carriers on regular post days and ensure that every copy printed was available to customers in the shortest possible time. The profitability of this venture was crucially dependent on the efficiency with which this was achieved.

Ben Jonson, a contemporary dramatist who wrote about foreign news publication at its height in the early 1620s, described 'a staple of news' in his play of that name. This was an office where news came in, was recorded and then sorted, sealed and issued. The chief clerk at the office was Nathaniel, a clear reference to Butter, whose first task was to sell a groatsworth of news to a 'butter-woman'. There were four 'emissaries' who were

> sent abroad
> To fetch the commodity
> From all the regions where the best news are made.

These included 'Hans Buz, a Dutchman; he is emissary Exchange', a reference to news from the Royal Exchange and Pope's Head Alley. The first news discussed in the play is the latest news of Spinola.[5]

---

[4]   H. Langer, *The Thirty Years' War* (Poole, 1978), 236.

[5]   Jonson, Act I i. 352, i, 353 and 361, Act I ii, 358–9; D. F. McKenzie, in *The Staple of News and the Late Plays; A Celebration of Ben Jonson*, ed. W. Blissett *et al.* (Toronto, 1973), 118. McKenzie, 194, fn. 19, also speculates on whether Cymbal is modelled on the editor Thomas Gainsford and the references to 'moiety, divided into seven parts' is a description of the share holding by booksellers.

Jonson's fictitious office was probably for scribal publication and suggests rivalry with the printed news, though this rivalry appears to have been overstated for dramatic purposes. In reality, Archer appears to have been engaged in simultaneous manuscript and print news production and John Pory, a professional newsletter writer, was closely connected with Butter's business. Jonson recognised the significance of an organised London news network run for profit, and portrayed this busy office as a coveted place to be. It was all to do with conspicuous consumption and fashion, and was based entirely on the motive of making money. At the end of the play, it prophetically collapsed on the failure of funds, but at the outset Thomas, the barber, was keen to get a job there as a clerk. A price of £50 was paid by his stylish young patron who, in return, asked to be kept up to date with all the very latest news. This suggested that even the work at the office had captured the imagination of patrons of quite substantial means. The figure of £50 may have been Jonson's idea of what it cost to become a partner in the syndicate, possibly based on the cost of membership in the London Stationers' Stock Company. The sum may not have been unrealistic, given that John Pory had estimated that for a patent to print 'a Gazette of weekly occurants', 'would be worth unto me £200 per ann[um]'. He was receiving £20 a year from Lord Scudamore in 1631–2 for a comprehensive news service including newsletters and printed foreign news. The five members of the syndicate, with the new apprentices (who would each also have brought with them a small capital sum towards the finances of this new enterprise), may have, therefore, drawn together initial capital of perhaps around £300 or possibly more.[6]

Jonson evidently expected his audience to recognise the references to Butter in the leading role, surrounded by a bevy of busy apprentices. He possibly also expected audiences to identify Tom as Thomas Archer, anxious to work in the office. The assistants at the Court of the Company of Stationers clearly would have agreed that Butter was in the lead.[7] His name was dominant in the registers of the Stationers' Company for the first series (ten issues were entered by Butter alone; eight by him with Bourne; five by him with Sheffard; and three by him with Downes), and on forry-five of the title pages, compared with twenty-six for Bourne, eighteen for Sheffard and seventeen for Archer. Butter also bound the most apprentices between 1618 and 1624 and again in 1639 to 1641, suggesting that he was at the heart of the activity. In addition, while publications for all five men increased overall in the early 1620s Butter was the most prolific. While the non-newsbook production of the others increased, he was the only one whose

6   Jonson, Act I, ii, 357, Act I, i, 352; Pory, 52–5; H. Love, *The Culture and Commerce of Texts* (Boston, MA, 1998), 10; D. F. McKenzie, *The London Book Trade in the Later Seventeenth Century* (Sandars Lectures, 1976), 6; L. Rostenberg, 'Nathaniel Butter and Nicholas Bourne, First Masters of the Staple', *The Library*, 5:12 (1957), 24.
7   *The Peace of France* (4 November 1622); Jackson, Fine Book (1957), 469.

non-newsbook production fell: Butter was dedicating more of his publishing capacity to this business than the others, making him the most committed syndicate member.[8]

Newsbook production quickly became a significant feature of the London print industry and was important to all the members of the syndicate. In 1623 foreign news periodicals accounted for an eighth of all surviving titles for that year and between 1620 and 1624 these publishers separately and together brought out nearly three hundred publications, two-thirds of which were newsbooks. There was also a complementary relationship between the newsbooks and their other publications. Fifty-three titles were religious, covering news related themes, and thirty-one were news (twelve of which were also foreign news). Archer published five unregistered news publications, while Sheffard and Butter produced religious works that provided a context in which to read and interpret the news. Commercial and political interests coincided. Only Bourne retained an interest in a more diverse publications list, including trade, education, logic and history.[9]

Production time and costs

Many cost elements were fixed irrespective of how many newsbooks were printed, including the purchase of foreign copies, shipping to London, translation, licensing and registration fees. The costs of printing and paper were significant, fluctuated and reflected the numbers of copies in a print run, so decisions about print runs were critical to profitability and sales. These in turn influenced the public impact of the news.

The full publishing costs are not known. We have no information on the charges for contracts with news networks for supplies of corantos, for shipping and any agent fees to bring copies over, or for translation. An editorial of 3 July 1624 contrasted these publications with others on the basis that their competitors 'have not taken the paines, had the meanes, or been willing to beare the charges which we undergoe to get good newes and intelligences' and there is a clue about the arrangements with suppliers in the issue of 4 October 1627 where the editorial refers to 'our great charge, being … a yearely charge'.[10] The syndicate had ended by 1627 and newsbooks were then produced by Butter and Bourne in partnership, but the yearly cycle of numbered issues in a series, each running for about fifty issues, continued. This suggests that the arrangements were secured with annual contracts and would help to explain the confidence with which the new arrangements were introduced in October 1622 and the decision to run each series with

---

8 Frearson, 100–1, 127–35.
9 S. Lambert, 'Coranto Printing in England', *JNandPH*, 8 (1992), 13; Frearson, 80, 83, 127–48, Table 2.2.
10 (3 July 1624), 1, STC18507.149; (4 October 1627), 1, STC18507.189.

fifty issues. It also tends to confirm the need for a fairly substantial starting capital.

The freshest news, generally from the Low Countries, would already be two to three days old when it reached London. By comparing datelines for continental copies and those for subsequent publication in London we can generally identify a lapse of five to six days between publication in the Netherlands and those in London. This gives a two- to three-day window for production in London.

From October 1622, the first task was to register issues with the Stationers' Company. Many were entered in the register for six pence, but not all. Even during the first series the syndicate only entered twenty-seven issues out of fifty. Retrospective entries to the register began on 23 February 1624 with the payment of 6s 6d made on that day covering issues up to, and including, the issue produced on that day. They may have paid a premium for this retrospective entry, since it only covered ten issues and the charge for ten would normally have been 5s.[11]

By the third series, we see the introduction of block entries and these continued into the next series.[12] From August to October 1627, in the fifth series, ten individual entries are related to control and inspection by a new licenser, Georg Weckherlin, but the block entries have no reference to licensing and seem to be related solely to satisfying the Stationers' Company's demand for fees. The second of these entries was 2 May 1628, during a break in production between January and June and seems to cover many issues already entered as having been licensed. It demonstrates the function of the Stationers' Company registers to record licensing for a variety of purposes of control, ownership and fees. So too, does the next entry, which was during the sixth series and dated 20 June 1629. This covers issues up to 20 March, including some that had already been entered as licensed by Weckherlin.[13] Retrospective block entries became the norm. Perhaps the oddest of the entries occurred after the ninth series had not only begun but also ended as a result of a royal ban. In December 1633, Butter and Bourne paid 7s to enter a retrospective block of fourteen newsbooks, taking them up to September 1633 although none had been printed since the ban in October 1632. They may have made this payment because they hoped to start again.[14]

The next task was to find a printer. The printer had only to cover his costs, overheads and profit and it was customary for the printer to charge for labour costs plus fifty percent. It was then up to the publisher to meet such costs as paper and editorial fees and to settle the retail margin.

---

[11] Arber, vol. 4, 74; Frearson, 103; C. S. Clegg, *Press Censorship in Caroline England*, 32–7, 144.

[12] Arber, vol. 4, 106, 124, 146.

[13] Frearson, 108–9; Arber, vol. 4, 146–62.

[14] Arber, vol. 4, 202, 222, 228, 234, 235, 246, 247, 248, 283.

The capital outlay for a printer was relatively inexpensive. The minimum equipment required was a workroom, a press, its accessories, sufficient type for at least one sheet and a supply of ink. Secondary needs were ornaments and devices for title pages. Woodcuts and engravings were rarely needed in pamphlets and binding materials were not used: pamphlets were, at best, sold stitched together without any covering. Purchasing type was more expensive. It was imported from France, and required renewal fairly frequently and replacement at a cost of around 3d a pound. However, once established, the plant required could be used almost indefinitely. Marjorie Plant noted a press valued in 1625 at £4. She estimated the capital value of a small print shop as between £150 and £165 in the mid-1620s.[15] Premises were not expensive since, with one press, the printer could manage with one fairly small workroom. Plant suggested that rents were low in St Pauls and around Fleet Street and unlikely to have affected the cost of individual books.[16]

Labour costs were more immediate and formed the basis of the calculation when quoting for a job. Plant noted 18d for a weekly wage for a journeyman in 1581, plus food, drink, laundry and lodgings while Moxon wrote of them being paid for 'all Church Holydays that fall not on a Sunday, whether they work or no'. Not all presses could usually be working simultaneously and continuously, so take home pay could fluctuate. The total numbers of printers per working press was probably in the region of three or four (taking master, compositors, pressmen and apprentices together), but again variations were common and crews could work more than one press and book at a time.[17]

In Geneva and Paris working days of twelve to fifteen hours were normal in the early seventeenth century, so Febvre and Martin estimated that compositors might complete between one and three forms a day according to the kind of work involved. A printer's output ranged from 2650 sheets per day in Paris to 3375 in Frankfurt and 3350 a day in Lyons at the end of the sixteenth century and 4000 a day in the Netherlands in the early seventeenth century. This gives a potentially high output of something close to two hundred sheets an hour for a hand press. Yet it seems that the general rates of pay across the Continent were only slightly higher than those for a less skilled or educated labourer, around 8d a day. McKenzie and Raymond have estimated a maximum output rate of two hundred and fifty impressions an hour. This is in line with the figures for Bowyers printing house in the 1730s for a full press, but McKenzie has cast considerable doubts on calcula-

---

[15] Gaskell, *A New Introduction*, 178; L. Febvre and H-J. Martin, *The Coming of the Book* (1976), 110–13; Plant, 172, 179.

[16] J. Moxon, *Mechanic Exercises in Printing*, ed. H. Davis and H. G. Carter (1962), 17; Plant, 165–9.

[17] Jackson, xxi; Plant, 156; Moxon, *Mechanic*, 327; McKenzie, 19–21, 23, 29.

tions of printing house outputs based simply upon multiplying out averages since this was not an automated industry.[18]

The economics of printing tended to keep edition quantities down so that the investment could be recovered. They also discouraged printers from enlarging their plant to an extent that would increase dependency on a flow of large orders. Even in cities where the number of presses was uncontrolled there was a preference for smaller printing houses.[19] In England, from 1586, the number of printers and presses was controlled. The number of printers varied between twenty and twenty-three in London up to 1637 and the number of printing presses appears to have exceeded the numbers specified, but remained low.[20]

Most printers would have welcomed the opportunity to print the news. Issues were short and could be fitted in between other tasks to help keep the presses busy. The publishers would have looked for a printer with a press available and the capacity to start immediately. They would, no doubt, have aimed to get the best price that they could too, but they probably would not have had much scope to negotiate since the industry appears to have been working with narrow margins of profitability due to the constant struggle to find enough business to keep their presses occupied.[21] Dahl identified the work of seventeen different London printers among editions in the 1620s, some being employed far more frequently than others. The main printers prior to the formation of the syndicate were John Dawson who, between 1613 and 1634, operated from the Three Cranes in the Vintry, and Edward Allde who may still have been operating from his premises in Old Fish Street at this time, followed by Bernard Alsop, from Distaff Lane near Old Fish Street.[22]

Prior to October 1622, the lesser coranto publishers sent their news to be printed by individual printers. Downes's corantos, for example, were printed by Nicholas Kingston, while the Sheffard–Newbery partnership employed John Dawson to print theirs. Butter, Bourne and Archer rarely used the same printer from one issue to the next. But the syndicate favoured printers with the greatest capacity: Dawson and Allde were both allowed two presses each, George Eld had two presses in partnership with Miles Flesher,

18 Febvre and Martin, The Coming, 131–2; McKenzie, 'Printing and Publishing', 562; McKenzie, 19; Raymond, 234.
19 Gaskell, A New Introduction, 175–6; Langer, Thirty Years' War, 15.
20 Seibert, 70; Lambert, 14; Febvre and Martin, The Coming, 192, 131; E. Arber, vol. 1, 242, vol. 3, 699–700, vol. 4, 529–36; Johns, The Book, 72–3; McKenzie, 'Printing and Publishing', 557; McKenzie, 57–60.
21 Bennett, English Books, 271.
22 Dahl, 14; H. R. Plomer, A Dictionary of the Booksellers and Printers who were at work in England, Scotland and Ireland from 1641 to 1667 (1907), 5; R. B. McKerrow, A Dictionary of Printers and Booksellers in England, Scotland and Ireland and of Foreign Printers of English Books 1557–1640 (1910), 160–1.

and Eliot Court Press was a partnership of three printers with five presses between them.[23]

The shift to printers with a greater capacity is both evident and significant. The Eliot Court Press had possibly only been used once for foreign news printing before the syndicate was formed in October 1622, being brought in by Butter and Archer on 27 September 1622. Similarly George Eld had only printed two issues before for Butter on 23 August 1622 and for Butter and Sheffard on 25 September 1622. Yet these quickly became the dominant printers of the series, with Dawson and Allde falling into second place. When Archer and Butter came together for their first joint issue they selected the Eliot Court Press, which was new to this business. Business was prospering and a larger print run for the first issue allowed for dissemination throughout both their distribution networks. The location of the presses was another factor. George Eld and the Eliot Court Press were located on the very west of the City in Fleet Lane and the Little Old Bailey, locations which were less convenient for Bourne, Sheffard and Archer than they were for Downes and Butter. Printed copies needed to be moved from the printer to the publisher for counting, packing and dispatching. The larger the edition the more it would have made sense to minimise the journey through crowded streets and alleys in the City. What we appear to be seeing here is a geographical shift that reflected the increasing importance of Butter at the centre of the dispatch and dissemination activities.

Later developments support this theory. When Archer left the syndicate and was working independently, he still used the printers Eliot Court Press, but reverted also to Bernard Alsop and William Jones for his news publications while Edward Allde, who at some time after 1612 had also moved west, continued to work for Butter and Bourne, producing seventeen of the extant numbers. George Eld produced four issues and Augustine Mathewes, also in the west in Bride's Lane off Fleet Street, one issue. By the end of the second series, the syndicate with a consortium of printers had been succeeded by Butter and Bourne in partnership and one printer, Edward Allde. This trio continued to work together throughout the third series. From 1625 to August 1627, Butter and Bourne used the imprint 'Mercurius Britannicus' and printers were not named, but this imprint was dropped in the sixth series. Towards the end of the seventh John Dawson became identified the main printer. He appears to have had a contract for the whole of the eighth series.[24]

By not committing themselves to long-term contracts with printers and negotiating issue-by-issue, the publishers gained maximum flexibility both on timing and on quantities. They turned first to larger printers because a

---

[23] Frearson, 101, 95–6.
[24] The exception was 3 August 1632 when two issues appeared the same day. The first mentioned 'I.D.' (Dawson) in the imprint, the second 'B.A. and T.F' (Allsop and Fawcett).

printer with several presses could probably respond quickly as soon as copy was available. They would have been less likely to have to interrupt other work to get started. Moreover, the use of printers with greatest press capacity allowed for an increase in production and, with presses running simultaneously, it also allowed for a more rapid turn around of copy. The syndicate printed longer runs than was normal for that time and a few numbers were even printed by more than one printer, such as those published in February 1623 at a time of heightened interest due to the departure of Charles and Buckingham for Spain. News of a plot to assassinate the Prince of Orange broke on 6 February 1623. The syndicate produced three newsbooks using three or four printers for each issue. With news of the Continent in everyone's thoughts at this time, the publishers aimed to cover it quickly.[25]

The syndicate had just lost the case in the Court of the Stationers' Company to Nathaniel Newbery about copyright to news of the *Peace of France*. The decision by the Stationers to uphold Newbery's copyright entitlement against them gave them, by the same token, confidence that no one would be allowed to compete with them by producing rival versions of the authentic Dutch texts concerning the conspiracy if they got the news on to the streets promptly. They were so sure of high sales that they commissioned high print runs in a hurry as we can see from the type setting of three issues in February 1623. The issue of 11 February 1623 concerned the discovery of a plot to assassinate the Prince of Orange. Only five days after the event, by means of duplicate setting, they were able to produce a thirty-eight-page (five sheet) issue using three printers simultaneously. Confidence about prospective sales cannot have been disappointed as the next two issues were printed in a similar fashion.[26]

Timeliness of news has always been a factor for news publications. Even without the rivalry of other news publishers, time could be significant when the news was sufficiently interesting to spread rapidly by manuscript, word of mouth and rumour. Thomas Barrington, for example, sent news to his mother, Lady Barrington, on 15 May 1632 about the duke of Bavaria's departure from Ingolstadt that appeared in the newsbooks the following day.[27] But English publishers were under less pressure than their Amsterdam counterparts to get news onto the streets quickly. Van Hilten reduced printing times by about four hours for each issue from 1632 by introducing

[25] Frearson, 102; McKenzie, *London Book Trade*, 6–7.
[26] (11 February 1623), STC18507.97; Dahl, 96–7; (19 and 28 February 1623), STC18507.98 and 99: sheet A printed by Eld and the Eliot Court Press, sheets C and E by Allde, and sheets B and D by another printer.
[27] R. Streckfus, 'News before Newspapers', *Journalism and Mass Communication Quarterly*, 75:1 (1998), 91; (Concurrent printing could also be practised to avoid detection; Johns, *The Book*, 289); A. Searle, *Barrington Family Letters, 1628–1632*, Camden Society, 4:28 (1983), 241.

duplicate setting. This enabled him to have corantos on sale earlier than his competitor Broer Jansz.[28]

The publisher had to supply the paper. This could easily be the largest single cost, equalling or exceeding the cost of printing. The quality of domestic paper was low and most white paper for printing was imported from France, Italy or Germany. The Cambridge printer, Canterell Legg, recorded 'average' book quality paper at 10 or 11s a ream and coarser paper at a 'conservative' valuation of 3 to 4s a ream in the 1620s. Thomas Walkley paid 4s 6d per ream in 1620. The lowest quality for printing ballads was set by the Stationers' Company in 1612 at 2s 8d per ream and we know that the foreign news was printed on low quality paper, since there is a complaint in 1625 in the Stationers' records. Taking a range of prices for cheaper print of 3s 4d to 5s 6d, David McKitterick calculated an average cost per ream of less than 0.1d per sheet. News editors aimed to make the best use of every page, but even so, the cost could have been as high as ¾d or 1d per copy for longer issues, making it a key consideration when planning issues.[29]

The length of each issue would influence the cost of production through the amount of labour involved in printing, the time it would take before copies were on sale and the amount of paper. In the early days publishers experimented with the length of issues varying them from eight pages (or one sheet) to thirty-two pages (or four sheets), the most common length being twenty-four pages (or three sheets). Usually the verso of the title page, the first leaf and the last page would be blank, giving nineteen sides of news. When numbered and dated series began in October 1622, they would leave only the verso of the title page blank, filling the remaining twenty-two sides with copy. This system was largely maintained for the next three series. After this, the length of the newsbooks was reduced to sixteen sides, including fourteen of news, and remained this length until 1632.

In 1638 publication was resumed, but costs had risen. The book trade had experienced a period of inflation. Raised tax duties bore heavily on the import of paper. In addition, under the terms of the new warrant, a new fixed price tax was introduced for foreign newsbooks involving the payment of 10s a year towards the repair of St Paul's. The appearance and mode of publication were transformed. More sources were available and Butter and Bourne took the risk of extending subscriptions to more news networks. Instead of combining reports into one weekly issue, they published short separate four sided London issues corresponding to the publications they were importing. Thus, three or four issues would appear on the same (or almost the same)

[28] F. Dahl, *Dutch Corantos 1618–1650* (The Hague, 1947), 19–20.
[29] D. McKitterick, *A History of Cambridge University Press: Printing and the Book Trade 1534–1698*, vol. 1 (Cambridge, 1992), 284–6; McKenzie, 38, fn. 61; D. Bidwell, 'French Paper in English Books', in Barnard, 586–8; H. Carter, in 'Early Accounts of the University Press Oxford', in *Studies in the Book Trade in Honour of Graham Pollard* (Oxford, 1975), 18, 122.

day. The pages were slightly larger and the title page summary was reduced to a quarter of the front page. Pages were numbered continuously; a device that presented all the issues as one continuous series to encourage the sale of all issues. The partnership may have hoped to avoid editorial costs and to increase sales, but the quality of these short, single-source issues was poor; the paper of such low quality that ink showed through and sales did not support the high number of issues appearing. To get a full picture of events it was necessary to buy several, thereby paying a significant premium and tolerating constant repetition. This experiment ended when Butter, who by April 1640 was the sole publisher, announced, 'Gentlemen, we have againe reduced the methode of printing the forreigne weekly Avisoes, into two sheets, and do promise, for the content of the buyer, to sell them at a cheaper Rate, if a competent number shall be vented weekly, to recompence the charge, we shall continue them; if not, we shall be forced to put a period to the Presse.' By 1641, and particularly in 1642, quality was very low. Butter was probably unable to afford to employ someone to oversee the press and check proofs.[30]

Establishing the likely size of print runs for newsbooks is remarkably difficult, yet it is important to our understanding of both the economics of the trade affecting the amount and cost of paper and the cost and time of printing. The sizes of editions of newsbooks also influenced the size of the readership, since the larger the print run the higher circulation a text was likely to have and the greater its potential influence.[31]

The smallest possible print run for which a printer would set up type for a short cheap print was 1 to 200 copies. In the earliest days, for books, editions of 2 to 300 were quite normal, but by the sixteenth century 1500 was more usual. The economics and financial arrangements worked in favour of printing at least 500 copies and no more than 2000 of a sizable book, but favoured larger prints of small, cheap books. Raymond has suggested 250 as the incremental unit for print runs. Composition of one sheet cost about the same in wages as the printing of 1500 copies. Printing more copies led to a pro-rata rise in costs for the pressmen's wages, but left compositors without work. From 1586 until 1637 edition quantities were limited by decree to 1250 to 1500 for ordinary books and 3000 for books in small type and small books like catechisms. These controls were to protect the work of the compositors, though we know that masters often ignored them. It is more likely that the real constraint on print size for foreign newsbooks was the estimate of how many copies could be distributed and sold in a week.[32]

---

[30] CSPD, 1638–1639, 182, quoted in Dahl, 223; Bidwell, 'French Paper', 590–1, 586; Dahl, 223; (23 April 1640), verso, STC18507.337.

[31] Raymond, 233.

[32] Watt, 11; Gaskell, A New Introduction, 160–2; Raymond, 233; Febvre and Martin, The Coming, 219; C. S. Clegg, Press Censorship in Caroline England (Cambridge, 2008),

Dahl initially estimated that only perhaps 200 copies of each were printed, later he revised his estimate upwards to 400 to the sort of number usually estimated for illicit pamphlets. He assumed that there were between 1000 and 1200 different issues. This made the total production 400,000, giving an overall survival rate of about 0.13 percent.[33] Frearson eliminated uncertainty about the number of issues published by excluding from his calculations the single sheet corantos, the unnumbered newsbooks and Archer's separate series between 1624 and 1628 because we do not know how many issues there were. Basing his calculations on the numbered and dated series gave him a figure of 641 for the number of issues published from 1622 to 1641. He then considerably increased the output estimate to an average of 1000 copies each overall, arguing reasonably that intensity of publication is shown by the frequency of editions, the rapid evolution of form, the large number of publications involved, and the number of publishers involved in the early 1620s. Together these indicated a rapid growth in interest in European affairs. This gave a total production figure of 641,000 copies from October 1622 to January 1641 and produced two very strong survival peaks corresponding with periods of heightened demand and more frequent publication. His calculations supported an argument that the significance and potential penetration of these publications had been consistently underestimated by historians.[34]

Another way to estimate print runs is through survival rates. Unfortunately, it is almost as difficult to pin down survival rates as to estimate print runs. Some variation in the survival pattern from issue to issue is credible. During times of heightened interest, the content was of greater interest and, therefore, it was possibly thought more worthwhile to keep copies in much the same way as commemorative issues of memorable news are kept today. In addition, people who did not habitually purchase an issue would have bought a copy at these times and may have been more likely to hold on to it for this very reason. However, it seems unlikely that survival rates would have fluctuated radically and print runs to have remained the constant, as Frearson's model assumes. We know from McKenzie's research that it was common for edition sizes to fluctuate, even for books, with a seemingly more steady demand.[35] Moreover, given the sensitivity of this trade to fluctuating interests and given that publication costs were so closely related to the quantities printed, the publishers had strong incentives to tailor each print run as closely and tightly as possible to estimated demand. Of course, they would not always have got it right and there is some evidence to suggest that from

147–8; P. Lake and M. Questier, *Antichrist's Lewd Hat* (New Haven, CT, 2002), 14, fn. 19; McKenzie, 60–1; McKenzie, 'Printing and Publishing', 559.

[33] F. Dahl, 'Short-title Catalogue of English Corantos and Newsbooks 1620–1642', *The Library*, 4:18 (1938), 45–6; Dahl, 22.

[34] Frearson, 116–18, Table 2.1.

[35] McKenzie, 24.

time to time they may have underestimated demand and ended up ordering a reprint or asking the printer to run off some additional copies. The issue of 30 October 1622 has two identical versions, except for the names of the publishers in the imprints. It is possible that Butter and Downes paid for the first printing and that, when demand outstripped supply, Butter, Bourne and Archer funded a second printing from the same type setting. In 1632, again at a time of high demand, there are instances where the text was amended in the course of printing. There are two different settings of issue 38, which appeared on 3 August, the same day as issue 37. There are also two surviving variants of the same issue for 1 September 1632.[36]

Overall, a credible profile of production is created by assuming a fairly even, and low, survival rate. Newsbooks were a weekly ephemeral product printed on cheap paper and rendered redundant by the arrival of a more recent issue. There was no single obsessive collector at work over the period of the Thirty Years War to unduly distort the survival rate, as there was with Thomason in the 1640s. It is clear from reading contemporary correspondence such as Mead's letters to Sir Martin Stuteville that there were many issues and only a small sample has survived. Contemporary comment explains why the survival rate is so low. Richard Brathwaite's *Whimzies: or, a New Cast of Characters* refers to 'A Corranto – coiner' and to the fact that his products do not last,

> A weeke is the longest in the Citie, and after their arrivall, a little longer in the Countrey. Which past, they melt like Butter, or match a pipe and so Burne. But indeede, most commonly it is the height of their ambition, to aspire to the imployment of stopping mustard pots, or wrapping up pepper, pouder, staves-aker, &c. which done, they expire.[37]

All pamphlets and newsbooks plus many broadsheets were no doubt treated similarly. Watt notes that the earliest surviving copy of William Perkins's chapbook *Death's knell* (1628) is labelled the '9th edition', but for that, we would have no idea of its popularity. McKenzie gives further examples of editions that have disappeared, especially those in smaller, shorter formats. Coupe, in his study of German illustrated broadsheets from the seventeenth century, drew similar conclusions about their low survival rate. He suggested an assumption that the ratio of sheets that have survived approximates broadly to the ratio of sheets actually produced. This seems realistic.[38]

---

[36] STC18507.85 and 86. Dahl, 88–9, suggested it was the other way around but it makes sense to assume that the financial burden was spread more widely for an unscheduled additional printing. (3 August 1632), STC18507.262; (3 August 1632), STC18507.261; (1 September 1632), STC18507.266 and 7.

[37] McKenzie, 'Printing and Publishing', 561, quoted in Dahl, 'Short-title Catalogue', 45.

[38] Watt, 259; McKenzie, 'Printing and Publishing', 557, 559, 560; W. A. Coupe, *The German Illustrated Broadsheet in the 17th Century* (Baden-Baden, 1966–7), 83.

We can assume that the survival rate for the two most successful series, the first and the eighth, was probably a little higher than for other series and that the survival rate in the least successful series is probably lower; partly because the news was so lacking interest that very few people were motivated to keep their copies, but also because the publishers may have been left with copies on their hands which they destroyed. This still gives a likelihood of some print runs of over the legal limit of 1250. But we know that in 1621 demand for printed corantos outstripped supply as the publishers struggled to get to grips with the production process. By 1622, several publishers and several printers were involved so they probably went for sizable print runs especially since, by early 1623, they needed reprints. In any case, the purpose of controlling the number of books printed was to create work for compositors for subsequent editions. There was no prospect of a reprint after a new issue was available and no reason to impose the legal limit.

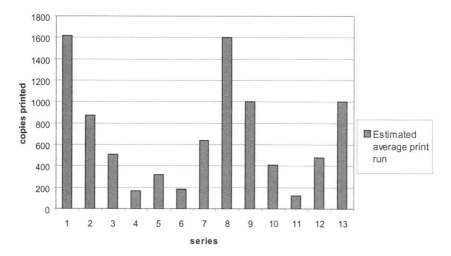

Figure 1: Estimated average print runs

Figure 1 reflects a fairly even and low survival rate of one in a thousand. It assumes print runs fluctuated in line with demand and yields a range of print runs that reflect fluctuating circumstances. The range accommodates Dahl's earlier estimates (200 and 400) for years of dwindling interest, while allowing for higher runs, which are more in line with Frearson's estimate of 1000, at times of heightened interest. This corresponds with estimates for German newspapers at this time and for France in 1630s. The estimate is quite modest, yielding average print runs not far off 500. In other words, at times when the business was neither booming, nor failing (for example, in the third, seventh and twelfth series), print runs were fairly normal for pamphlets in the early 1600s. Similarly, this approach gives an overall average of around 600 copies per issue, which again, is closer to what might reasonably be expected for a news pamphlet at that time.[39]

What makes periodical newsbooks so significant is not so much that many print runs were large, but that, even on a modest estimate of print runs, frequency of publication meant overall output was remarkable. Contemporary criticism of the periodical news, especially by dramatists, was a recognition that the social mechanisms for communication had shifted from the theatre to the news periodical.[40] The volume and accessibility of periodical news meant its presence was experienced more keenly and continuously than ever before. The number of issues was particularly high in the early 1620s and again in the early 1630s. Once the frequency of publication, for which we have sound evidence, is built into the calculations, a credible profile of production emerges, reflecting the fluctuations in trade and the down turn which almost put the publishers out of business in the late 1620s. Figures 2 and 3 demonstrate the large numbers of copies in circulation in the busier periods, of possibly over seven thousand copies a month in 1622–3 and again in 1631–2. This outcome brings forward by two decades the date at which 'pamphlet culture was impossible to ignore', as suggested by Michael Mendle.[41] These numbers are not so high as to call into question the capacity of the trade or the availability of paper to meet this demand, but they are consistent with the fact that five publishers were involved at the height of the trade, and with the extent to which these publications are mentioned in contemporary correspondence and journals and with the level of interest depicted in Ben Jonson's work.[42] It is periodicity, their single distinguishing characteristic, that pushed production numbers up to unprecedented levels and meant that in the first decade of the numbered series well over a quarter of a million newsbooks went in to circulation.

As for the time it would take to print the copies, much would depend on the availability of press and pressmen and the priority given to the work. Raymond, working with the newsbooks of the early 1640s, arrived at an estimate of perhaps fourteen hours or less to compose the text.[43] The quality of the foreign newsbooks was similar, so the time was probably similar. This

---

[39] T. Schroder, 'The Origins of the German Press', 133, and J-P. Vittu, 'Instruments of Political Information in France', 167, both in DandB; Raymond, 233; J. Raymond, *Pamphlets and Pamphleteering in Early Modern Britain* (Cambridge, 2003), 80.

[40] Ibid., 129, 138; McKenzie, *The London Book Trade*, 3–5, 10.

[41] M. Mendle, 'News and the Pamphlet Culture', in DandB, 57; B. Reay, *Popular Cultures in England 1550–1750* (New York and Essex, 1998), 48; M. Spufford, 'The Pedlar, the Historian and the Folklorist: Seventeenth-century Communication', *Folklore*, 105 (1994).

[42] McKenzie, 'Printing and Publishing', 557; McKenzie, 130; P. Stallybrass, '"Little Jobs": Broadsides and the Printing Revolution', in *Agent of Change: Print Culture after Elizabeth L. Eisenstein*, ed. S. A. Baron, E. Lindquist and E. Shevlin (Amherst and Boston, MA, 2007), 333–7.

[43] Raymond, 235; McKenzie, 19–21.

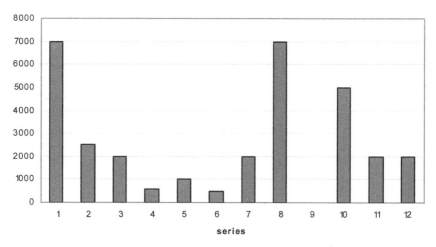

Figure 2: Estimated number of copies per month

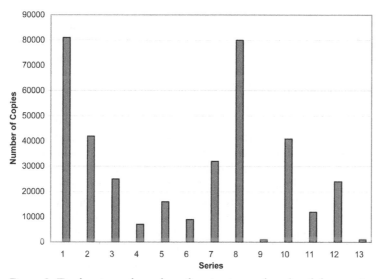

Figure 3: Total estimated number of copies in numbered and dates series

means that even a two thousand-copy edition might, at least theoretically, be turned around by a printer within twenty-four hours. However, although the foreign news was current and time sensitive, the syndicate was not under the same pressures as the publishers of competing newsbooks in other European cities, nor were they under the same time pressures as publishers of competing publications in London in the early 1640s. Most translation probably took place in London. Publishers also took time to edit and amalgamate texts from different sources. Printed copies could be on the streets in two to three days after reaching London. A thousand print run in the early 1620s with three sheet issues would take one long day's work. By the mid-1620s with only two sheets to print and print runs down to five hundred copies or less, a turn around of copy in one to two days could have been fairly easily accomplished.

Arriving at a total production cost is even more difficult, despite all that is known about the trade and the fact that the parameters of charging by the printers are fairly well known. It is clear, given that the time it took to compose and print and the labour involved were all quite standardised in practice, the costs passed on to the publisher were likely to have been predictable at the time.

Raymond calculated that if newsbooks with a plausible run of two hundred and fifty copies were then sold for a penny, the cost of 9s would provide a profit of 11s 10d to be shared between the supplier, publisher, editor (if any) and sellers.[44] Other calculations yield different results, some considerably lower than this. For example, 8d to 10d a day for a compositor, plus four people on a press for two working days would be a maximum of 7s 6d, and if the printer added fifty percent, we get a maximum of 11s 3d for three thousand plus sheets (plus the cost of paper which would at least double the cost). Marjorie Plant suggested that in the mid-1620s eight sheets for 1d would cover the printer's costs. News production, even at ½d per copy for a two-sheet issue, could be very profitable if print runs were high since the initial costs were fixed. As soon as print runs rose, the profits would increase, making issues with a thousand copies or more quite lucrative. Raymond's calculation of a minimum print run is also instructive because it demonstrates how tight the margin could be on a low print run, particularly by the early 1640s, with short runs of 1d for short publications. This would have been a very small margin indeed, since there were additional initial outlays to obtain the copies from the Continent, register and translate them. Production prices rose in the 1630s, with paper costs rising by twenty-five percent and an overall rise of possibly as much as forty percent throughout the trade.[45] It is perhaps not so surprising that Butter struggled financially after the partnership ended in 1639. It is also quite possible that some of the issues in the fourth and sixth series with low print runs were produced at a loss.

For Butter, in particular, the experience of more profitable times provided sufficient incentive to continue through a number of leaner times. He persisted in difficult times for too long. Instead of diversifying in 1639, Butter mortgaged his copyrights to secure loans totalling £600 to raise money in time for the next year's news network subscriptions. Thus, the tenacity and

---

[44] Febvre and Martin, The Coming, 110–13; Raymond, 233–4.
[45] Gaskell, A New Introduction, 177–8; F. Johnson, 'Notes on English Retail Book – prices 1550–1640', The Library, 5:5 (1950), 90; Carter, 'Early Accounts', 18, 122; Plant, 221. Plant, 198, 188; Febvre and Martin, The Coming, 112, 114.

optimism that had seen him through earlier rough times proved his undoing because he did not know when to give up. Bourne was the shrewder financial operator, not only diversifying but aligning himself with the interests of the Stationers' Company and the House of Commons in the 1640s.[46] But does Butter's tenacity mean that he had a religious rather than a commercial motivation? I doubt it. If the Protestant cause had been his overriding motive, in the early 1640s he would have switched his attention to London news. Though his interest in the international Protestant cause is undeniable, his chief motivation was the foreign news trade and, by this time, his reputation in this field.

Prices and wages

Just as the charge for printing was based upon costs, so too was the retail price and, as in so many aspects of early modern English life, the government stood ready to intervene and to enforce the sale of books at reasonable prices if there were signs of profiteering. In practice there was little need. Prices were calculated on a cost basis, allowing a margin for booksellers and hawkers. From 1560 to 1635 the calculation for most publications was in the region of one half penny per sheet for those composed in pica types, with higher prices for publications including illustrations. Prices also varied slightly according to the type of work subject matter, and a small pamphlet tended to be sold at a higher rate proportionate to size.[47]

Barry Reay has described a hierarchy of accessibility of printed works, based largely on length with the penny ballad at the bottom, two and three penny almanacs and chapbooks in the middle. At the higher end, chivalric romances and histories sold for one or two shillings or more by the 1640s.[48] Printed broadsides were the cheapest. By 1641, the normal price was a penny and Tessa Watt suggests they may have been lower before 1635.[49]

Pamphlets generally sold at a penny a sheet. Two pence was the expected price of a short pamphlet of two sheets (sixteen pages). Murder pamphlets published in cheap quarto, twenty-four-page format with blackletter type. Longer ones ran to forty-eight or fifty-six pages: they all sold for a few pence. After prices rose in 1635 it is likely that lengthier pamphlets no longer sold at two pence. Because book prices remained stable between 1560 and 1635 they became more affordable as wages rose by half to two-thirds. Raymond noted 2d for 'two printed declaracons' in 1642 and 1s 6d for a manuscript of 'parliament Occurrences'. Watt concluded that, given the wages in the early

[46] ODNB, Butter, Bourne; pp. 250–1, 256–7, 263.
[47] Plant, 238–9; F. Johnson, 'Notes', 83–112.
[48] Reay, *Popular Cultures*, 56.
[49] Watt, 11, quotes Henry Peacham, *The worth of a penny* (1641); Plant, 239, gives a ballad sheet at least ½d.

seventeenth century, 'a two penny pamphlet every fortnight or so looks like a possibility for even a fairly ordinary household, although it might mean sacrificing two quarts of beer at the alehouse. A lesser yeoman with £40–50 income a year would hardly have to think twice about buying pamphlets of ballads and probably presented a more regular market.'[50]

Fortunately, we have contemporary evidence for the price of foreign news-books. The 8 June 1627 copy in the Burney collection has 'Liber Nathan: Bowman ... ijd' written in hand on the front. Ben Jonson gave 'Two-pence a sheet' as the price to secure copy by order in advance in *The Staple of News*. However, newsbooks in 1625, when the play was written, were twenty-four pages long and by 1627 they were sixteen pages. So Jonson's price of 2d for a sheet would seem to be a generic and familiar one. The price rose in the 1630s in line with other publishing prices. A copy from 1 September 1632, has on the title page, '1632.pr[e]t[iu]m 3d', for a sixteen-page issue.[51] Further rises in cost may have meant that a charge of 4d would be necessary to cover a similar publication by the late 1630s. When, in the tenth series, Butter and Bourne changed the format and began to produce three or four one-sheet issues simultaneously, each covering the news from a different European city's publication for that week, these one-sheet issues could be sold for one penny. This would make them more affordable for poorer customers. Unfortunately, the experiment was doomed to failure because, while it may have attracted addition sales from lower down the market, it could only do so at the risk of failing to maintain sales of all three or four issues to wealthier and more consistent customers. The experiment ended and the sixteen-side newsbook was reintroduced in the twelfth series in 1640 with the promise to sell them 'at a cheaper Rate'. Butter needed to keep the price as low as he could to reach down market and secure as many sales as possible, but he also needed to give value for money to customers who could afford more.[52]

These prices put newsbooks within the grasp of most people. They represented a reasonably small sum to most literate Englishmen. We know that, even at twice the price of these issues, a topical pamphlet could sell well. Sir Simonds D'Ewes in a letter of 2 February 1627 refers to a scurrilous book or pamphlet selling at 6d. It was clearly a good commercial proposition because he tells us it was on sale at every shop.[53]

Wages varied from 7d to 1s a day for agricultural workers. An artisan in London could earn 7s a week and would pay between 1d and 1s to see a

---

[50] Lake and Questier, *Antichrist's Lewd Hat*, 3; M. Ashley, *England in the Seventeenth Century* (1952/1977), 23; Raymond, 91; Watt, 261–2.

[51] Dahl, 153, 214; Jonson, Act I, ii, 357.

[52] (23 April 1640), verso, STC18507.337.

[53] Schumacher, 68; J. O. Halliwell, ed., *The Autobiography and Correspondence of Sir Simonds D'Ewes*, vol. 2 (1845), 193.

play and 4d for a quart of ale, 8d for a quart of sack. A penny would pay for a 6.5lb loaf. A peasant family's weekly average income may have been little over 3s, to pay for rent, clothing, food and drink, with a woman only earning a shilling a week, even doing men's work.[54] However, while the price of a single issue was about the same price as other forms of cheap print, such as ballads, chapbooks and almanacs, and, therefore, brought them within the reach of the most humble potential customer, this only meant they could afford to buy a copy occasionally. At 2d a copy, it cost more than 8s to buy a series of fifty numbers, plus the cost of carriage could double or triple the price for anyone beyond the vicinity of the City. So, although these publications would have been encountered at all levels of society, the market of purchasers was 'probably much less amorphous'. Readers who supported the expanding news industry of the early 1620s were those who could afford to purchase copies regularly. The real cost of following the foreign news must be considered in terms of the consistent purchase of weekly copies. Comprehension of the often complex and confusing news reports depended on regular reading, putting newsbooks beyond the reach of many poorer readers. Subscription also demanded a degree of loyalty and commitment, to continue to make a financial outlay through times when there was little of interest being reported. Mead commented on this to Stuteville, 'because I am a customer I must refuse nothing they send me'.[55]

The London market for printed news was adopting a subscription system that was already familiar in local manuscript newsletter networks and a growing phenomenon on the Continent. Schroder suggests that in Germany subscription lists were strong, appealing to well-educated and wealthy citizens, including the high nobility and smaller German courts. By 1611, the Wolfenbuttel *Aviso* had subscribers at the local court, among jurists and aristocrats and was circulated in the countryside by messengers to subscribing aristocrats, pastors, estate managers, mayors and governors. Communal subscriptions lowered the costs for individuals in private reading circles with some aristocrats and patricians sharing issues and copies going to monasteries, convents, charitable institutions and municipal councils. He estimates German readership as 24,000 to 60,000 people before the Thirty Years War, rising to 200,000 and 250,000 after the war with a larger public being reached through oral news circulation. It is very difficult to guess what multiplier could be used to establish the level of readership, especially as many would hear the news by gathering in places such as alehouses and

---

[54] Ashley, *England*, 197; C. Bridenbaugh, *Vexed and Troubled Englishmen* (Oxford, 1968), 51, 79, 148, 211.
[55] Frearson, 'The Distribution', 17, 22; Harl. MS 389, fo. 289, quoted in D. Randall, 'Joseph Mead, Novellante: News, Sociability, and Credibility in Early Stuart England', *JBS*, 45:2 (2006), 302.

market squares where they could listen as it was read. Estimates of multi-pliers range from five or six to as high as fifty per copy.[56]

The interplay between periodicity (with its dependency upon a stable market of subscribers) and one-off street and bookstore sales also helps to explain the pattern of sales. High sales were achievable when noteworthy events occurred, such as, in February 1623, when interest in continental events was already high because of Prince Charles's trip to Madrid. At these times the newsbooks could have sold like any topical one-off pamphlet. Sometimes the content, like other pamphlets, was almost completely dedi-cated to that single topic rather than a variety of items from many loca-tions. The challenge was to maintain a consistent level of interest. In this case, it seems that printing returned to normal by the first issue in March, even though the story of a Dutch plot was still running with accounts of the apprehension and torture of suspects. In what was virtually a subsist-ence economy, bad harvests in 1623–30 and 1636–7 and summer plagues in the mid-1620s and late 1630s, would also have reduced the disposable income of poorer buyers leaving them with less to spend on inessentials like foreign news.[57] While out of town subscribers might remain loyal, for London readers it was easier to be more selective. So it proved difficult to retain the same high level of regular sales through summers of campaigns with inconclusive skirmishes taking place in regions that readers knew little about. It was more difficult still to maintain interest through winters where the armies were disbanded, in winter quarters or uneventful sieges.

Long-term financial success was critically dependent upon the number of committed subscribers. Newsbooks needed a readership prosperous enough to commit around 8d to 10d a month in the 1620s and 1s to 1s 3d in the 1630s. Continuity maintained interest and the publishers, like any good director of a modern TV soap opera, ensured that the title pages stressed the fact that they were reporting on continuing stories of main actors and critical campaigns covered in earlier issues. This stress on continuity was so great that, by 1624, the title itself had become almost standardised to read, *The continuation of our weekly newes* (or later, *our forraine/weekly avisoes*).[58]

Sales and distribution

The final factor in an assessment of the impact of foreign newsbooks is the extent to which they were disseminated beyond London.

The publishers needed to distribute copies quickly. Between them the syndicate had bookshops in the south at St Paul's, further east at the

---

[56] Schroder, 'The Origins', 133–5; T. C. W. Blanning, *The Culture of Power and the Power of Culture: Old Regime Europe 1660–1789* (Oxford, 2002), 156–7.
[57] J. Raven, 'The Economic Context', in J. Barnard, 572–4.
[58] Plate p. 126.

Exchange and in Pope's Head Alley, and in the west near the Fleet. They could trade their newsbooks with other publications to get them into more bookshops and ensure there was a wide availability on the streets of London. In London with literacy levels high by the 1620s and print prices at an all time low compared with wages and other potential purchases there was a strong potential market. However, most of the readers of foreign news known to us today were living outside London, receiving news in correspondence and recording events in journals. Most appear to have had personal arrangements to ensure a steady supply of information from the capital, but some, like Davenport in Stockport, in Cheshire, appear to have belonged to news networks that provided at least an infrequent supply. Efforts to explore the distribution of printed material have increased in tandem with a growing interest in popular culture. Jonathan Barry's assessment is cautious, suggesting that there may have been many barriers to reading, 'whatever the theoretical reading capacity of the public', and that while publishers always aimed to broaden markets they may have concentrated on the luxury end of the market and on letting buyers come to London. Tessa Watt has argued that, while before 1640 it is likely that a large proportion of the buyers of cheap print were drawn from the middling ranks of yeomen, husbandmen and traders, and would have included gentry readers, cheap print can be seen as an instrument of social cohesion, bringing more people into the reading public.[59]

Ben Jonson pointed to an extensive distribution system for news, including

> Factors, and agents –
> Liegers, that lie out
> Through all the Shires.

London's onward-selling markets were expanding and there is growing evidence of the wide geographical distribution of news trade networks in the seventeenth century. By 1654, a contemporary was commenting on London as 'the sea of news from which smaller rivulets often flow to us in the country'. Frearson has demonstrated that periodical foreign news 'informed a much larger body of public opinion than illicit pamphlets and manuscript newsletters'. They 'were intended for a large market of readers, and they were encountered at all levels of society'. He argued that 'London news was much more influential beyond the capital than historians have

---

[59] J. Barry, 'Literacy and Literature in Popular Culture: Reading and Writing in Historical Perspective', in *Popular Culture in England c1500–1850*, ed. T. Harris (Basingstoke and London, 1995), 79–80; Watt, 5; A. Fox, 'Ballads, Libels and Popular Ridicule in Jacobean England', *PandP*, 48 (1995); Atherton, 44.

previously supposed, especially in the "corridors of communication" which linked the capital with the localities'.[60]

Records from booksellers kept after the Fire of London give evidence of trade networks and private customers essential for successful distribution. Supplies were reaching booksellers in Oxford, Cambridge, Shrewsbury, Lichfield, Market Harborough, Coventry, Ludlow, Bristol, Norwich and Exeter with most provincial booksellers keeping a running account and frequent communications with London suppliers. Some also traded with cities in a wider circle. For example, Oxford maintained supplies from London and, in turn, provided books to the west and Wales. Bristol supplied Ireland. Dealings and communications between booksellers were probably very little different across Britain to those on the Continent where booksellers would correspond and trade from city to city, employing an agent to act for them or taking to the road themselves to improve business links.[61]

Frearson established a link between Butter and a bookseller in Bristol and listed twenty-nine cities, from Newcastle and York in the north to Exeter and Wells in the west and Canterbury and Ipswich in the east, with booksellers at this time. However, 'small books' were rarely itemised in the inventories of provincial booksellers and booksellers were probably not the main vendors. Packhorse and carrier services probably provided the best means of distribution available.[62] Watt showed chapbooks and ballads were distributed together using the same networks. She added these traders to the London based pedlars who 'alone covered much of the country in their wanderings', and to the routes covered by the carriers, to conclude that 'we should think of a national market for cheap print, not merely the metropolitan area'.[63]

Packhorse and carrier services were cheaper than the official post, introduced in 1635, and faster and more reliable than river and coastal services. Evidence from provincial readers shows they used these services and were regularly supplied with the latest printed news from the capital. The weekly journeys of common carriers and packhorse drivers between the capital and numerous provincial destinations provided a fast, frequent, regular, reliable and inexpensive service.[64] Packhorses needed tracks rather than roads and

---

[60] Jonson, Act I, ii, 358; McKenzie, The London Book Trade, 7; M. Spufford, Small Books, Ch. 5; Reay, Popular Cultures, 48–50; The Faithful Scout, 188 (14–21 July 1654), 1492, quoted in J. Friedman, The Battle of the Frogs and Fairford's Flies (New York, 1993), 6; Frearson, 5, 14; Frearson, 'The Distribution', 2.

[61] Mandebrote, 'From the Warehouse', 73; F. J. Levy, 'How Information Spread among the Gentry 1550–1640', JBS, 21 (1982), 20; P. Morgan, 'Letters Relating to the Oxford Book Trade Founding Bindings in Oxford College Libraries c1611–1647', in Studies in the Book Trade, 18 (Oxford Bibliographical Society, 1975), 77–84; Febvre and Martin, The Coming, fn. 205.

[62] Frearson, 'The Distribution', 7; Frearson, 15–17.

[63] Watt, 27–9.

[64] Frearson, 24.

had less difficulty with winter conditions than wagons, so the roads were good enough to support a complex network of scheduled public carrying services that provided the basis for most trades. London was connected to most parts of the country with a web of highways and cross-country roads keeping them in regular contact with the capital. Road books demonstrate that most of the cities and towns of England, and a number of those in Wales, could be reached regularly. The main highways had inns and alehouses from which all the local roads and byways could be penetrated ensuring London news filtered through to the localities.[65]

Provincial inns and alehouses were the main centres of news for country people. People collected letters, parcels and news, met others, conducted business and exchanged information and gossip. It was common to leave letters at inns and hostelries for collection. There were up to about four thousand of these inns and alehouses outside London in the seventeenth century, so that everyone must have had access to such an establishment. At the London end of each route inns were grouped. In *The carriers cosmographie* (1637) John Taylor listed inns, hostelries and other lodgings in and near London where carriers could be found on specific days of the week, bound for more than two hundred towns across Britain, 'and able to deliver goods and letters to the remotest regions of Scotland, Wales and Cornwall', with regular services to all the main towns in the north and many other towns in between. Examples included the Bell Inn outside Ludgate where carriers arrived every Friday and left again on Sunday or Monday for York. From there, further services were available to Berwick and into Scotland. While from Lancaster they could travel on to Kendall and Cockermouth; from Worcester, goods could travel on to Carmarthen, from Exeter to Plymouth and from Chester to Caernavon. Southwark served Kent, Sussex and Surrey while Fleet Street and the Strand served roads to the south-west; Bishopsgate, those to the north and east. The Oxford road terminated at Holborn. Watt, convinced by the evidence of such extensive services, concluded that 'we should think of a national market for cheap print'.[66]

However, costs for readers were significantly higher outside London. The charge from London to Ipswich and Oxford was 1d at this time and to Coventry, 2d. This would have been enough to ensure that only a wealthier reader could afford to subscribe and it is these customers whose news correspondence historians know most about. But many carriers and pedlars would have taken newsbooks by the bundle along with other cheap print and then aimed to get the best price they could. Their readers may not have had every copy and would not have been able to follow the news as effectively as subscribers, but the frequent arrival of news at the local alehouse would

---

[65] Ibid., 27–9, 33–41, 46–52, 59–70; Frearson, 'The Distribution', 10, 13; Watt, 'Publisher, Pedlar', 63.

[66] A. Fox, *Oral and Literate Culture in England 1500–1700* (Oxford, 2000), 374; Watt, 71–2.

have generated its own momentum and interest. Those who could not afford to buy could still enquire about the news.[67]

Provincial readers would not have received news as quickly as the immediate London market. Estimates of the distances covered by carriers in a day vary from ten to twenty miles. News reached Colchester and Cambridge in two days and it took three to four days to reach Bristol, Southampton, Salisbury, Oxford and the Midlands; six days to reach Manchester and Liverpool and a week to reach Devon, Wales, Lancashire and York. While the southeast of England was probably best informed, by the 1640s newsbooks were reaching every corner of England and were available in Wales and Scotland. Readers would usually have received one issue before the next was on sale in the streets of London.[68] The scale of weekly services can sometimes be found from the records of the towns served. For example, Tiverton employed twenty-two carriers to London between 1617 and 1636. Up to five were working at any one time. Taylor showed that most services were bi-weekly, with most carriers arriving on Tuesdays and Fridays and leaving the next day.[69]

Many writers of newsletters used carriers and included printed foreign news in their shipments and John Pory even used Butter's address as his own. A notice published 19 March 1624 demonstrates that provincial readers were an important part of the publishers' marketing strategy and that they aimed to make the best use that they could of the bi-weekly carrier services:

> both the Reader and the Printer of these pamphlets, agree in their expectation of weekly Newes, so that if the Printer have not wherewithall to afford satisfaction, yet will the Reader come and aske every day for new Newes … either to please themselves or satisfie their customers. Therefore is the Printer, both with charge and painstaking very carefull to have his friends abroad supply his wants at home with pertinent Letters, and acquaint him with the Printed copies beyond the Seas, that hee may acquaint you with such true intelligence … so that … sometimes you may have two Corantoes in one Weeke which seeing it is for your sake, and especially that you may make the Country far off partake of our London Newes, be so far generous to acknowledge his kindnesse.[70]

Because of the uncertainty of supply from across the Channel newsbooks did not have a fixed day of the week for publication. However, most were published between Tuesday and Friday with the others appearing on either Monday or Saturday.[71] The main task of the apprentices would have been to assist with batching, recording and dispatching printed copy as soon as

---

[67] Raven, 'The Economic Context', 578.
[68] Frearson, 21, 71–6; Raymond, 238–41.
[69] Ibid., 57–8.
[70] Levy, 'How Information Spread', 23; Pory, 51–3; (19 March 1624), 1, STC18507.145.
[71] Frearson, 76.

it came off the presses. The additional hands would have assisted a speedy turn around of copies to catch the carriers. Butter was centrally located in the St Austin's Gate end of Watling Street, near St Paul's, convenient for the carriers for Oxford, the Midlands and the north-west who used inns in and around Smithfield and Holborn. Southwark Bridge gave access to the south. Publishers by the Exchange had easy access to Bishopsgate for the north and east, and to London Bridge for the south-east. Downes may well have been brought into the syndicate because of the westerly location of his shop, near the Fleet. This would have supported the rapid distribution of copies to the south-west, as well as improving access to the carriers around Smithfield and Holborn.

The foreign news syndicate may well have provided the inspiration and blueprint for the operation of the ballad partners who first registered 127 ballads in 1624. Like the syndicate, the ballad partnership focused on the dissemination of cheap, small and easily carried printed works. It also, like the syndicate, comprised booksellers located to provide access to different carrier services with a communal warehouse from which they sold their ballads to hawkers at a standard rate of a third of a penny a copy.[72]

Spotting a new trend, Jonson's depiction of the new news office seems to have had a distribution function. Many of the hawkers, most of whom were women, as shown by Jonson's 'butter-woman', would have provided a service through the streets of London, supplementing retail sales through London bookshops. They seem to have been the main means for distributing ephemeral material rapidly and anonymously. In addition, 'Mercury Women' sold them wholesale. Both hawkers and carriers would then take them out, beyond London.[73]

Conclusions

Publication in London required a significant investment. Subscriptions for the supply and shipping of news, registration with the Stationers' Company, printing and paper had to be paid for before copies were available for sale. In addition, the publishers took on apprentices for the batching and dispatch process to speed dissemination throughout London and out to the provinces. There is no evidence of a wealthy politically or religiously motivated sponsor and, although some of the publishers were more clearly committed to Protestantism than the others, there can be little doubt that they were first and foremost engaged in a business enterprise. Their decisions also seem to have been based on business considerations.

---

[72] Watt, 'Publisher, Pedlar, Pot-Poet', 66.
[73] Jonson, Act I, ii; Mandebrote, 'From the Warehouse', 53.

Understanding the business methods of the publishers helps us appreciate the extent of the trade and the degree of penetration into the market for print. The number of issues, their frequency and the size of print runs in buoyant periods suggest that the newsbooks were by far the most dominant publications on the market in the early 1620s and early 1630s. Periodicity pushed production numbers up to unprecedented levels and newsbook output became greater than any other news or topical publication that had been experienced in England at that time and distribution was well organised.

Given what we now understand about the interrelationships between oral and written cultures and the role of inns and alehouses as centres of communication, it is reasonable to conclude that foreign news penetrated every corner and every level of society. However, it is unlikely that many below the yeomanry class could afford to subscribe. The stop-go economy of the early seventeenth century meant a working man, living in or near London, could almost certainly have afforded a copy from time to time, but not weekly. This factor ultimately led to a struggle for survival for publishers dependent on regular sales. Nonetheless, newsbooks performed a significant role in the education and politicisation of the public. Even illiterate visitors to the inns and alehouses on the highways could regularly catch up with the affairs of Europe. Interpretation and understanding were a problem, but the publishers thought of that too, and they addressed it with the publication of complementary and interpretive material and, as the following chapters show, through editorial work intended to make the newsbooks more accessible to the less educated of their readers.

Part Two

News Editors and Readers

5

Editing and the Work of Thomas Gainsford 1622–4 and William Watts 1631–2

'I will come toward you with honest information,
and not hide my talent in a Napkin.'[1]

In addition to the publishers, a number of different editors who were involved with the news press in London during the Thirty Years War made a contribution to the evolution of the news periodical. Of these, the editors Thomas Gainsford and William Watts are best known for their efforts in shaping news publications and building a relationship with readers by speaking directly to them in editorial prefaces. They are associated with two periods of intense demand for news at times of heightened interest in European events, when editorial innovation and experimentation with the methods for gathering and presenting the news significantly accelerated. These two rationalised the reports that arrived at irregular intervals from a variety of continental sources and converted the material into newsbooks suitable for an English readership. They helped to educate and inform an emerging market of newly literate customers about the crisis in Europe.

The publishers needed to expand their base income by reaching out to increase the frequency of sales to poorer readers. Only the most affluent readers could be relied upon to subscribe as purchasing on a weekly basis was too costly for many, however, the price of a single issue was affordable to a wide range of the literate public. Though most other obstacles to reading were beyond the control of the publishers, including lack of leisure, privacy and even the effectiveness of candlelight, this did not deter them from tackling the barriers they could.[2] They aimed to increase the appeal of issues to make them accessible to new readers by editing to transform imports, compiled from multiple sources, into something with a closer resemblance to popular news pamphlets. To extend sales to many who were first genera-

[1] Concluding words of the editor, probably Thomas Gainsford (29 August 1623), 22, STC18507.124.
[2] J. Barry, 'Literacy and Literature in Popular Culture: Reading and Writing in Historical Perspective', in *Popular Culture in England c1500–1850*, ed. T. Harris (Basingstoke and London, 1995), 79–80.

tion literate and unfamiliar with European politics and geography, or military matters, they needed explanations to make them more comprehensible.

Most Londoners had an interest in the foreign news but lacked knowledge. This is illustrated in John Taylor's account of his reception in London on return from Bohemia in 1620 when he encountered widespread ignorance:

> John Easie … will needs torture some newes out of me from Spinola, whom I never was neere by 500 miles: for hee is in the Palatinate country, and I was in Bohemia … an Alderman of Gotham, catches me … demanding if Bohemia bee a great towne, and whether there be any meate in it, and whether the last fleet of ships be arrived there.

Thomas Cogswell has argued that 'in the decades before Edgehill, a rapidly expanding percentage of the population underwent a crude adult education which left them keen observers of national events and ultimately eager participants'.[3] This chapter shows that the education offered by the press made no direct criticisms of government yet was instructive. By studying the extent to which the needs of readers were accommodated we can better assess the reach as well as the role newsbooks played in raising awareness and influencing the development of public opinion.

Identity and format

The publishers gave their product a 'selling face', adopting some elements of modern news presentation as they experimented with marketing.

The brief bulletin reports they received in the early 1620s were a far cry from the eye-catching headline news and colour photographs in newspapers today. En route to London, vivid detail could be lost, sometimes resulting in what Arblaster has described as a 'bewildering ragbag of unexplained events'.[4] Ingenuity and editorial effort were required to produce attractive issues that were readable and credible. By the summer of 1622, the publishers were tackling these issues. Like Abraham Verhoeven in Antwerp, who similarly had the protection of a monopoly and used a book format, they could allow time for editing. A delay of a day or two for improving an issue was worthwhile if it increased sales.

Even before the syndicate was formed, publishers changed the format from single sheet corantos used by the Dutch and Germans, to quarto newsbooks with a front page devoted to the title and description of contents.

---

[3] John Taylor, *Taylor his Travels* (1620), A2, STC23802; T. Cogswell, 'The Politics of Propaganda: Charles I and the People in the 1620's', *JBS*, 29 (1990), 278, 294.

[4] P. Arblaster, 'Posts, Newsletters, Newspapers', in *News Networks*, ed. Raymond, 31; Plates, pp. 46 and 132.

Then, by skilful manipulation of layout and careful organisation of texts, they developed a style that was attractive, intelligible to readers and economical to produce. The pamphlet format was in general use in England for news of all kinds. It had been used throughout the previous century for news pamphlets, including John Wolfe's news publications from 1589 to 1591, so the adoption of a format familiar to the readers may well have been an important factor. The change was so successful that the Dutch form was never used again by any publishers of European news in English in this period. Even during the 1632–8 ban on London production of weekly news, when news began to be published again with Amsterdam imprints, the newsbook format was used.[5]

An anonymously published issue as early as March 1622 shows the publishers were already aware of the benefits of adapting and addressing themselves directly to their readership. *More newes ... for the satisfaction of every true English heart* complains that,

> Corantos in England are so translated, and obsequious to the Dutch Coppies, that they never mention any exployt of the English, nor vouchsafe to attribute the glory of any enterprise; unto them, as forgetting Captaine Boroughs, at the siege of Frankendale, and divers valiant Gentilmen in other places nay, they scarce mention Generall Vere himselfe.[6]

Modern editors always try to give their papers a striking visual impact and, in this respect, London editors were well ahead of their Dutch counterparts. Instead of a heading or a few lines on the first page, except during the period January 1639 to April 1640, they followed the practice in popular pamphlets of developing title pages designed to tickle the curiosity of the prospective reader browsing through a bookstall. Just as today the main feature of a front page is the headlines, so too, on these title pages the content is emphasised. They drew attention to sensational or good news and to news of particular places or people. The issue of 17 April 1622 began with the promising title, *Good newes for the King of Bohemia? Or, a certaine relation of the last and great overthrow, given by the Duke of Brunswicke to the Bishop of Cullen, and Duke of Bavariaes forces ... With the proceedings of Count Mansfield ... [in] the Palatinate.*[7]

In the summer of 1622, Butter, who was establishing a series in competition with Bourne and Archer, appears to have been the first to recognise the need for an original consistent identity and appropriate 'selling face' for his publications. He told readers his issues could be identified by their 'like title, with the Armies of the King of Bohemia on the other side of the title page'.[8]

---

5 Dahl, 280–3.
6 (late March, 1622), 10–11, STC18507.38 quoted in Dahl, 57.
7 (17 April 1622), STC18507.40.
8 (23 August 1622), 19, STC18507.72 quoted in Dahl, 78–9.

Nouemb. 21. 1622.   *Numb.* 8.

The Continuation

of the former Newes.

WHEREIN IS RELATED
the difcontents of the Duke of *Saxony* ; for
the ill vfage of the Proteftant Minifters, in *Bohemia, Morauia, Silefia,* &c. with the prefent
troubles of the Churches of
thofe Countries.

Together with a large ftory of the
prefent diftreffe of the *Grifons*, and the
hopes from the *French* King for their affiftance :
And alfo fome miferies in *Leopoldus* Army :
As alfo the names of thofe *Englifh* Captains
and Lieutenants, which came out from
Manheim ; with the prefent eftate
of *Franckendale.*

L A S T L Y,

The holding out of the Fort of *Papenmutz*,
with the paffing vp of the Prince of *Orange*, and the
Marquefle *Spinolaes* Armies vnto Count *Manf-
field* in *Weftphalia*, and diuers o-
ther *particulars.*

LONDON,
Printed for *Nathaniel Butter, Bartholomew Downes,*
and *Thomas Archer.* 1622.

Plate 2. A fairly typical title page (21 November 1622) of a quarto newsbook from the first series of the news syndicate; with an issue number, date, a selection of publishers' names, and a list of contents. Protestant concerns about the re-catholicisation of Bohemia and interest in English officers serving in the Palatinate are selling features. The title was not firmly established. (The next issue in this series was called *Weekly Newes.*)

From June onwards in 1622, the appearance of title pages began to settle down and titles began in a similar fashion with the words, A *continuation*, or *Our last newes*, *Weekely Newes*, or *More newes*. In the first series of news-books produced by the syndicate from October 1622 this standardisation was taken a step further: on the top right hand corner of each title page there appeared an issue number and, in the top left, a date.[9] Initially, this dating and numbering may have been a requirement for licensing, rather than a device for customer recognition. The publishers did not make the next step of realising that a consistently used name could be helpful. This is perhaps surprising since Butter, when he registered copies with the Stationers' Company, simply entered 'A currant of news'. We also know from contemporary references that customers spoke of the latest 'currant', 'aviso' or 'weekly relation'. Without competitors the publishers may have felt no need for a consistent title. When the issue of competition resur-faced in late 1624 the publishers sought simply to demonstrate that theirs was the authentic series, confident of their monopoly and not seeing them-selves as marketing a particular brand. As a consequence, as late as October 1627, they were fumbling for a way to refer to their publications, calling them 'passages of forreine Intelligence' and the rival publication (probably Ralph Mabbe's) as 'another unknowne Mercurie'. They advised readers to 'compare him with the continuation of our weekly Newes'. This formula was awkward, yet *The continuation* became the most usual opening of the title, especially from the late 1620s. Moreover, they never quite decided what, exactly, it was that they were continuing. They referred variously to 'weekely intelligence', 'weekely newes', 'forraine newes', 'forraine avisoes' and 'weekely avisoes', until during a brief spell in the tenth to twelfth series, while adopting a format where one issue was simply a translation of a single issue from another city, they used the term 'curranto'. For these, Butter simplified the title to *The Curranto for this weeke from Norimberg, or Holland* or *Franckford*.[10]

Editorial notices and Gainsford's Protestant perspective

One of the most distinctive features of the English newsbooks were the notices addressed 'To the Reader', added in London to assist those following the news from week to week by explaining editorial policies whenever these were criticised or changed. Occasionally, they also expressed views or offered an interpretation of events. The device was used frequently and they provide a wealth of evidence on many aspects of the trade and formed part of an effort to bring the publication to readers in ways that were interesting and comprehensible.

[9] Plate 2, p. 126.
[10] (4 October 1627), 1, STC18507.189; Arber, vol. 4, 150; Plate, p. 244.

Editorials were not an entirely new feature. In 1591 when John Wolfe approached the idea of serial publication, he announced in an introduction:

> To the Reader Least that the better sort shoulde be mis-ledde by the malicious, who hearing of some smal garboyl betweene the French and the English, enlarge it so on Tenterhookes, that they proclaimed it a ruin of both armies. I thought it good to publish this Journall of Advertisements, which I received out of Brittaine as well to make it knowen how well our slender and weake Forces daylie confront the enemie as also with what good agreement (by the great wisdome of the Commaunders) the two Nacions joyne in a common quarrell against a common enemie. If I may finde this to be acceptable to the Reader, I shall be willing to acquaint him with the rest, as it shall come unto my handes. Farewell.

Abraham Verhoeven in Antwerp used the same method of addressing readers and promised in 1622 that, 'With God's help we shall not fail to continue every week'. The preface functioned as a means of courting readers. Direct speech was used to establish a more intimate relationship with readers, to seek consensus around a shared Protestant belief in the need to resist the Catholic armies and to draw readers into an agreement about the value of the newsbooks themselves. Editorial notices mimicked the style of newsletters where the writers and recipients are known to one another. An introductory greeting indicated an aspiration to gentility that would have been complementary to readers whatever their social standing. The language therefore aimed to establish a close relationship with readers, to assure them of the editor's commitment to provide a satisfactory product and encourage readers, in return, to recognise and appreciate the high standard of workmanship. It seems, therefore, that both Wolfe and the news syndicate associated a printed periodical news service with the familiar manuscript newsletter service, mimicking its tone of deference and offer of assistance. Like Verhoeven, they were reaching out, placing their newsbooks beyond the confines of a subscription list and into the public sphere, while seeking to bind readers into a relationship of trust and mutual understanding.[11]

The first known examples of editorial notices in the newsbooks are in Bourne and Archer's issues of 3 and 26 July 1622. The first consoles readers for news of the duke of Brunswick's defeat at Hochst and assumes that readers are enthusiastic supporters of Brunswick. They are advised not to,

---

[11] P. M. Handover, *Printing in London from 1476 to Modern Times* (1960), 108; P. Arblaster, '"Dat de boecken vrij sullen wesen" Private Profit, Public Utility and Secrets of State in the Seventeenth-century Habsburg Netherlands', in Koopmans, 86; J. Raymond, *Pamphlets and Pamphleteering in Early Modern Britain* (Cambridge, 2003), 95; N. Brownlees, 'Spoken Discourse in Early English Newspapers', in *News Networks*, ed. J. Raymond, 69–74; D. Randall, *Credibility in Elizabethan and Early Stuart Military News* (2008), 2–3, 10, 15, 97, 130, 146–9.

discourage a young brave Warrior, by lamenting for some small losse by him sustained, seeing also that commonly the issues of Battailes and Warlike Actions are variable and inconstant, and many times it happeneth, that those that the one day have the worst, the next day have the better hand.

The second consoled readers for the absence of news from the Palatinate, 'But whereas you expect, and that with great longing, the Businesse of the Palatinate: ... you must not looke for fighting every day.... In the meane while, take this in good part: For as I conceive, it will afford you much pleasure.'[12] We have no direct evidence from newsbooks on who wrote the first editorials or, indeed, on the identity of any editors. However, the style and sentiments are unmistakably those of many subsequent issues. The writer may have been Thomas Gainsford, an editor who never signed his name to any material in newsbooks, but who was popularly known as 'the Captain' and widely acknowledged by readers and contemporary commentators to be an editor between 1622 and 1624.

The first contemporary mention we have of his news work is in a poem written by Ben Jonson in 1623:

> Captaine Pamphlet's horse and foot that sally
> Upon the Exchange, out of Pope's Head Alley,
> The weekly Corrents with Paul's Seal and all[13]

Thomas Gainsford had a long established connection with Pope's Head Alley, having inherited part shares in eleven neighbouring Lombard Street properties that he sold in March 1590. This rhyme suggests that Gainsford's place of employment was Archer's shop in Pope's Head Alley. It seems, therefore, that, once again, Thomas Archer can be associated with a new development in the trade. Archer not only became the first publisher, but also employer of the first known London editor.

However, Butter was not to be out-done: within a month his competing series began. His issue of 23 August 1622 included a reference in the notice to readers to 'the Writer or Transcriber' and a promise to continue the 'manner of writing and printing ... weekly by Gods assistance from the best and most certaine Intelligence'. The style of this announcement is more formal than the July notices. Probably written by Butter himself, it demonstrates an understanding of what was needed to distinguish his issues from those of rivals, announcing the introduction of not only the logo, but also the appointment of a 'Writer or Transcriber'. (The term editor had not yet

---

[12] (3 July 1622), verso, STC18507.59 quoted in Dahl, 68; (26 July 1622), verso, STC18507.66 quoted in Dahl, 73.
[13] M. Eccles, "Thomas Gainsford, 'Captain Pamphlet'", *HLQ*, 45 (1982), 259–60; B. Jonson, 'Execration upon Vulcan', 1623 or 24, in *Ben Jonson: The Man and His Work*, ed. C. H. Herford and P. Simpson (Oxford, 1925/1954), 2, 174.

come into use but the role proposed here was that of an editor, not a trans-lator.) Butter invited readers to choose between rivals on the strength of their style and presentation while claiming that his series had the best and most reliable reports. As Butter explained, this 'Writer or Transcriber' had taken command of the content of the newsbook to make it more intelligible for readers. Of course, Butter may have found another editor to do this, but, given the novelty and unique range the skills displayed, this is unlikely. The editing style in the August issues of Nathaniel Butter bears hallmarks of the approach Gainsford had already begun to develop in July for Bourne and Archer; an approach that was also subsequently to work for the syndicate. It seems therefore that Butter poached Gainsford. We do not know if he offered more money, but Mead tells us the editor had a year's contract: once again we can see Butter acting as a financial risk taker, believing strongly in the potential of this new trade. When the publishers joined forces to form the syndicate this contract continued into the following summer and expired with issue 42 of the syndicate's first series.[14]

Editorial work is evident in most issues during the period up to the summer of 1624, which Chamberlain tells us was when Gainsford became ill and died. He describes the progress of the 'spotted feaver' due to the hot, dry summer, and lists among the victims 'Captain Gainsford our newsmonger or maker of gazetts'.[15]

Gainsford did not work on every issue: some were not edited and there was also at least one period when, after the expiration of Butter's one year contract, other editors were tried. Mead described efforts to replace the first 'Corrantoer' and believed that the editor of issue three on 11 November 1623 was the second newcomer to the role since August. This issue also introduced some previously untried editorial innovations that were success-fully embedded in subsequent issues, so it is possible that there was a permanent change of editor at this point. However, it seems unlikely that a completely new editor could have achieved editorial control over the material and become so confident and competent so quickly. Underlying continuities in style suggest Gainsford was reinstated. Moreover, a comment on the new method in the issue of 11 December 1623 appears to refer back to events in the interregnum, 'I cannot use a better Methode, then I have ventured upon in the division … I will follow that tract.' This suggests that Gainsford and the syndicate were divided but came back together again and that the break enabled him to further refine his approach.[16]

We must also consider the notoriety Gainsford achieved. Contemporary comment on Gainsford only began in 1623, but it takes time to acquire a reputation and writers had little status then. Yet Gainsford became so well

---

14 (23 August 1622), 19, STC18507.72; Harl. MS 389 fo. 381.
15 *Chamberlain*, vol. 2, 579, Chamberlain to Dudley Carleton, 4 September.
16 Harl. MS 389 fo. 381; (11 December 1623), 2, STC18507.135.

recognised among Londoners that, despite his lack of identification in the newsbooks, there were many contemporary references to him. He made a strong impression on Ben Jonson and others were still writing about him after he died. In 1645, in *Mercurius Anti-Britanicus* he is referred to as,

> the Captain who heretofore wrote weekly intelligence from Popes-Head Alley; who usually took Townes in Cyder, and after his second draught in Metheglin still ... in lesse then two Houres operation ordinarily over-runne all chiefe parts of Germany. I never knew any professed sword man but this make Gazets his Trade of living.

Mercurius Anti-Britanicus and another series, *Mercurius Britanicus*, were both 1640s periodicals named in 'railing' references back to the 1620s imprint of Butter and Bourne. In *The Staple of News*, Jonson alluded to Gainsford's death, when the Register of the news reprimands a 'Butter-woman', 'Do, good woman, have patience; It is not now, as it was when the captain lived'. Also referring to the partnership's imprint, he added that Mercurius Britannicus 'was want to get In hungry captains, obscur statesmen . . . Now all that charge is saved'.[17] Fletcher's play, *The Fair Maid of the Inn* repeated several of the same ideas including the pun on Butter's name and the suggestion that Gainsford wrote the news. Like Jonson's *Staple*, it introduced the idea of 'a new office for writing pragmaticall currantos'. The character Forobosco, a conjurer, offers to call up the ghost of some lying Stationer, 'a Spirit shall looke as if butter would not melt in his mouth'. Coxcombe remarks, 'I would set up a press here in Italy To write all the Corantos for Christendome, O There was a captaine was rare at it' and Forobosco replies, 'that Captaine writ a full hand gallop, and wasted indeed more harmlesse paper than ever did laxative Physick. Yet will I make you out-scribble him.'[18] The debacle in 1623 and his reinstatement may well have established his identity and unique standing in the trade.

Kevin Sharpe has drawn upon Gainsford's earlier work to demonstrate the glorification of James I as 'true champion of the Christian weale' and the celebration of the virtues of the royal Court and courts of justice in print, while Simon Adams and Michael Frearson have focused on Gainsford as a Protestant propagandist, noting similarities between his views and those of Thomas Scott. Adams has explored his association with the writing of *Sir Walter Rawleigh's Ghost or Vox Spiritus*, a pamphlet opposing the Spanish marriage and urging the king to support his son-in-law. The discovery of the manuscript during a search by Secretary Calvert for scurrilous pamphlets

---

[17] *Mercurius Anti-Britanicus* (22 August 1645), 24, quoted in Raymond, *Pamphlets*, 137; Raymond, 152–4; Herford and Simpson, *Ben Jonson: The Man*, 2, 175; Jonson, Act I, ii, 357, 358.

[18] Beaumont and Fletcher, in A. R. Waller, ed., *Cambridge English Classics*, 10, Act IV, ii (Cambridge, 1911).

(1)

Relations of Newes from most parts of the world, translated out of the low Duch Copies printed in *Holland.*

From Venice the 9. of December.

 IT is confirmed from *Con-stantinople*, that there is arriued a Perfian Am-baffadour which hath brought rich prefents from his King to the great Signior, who defi-reth to confirme the peace made here before.

The Souldiers of the Archduke *Leopoldus*, which lay in the Countie of *Tirol*, and *Alfa-tia*, beginne to mutinie for want of payment.

Out of Wedderan the 18. of December.

THe Bauarian Forces inquatter them-felues in thefe parts, notwithftanding that we are vnder the Emperours fauegard, or protection, and we vnderftand that they are to abide there vntill Saint *Peters* day, to winter themfelues in the meane time, they are likely to ruine the Boers and other people, li-

A 2   uing

Plate 3. The first inside page (recto) of the *Weekly Newes* (28 January 1623), showing the ornamentation and datelines typical of the early series. There is no suggestion here of any editorial hand in London. A Dutch coranto has been translated. ('Wedderan' was probably the Wetterau region in Hesse that suffered many times during the war.)

and Gainsford's arrest were reported to Buckingham in a letter dated 28 November 1620. Calvert described the author as 'a pooree Captaine about London one Gainsford, whom I have committed to prison'. *Vox Spiritus* purports to record a conference between Gondomar and a Jesuit, in Ely House, Holborn that took place on 21 November 1620 and was intended to appear as a sequel to Thomas Scott's *Vox Populi*. *Vox Spiritus* proposed a programme for Parliament, including assistance for the king of Bohemia and investigating the Spanish match. Adams concluded that Scott continued his propaganda from the United Provinces after fleeing, whereas Gainsford used the periodical news as part of a Protestant campaign to engage England in the cause on the Continent.[19]

Whether Gainsford should be seen simply as a hack writer who readily changed his arguments to suit the market or whether his news editing work could be depicted as anti-royalist is, however, debatable. Gainsford was working in Pope's Head Alley, which in the 1640s came to be known for its anti-royalist propaganda, but in 1625 Archer published *Epithalamium Gallo Britannicum* to celebrate Charles marriage to Henrietta Maria with emblems suggesting potential for greatness in war and peace. Reports from abroad inevitably encouraged fears about religious security at home and popish influence of government, but whether this meant that the news was, as has been argued, 'a thinly disguised vehicle for sustained critical comment on the English government' is questionable. The preface of 6 March 1624 claimed 'There are few English eares, but would be glad to have Paletines restitution' and in 1622–4 newsbooks amplified contemporary 'hawkish' propaganda that advocated a militaristic policy based on war with Spain in support of the European Protestant cause by simplifying affairs in Europe into a holy war. There is no exploration in the newsbooks of Spain's differences with the emperor, nor of the differences between the Pope and the Habsburgs, the Jesuits and the Capuchins. Instead, reports of recatholicisation of previously Protestant territories, the Pope's support for military action in Europe and Spanish support for the emperor helped build a picture of Catholic aggression. There was also a consistently optimistic view of the Protestant position intended to strengthen English support for the European Protestant cause, but any criticism of James was not explicit and public perceptions of his position at this time were, in any case, far from certain. The newsbooks championed Frederick's Bohemian claims and always called him 'the King of Bohemia'. Gainsford was adding his voice to the active debate within England about how best to respond to the evolving dynastic crisis. But, if the newsbooks identified Spain as an aggressor and conveyed

---

[19] K. Sharpe, *Image Wars; Promoting Kings and Commonwealths in England, 1603–1660* (New Haven, CT and London, 2010), 51–3, 113–5, 119–29; S. L. Adams, 'Captain Thomas Gainsford, the "Vox Spiritus" and the "Vox Populi"', *Bulletin of the Institute of Historical Research*, 44 (1976), 141–4; S. R. Gardiner, *The Fortescue Papers*, Camden Society, new ser, 1 (1871), 143–4; Frearson, 213–7.

a message to readers that pacific diplomacy was an ineffective response to the threat posed by the Hapsburg conquest and Counter-Reformation, they were representing a popular perception of the situation.[20]

To determine how far their message can be attributed to London editing we need to consider newsbook sources and their use. Chapter 2 shows that, while most material from the United Provinces and Germany in the early 1620s was Protestant, the provenance and content of news was more complex than is immediately apparent and that the only control the publishers and editors had was over what to include and what to omit. There was little prospect of wasting material: reports directly from Catholic cities were used when available. Gainsford might protest, 'I acquaint you with nothing but what is extracted out of true and credible originals' but not all were equally credible. Catholic sources were suspect and Gainsford expressed caution. Thus, in January 1623 he wrote, 'we set downe some things as we receive them from the High Dutch Copies, and some from the Low Dutch, printed at Antwerpe which peradventure may speak partially, which I desire you to … judge accordingly'.[21]

When the first year's contract for Gainsford's editorial services ended, the syndicate used what was at hand from Antwerp while trying to fill their vacancy. A notice 'from the Printer' 27 August 1623 acknowledged that local news, even from Catholic sources, could have merits, and that Italian Gazettes may be trusted to be accurate 'in their own businesse', but this must be regarded as special pleading. The next notice again covering Catholic sources suggested that 'Dutch-men were partiall on their owne side', but as the notice continues we find a greater concern to explain away the lack of editing:

let the Letters answere for themselves, onely by way of caution let me intreat you neither to expect an order ffrom Prioritie of date, nor any such exactness, as men are tyed to a continued story: For in plaine tearms for any thing I see, they that writ these Letters had them by snatches.[22]

As we have seen, much of the news coming from within the Habsburg territories came originally from residents there, probably Catholic. This was true, even though the news generally reached London via Dutch or Protestant German publications, and not all reports painted an attractive picture of Protestant activities. Some have embedded references that point to Protestant partisan authors, for example, the 30 October 1622 issue refers to 'our campe before Manheim', but the issue of 28 January 1623 included a report of Mansfeld's army pillaging. In the issue of 31 January, news from Antwerp

---

[20] Ibid., 3–8, 156–8, 165–75, 191–7, 212–21; Sharpe, *Image Wars*, 211–3, 265; (6 March 1624), 1, STC18507.143.

[21] (13 December 1623), 1, STC18507.136; (31 January 1623), verso, STC18507. 96.

[22] (27 August 1623), 21, STC18507.123; (29 August 1623), 1, STC18507.124.

was included again but with a note responding to criticism by acknowl-edging that 'some write partially' and advising readers that they must judge for themselves. Again, in August and November 1623 we see news from Antwerp included with a caution that the post from Antwerp brought 'many unjustifiable things', while in February 1624 news from Antwerp was described as 'so much smoake'.[23]

It is a difficult task, involving close scrutiny of the text of reports (rather than the London editorials), to separate what was contributed in London from source material, to identify the authentic 'voice' of a London editor. Sometimes Gainsford appears to have been writing in reports. In the issue of 16 November 1622, the 'voice' could be that of a correspondent from Vere's camp at Manheim explaining the surrender, 'But first you may please to heare the extremities our countrimen were driven unto before the reso-lute Generall would give it up.' The terms of surrender are given, but the conclusion drawn could have come from anywhere: 'upon these conditions, (then which his friends could scarcely have desired more honourable, and none here lookt for any so good) was the castle surrendered'. By contrast, in 28 October 1623 issue, the new London editor's voice comes through with flowery language, 'Fortune is never constant ... some will thinke it strange that they have begun now so late in the yeare to set upon the Emperour, we will give the Reader (touching this point) as good satisfaction as wee can.' The mixture of voices makes it difficult to tell what was added where, except where familiar editorial phrases signal changes of subject and remind readers of the news in the last London issue.[24]

There are some 'hallmarks' that allow us to give a positive identification in some issues, such as when the London editor addressed his readership directly as 'the Reader' and disassociated himself from current speculation. For example, on 28 October 1623, 'whether the Protestants in Germany may conceave any hopes of their re-establishing (as many believe in Holland) by the cumming downe of Bethlem Gabor, it is not our intention to speak of it at this present: But we will rather wish that it were already done.'[25]

It is, however, fairly clear that in the uncertain editorial period from August to October 1623, the substitute editor had less of a grip on his mate-rial. Comments appeared that were unlikely to have come from London, but escaped editorial attention. Thus, for example, in the issue of 2 October 1623 we learn, 'thus are the Emperors Designes likely to go forward apace, and prosperously, the successe we must leave to time' and, on 28 October,

---

[23] (30 October 1622), 15, STC18507.86; (28 January 1623), 14, STC18507.93; (30 and 31 January 1623), title page verso, STC18507.94 and 95; (29 August 1623), 1, STC18507.124; (20 November 1623) 21, STC18507.133; (24 February 1624), 17, STC18507.141.
[24] (16 November 1622), 16, 20, STC18507.89; (18 July 1623), STC18507.119; (28 October 1623), 1–4, STC.18507.131; (16 June 1623), STC18507.115.
[25] (28 October 1623), 3–4, STC18507.131.

that 'it is knowne almost to the universall world, what great successes the house of Austria hath had within these few yeares'.[26] Generally, through into the 1640s, where an opinion was expressed within a report in a newsbook, it was most likely from the original, as received in London. In the absence of anything showing it was added in London, it is safest to assume that it was not. Even where England or the English were mentioned it could be because news from England was recorded in Amsterdam, Antwerp or Cologne then allowed to stand when the text arrived back in London. The issue of 24 February 1624 has a comment aimed at English readers but the words 'you in England were' indicate they were not written in London.[27] Taking the whole period, rather than years when we know issues were edited, it is possible to see that Protestant reportage dominated, but this is not as coherent as in 1622–4. While it is not always possible to be sure when Gainsford or another London editor was adding, it is safe to conclude that editors in London generally amplified the pro-Frederick dimension in particular. By emphasising even minor victories and making as little as possible of defeats, newsbooks cultivated false hopes and inevitably left Protestants feeling cheated as the news of failures steadily accumulated.

However, there is nothing to suggest that Gainsford or anyone else was omitting any explanatory material covering the stresses and conflicts within different Catholic factions. Publishers did not have access to diplomatic correspondence, only to published Treaties. Gainsford appears to have been completely unaware of how close some of James's diplomatic initiatives came to securing Frederick's hereditary lands, since the results of these efforts did not conclude with public announcements. The Brussels Conference in the summer of 1622 was overtaken by events. Similarly, the agreement reached in Madrid to cease military action in the Palatinate was not publicly known. The fact that during these discussions Tilly and Cordoba acted independently of Isabella could not have been known from printed material arriving in London. So reports of military action simply covered the siege of Heidelberg and its fall, followed by Mannheim and Frankenthal in December 1622, then in the autumn of 1623 the distribution by Ferdinand of Frederick's lands.

Gainsford did not explore motives, nor venture opinions on the role of Saxony during a period when the duke's position was critical and topical. The issue of 7 May 1623 showed the way Gainsford handled the duke of Saxony's negotiations with the emperor. It simply said wait and see what the news brings. There was no attempt to explain. Editors worked with what was written. Correspondents were not much inclined to probe motives. They reported on visible, actions and consequences of actions and sometimes they

---

[26] (2 October 1623), 9, STC18507.129; (28 October 1623), 1, STC18507.131.
[27] (24 February 1624), 21, STC18507.141.

speculated on intentions.[28] As news got nearer to London it came predominantly from Protestant writers with whom Gainsford shared sympathies. He had, to use his own words, to 'trust other men's relations' and he tried to persuade readers to do the same while acknowledging difficulties in trying to discern the truth when faced with a range of reports of military actions and diplomatic movements.[29]

Editing newsbooks

To form a true assessment of Gainsford's unique contribution to the newsbooks it is necessary to examine what he claimed he achieved, namely, 'the orderly setting downe of the businesse'. Through this, Gainsford provided a valuable service that helped to create a marketable commodity at a time when newly literate readers were facing a steep learning curve and were unfamiliar with military or political reporting or with the European-wide dimensions of religious conflict. David Randall has expressed this in terms of assisting readers at a transitional stage when news reporting evolved from reliance on the honour, status and social credit of known correspondents to an impersonal news media where confirmation involved extensive reading of third party sources. In the process, again in Gainsford's own words, he 'got the start of opinion'.[30]

Mark Eccles has investigated how Gainsford became 'an expert in collecting and editing foreign news': Gainsford was an impoverished career soldier who made a living writing histories and foreign news, despite being born into a moderately wealthy Surrey family and educated in Cambridge and the Inner Temple. In addition to his property shares in Lombard Street he inherited a large house with associated gardens and houses in Holborn. But in his youth, he lived beyond his means and ran into debt, selling off properties to keep debtors at bay. When his inheritance was gone he joined the army and went to Ireland where he served as a captain from 1601 to 1603. In 1606–07 he travelled in Italy, Switzerland and Turkey, then in Cyprus and Israel in 1607–08. He served under Prince Maurice of Nassau in the war of Cleves in 1610 and 1614 and began his writing career during this period. *The Secretaries Studie* (1610 and 1615) demonstrated a professional interest in the craft of writing and skills required to provide news reports from abroad addressed to those back home in England. It includes sample letters of news that appear to have been written by him from Italy, Crete, Cyprus, Malta and Israel. In addition, many newsbooks about the Cleves war were entered in the Stationers' register. He also had an interest

---

[28] Schumacher, 71–2; Arblaster, '*Dat de boecken*', 81–2; (7 May 1623), 8, STC18507.109.
[29] (11 November 1623), 12, STC18507.132.
[30] (13 December 1623), 1, STC18507.136; Randall, *Credibility*, 126, 130.

in history and story telling. His years of travel led him to the view, expressed in *The Glory of England, or a True Description of many ... Blessings whereby she triumpheth over all the Nations of the World*, that England was the best place to be.[31]

His Protestant background found expression in *Vox Spiritus*, but he needed the income from writing and editing. Gainsford had honed his skills and had extensive experience both of military matters and of the relevant geographical and diplomatic factors that were influencing events on the Continent. He had been to many of the places from which reports came and had even served as an officer in action in Europe. This helped him to make sense of the reports that came his way. Once established as the syndicate's editor, he experimented with different ways to make a clear and orderly account and he was untiring in his efforts to communicate effectively with readers.

Beginning with the issue of 26 July 1622, we see attempts to render order and coherence to the presentation of reports, 'dayly Letters afford matter sufficient both of pleasure and varietie ... for thy contentment, . . . I have contracted them, as you see, and culled them out to give you notice of the affaires of Europe and what is likely to be the issue of these troubles'. He made sense of the array of material reaching London by this stage and put events into a historical context for readers, 'This attempt of Spinola's on Bergen makes me remember that famous siege in 1590 or, thereabouts, when the Prince of Palma came before it with 30000 and continued the battery almost halfe a year.' He referred to events that followed the Armada and introduced the latest news of the siege with an explanation of Bergen's geographical and strategic significance:

> The Towne of Bergen is of as great importance to the States in Brabant, as Sluice in Flaunders: For as this watcheth Ostend, Newport, Dunkirke, and other maritine Townes, yea openeth a doore to Ipres, Gaunt and all the land Countrey, that keepeth the Rivers, and is the key of the continent letting you in to the fields of Antwerpe, ... and all the great Townes of Brabant.

He also acknowledged news of particular relevance to English readers; 'I will not speake a word of neither Armies, nor their skirmishes ... but of the bravery of the beseiged and the glory of the English, whose fame flourished over the world.' He dealt with the loss of six hundred men, 'most of the Irish and English newly come out of their Countries ... [and] a valiant Colonell Scotchman [who] lost his life', by showing these were outweighed by Spanish losses.[32]

Gainsford took the trouble to explain not only the news but also presentational changes and how he was handling them. In the issue of 4 October

[31] Eccles, 'Thomas Gainsford', 259–63.
[32] (26 July 1622), verso, 2, 11, 12, STC18507.66, quoted in Dahl, 72–3.

1622, a logical arrangement was imposed on the material and his method was explained. Under the first heading 'Naples' he stated,

> I begin with Naples, because as neere as I can I will come orderly forward with the Provinces as they lye, and in regard the several Letters beare not one date, I have thought good to muster the newes, which belongs to the same place, as it were into one Armie, and so you shall receive the occurrences all together.

Under Venice, he explained, 'Because commonly our Post letters of Italy come from Venice, or at least those of Venice make mention of the affaires of the petty provinces, especially Milaine I have thought it convenient to put in the items of Italian affaires into this section.' Under Vienna, he continued:

> You see what Method I have used to draw the account of Europes Businesse by items, which I am perswaded is not unpleasing, and therefore I will continue the same.... There are so many Letters ... and so much contradiction, as men on either side favour the cause, that I know not how to satisfy the Reader: yet considering there is but one truth, and to be honest in a plaine enarration of the same, is allowable, therefore as neere as I can, I will relate, what is most probable and worthy of your acceptation.[33]

The reference to what 'is allowable' refers to the clash with Cottington the month before. Here we learn that Cottington would allow an honest plain narration. The task was to produce a factual account without speculation or entering into sensitive areas of international diplomacy. The lesson of the clash with authority was learned.[34]

Gainsford enjoyed this work and was agreeably challenged by the process of attempting to make sense of the many overlapping and conflicting reports to tell a coherent story as honestly as he could, quite possibly because this was more than a job to him. He had been to these places. He probably knew many soldiers in active service and he wanted to unlock the reports and discover the facts. He did not claim to know or to be able to understand everything and openly accepted that there was a limitation on the confidence with which he could report some news.

Gainsford's temperament was inclined to be philosophical and nationalistic rather than confrontational. Thus, for example, explaining the shortage of fresh news over the winter months in the issue of 6 February 1623, he commented,

> you have a long time expected some relation of newes ... alas you must consider what you doe, when you come into a well furnished Garden, you see the frost and

---

[33] (4 October 1622), 1, 3, 5, 8, 16, 17, 35, STC18507.81.
[34] (14 September 1622), STC18507.77; see pp. 88–91, 189–91.

snow hath nipped the flowers, and there is scarce any appearance either of sweet herbes or flourishing plants ... so hath winter delt with the affaires of Europe, the Souldiers have beene glad of refreshing, and the Princes taken care to make them strong with ease and quietnesse, but now ... you shall see ... a face both of terrour and pleasure.[35]

We can follow the process of discovering how best to produce an honest narration. The issue of 22 October began reflectively:

Smart usually makes not such an impression in us, as Feare, nor doth the Thunderbolt it selfe so generally amaze the world, as the Thunderclap: And the feare of Warre, oftentimes workes more in us, then the blowes; for while we expect an evill to come (which is the very materiall cause of feare) wee are not able in that puzzel so suddenly to remember or fore-think how manhood can suffer.

Later, in reference to whether a Diet will be called, he commented, 'as eye-witnesses are more fully to be beleeved, then those that report upon hear-say'. He reported a plan to move Matthias's body to a new location and added that he wished the emperor would consider 'those poore soules, both in his owne and the Protestant Armies, whose carkases have no other Tombe, then the bowles of wilde beasts'. Then he warned readers not to be too hopeful about news from Frankfurt of a rift between the duke of Saxony and the emperor, 'peradventure these Relations may bee streyned too high, or these two Princes may be friends againe and we may never heare of it, which will make people suspect these reports for lies'. Readers should be wary of the reports they might most want to believe.[36]

He had to decide what to include when many reports said much the same thing, and what to do with material that was blatantly Imperialist. Under the report from the Val Telline, in the 30 October issue, he admitted,

Much of this we confesse you have heard before though not in so continued a discourse, but this we repeat, not only to show you how true intelligence we have of Forraigne occurrences, but also that you may see how the businesse of the times ... conspired ... to give their enemies leasure and means to subdue them. And this is the reason that this manly and stout Nation hath beene compelled to accept such poore conditions in the Diet of Lindaw.[37]

Gainsford wrote as if oblivious of the king's very different agenda and ambitions for a resolution in Europe, focusing entirely on the activities of war as they unfolded. He demonstrated skill at recognising what explanations readers might need and providing them. Gainsford told readers, 'we had

---

[35] (6 February 1623), 1, STC18507.96.
[36] (22 October 1622), 1, 4 (2 but misnumbered), 8, 14, STC18507.84.
[37] (30 October 1622), 4, 15, STC18507.85.

a purpose to have left nothing which is hard to be understood unexplained'. Nearly six years before the Edict of Restitution he explained that one of Tilly's objectives would be to restore church lands which were currently held by temporal princes and their younger brothers. At this level, little seems to have escaped Gainsford's attention, even among the smaller details: he would explain a word if he felt readers needed this. An Amsterdam 'spinster house' was explained as 'a place of punishment like Blew coats in Bridewell'. His issue of 30 October 1622 included an explanation of the method of dating, referring to the letters of 23 October '(which is our 13th)'. Other examples of explanations of the implications of differences in dating and travel times include, 'You may see by the date of this proclamation, October 19 that it could not here be knowne ... although their 19 be three daies before our 12'. Usually the original dating was allowed to stand, thereby giving impression that the news was consistently 'fresher' than it was, though, of course, this would not hold good for really 'fresh' news from the Low Countries.[38]

Gainsford's greatest accomplishment was to produce issues that provided a well-ordered and coherent account. His issue of 21 November 1622 is a good example. In it he ended the Palatine news with a common sense verdict on Frankendale, unadorned by comment or by questioning of the inescapable fact that England had manifestly failed to provide the necessary support, 'neither doe we looke for any other newes but that it is given over by this time, or shortly will be when provisions be more spent; if they many have honourable conditions and faire quarter granted them, unless the seige by authoritie be removed'. There were many examples. The issue of 7 May 1623 explained that Silesia was surrounded by Imperial forces, 'For they write from Vienna (which should have been tolde you in the last booke)'. Then he explained that because Bethlem Gabor's forces were mostly horse they could not march until the grass has started to grow and hay and oats were available. The next issue moved from the journeys of the emperor and empress to Prague to Bethlem Gabor's negotiations with the Turks. A meeting between the duke of Saxony and Darmstadt followed, with news that the duke of Bavaria had agreed to a tax of one rix dollar per man to support the wars and to maintain 3000 foot and 500 horse: one in every five men was to be conscripted in the towns and one in every ten in the countryside. 'Thus farre the Letters, which if punctually true, is a very large proportion both of men and money. And what need there will be of them, time will hereafter show.' The following issue explained etiquette

---

[38] (2 May 1623), 3, STC18507.108; (11 November 1623), 17, STC18507132; (30 October 1622), 13, 19, STC18507.86; (5 November 1622). 1, STC18507.87. (Later the publishers said they used new style dating in line with European publications (23 May 1626), 11, STC18507.179.)

around the emperor, throwing in an explanation of the behaviour of local magistrates, '(for you must understand that Prague is three Cities in one)'.[39]

With news of this quality and almost weekly regularity, newsbooks were ensuring that a reader could be well informed about a wide range of events. Newsbooks had become more regular, more educative and a vehicle for making news accessible to a wider readership. The quality varied, but well-edited newsbooks would have items abridged with most personal comments from the original letters, such as the addresses 'Worthy Sir' or 'loving friend', removed. News would start with the oldest, the latest last. News on one topic was broadly grouped together. Arrangements remained flexible: from time to time, an issue was divided to draw attention to a significant item, quoting the official text or an original letter in full. For example, the issue of 7 April 1625 made a fresh start towards the end with a heading, 'A Short Relation & Of the guifts which the Kingdome of Spaine have lately offered to his Majestie towards the maintenance of the war: Printed at Antwerp the 29 day of March 1625.'[40] Organisation aided continuity from issue to issue on major stories.

Gainsford edited at a time of energy and innovation that corresponded with a period when news readership expanded and reached a wide group in society. He made the news readable, educating his readers about European politics, military matters and geography. He continually helped readers interpret what they were reading. At a more detailed and technical level, however, Gainsford was not a particularly good editor. A close inspection of runs of newsbooks reveals repetitions and overlapping items that might have been consolidated.

After his death there was relatively little editorial work until interest revived with the entry of Gustavus Adolphus into the war. There were some notices to readers but these were headed 'The Translator to the Reader' and the author is unidentified. Sabrina Baron has suggested that this may have been John Pory.[41] If so, he successfully maintained a low profile and kept editing to a minimum consistent with orderly transcription. Meanwhile, poor sales and the consequent low survival of issues provide insufficient evidence to see what readers could have made of the tangle of negotiations and informal alliances and groupings behind the Diet of Regensburg.

[39] (21 November 1622), 16, STC18507.90; (7 May 1623), 4, 7, STC18507.109; (12 May 1623); 4, 7–8, 9, STC18507.110; (17 May 1623), 2, STC18507.111.
[40] Schumacher, 70–3; (7 April 1625), 21, STC18507.165.
[41] S. A. Baron, 'The Guises of Dissemination in Early Seventeenth-century England', in DandB, 45–6.

The editorial work of William Watts

An editorial notice in July 1630 signalled an anticipated upturn in trade and reflects the publishers' concern with the need for 'better encouragement [having] lost by our publication, both our labour and a great deale of money'. Soon after, in the issue of 2 September, we see a new, confident, Protestant voice emerging: 'In our last ... wee printed severall passages of the late good success and Victories of the King of Sweden ... God grant him the multi-plication of the like victories and good successe until all his Enemies be vanquished, and a generall Peace settled in all the parts of Germany.'[42]

Anthony Wood tells us that the editor during Gustavus Adolphus's successful campaign was William Watts who published forty newsbooks or more. He was a linguist and a graduate of Cambridge who became chaplain and fellow of his college, Gonville and Caius, in 1616. He had acted as chaplain to Morton when he delivered £300,000 to the Protestant princes of Germany in 1620. He was not a puritan, but a pluralist, vicar of Barwick in Norfolk and rector of St Alban, Wood Street, London, from 1624. His other publications included translations of St Augustines Confessions and The Catholic Monitor. He wrote Mortification Apostolicall (1637), which Wood noted gave great offence to puritans, a Treatise of the Passions and a Treatise of the Surplice, plus several sermons, and he edited Matthew Paris's Accesse-runt duorum offarum (1638) and Historia Apostolical (1640). In January 1632, Watts also started the substantial serial publications that appeared every few months called The Swedish Intelligencer. They gave an organised account of events, supplementing newsbook information with subsequent reports and focusing on the activities of each army in turn. They are perhaps the best known of his works and were followed by other lengthy news compilations.[43] Watts was soon able to boast,

> To the Favourable and judicious Reader, This is a Booke thorowly allowed, when Seene and Allowed: when the Readers have approved it, as well as the Licencer. With this favourablenesse (as I thankfully must acknowledge) have my former Bookes beene entertained; yea, most favourably, by the most judicious.[44]

Schumacher saw Watts as a writer who saw the king of Sweden as 'a gift from Heaven, [that] his achievements [were] beyond all proportion to his resource ... [was] proof of divine assistance'. Watts news editing was part of an 'intense but transitory revival of interest in the war' and he ended his participation when the king died. Watts wrote from the beginning of Gustavus, 'His justice, finally and his mercy: his exemplary and his inde-

---

[42] (16 July 1630), 1, STC18507.205; (2 September 1631), verso, STC18507.221.
[43] ODNB, Watts; A. A. Wood, Fasti Oxonienses, ed. P. Bliss (1815), col. 383–4.
[44] Arber, vol. 4, 234, 244; The Swedish Intelligencer, Part 2 (1632), 3, STC23524.

fatigable industry: his affability, and his easinesse of accesse: the goodnesse of his cause, and the common Libertie which his victories bring with them: have conquered more than his sword.' His allegiance and circumstances make Watts unlikely to have had a primarily financial motive for this work. In *The Swedish Intelligencer* he reflected on whether editing for the press was an appropriate activity for his station in life:

> That God had begun to send a Deliverer unto His people. This (me thoughts) in a time of my leisure, was a worke not altogether beneath me: and that to bring Glad tidings, was next unto the preaching of the Gospel. To the going on with this Second Part, hath the united and repeated desires, of well disposed people provoked me.

When Gustavus Adolphus was killed Watts continued to the conclusion of the account of his victories through to the Battle of Lutzen, returning only to add an account of the conveyance of the body back to Sweden. An editorial explained, 'the Author of the former parts of that History, as he served the King of Sweden, faithfully, while he lived, so hath beg'd us that favour that hee might do him the honour to bring him to his grave'.[45]

Butter and Bourne, building on their experience from the earlier period of prosperity in Gainsford's time, knew how to make the most of this opportunity to maximise sales. In Watts, they employed a capable editor to engage the sympathies of their readers and they built contacts to secure a good supply of fresh reports back to London. Watts had the benefit of a wider range of sources than ever before. The network of European news centres had expanded and more cities now had printed news. Hamilton's volunteers had joined the Swedes in northern Germany and Charles had embassies in Vienna and the king of Sweden's camp. The reports Watts received from serving officers, plus information from contacts at Court, gave him access to copy with a distinct sense of a shared interest in Protestant success with references to 'Our soldiers of Wesell [in Cleves]' and 'My Lord Craven', who had been commissioned in August 1631. A letter from Frankfurt included a prayer to 'The same God that stood on our side, and fought for us ... give us all truely thankfull harts'. From an ardent admirer of Frederick in Bohemia came news that, 'Almost all Townes do openly rejoyce and declare for [the Swedes]' and from the Palatinate came news of people waiting for the king 'with a fervent and longing desire'. Eyewitness accounts like this made Watts's issues particularly lively.[46]

45 Schumacher, 195, 221, 233; *The Swedish Intelligencer*, Part 1 (1632), A2, STC23522; Part 2 (1632), 5, STC23524; *The Continuation of the German History*, Part 5 (1633), A3, STC23525.3.

46 Schumacher, 209, 216, 227–30; (25 June 1631), 12, STC18507.218; (24 January 1632), 2, STC18507.238; ODNB, Watts; (13 October 1631), 5, STC18507.226; (29

Catholics remained the real villains of most reported atrocities and Watts blamed them for the war and its continuation. Watts had longer to refine and interpret texts and express his own opinions in *The Swedish Intelligencer*. For example, the report of the arrival of Hamilton's forces at Elsinore is amended on the advice of a Commander 'of our Nation' and reported carefully, showing that the British forces were well managed, while addressing any rumours of criticism with a counter claim of dissent and treachery from home-grown Catholic and Spanish sympathisers. It reports that the Scottish and English contingents met up in Norfolk and sailed from Yarmouth on 19 July and landed in August, 'being upon Muster found to be above 6000 able men; amongst which but a few sicke, and two dead in all the voyage. The two dayes next they were all armed', then billeted to wait for the Swedish army to arrive. He then reports that, in Vienna this news:

> did something startle and amaze the Courtiers: but the Hubub was ere long well allayed, by a letter (from a good Catholike hand no doubt received out of England) [claiming the men were gathered through] … a most strict presse … upon which few or none except rogues or jayle –birds were taken; so that those Forces were not much to be feared. You see how much this Army was beholden to their Country-man, this Spaniolised Intelligencer.[47]

By contrast, the schedule for turning round newsbook copy and getting it into print was far too tight at this time to permit extensive editing and rewriting. In the ten months of the eight series, which began December 1631, fifty issues were published, three times there were two issues in the same day and three times there were three issues within seven days.[48] Their content continued to be mixed. Rather than waste copy for which there was an eager market, Watts used all sources available to him, including Catholic reports, such as those on the collection of contributions in Vienna from Spain, Hungary, Bohemia and the church; the Pope's 'admirable eloquence (wherein indeede he doth excell)' in Rome; and from Cologne of the Swedes crossing the Weser and making 'terrible ruines & doe[ing] much harme'. To manage the flow, he split material from a full postbag into two parts, generally according to its place of origin or focussed on an event. He indicated on title pages when two parts came from the same shipment of news. Sometimes Watts would carry news over from one issue to the next. The issues of 24 January and 14 April 1632 included reports that he had not managed to fit into either of the two preceding issues. He used the issues of 6 and 15 March 1632 for German reports and letters and Dutch news. Simi-

---

November 1631), 1–8, 11, STC18507.233; (24 April 1632), 1, STC18507.247; Dahl, 166.
47 *The Swedish Intelligencer*, Part 1, 73, 108–09.
48 Dahl, 187.

larly on 20 August he kept the reports on the kings of France and Sweden back for subsequent issues.[49]

Despite access to an unprecedented flow of material, he included the usual mix of the Dutch and German sources and affiliations. For example, he included 'The Contents of a letter written by a Papist ... and sent to London', and the title of the issue of 14 March 1631 refers to *the good successe of the King of Sweden in ... Mecklenburgh*, but inside, a Catholic report alludes to secret discussions between the French, Swedes and the Protestant states. On 24 January 1632 news from Brussels even referred to 'the turbulent Hollander' and 'Our Spanish Generalls', and informed readers that citizens of Mainz were paying 80,000 Rixdollars to the Swedes to avoid pillage. In September readers learned of the callous and matter of fact attitude to pillage and destruction by the Swedish army.[50]

Watts maintained the victorious Protestant king theme through titles such as *The late happy and victorious successe of the King of Sweden against the forces of the Emperour. 2. The taking of the citty Francford ... with the slaughter of neere 6000 of the Imperialists*, and on 25 June 1631 the title referred to *The malicious inhumane cruelty offered to the dead bodies of those which were martyred at the taking of Magdeburgh, and Tillies causing a Te Deum to be sung for his bloody massacring of innocent Protestants*. However, despite this billing and the fact that the sack of Magdeburg was the most outrageous of the disasters and atrocities of the war, the newsbook made less of the opportunity for attributing blame to the Imperialists than might have been expected. Protestants in Leipzig reported that due to the 'late miserable and hideous disaster [Magdeburg] is reduced to an heape of stones, being quite and utterly ruinated'; but from Magdeburg itself the tone was more neutral, reporting that nearly all the bodies had been removed and that 'Yesterday there was sung for Joy of the taking of this Citie, Te Deum Laudanum'. Reports from escapees and other contributors reflected their views rather than those of Watts's title page. However, through gathering further evidence and subsequent editing, in Part 1 of *The Swedish Intelligencer*, Watts was able to provide both a map and a more considered account of what was destroyed and what saved. He distinguished between the actions of Walloons and Croats (who would spare few people) and Tilly's orders on arrival to bring order to the situation. Watts acknowledged the significance of this destruction, comparing it with the fates of Troy and Jerusalem, explaining why the

[49] (30 January 1632), 3, STC18507.239; (6 June 1632), 1, STC18507.254; (1 September 1632), 11, STC18507.266; (24 January 1632), STC18507.238; (14 April 1632), STC18507.246; (6 March 1632), STC18507.242; (15 March 1632), STC18507.243; (30 August 1632), title page, STC18507.265.
[50] (3 October 1632), 12, STC18507.273; (14 March 1631), title page, STC18507.209; (24 January 1632), STC18507.238; (1 September 1632), 8–9, 11–12, STC18507.266.

Swedes did not arrive in time to save the city and claiming they, 'vowed (some say) to be revenged'.[51]

Just as Gainsford made no direct criticism of James, Watts made none of Charles. The closest he came was implicitly, in his conclusion after the Battle of Lutzen, describing Gustavus Adolphus as 'the most incomparable valiant and good Prince; that ever (yet) honoured any age or Story'. Watts, like Gainsford before him, did not report on diplomacy. After Gustavus Adolphus took control of Stralsund, Watts explained its strategic importance in *The Swedish Intelligencer* but provided little discussion of Sweden's military interests. Similarly, the Treaty of Barwald was covered, as was other evidence of French support for Sweden but with little comment on French diplomacy. The handling of Saxony's position continued to be problematic even after the Protestant Convention at Leipzig. As in the early 1620s, it remained unexplained, though in *The Swedish Intelligencer*, Watts noted Saxony's record of inconstancy. Similarly there was little news of splits on the Catholic side and no discussion of either French or Spanish dealings with the Papacy. Omissions can, of course, readily be ascribed to the nature of the sources available. However, given Watts's unprecedented access to original material from participants in both military and diplomatic spheres, the lack of comment on Britain's role is more conspicuous. Instead, Watts aimed to show a Protestant consensus, for example in *The preparation of the Duke of Saxony and all the Protestant princes, and their unanimous joyning with the King of Sweden, for the recovery and preservation of theyr liberties, against … unjust persecution*, and his comment on the meeting of the Heilbronn League was included in *The Swedish Intelligencer* to show the Protestants are 'well disposed to the continuance of the warres, for so good a Cause'.[52]

Watts benefited from the earlier editorial experiments and was able to organise his material coherently, grouping reports on the same topic, giving a sense of order and stating origins. Watts provided little explanation of his methods in newsbooks. This debate had already been had. However, he wished to explain *The Swedish Intelligencer*, since it was longer, innovatory, and more thoughtful, 'Our methode is this: to handle every story by it selfe, and then bring all together at the day of Battell'. It allowed him to take, for example, all the October and November 1631 reports of Swedish victory Breitenfeld and turn them into the best contemporary account now available. Contacts through British forces serving under Gustavus Adolphus paid off with accounts so well written that they were widely read and

---

[51] (9 May 1631), title page, STC18507.213; (25 June 1631), title page, 4, 3, 5, 10, 13, STC18507.218; *The Swedish Intelligencer* (1632), Part 1, ed., 3, 118–9, STC23523; Wedgwood, 285–91.

[52] *The Swedish Intelligencer*, Part 3 (1633), 180, 212, STC23525; Schumacher, 201, 210–11, 224–5; Wedgwood, 280–5, 291–5; (25 June 1631), title page, STC18507.218.

understood.[53] The first issue was so well received that it ran to four editions and many sequels. Watts introduced features of a book, including an index and contents page. Marginalia were added and even a tabulated timeline. Sales were so good they supported the production of associated maps and engravings. In the third part, Watts was even moved to respond to praise, 'in thankfulnesse to your courtesies ... I have done all with as much diligence as a scholler'.[54]

Watts was less intimate with readers and lacked Gainsford's 'common touch' but he was a better editor, and more confident of what was required. Working at speed, he applied a light touch, grouping and labelling sources. He provided an upbeat title page that generally reflected a confident view that readers were Protestant, supported the Swedish campaign and hoped for the restoration of the Palatinate. The success of *The Swedish Intelligencer* demonstrates that readers had an appetite for both the news as it appeared and for the larger digests every few months that revisited events.

Watts placed higher expectations on readers, provided less interpretation than Gainsford and explanatory background information on topics such as dating, distances, currencies and topography, was confined primarily to margin comments in *The Swedish Intelligencer* and explanations of the maps that accompanied that series. However, he was working a decade later and readers probably needed less help. Readers had become accustomed to the genre, and gained familiarity not only with its conventions and limitations but also with the place names of main theatres of action, the principal military leaders and chief civilian protagonists.

Conclusions

Some useful organisational signposts were introduced early to the front pages of these periodicals (title, dating and numbering). These facilitated customer recognition, encouraged return sales and were adopted for domestic news periodicals in the 1640s. News publishers, however, did much more in their efforts to reach out to an extended readership. They aimed to include in their market the newly literate of the middling classes who needed to be informed and trained to assess and understand the reports and so participate in the news culture that gripped society from the outset of the Thirty Years War. For this, editorial innovations and editors were needed to cultivate readers and their relationships with them. For the editors, 1622–4 and 1631–2 were periods of experimentation and learning what was possible and acceptable to their readership. They strived to present a coherent and acces-

[53] *The Swedish Intelligencer*, Part 1, 3; (13 October 1631), 3–5, 9, STC18507.226; (9 November 1631), STC18507.228; Dahl, 183–4.
[54] *The Swedish Intelligencer*, Part 1, ed., 3, 34, 117, 178, 241–6; *The Swedish Intelligencer*, Part 3, 1. Plate, p. 164 and front cover.

sible story from each of the main theatres of action, along with evidence of the provenance of the reports. The progress that they made is evident in the copy they produced and in the following of active readers, as reflected in their editorial responses and frequently renewed efforts to improve their work. This learning and refinement of editorial skills culminated in the production of *The Swedish Intelligencer*.

The lessons learned from Gainsford and Watts were well digested and can be observed in the work of many of the editors of the 1640s. Dateline headings were adopted for reporting the progress of the English Civil War, giving periodicals of that period a simple organisational principle and a diary like appearance. By the time John Dillingham took up his pen in the 1640s, with usually only four or five pages a week to dedicate to continental news, he would simply summarise the key stories from Dutch and Parisian sources under dateline headings and use a succinct sentence or two to note points of particular relevance or interest to English readers.

6

Readers and Press Reactions 1622–48:
A Developing Dialogue

As we have seen in Chapter 4, we know something about the readership of news during the Thirty Years War from the frequency of news publication, from print runs and from the format of issues. To understand how the news was read and how readers reacted we need to know more about the readers themselves. Some, particularly those who were among the middling sort, have left records of their reading in diaries, correspondence, commonplace books and even, occasionally, in marginalia on the newsbooks. Other contemporary commentary can be found in sermons, plays and poetry, though this was from writers who were themselves part of the media. Dramatists and preachers, while reflecting on society and its interests, were also often addressing and seeking to influence the same audiences and were, consequently, in competition to some degree with the periodical press: a penny or two spent on a newsbook might otherwise go to the theatre or to the church. News editors are another source of information: they reflected on customers' comments and responded in print, and tried to anticipate reactions to the issue in preparation. Their motivation was to explain their product to readers and to connect with them to increase sales. This chapter follows the periodical press through three decades and explores the evidence that has been left by readers and by those in the media who commented on news reporting, to assess the extent to which we can learn about the penetration of Thirty Years War news in early seventeenth-century society and about the way it was received.

Readers who left records in their diaries and correspondence include those frequently commenting and combining news from a variety of sources often because their livelihood was to a degree associated with the business of the news. These include the correspondent John Chamberlain; Dudley Carleton, Viscount Dorchester, the diplomat and secretary of state, and the magistrate, merchant, and MP in 1626; and William Whiteway, in Dorchester, who traded in France and whose records in both his diary and commonplace book cover domestic, foreign and shipping news up to 1635. To these we can add Walter Yonge, a merchant and puritan, educated at Oxford and the Middle Temple, who became Sheriff of Devon in 1628 and MP for Honiton in 1640. His diary for the years 1604–28 shows that he relied on the correspondence to help him keep abreast of the news. He was in receipt of news throughout most of 1620 to 1622, probably as often as once a month that he recorded in his diaries. Then in January 1623 he wrote, 'We give the Palatinate as wholly lost.' After this, his interest in European news appears to have dwindled and his recording of European events became sporadic.[1]

Other readers include James Howell, Thomas Crosfield and John Rous. Printed news from Howell's correspondence became part of the duke of Rutland's collection and includes a newsbook of 24 August 1626 annotated in a contemporary hand with such comments as 'good yf true', indicating the Protestant and Palatine sympathies of the reader. Faith in Mansfeld is shown in the comment 'tis sooner said then done', which appears alongside news of plans for the emperor's army to go to Silesia to oppose Mansfeld. Thomas Crosfield, a Fellow of Queen's College, Oxford, mentions 'curr-antos' in several dairy entries from the mid-1620s, weaving notes about Parliament with progress of Tilly and Christian of Denmark in Germany in 1626, news of the Rhé Expedition, success of the Swedish campaign in 1631–2 and thoughts on the willingness of Londoners to pay ship money in 1635–6. Yet he made very little comment on either the sources or his views. John Rous was a clergyman, educated at Cambridge (MA, 1607), whose diary shows he was following the European news intently from his home in Norfolk. An entry for 1627 tells us, 'Newes came in October of count Mansfeld, that he had given diverse overthrowes to the emperor's part, and slaine the duke of Friedland in the field.' This was false he adds, but 'Newes is newes. Many corantoes confirmed an overthrowe given to the duke of Friedland.' An entry for 29 October 1628 tells us, 'I had a coranto at Norwich, wherin was a liste of the names of fifty-two shippes, Rochelers and English, that joyned with our navy at Plimmouth, wher I was tould, that a former coranto had a liste of the navy from Portsmouth.' His diary shows his interests to be first local news of the assizes and Parliament, then news of relations between England and France and Spain, then German news, lastly shipping and mercantile news. It seems he could rarely get his own copy of a newsbook, but he could pick up information about the latest issues, or see a copy in Cambridge or in Norwich when he visited.[2]

In London, Sir Simonds D'Ewes, a puritan, and Sheriff for Suffolk in 1639 and MP for Sudbury in 1640, was an enthusiastic reader of news-books, broadsheets, pamphlets, proclamations and ballads. His reading often furnished him with materials for notes in his diary that record his feelings about the news. In the early days of the war he noted the difficulties he encountered in getting 'certain truth though I resided then in London, and

---

[1] CandT, 2 vols; Frearson, 286–313; W. Yonge, *The Diary of Walter Yonge*, ed. G. Roberts, Camden Society, 1:41 (1848), 67.
[2] (4 August 1626), STC18507.181; Dahl, 149; F. S. Boas, ed., *The Diary of Thomas Crosfield, Fellow of Queen's College Oxford* (1935), xxvi–ii; *Rous*, 7, 31.

daily inquired ... [and] partook of the best intelligence the towne afforded'. Later, when printed news from Europe was in more plentiful supply, he carefully reported it, summarising and assessing what he learned. He blamed the loss of the Palatinate on the duplicity of Spain and the dissolution of the 1621 Parliament before sufficient funds had been voted: 'Thus, by the failing of seasonable assistance, were the Prince Elector's whole dominions vested by his bloody enemies.' Nonetheless, he maintained an active interest in foreign policy into the 1640s.[3]

D'Ewes's correspondence includes letters from Robert Gell, a Fellow at Christ's College Cambridge, to Sir Martin Stuteville and these, in turn, include references to newsbooks indicating that some copies were being enclosed with his letters. John Pory's circle of correspondents included Sir Thomas Puckering, Lord Brooke and Sir Robert Cotton. Dr Meddus also wrote to Mead and Mead to one of his students, Geoffrey Finch in Cambridge; while Lady Judith Barrington corresponded with her mother-in-law; and Francis Harris in London with his aunt, Lady Joan Barrington in Essex, sending her copies of the latest foreign news. Their letters are among a collection of family letters that she received between 1629 and 1632. They complemented the supply of news purchased by Thomas Barrington in that period, plus his own commentary on recruiting in England and reports of diplomatic developments gleaned from conversations in London. Peter Moreton wrote from Westminster to his father in Chester, while William Davenport, also living in Cheshire, recorded reports of Mansfield's and Gustavus Adolphus's campaigns and news of the Isle of Rhé Expedition in his commonplace book.[4]

Jacqueline Eales's study of the puritan correspondence of Sir Robert Harley's third wife, Lady Brilliana Harley, shows how the 'cause of right religion and their sympathy for the reformed Churches of Western Europe also gave their religious beliefs an internationalist dimension'. News was crucial to their understanding. Harley corresponded with Robert Horn, rector at Ludlow in Shropshire who recorded his interest in foreign policy in his commonplace book, and with Sir Horace Vere while he was leading the volunteer forces in the Palatinate. Lady Vere received regular news from her husband and also corresponded with a wide circle of puritan ministers. Harley spoke in favour of war against Spain in the 1628 Parliament as a

---

[3] E. Bourcier, The Diary of Sir Simonds D'Ewes 1622–24 (Paris, 1974), 43; J. O. Halliwell, ed., The Autobiography and Correspondence of Sir Simonds D'Ewes (1845), vol. 1, 143, 159, 153–4, 173, 222, vol. 2, 291–2.

[4] Ibid., vol. 2, 200, letters, 25 July 1628, 205–06; 212–13, letters, 8 and 9 August 1628; Frearson, 205–06; A. Searle, Barrington Family Letters, 1628–1632, Camden Society, 4:28 (1983), 190, 195, 235, 238, 242; D. Randall, Credibility in Elizabethan and Early Stuart Military News (2008), 55, 25, 30, 80, 84, 14; J. Morrill, 'William Davenport and the "Silent Majority" of Early Stuart England', Journal of the Chester Archaeological Society, 58 (1975), 118–22.

way to protect English Protestantism while Lady Brilliana's letters show her sympathy for the Scots and an apocalyptic interpretation of international developments. She followed the news closely between 1623 and 1643.[5]

Together, these customers comprise a well-educated, thoughtful and discerning readership with Protestant leanings and affection for Princess Elizabeth and the Palatine cause. They were English Protestants who wished to know when to praise and when to pray for mercies and punishments shown by God to their brethren abroad. Both sinfulness and piety were thought to affect the course of the war. They were a receptive audience that held anti-Spanish views before they started to read this news.[6] These were the representatives of the people to whom the Crown was obliged to turn in Parliament for subsidies to support foreign policy. They also had similar educational backgrounds to Gainsford and Watts, a factor that demonstrates the business sense of the publishers who employed editors with sentiments likely to resonate with regular customers.

We know these readers scrutinised editorial skills closely. Mead's correspondence refers to the dismissal of one editor in October 1623 because he 'was not liked'. His verdict on the subsequent editor (that 'in time he will do well') proved true.[7] However, these discerning readers were the wealthier clients who could afford subscriptions. They were probably not the people to whom Gainsford was primarily addressing himself in editorials. It seems reasonable to speculate that he would have adopted a rather different tone to those with whom he was educated and from whose company he was somewhat distanced by poverty and his lowly news trade status. It is more likely that in editorials Gainsford was at times reacting irritably to those who came round to Archer's shop in Pope's Head Alley or drank with him in the local tavern. These customers would have been a mixture of those buying to send into the country and buying to read. Newsbooks probably filtered down to all levels of society but, given the high cost involved in the regular purchase of copies, customers would have been mainly among the middling ranks of the prosperous who could afford them.[8] These included newly literate customers – people that the publishers would have been most keen to attract to expand their customer base, people who left little first hand evidence of their growing interest in contemporary affairs.

---

[5]   C. Durston and J. Eales, ed., *The Culture of English Puritanism 1560–1700* (1996), 5; D. Colclough, *Freedom of Speech in Early Stuart England* (Cambridge, 2005), 219–24; J. Eales, *Puritans and Roundheads: The Harleys of Brampton Bryan and the Outbreak of the English Civil War* (Cambridge, 1990), 11–13, 42, 71, 78–80, 88–9, 94; J. Eales, *Women in Early Modern England 1500–1700* (1998), 42.

[6]   Frearson, 273, 292–3, 284.

[7]   Harl. MS 389, fo. 381 (possibly because of his acceptance of Imperial successes – see pp. 135–6).

[8]   Frearson, 279.

In London, even by 1620 there was a large class of tradespeople who were literate though few left behind personal journals and correspondence. These readers were, in a sense, learners. As Malcolm Smuts notes, they also needed to learn to apply analytic observational skills to the gathering of information, to develop a sense of how politics worked, and a skill in distinguishing misleading appearances from meaningful information. This process of learning was encouraged. As early as 1621, Thomas Gataker recommended reading foreign news publications to develop compassion for the Protestant brethren in Europe and inspire support for their cause. By 1624, Thomas Lushington was encouraging his Oxford congregation to weigh news carefully and learn to distinguish between the opinions of writers of different religious affiliations. Seaver argues that a puritan culture of study and reflection 'joined artisan and husbandman, minister and gentleman' in the study of public, political developments. They saw their own personal spiritual struggle as part of their search for understanding the unfolding of God's purpose in the world. Wallington, a London puritan wood turner who followed the news closely from 1637 to 1645 and kept a journal, provides us with insights into the way he interpreted events in the world. News publishers were targeting these readers rather than the least literate. Even though blackletter remained the most accessible text for the least literate, they switched to roman at an early stage, as well as switching from single sheet to pamphlet format. This demonstrates they were expecting readers to be moderately sophisticated.[9]

Increasing literacy was widening the horizons and awareness of people.[10] The newsbooks broadened the political perspective of readers, helping them to see events in Westminster in a European context and they trained readers to become discerning in their use of written evidence. We can observe Gainsford confidently and directly addressing this audience in a way that suggests an open dialogue, but, since most of the known records of news-readers do not belong to this extended readership, is it possible to form a view about their attitudes and interests?

Contemporaries did: Ben Jonson reacted to the surge of interest in the early 1620s. His work tells us about an expanding readership and a new

[9] T. Harris, 'The Problem of Popular Culture in Seventeenth-Century London', *History of European Ideas*, 10:1 (1989), 43–4, 48–51; M. Smuts, *Culture and Power in England 1585–1685* (1999); T. Gataker's sermon, *A Sparke Towards the Kindling of Sorrow for Sion* quoted in J. Raymond, *Pamphlets and Pamphleteering in Early Modern Britain* (Cambridge, 2003), 145, as is T. Lushington's sermon, *The Resurrection Rescued from the Soldiers Calumnies*, 146–7; P. S. Seaver, *Wallington's World, A Puritan Artisan in Seventeenth-Century London* (Stanford, CA, 1985), viii, 3, 8, 10, 152, 156–7; K. Thomas, 'The Meaning of Literacy in Early Modern England', in *The Written Word: Literacy in Transition*, ed. G. Baumann, 1986, 101; J. Barry, 'Literacy and Literature in Popular Culture: Reading and Writing in Historical Perspective', in *Popular Culture in England c1500–1850*, ed. T. Harris (Basingstoke and London, 1995), 80–2.
[10] Thomas, 'The Meaning', 119–21.

class of literate customers for the printed news. Jonson commented upon contemporary life in London and showing how newsbooks made inroads into a market well beyond graduates and the legal profession. News became as a social asset to take to a dinner party or to the tavern and to exchange on the streets. He drew a picture of a growing and curious class of critical readers within a politicised artisan culture. He depicted greedy news seekers with few powers of discrimination, introducing them in *The Staple of News* as 'Gossip Mirth, Gossip Tatle, Gossip Expectation and Gossip Censure, four Gentlewomen, lady-like attired' who describe themselves as 'persons of quality ... and women of fashion'. Those aspiring to rise socially clearly needed to be aware of the news.[11]

Newsmongering was potentially big business: sales penetrated into different social groups, following visitors back to the counties and reaching down the social scale. Jonson mentions barbers' news and tailors' news. A countrywoman comes in asking for, 'A groatsworth of any news, I care not what, To carry down this Saturday to our vicar.' As a retailer of news she is called a 'butter-woman', making one of many obvious plays on Nathaniel Butter's name. Customers are 'of all ranks, and all religions – Through all the shires of the kingdom'. Jonson's 'staple' or news office is to see that readers,

> No more shall be abused, nor country parsons
> Of the inquisition, nor busy justices
> Trouble the peace, and both torment themselves,
> And their poor ignorant neighbours, with enquiries.

His observation that everyone has access to news is linked to a concern about both the credibility of the news and the credulity of readers. The head of the new office is asked,

> Why ... if the honest common people
> Will be abused, why should they not have their pleasure,
> In the believing lies are made for them;
> As you in the office, making them yourselves?

The reply is that they oppose printing,

> for when news is printed,
> It leaves, sir, to be news ...
> The very printing of 'em makes them news:
> That have not the heart to believe any thing,
> But what they see in print.[12]

---

11 Jonson, Prologue, 347.
12 Levy, 15, 32–4; Jonson, Act I, i, 352; Act I, ii, 357; Act I, ii, 358–9.

Jonson, despite his own origins as the stepson of a bricklayer, worked for the Crown providing masques and plays. His views on the press and their readers must be seen in the light of his preferences for peace and stability. He did not celebrate the marriage of Elizabeth and Frederick in 1613 and, in 1621, his *Pan's Anniversary* was criticised for its lack of sympathy with puritan concerns at a time when things were going badly for Protestants in France and Germany. In *Time Vindicated* in 1623, he satirised George Whither, proponent of an actively engaged Protestant foreign policy. However, he was a sharp observer of the social and political importance of the emergence of news reporting in the 1620s. McKenzie argues that his lack of sympathy or understanding of the process of education and awareness-raising meant that he isolated himself. Jonson understood what the editor and publishers of newsbooks came to understand through practical experience, that reporting requires analysis, but his reaction to their efforts was arrogant. He vilified Nathaniel Butter and looked down on his readership, just as he blamed his audiences for their failure to understand his plays, condemning them all as fools.[13]

Jonson's view was nonetheless informed by the accuracy of the eyewitness observation. He saw that this was an economic development with potentially enormous social and political consequences. He recognised that the popular press was a reflection of an egalitarian movement and immensely educative in forming a new language for talking about politics. McKenzie described *The Staple of News* as a 'supremely perceptive ... deeply conservative but powerfully sanctioned, [reaffirmation] of the poet's public role as spokesman for his age, a role which the development of the press, with its unsifted reports and vulgarity of language, threatened to usurp'. He pointed out that Jonson took a long time to write this play and produced a deeply considered comment on where he saw the nation going but he had little faith in human nature. The play 'shows no understanding at all of what a painful struggle it is for the ill-educated to learn a new language of conscience and independent political judgment'.[14] It made no allowance for the fact that the press could be a teacher, and failed to recognise any potential for good from the emerging media.

Jonson was not alone in stigmatising 'commoners', described by Zaret as those who read but had not had a grammar school or university education. The growth in reading and comment was scorned in *Mortalities Memorandum*:

---

13 M. Butler, 'Ben Jonson among the Historians', in Lake, 98–9; D. F. McKenzie, in *The Staple of News and the Late Plays; A Celebration of Ben Jonson*, ed. W. Blissett *et al.* (Toronto, 1973); McKenzie, 176–7, 181, 197.
14 McKenzie, *The Staple*, 107, 95, 116, 111, 118; McKenzie, 184, 187.

> Readers too common, and plentiful be;
> ... utter their verdict on what they doe view,
> Though none of the Muses they yet ever knew.[15]

Jonson identified a problem that has survived into the twenty-first century. While people are aware that information they receive by word of mouth or in a manuscript may be fallible, they tend to accept printed information allowing the act of printing to give the written word greater authority. Jonson criticised the public for lack of discrimination in their thirst for news. He described them as,

> both the curious and the negligent,
> The scrupulous and careless, wild and stay'd,
> The idle and laborious
> ... the vulgar: baits, sir, for the people;
> And they will bite like fishes.[16]

The news trade was booming. The gullible throughout society were hungry for news and newsmen were only just managing to satisfy demand. Jonson's parody of their product confirms the significance of this news by the mid-1620s and shows he was aware then of what historians have been remarkably slow to recognise: he was witnessing change of enormous potential significance. It was so important that he parodied the news media at the start of the decade in the masque *Newes from the New World Discover'd in the Moon*, and continued to the end of the decade with *The New Inn* where the character, Jug is described as 'the tapster, a thoroughfare of news' with a reputation for incredible stories. When the news trade boomed again in the early 1630s, *The Staple of News* was staged again in 1631 and Jonson oversaw the publication of his works on the news press.[17] Whether or not Jonson was prompted to criticism by his political opposition to intervention in the Palatinate, his negative view of the powers of discrimination of new readers blinded him to their potential for education, change and growth. These new customers had ideas about what made for a good and readable newsbook and they weren't afraid to express them.

---

[15] D. Zaret, *Origins of Democratic Culture: Printing, Petitions, and the Public Sphere in Early-modern England* (Princeton, NJ, 2000), 42, 50, 154; Rachel Speght, A3 verso, STC23057, quoted by Zaret, 155.

[16] Jonson, Act III, i, 386.

[17] P. R. Sellin, 'The Performances of Ben Jonson's "Newes from the new world discover'd in the Moone"', *English Studies*, 61:6 (1980); P. R. Sellin, 'The Politics of Ben Jonson's "Newes from the new world discover'd in the Moone"', *Viator: Medieval and Renaissance Studies*, 17 (1986); S. Lambert, 'Coranto Printing in England', *JNandPH*, 8 (1992), 5; N. Malcolm, *Reason of State, Propaganda, and the Thirty Years' War: An Unknown Translator by Thomas Hobbes* (Oxford, 2007), 83–4; Raymond, *Pamphlets*, 129; Jonson, 429.

Reflecting upon customers' views and responding to criticism

Newsbook editorials reflected the relationship between the publishers, editor and readers from the perspective of the trade. In them we can observe how the publisher and editor responded to comment and criticism by trying to make the product more acceptable and appealing, and what they were saying or assuming about their readers. As texts inevitably tell us more about their producers than their consumers, however, we must proceed with care in attempting to 'read across' from what remains of printed material from the past to assess its reception among readers.[18] We must be especially alert where production was subsidised, print was distributed as propaganda or controlled by government. When readers have left no records, we cannot know to what extent they agreed with what they read.

We know these editors knew their readers. In the small world of news-print in the City of London in the early seventeenth century, readers, editors and publishers met and aired views freely. John Sommerville has reflected that the modern industry would envy such intimacy and, as news was being published for profit, publishers needed to be responsive to audiences and to their assumptions and prejudices. Sharpe has noted how prefaces more generally at the time demonstrate a mounting concern about readers and a need to explain. He and Zwicker have written of 'continuous transac-tions between producers and consumers' and 'the power and centrality of the reader in all the commerce of the book'.[19] News publications could show people's attitudes and, since these publications were periodical, we can observe the progress of a dialogue with readers. Editors may have intended to educate the readers but in practice, over time, they found themselves in a process of negotiation rather than domination. A study of successive issues of newsbooks illustrates this: the publishers could not afford to ignore customers' opinions and both sides understood where the power lay. Accord-ingly, especially in the 1620s when the relationships were first being defined and developed, newsbooks often give an impression of a rather beleaguered

---

[18] K. Sharpe, *Reading Revolutions: The Politics of Reading in Early Modern England* (New Haven, CT, 2000), 15–20; Barry, 'Literacy and Literature', 79; A. Fox, 'Ballads, Libels and Popular Ridicule in Jacobean England', *PandP*, 145 (1995), 48; B. Scribner, 'Is a History of Popular Culture Possible?', *History of European Ideas*, 10:2 (1989), 180, 176, 186; A. Patterson, *Censorship and Interpretation* (Madison, WS and London, 1984); A. Patterson, *Reading between the Lines* (1993).

[19] C. J. Sommerville, *The News Revolution in England; Cultural Dynamics of Daily Information* (New York and Oxford), 1997, 30; Sharpe, *Reading*, 56–7; K. Sharpe and S. N. Zwicker, *Reading, Society and Politics in Early Modern England* (Cambridge, 2003), 3, 8; D. Underdown, *A Freeborn People* (Oxford, 1996) 88; M. Nevitt, 'Ben Jonson and the Serial Publication of News', in J. Raymond, ed., *News Networks in Seventeenth-Century Britain and Europe* (London and New York, 2006), 51–62; Barry, 'Literacy and Literature', 88.

editor or publisher being criticised, striving, yet unable to live up to the demands and expectations of readers.

This process was so marked that by the 1630s publishers and editors openly anticipated comment. After Watts resigned editorials were quick to warn readers,

> you must not expect ... that abilitie (for all things) which was, and is in that man, onely you shall finde as much truth as could be sifted out ... [also] consider the season of the yeere, Winter: and the sad disaster on both sides, the one to loose the battell, and the other their king.

The new editor, appointed for the seventh part of the *German History*, evidently decided that attack was the best form of defence, beginning,

> Hee that shall adventure to set forth a Story, is as sure to meet with scoffes, as a souldier is with knocks. The best Historians hath not scaped uncensored.... I am ready to undergoe the common fate, armed against ill Language, with that innocency which accompanieth Truth, and my desire of communicating that Intelligence, (which at first was private) to the publick benefit: Hee that in grosseth all to himselfe, may thinke himselfe wise, but will scarce prove himself honest, and they which censure the labours of them, who intend a common good, give evidence against themselves of a snarling Cynicisme, not Scholasticall ingenuitie.[20]

For a very different approach a decade later, we can observe John Dillingham, editing *The Moderate Intelligencer*. He attempted to defuse discord among readers with the theme of 'the non-dangerousnesse of Opinions', arguing that these need not disturb the kingdom or divide friends. He flexibly abandoned this when readers objected, saying he intended to 'touche weekly [on] the cause of their increase, with the remedies' but was 'wholly discouraged from going any further with this busines'.[21]

Newsbooks were often criticised for presentation, content, and sources. In the autumn of 1623, for example, after the shattering defeat of Christian of Brunswick at Stadtlohn in August, Frederick signed an armistice with the emperor. This left Mansfeld and his army surviving through the winter months on plunder in East Friesland while in London there was a different front line: the press was facing disappointed readers (who perhaps recognised the significance of this defeat). The editor responded to their complaints,

> Gentle Reader, how comes it ... that nothing can please you? ... if the newes bee forcible against the Emperour, you breakeforth, it is impossible, and all is

---

[20] *The Continuation of the German History*, Part 5 (1634), 'Printer to the Reader' verso, STC23525.6; *The German History Continued*, Part 7 (1634), 'To the Reader', STC23525.7.
[21] *The Moderate Intelligencer* (5–12 March 1646), front page, N&S419.053, E.327(25).

invention: if it tend to the dejection of the Country, you seeme to commiserate and wonder at the misfortune: if we talke of novelty indeed you make doubt of the verity: if wee onely tell you what we know, you throw away the booke, and breake out, there is nothing in it, or else it is repetition of the former weekes newes ... what ever we endeavor is wrested by the scrue of passion; and whether good or bad, is fashioned to strange formes by the violence of humor, and over-swaying of opinion. ... yet ... we will not be affrighted from ... acquainting you with the occurents of the time.

They were still complaining two weeks later: 'many have laughed to scorne some of these reports: and because they heare not present sacking of Townes, possession of Countries, crowning of new Kings, slaughtering of whole Armies, and taking of great men prisoners, they peremptory conclude, there is no such matter'.[22]

Nevitt suggests that 'publishers had little idea of what their readers wanted'.[23] Yet it is clear they were receiving considerable feedback. The question was whether they could hope to satisfy customer demands. News-books could not be all things to all people. A January 1624 notice acknowl-edges a range of different views and demonstrates how keenly the news was being followed:

For some are yet so transported with conceit, or opinion of the Emperours prevailings against all the protestant Countries in Germany, that they will not allow more then a rumour, and some suming reports of such an Enemies proceed-ings, as the prince of Transilvania, and flatly deny the successe of such attempts, as have beene formerly divulged. Others, who seeme to understand the businesse, and are apprehensive of the danger ... doe not deny his descent into Hungary.... Others suppose, that there hath beene a kinde of forbearing ... and the Transil-vanians were willing to desist ... In this manner at this houre is the businesse variated even in England it selfe betweene the Emperour and Bethlem Gabor, and although men doe read both letters and credit, and peruse the very printed Dutch Corantoes, yet doe they either disesteeme then, as untruths, or deny them as partiall.

Gainsford knew his readers, their range of opinions, strengths and weak-nesses in understanding and was resolved 'I will not be disheartened'.[24] He acknowledged that there were factions and they could not please everyone:

Gentle Readers: for there are two sorts of you I know: the one wishing well to the Emperor and his proceedings: the other, murmering and repining that the Palatine's cause and Bohemia's business thrives no better: Now how can you

---

22 (20 November 1623), 1, STC18507.133; (11 December 1623) 1, STC18507.135.
23 Nevitt, 'Ben Jonson', 58; Raymond, *Pamphlets*, 147–8.
24 (7 January 1624), 1–2, STC18507.137.

both be satisfied with any reports or newes that concerne either party: therefore to avoid partiality and take an eaven course concerning the reports abroad, and passions at home, I will directly proceed in my accustomed manner of searching and opening the Letters that came from beyond the seas, and so acquaint you with their secrets.

Gainsford added that, if they were not satisfied, they should blame the letters, not him or the printer. He soon retracted, acknowledging a dominant interest in the restoration of the Palatinate, 'little pleasing newes hath bin exposed … I call it pleasing for there are fewe English eares, but would be glad to heare of the Palatines restitution'.[25]

However, Gainsford's portrayal of himself as simultaneously a blameless middleman and commentator upon the news, with a sympathy for readers' views, was overridden by the publishers' determination to keep the presses going. As winter was drawing to a close in early 1624 they had little news to report. He commented,

Gentle Reader: I make no question, you heare how loudly Rumor threatens the Low Countries, as if the King of Spaine had found out a new Myne, as he hath raised new armies. For now they say, that 15000. Italians, Spaniards, and Swisse, are come into Brabant and Flanders: So that … there is nothing to be expected, but overrunning all Holland immediately. And yet for all this, there is no newes … I confesse your hearts are even sadded againe at the first view, when you thinke you shall reade of nothing, but the happie proceedings of the Emperour; and that the States, with the Prince Palatine, are now threatened to their utter ruine.… Notwithstanding … you shall be supplied with one Newes or other.[26]

Although William Watts did not attain the personal notice or notoriety of Gainsford, commentators quickly registered the renewed news interest of the early 1630s. Richard Brathwaite commented upon the evolving trade of journalism in *Whimsies: or A New Cast of Characters*, which included a description of a 'Corranto-Coiner'. We are told there are journalists who actively seek foreign news and write down whatever is heard. The publisher's motive is 'to get him currant money and delude the vulgar'. Because of the great appetite of the public for news, he is thriving, 'His mint goes weekly and he coins money by it'. Jonson, too, in *The Magnetic Lady* in 1632, returned to the familiar pun on Nathaniel Butter's name, 'News, news, good news, better than butter'd news'. This play included a character called Bias, an intelligencer, described as, 'a vi-politic or sub-secretary … all the lords Have him in their esteem for his relation'. Christopher Foster prayed in 1632 that God would 'inspire the curranto-makers with the spirit of truth,

---

[25] (24 February 1624), 1, STC18507.141; (6 March 1624), 1, STC18507.143.
[26] (12 March 1624), 1–2, STC18507.144.

that people might know when to utter praise for the King of Sweden's victories, and when to pray for him in his distress'.[27]

There is less evidence about how well Watts knew his readers. He benefited from the popularity of Gustavus Adolphus who embodied a Protestant ideal and was acting as the military saviour of the afflicted Church.[28] His successes were greeted enthusiastically and Watts's work was so well received during Gustavus Adolphus's time that it opened up a market for longer compilations in *The Swedish Intelligencer*. Watts followed the precedent of manuscript news writers and solicited for news, indicating the sympathies of readers and the type of material he was seeking:

> God blesse the King of Swedens Maiestie: and thoroughly enable him to be the glorious Assertor of the Germane Libertie. If the Reader desire the continuance of our Relations, our Intelligencer shall be much the better furnished to give Content, if they please to send us their owne Intelligence.

The first part of *The Swedish Intelligencer* sold so well it ran to four editions. By the second part he expressed his purpose as addressing 'well-affected English, as desired in their dayes, to see some ease and consolation to the miserably afflicted Churches of Germany'. His aim of 'Truth and Plainenesse' led him to become not only editor but an investigative journalist, 'my care was, to learne out, and get acquainted with such understanding Gentlemen as had been personally present in the Actions' and his references to continental sources suggest he knew his readers to be familiar with them. Responding to comment from those who were less enthusiastic about the news of Protestant success, he turned the table, inviting them to supply evidence, 'had the Imperialists well beaten the Swedish now and then; I would not have omitted it, if any claim [otherwise] … they should have done well to have sent me in their Intelligences'. This challenge evidently served well enough for us to see it repeated in subsequent compilations. *The Swedish Intelligencer* was a compilation of news akin to the German news digest *Mercurius Gallobelgicus*, a semi-annual publication in Latin that first appeared in 1594 in Cologne and was later published in Frankfurt. This aimed to provide an overview of events and Watts evidently referred to it frequently. He boasted repeatedly of the superiority of his product over *Gallobelgicus* (which he claimed he only used sparingly) pointing out where it was less accurate than his own sources. He frequently covered the 'British interest' through reports

---

[27] A. B. Worden, 'Literature and Political Censorship in Early Modern England', in *Too Mighty to be Free Censorship and the Press in Britain and the Netherlands*, ed. A. C. Duke and C. A. Tamse (Zutphen, 1987), 53–7; R. Brathwaite, *Whimzies: or a new cast of characters* (1631), quoted in *The Times Tercentenary Handlist*, 9–10; B. Jonson, 2, 'The Magnetic Lady', Act III, iv, 545; Act III, i, 533; Dahl, 23.

[28] M. A. Breslow, *A Mirror of England, English Puritan Views of Foreign Nations, 1618–1640* (Cambridge, MA, 1970), 125–31.

and fulsome praise of those officers and others, great and small, that readers might know of, such as Hamilton, Hepburn, James and Robert Ramsay, Reay, Lord Craven, Jacob Ashlye, Patrick Ruthven and the 'young Sparke ... gentilely bred', William Harvey. And he explained his editorial decision to deal with the death of Gustavus Adolphus before ending his account of the action of Lutzen by noting he has observed 'how curiously inquisitive men have beene, after the manner of the King's death'.[29]

Watts appears to have had a more confident relationship with readers than Gainsford before him or those who followed him. Teething troubles had been dealt with by Gainsford. Access to news sources had improved. Significantly, in Watts's time the news itself was more palatable to Protestant sympathisers. His successors in the 1630s were less at ease with their readers. Watts confident request of 1631 became a more defensive reaction by 1635 with an invitation addressed only to the most educated, 'If any Loyalist thinke I have failed in the discovery, or hath attained more perfect knowledge, I shall intreat him in the words of the Poet, si quid novisti rectius istis Candidus imperti, si non, his utere mecum.'[30]

In what Ann Hughes dubbed the 'enigmatic decade', it is more difficult to assess readers' reactions. There were no Parliaments and, due to a ban from 1632 to 1638, we have no newsbook editorials engaging in the shop dialogue with customers.[31] The infrequently published compendiums of news that succeeded *The Swedish Intelligencer* were called 'histories'. They were lengthy and took the price way beyond the reach of many readers that earlier newsbooks had aimed to attract. Sir Thomas Barrington could afford to spend around £7 a year on books and foreign newsbooks. His book bill from Richard Whittacker in St Paul's Church Yard, for 1636–9, came to £28 9s 4d. He paid 1s 6d in for *The Modern History* and the same again six months later for an issue of *Mercurius Gallobelgicus* and 2s 6d on *Poma Palaestina*, a remonstrance against the transfer of the Palatinate to the duke of Bavaria. These prices effectively restricted the market, though not so narrowly as to exclude all but those who might afford to pay for a newsletter service at between six pence and three shillings per separate. Butter later described this period as leaving 'every man to the pleasing of his own fantasy, by a more uncertaine restrained way of private letters, or verball news which cannot but suffer much alteration, according to the affection of the Relater'. D'Ewes drew on correspondence, including personal arrangements for letters from the United Provinces, but adapted in his *Autobiog-*

[29] Dahl, 202–05; *The Swedish Intelligencer*, Part 1 (1632), 3 and verso, STC23522; *The Swedish Intelligencer*, Part 2 (1632), preface, 1, 12, 62, 75, 77, 81, 176, STC23524; *The Swedish Intelligencer*, Part 3 (1633), 2, (quoted p. 176), 39, 40, 131, 141, 153, STC23525.
[30] *The History of the Present Warres*, Part 6 (1634), A3, STC23525.5; *The Modern History*, Part 8 (1635), 'To the Reader', 3 (misnumbered) and verso, STC23525.9.
[31] A. Hughes, *Politics, Society and Civil War in Warwickshire, 1620–1660* (Cambridge, 1987), 99.

142   *The Swedish Intelligencer.*

* The *Swedes* generally one with another, are all *Carpenters*: and the *Fins*, being a plaine, simple and droyling kinde of people; are more used for the *Spade*, then for the *Sword*: notwithstanding wee have here heard so much, of the great exployts of these *Finlanders*. The *Swedes* and *Finlanders*, plainly, are not the best souldiours of the Army: tis the *Scots* and *Germanes* that have done it: and yet have both the other, done their parts also.

The most famous Story, of the Kings passing the river *Lech*.

of advantage for the bridge; the King gives order unto the *Swedes* * his Carpenters, and unto the *Fins*, his Pioners; to breake downe the houses of the neighbour villages; and to bring such timber, plancks, and boords, as might be fit for a bridge-worke. The place appointed for the working of the bridge, was at *Oberendorff*; a small Dorp some halfe an *English* mile from the very point, where the King intended to lay it over. The place resolved upon, was betwixt *Rain* and *Thierhaubten*; just upon a point of land: made so, by the crooking or bending of the River. The ground on the Kings side, was a pikes length higher banckt, and playner withall, then that on *Tillyes*: which was both lower, and wooddy. There was a tryall made first of all, to lay a floate-bridge; but the River would not endure that: for notwithstanding it be not above thirty or forty paces over at the most, yet by reason of the straight course of it, the streame sets very swift and violent.

All the materials being now prepared; the King about nine at night, upon the fourth of *Aprill*, advances some 1000 *Commanded men*, unto the place aforesaid. Two houres after, they begin to worke a *running Trench* round about the crooked banke of the River, that the Muskettiers out of that, might with more security give fire into the Wood on the other side of the River. This *Line* or *Trench*, had a great Battery at each end of it, for halfe and quarter Cannon: together with many lesser *Batteryes* betweene, all along about the *Point*, for the smaller field pieces to play upon: which were every-where intermingled with Muskettiers also. Whilest the Pioners are thus a working, the King in divers other places (both above it and below) gives false fires and Alarms, both with Muskets and smaller fielding peeces, for to amuse the enemy; that till the morning they could not imagine where to find him.

By sixe on the Thursday morning, Aprill 5. was this worke finished, the Cannon mounted, the Arches or Tressels for the bridge, with the planckes and other materialls, all brought;

Plate 4. Page 142 of *The Swedish Intelligencer. The first part* (1632) which, as it boasted, was revised and augmented for the third time. It illustrates the level of detail and editor's extensive comments (intended for English and Scottish readers) in both the text and margin. Crossing the River Lech, in April 1632, was (as noted) one of Gustavus Adolphus's greatest achievements, allowing him to enter Munich in May.

raphy to summarising 'the sad and dismal' international news toward the end of his account for each year, aligning it with the appearance of news compilations that succeeded *The Swedish Intelligencer*. John Rous was able to continue to follow issues of the successors of *The Swedish Intelligencer* but he did this without comment on the content while maintaining an eye for factual accuracy.[32]

At the end of the decade Lady Brilliana Harley, writing to her son in Oxford, looked forward to the resumption of regular news publication following the grant of a patent to Butter and Bourne in December 1638.[33] She was probably disappointed by the product when it arrived. The next series marked a distinct regressive step. Dutch and German publications were reproduced without any editorial contribution in London that might enhance their appeal. They had little to commend them to popular taste. They were repetitive, giving telegram-like reports of the same news from all directions. A reader might have been fortunate to find one interesting report with eyewitness detail or a story line in a week's batch of three issues. There was no analysis and no engagement with readers in dialogue. We only know that, after an initial period of good sales that sustained an initially high output, they could not compete with the growing market in short ephemeral pamphlets appearing in London. Readers voted with their pennies and foreign news ceased to be a viable enterprise. As Butter explained, 'if a number shall be vented weekly, to recompence the charge, we shall continue them; if not, we shall be forced to put a period to the Presse'.[34]

In the more vociferous decade of the 1640s, there was a transformation in the circumstances for public debate. A multitude of pamphlets brought contemporary domestic as well as foreign issues into print. Wallington and Rous's reflections showed how the increase in print in 1640–2 at times seemed to readers overwhelming, adding to unease and uncertainty in the heightened climate of 'anxiety, mistrust and fear'. Meanwhile, those who left no written record, but could read or hear the news by gathering around someone who could read it aloud, were more visibly participating in public discussion. Artisans, apprentices, chapmen and hawkers took politics out of doors into the streets and theatres, and people read and argued over pamphlets while standing in stationers' shops. (In 1642, one such altercation even came to the attention of the House of Commons.)[35] Controver-

[32] M. E. Bohannon, 'A London Bookseller's Bill', *The Library*, 4:18 (1938), 421, 423, 428–9, 437–8, 440; (23 April 1640), 'Printer to Reader', verso, STC18507.337; *Autobiography D'Ewes*, vol. 2, 119–22, 128–9, 223–9; *Rous*, 72–5, 81–2.

[33] Eales, *Puritans*, 92.

[34] (23 April 1640), 'Printer to Reader' verso, STC18507.337.

[35] D. Cressy, *England on Edge; Crisis and Revolution, 1640–1642* (Oxford, 2006), xi, 116–7, 298, 301; D. Freist, *Governed by Opinion; Politics, Religion and the Dynamics of Communication in Stuart London, 1637–45* (London and New York, 1997), 110–18, 122–4,

sial debate appeared in what McKenzie has called 'a form of communicative interchange' that was speech-like in the way it was presented in print and gives us an exceptional view of contemporary opinions and arguments as they emerged. Readers could respond as writers. Peacey has demonstrated the propaganda dimensions of this dialogue, probing the heady mixes of political and commercial motives behind publications. He argued that there was a growing sophistication in 'news management' by the proponents of both parliamentary and royalist views. There was also a greater awareness of the tactics the press employed as the decade progressed. Views emerged in parliamentary debate and among correspondents.[36]

It was not, however, until the mid-1640s that we again have evidence of a new generation of periodical editors reflecting on a potential readership for foreign news and tailoring their product accordingly. John Dillingham believed that 'the *Times* is the only study' and 'the good of the King and Kingdome' would be served by information. He began cautiously at first with overseas news in *The Parliament Scout*, offering explanation, not simply reproducing reports. For example, he explained the significance of Poland's entry into Germany as likely to distract the Swedes, adding 'whether this will please you or displease you, I know not'.[37] By 1644, with as many as thirty-seven serials on the market and hundreds of issues appearing annually, publishers were looking for ways to distinguish their products. William Ewry, seemingly inspired by the landing of a shipment of 'Corrants for England', decided to appeal to a readership that was probably lower down the social and educational scale than Gainsford had ever ventured, with an account of why they should look beyond the seas. In his second issue of *The Military Scribe* he explained,

> Forraigne Newes is little welcome to the Plebian or Vulgar sort of People, because they doe not comprehend how much the present affaires of Christendome are interwoven and connected, and therefore our Scribe hath reserved such kinde of Military Relations, for those that are ... Judicious; yet the meanest capacity may gather good fruit from the Results, and see the evident hand of God in the Actions and motions against the Protestants enemies.

Perhaps some readers were goaded into striving to identify with the judicious rather than the vulgar, but he was dependent for his foreign news on what he could glean from arriving merchant ships and hard pressed to

250–3; Harris, 'The Problem', 50–1; T. Harris, *The Politics of the Excluded, c.1500–1850* (Basingstoke and New York, 2001), 7–9.

[36] D. F. McKenzie, 'The London Book Trade in 1644', in McKenzie, 135; J. Peacey, *Politicians and Pamphleteers: Propaganda during the English Civil Wars and Interregnum* (Aldershot and Burlington, VT, 2004), 11, 39, 245.

[37] Raymond, 30; *Parliament Scout* (10–27 June 1643) 1, N&S485.1, E.56(7); (29 September–6 October 1643), 138, N&S485.15, E.69(27).

demonstrate simply and briefly why it was good news that the prince of Transylvania had invaded Imperial Hungary or that the Turks and Tartars were threatening the Polish borders. It was probably easier to see the benefit of a merchant dying in Italy and leaving £1000 to London's Parliament and of Parliament receiving good wishes from the king of Portugal. The publication did not last.[38]

The Weekly Account was more cautious. In the issue of 6 March 1644 continental news accounted for two out of twelve items; four, if we also count Dutch merchants receiving the National Covenant and the reception in London of the Swedish Ambassador. However, it provided a variety of short bullets of dateline headed reports in subsequent issues. In December the editor introduced a report on Swedish progress in Germany in a manner that showed a continuing expectation that readers liked to hear of Protestant successes:

> I use not much to trouble you with forraige newes, neither should I at this time (because I have many matters of a homebred concernment to write) but that I perceive the success of the Protesttant forces in Germany is of that great concernment, that the eye of all Europe is upon it.[39]

The Moderate Intelligencer at this time was also modest in its expectations of an interested readership explaining in April 1645 'because this day afforded little new newes, we will trouble the Reader with what we received from beyond Seas'. *The Exchange Intelligencer* provided a deeper insight into the evolution of the potential readership for foreign news in the 1640s, acknowledging that home news would come first in a time of domestic upheaval:

> Years ago we lived 'in so blessed a Time, that wee were onely curious, and desirous to heare forraign Newes, and to know the fate of other Kingdomes and Nations. And now ... wee talke of nothing else but what is done in *England*: and perhaps once a fortnight. Wee hearken after Newes out of *Scotland*.... our owne Domestique affaires are of greater concernment, then foreign businesses; but yet we may looke farther than home ... [to be reassured that they are too busy to be a threat or (as in the past) to rejoice or commiserate with our friends for their successes or failures]. Besides, it is requisite for Marchants, and for those that travell ... to know ... what forces are upon the Seas, and where Armies quarter.... These reasons have moved me to undertake this Weekly labour.... You shall know our owne affairs first, and in the next have Informations almost from all parts of the

---

[38] McKenzie, 'Trade in 1644', 143; *The Military Scribe* (20–7 February 1644), 16, N&S404.1, E.34(16); (19–26 March 1644), 40, N&S404.5, E.39(11), (5–12 March 1644), 24, N&S404.3, E.37(4); (12–19 March 1644), 27, N&S404.4, E.38(4).

[39] *The Weekly Account* (6–13 March 1644), title page, N&S671.137, E.37(6); (4–11 December 1644), Vuu2, N&S671.167, E.21(12).

world. The best of the *French* and *Dutch* Coranto's ... besides many things out of Marchants and Gentlemens letters.[40]

This analysis, identifying a niche for overseas news, seems to have been correct. Dillingham, with experience as a newsletter writer in Paris from 1639, was well positioned to secure a regular supply of material and had, it seems, a good grasp of the London news market. After a cautious start, he found a sufficiently committed readership in 1645 to continue to offer continental news in *The Moderate Intelligencer* through to the Peace of West-phalia, thereby giving readers the opportunity once again to follow events week by week as they unfolded.

Accuracy and accusation

Accuracy was the topic on which editors and readers had most to say to one another. Marcus Nevitt, recognising that contemporaries such as Holland, Lushington and Shirley shared a view that newsbooks contained fabrications and lies, has argued, 'If the publishers and editor were "not fully sure of" what they were printing, one can understand why so many readers were quick to lampoon their work'. However, Kevin Sharpe has demonstrated how learned texts were used by educated readers: he showed that Sir William Drake 'did not regard texts as truths' and John Rous 'read his own world'. Intellectual discipline created active readers. Claims about facts and truth helped to create an audience that desired facts and evidence. Truth was always the goal, but it was not always easy to obtain and reports often needed revisiting and revising. The language adopted in foreign newsbooks to reassure readers and help them develop discernment continued in use through the seventeenth century and into the next. News reporting consequently bolstered concerns for verifiability.[41]

There were unique difficulties inherent in discovering the truth, even about one seventeenth-century battle. No one person could observe more than a small part of the action and reports, written from an uncoordinated range of experiences and perspectives, went to readers unlikely to have visited the areas or experienced war first hand.[42] This made verification exceptionally difficult and led to the development of what Randall has described as a 'still surviving standard of extensive credibility derived from ... multiple anonymous texts'. There was 'much practical acknowledgement that individual pieces of news turned out to be false' and 'intelligent

---

[40] *The Moderate Intelligencer* (17 April 1645), 58, N&S419.008, E.278(26); *The Exchange Intelligencer* (1 May 1645), 1–2, Wing145.1 fo. E.284(12)), quoted in Raymond, 144–52.
[41] Nevitt, 'Ben Jonson', 54–6; Atherton, 45–8; Sharpe, *Reading*, 342, 297; B. J. Shapiro, *A Culture of Fact: England 1550–1720* (Ithaca, NY and London, 2000), 89, 91–3, 104.
[42] See p. 172.

news reading became a test of character'. Gainsford assisted: in some cases he acknowledged known sources and extolled their virtues, elsewhere, he relied on dates and the locations and extent of reportage. Joseph Mead's correspondence illustrates 'active and extensive' news reading in the 1620s. Mousley has used the works of Pory as a news writer and the news diaries of Walter Yonge and John Rous to demonstrate how knowledge through information, observation and confirmation from reliable sources affected their sense of themselves and their relationships with the state.[43]

Pory, in his scribal news service, used the dates of European correspondence as a means of assessing reliability. The Barrington family, with access to a wide range of news sources, could suspend judgement and wait for something more. Seasoned correspondents like Mead could wryly and routinely assess reports and spot discrepancies: transcribing from a newsbook on 15 October 1625, he wrote, 'from Frankfurt & Aken Sept 26. new style that the king of Denmark had over Tilly a very greate over throw slaying 100000 of his men. You see we are not the greatest multipliers, for we had but 9000 when it was highest.' Robert Gell similarly compared sources to get closer to an accurate assessment of the size armies.[44] But the continued topicality of European news combined with editorial work in the early 1620s opened the trade to a wider readership and ran into a problem of distrust. New readers were less familiar with, and less tolerant of, the inevitable shortcomings of the medium and they were primary targets for Jonson's sarcasm. The Prologue of The Staple of News depicted readers with unrealistic expectations and a limited understanding 'only we would entreat of Madam Expectation.... That your ladyship would expect no more than you understand.' He reprimanded a reader, saying she expected 'too much, lady; and teach others to do the like'.[45]

Criticisms of dramatists and poets struck at the news publications and at readers by association. Jonson's Newes from the New World, was concerned with intelligencers who 'do write my thousand letters a week ordinary, sometime twelve hundred ... [to] friends of correspondence in the country' and the printers of pamphlets on incredible events (such as the appearance of a nine foot long serpent in Sussex), 'for the common people ... [who have] pleasure in beleeving of lies [that] are made for them'. In this, the Printer says, 'Indeed I am all for sale, gentlemen, you say true. I am a printer, and a printer of news and I do hearken after 'em wherever they be,

[43] Randall, Credibility, 3, 10–1, 69, 126, 130; A. Mousley, 'Self, State, and Seventeenth-century News', The Seventeenth Century, 6 (1991), 149–68; D. Randall, 'Joseph Mead, Novellante: News, Sociability, and Credibility in Early Stuart England', JBS, 45:2 (2006), 293–5.
[44] CandT, Pory to Sir Thomas Lucy, 1 November 1632, 2:190; Searle, Barrington, 210, 217–18, 244; Harl. MS 389, fo. 496; Halliwell, Autobiography, 2:212, Gell to Stuteville, 8/9 August 1628.
[45] Jonson, Prologue, 348.

at any rates, I'll give anything for a good copy now, be't true or false.' Jonson associated the work of the clerks in the office in *The Staple of News* with gossip and condemned it as inaccurate: reports were obtained from 'hungry captains, obscur statesmen' and the like, who 'dish out news, Were't true or false'. The news was also often stale, 'worth nothing, mere pot butter' or worse, old news, reissued when 'the stationer cheats upon time, By buttering o'er again'. He linked both these complaints to Gainsford, referring to 'a stewed poet (with) two heads, as a drum has; one for the making, the other repeating! (who has) put himself to silence in (a) dead sack'.[46]

The idea that greed could override concern for truth grew as trade prospered. Thomas Middleton's political allegory about English/Spanish relations, *A Game at Chess*, included a scene where the Black Knight representing Gondomar, the Spanish Ambassador, received newsletters from England, France, Germany, Italy and Spain. He commented, as he was handed the German letter, 'Thinke they've sealed this with Butter'. Middleton evidently also assumed that Nathaniel Butter's name was already widely known and closely associated by audiences with the European news and with dubious content.[47] Abraham Holland's criticism of Gainsford's work in *A Continu'd just inquisition of Paper – Persecutors* was heated, referring bluntly to 'shamefull lies', and conveyed indignation and a suspicion that much of the weekly news is fabricated, yet widely regarded:

> hungry braines compile prodigious Books,
> Of Bethlem Gabors preparations, and
> How terms betwixt him and th' Emperor stand:
> Of Denmarke, Swede, Poland, and of this and that …
>
> To see such Butter everie weeke besmearre
> Each publike post, and Churchdore.[48]

Shirley's *Love Tricks or The Schoole of Complement* first appeared in 1624 and suggested there was money to be made from soldiers' lies and the fabrication of war news while sitting in a tavern:

> They … will write you a battell in any part of Europe at an houres warning, and yet never set foot out of a Taverne, describe you Towns, Fortifications, Leaders …

---

46 B. Jonson, 'Newes from the New World Discover'd in the Moon', in *The Works of Benjamin Jonson*, vol. 2 (1640, presented 1620, 1621?), 39–41; Jonson, Act I ii, 357; Act I ii, 358–9; Act II i, 381 and Prologue, 348–9.

47 T. Middleton, 'A Game at Chesse', Act I, i, in *The Revels Plays*, ed. T. H. Howard Hill (Manchester, 1993), 88; E. C. Morris, 'Allegory in Middleton's "A Game at Chesse"', *Englische Studien*, 38 (1907); T. Cogswell, 'Thomas Middleton and the Court, 1624: "A Game at Chess" in Context', *HLQ*, 47 (1984).

48 Part 2 (1625), 10, STC6340, appended to John Davies, *A Scourge for Paper – Persecutors*, partially quoted in Dahl, 22–3.

not a Souldier shall loose a haire, or have a bullet fly between his Armes but hee shall have a Page to wait on him in quarto, no thing destroyes 'em but want of a good memory, for if they escape contradiction they may be chronicled.

By comparison, Lushington's comment was mild:

This week the Spanish Match goes forward, and Bethem Gabor's troops are broken; and the next week Bethem Gabor's troops go forward, the Spanish match is broken . . . they cross and counter each others News . . . False news follows true at the Heels, and oftentimes outstrips it.[49]

Printed news was not official, not traditionally ritual, not socially honour-able, but commercial, vulgar and, perhaps most damagingly, anonymous.[50] In defence, editorial notices repeated reassurances that everything came from recognised sources, publications and letters from reputable writers. Gainsford also aimed to give readers enough information to form a view for themselves on what might be believed. Thus, for example, the issue of 12 May 1623 included a report that Brunswick had a successful encounter with Cordoba but with a note:

The newes is possible: but fearing that it may be but made Newes to put a Tricke upon us, that when the Truth comes, we may not know how to believe it, we will not make a Tempest of an uncertaine businesse to no end. Desiring our Readers in the meane time, to expect either the Confirmation or the Confutation of it.[51]

Gainsford explained his approach to rumours:

I thinke it not unfit to resolve a question which was lately made unto mee, viz. wherefore I would publish any tydings which were only rumoured without any certainty: I will answer, that I doe it to shew both my love and diligence to the impartiall Reader. And that I rather write true tidings only to be rumoured, when I am not full sure of them, then to write false tidings to bee true, which will afterwards prove otherwise.

Truth could not be kept from the readers indefinitely: if they were misled, he was answerable. If he felt sure, he told readers. For example, in the issue of 2 May 1623, he reported agreement between Mansfeld, the king of France, Savoy and Venice for the relief of the Val Telline with the assurance that 'wee have received them, from very good intelligence'. There are clear details about the numbers of men, horses and the sums of money involved

[49] J. Shirley *The Schoole of Complement* (1631), Act I, I; Lushington's sermon, *The Resur-rection Rescued from the Soldiers Calumnies*, quoted in J. Raymond, *Pamphlets*, 147.
[50] Randall, *Credibility*, 86–7.
[51] (12 May 1623), 10, 12, 18, STC18507.110.

from each party but the scheme came to nothing. Disappointments like these helped to feed the mistrust of enthusiastic Protestant readers who were hoping for a better turn of events. Still Gainsford persisted in his efforts: in the issue of 12 May 1624 he explained,

> I know that the one Letter makes mention of more or lesse slaine then the other, but they doe not marvell at this, seeing that commonly after all conflicts the number of the dead are increased or diminished as men are drawn by their affections, or otherwise guesse, for it happens many times, that the just number cannot be knowne at first, before it be found out how many escaped by flight.

He frequently warned people to be cautious about accepting a report simply because the news seemed good and recommended they wait until reports were confirmed. Readers learned and checking the facts became a common-place activity with many reading the news, seeking the truth as part of their search for a greater Truth of Divine will.[52]

There are also examples of times when, far from inventing news, news-books simply told the readers that there was nothing new. Responding in June 1623 to a rumour in London of conspiracy against Mansfeld, Gainsford replied 'of this we confesse that we have seen nothing'. On 12 March 1624, there was also a statement that 'there is no newes to acquaint you' (of the Low Countries).[53] However, the editor needed to ensure that issues filled the right number of sheets of paper. As paper was expensive a lengthy issue would mean charging a higher price to cover costs. Equally, empty pages at the end were wasteful. So the practice of using what was available, even if doubtful or repetitious, continued. Sometimes there was so much good material available that the editor was able to say 'the Letters and Dutch Corantos are come so thick into our hands this weeke, that we can spare you no wast paper if we would', and in July 1624 Gainsford claimed, 'Reader I cannot let the have the Letters of the Truce for want of roome, untill next weeke'.[54]

The last page or two of newsbooks often included news arriving at the last moment (a sort of 'stop press'), or it could be filled with odds and ends, 'Other such broken stuffe we have, which we think not fit to trouble you with the reading for that we believe you have not so much leasure to trouble yourselves with the remembring, and this that we doe, we doe rather to fill up a blanke page, than to stuffe out a Booke.' When there was little to report they made the best of what they had. The issue of 12 March 1624 was padded with fairly unnecessary explanation and several similar reports on the same topic and led to complaints. These were duly countered the

52 (3 July 1624), 1–2, STC18507.149; (2 May 1623), 17 STC18507.108; (12 May 1624), 4, STC18507.148; (12 May 1623), 8, 12, STC18507.110; Levy, 33; Atherton, 45–7.
53 (10 June 1623), 14, STC18507.114; (12 March 1624), 1, 3, 9, 15, STC18507.144.
54 (15 January 1624), verso, STC18507.139; (3 July 1624), end, STC18507.149.

following week with a complaint about readers asking them 'every day for new Newes'.[55]

On 16 April 1625, Mead reported that he saw a newsbook with 'a Catalogue of I know not how many men to be raised in Spaine in the severall provinces thereof above 100 thousand but I suppose it is but a bragg or at most but a story of what ... each province could afford if need were'. Then on 28 May, 'I send you a Corrant but the most part of the news is elder then the 2 last told us of. Thus the naves plague us.'[56] Repetition was common and not to be confused with invention: there is extensive evidence of caution. Recycling old news ceased to be a problem: after a feast of news in the early 1630s, the compendiums of news in the mid-1630s were sufficiently infrequent to appear only when there was sufficient material, though, of course, the longer the gap the more dated some of the earlier content by the time it was printed. In the 1640s news periodicals had ample domestic and foreign news and could choose how much space to dedicate to news from overseas.

Evidence of the value readers placed on information about sources was provided when more radical modification of the format was attempted in the autumn of 1623, eliminating references to the letters themselves. It was explained,

> I will promise you in a manner the whole business of Europe the last moneth of October: now you must consider that what extractions wee have, are out of Letters, peradventure of a whole moneths antiquity, so that though we expose to your view the 7 or 8 of November, yet are the actions of former date, and so to avoid breakings off, and fractions of matter, I will not precisely name either the Letters, or the time of their mission: Let it suffice that you know we were not eye-witnesses of the businesse but we must trust other mens relations.

There were no datelines in this issue, but topic headings such as 'The State of Spinola's Army' and 'The Affairs of Holland'. It is easier than usual to spot text throughout that appears to have been inserted in London, for example, he asked why good men are 'sometimes afflicted' and later commented, 'I had not thought to have published any Newes out of Italy at all, because there is nothing there befitting my Advertisement, or pertinent to our inquirie'. The public response was evidently sharp. In the next issue the editor replied bitterly about readers 'finding faults'. 'If we afford you plaine stuffe, you complaine of the phrase, and peradventure cry out, it is Nonsense; if wee adde some exornation, then you are curious to examine the method and coherence, and are forward in saying the sentences are not well adapted.' Instead of datelines, in this issue he noted the origin of letters

---

[55] (17 April 1623), STC18507.105; (12 March 1624), STC18507.144; (19 March 1624), 1, STC18507.145, quoted p. 118.
[56] Harl. MS 389 fo. 424, 448.

in the margin in some places and a few key subheadings such as 'From the Hage, with Letters from Amsterdam', while keeping to the new structure.[57]

This argument rumbled on into a December editorial where he acknowledged, 'Fame hath plaid a womans part, and rumour hath exposed unto you, as many lies as tongues, so that if you looke truly upon her, shee hath a deformed visage, but yet will show you rather a ridiculous face, then an affrighting countenance.' He would, however, keep going because 'there are judicious men, and temperate spirits to be satisfied'. He then listed ten topics he would deal with in turn.[58] It was business as usual and clearly what readers preferred. They had difficulty enough trusting the reports when their dates and places of origin were mentioned. It was too much to ask, that they 'must trust other mens relations'. They did not. However, with some encouragement, Gainsford continued on 13 December,

> Gentle reader.... Now because the last Methode I used was acceptable unto you, and the orderly setting downe of the business got the start of opinion and prevented rash censure concerning devices, and partiall invention, I will still keepe myselfe within the same limitation, and so desiring your pardon, if I doe not precisely name the date of the letters or the parties to whom they were missive: I will proceede to give you the same satisfaction which you yourselves confesse, you received by the former.[59]

The art of news editing was being learned quickly and it was a two-way process. There was a direct link with the reading public through the bookshops from which many customers obtained copies. There was 'over the counter', regular and spontaneous feedback on the material. Editors responded, leaving evidence of a continuous and sometimes heated dialogue. This exchange appears to have cleared the air and determined a method that was to outlive its creator.

Randall has looked at ways readers could assess credibility for themselves, for example, from a detailed oral account from a known witness, news of ritual celebrations and thanksgivings for victories, checking dates and waiting for confirmations. Comparison techniques can still be applied today: Schumacher compared events with reports and concluded that, on the whole, 'the news was rarely completely false ... the news was usually worth reading and provided Englishmen with a fairly accurate picture of events'. However, he noted that in 1623 the Protestant leaning of the newsbooks created the impression that Brunswick was conducting a successful campaign when in fact his successful minor skirmishes were completely cancelled out by his defeat at Stadtlohn. Other errors included the desti-

---

[57] (11 November 1623), 1, 6, 12, 21, STC18507.132; (20 November 1623), 1, STC18507.133.
[58] (11 December 1623), 1–2, STC18507.135.
[59] (13 December 1623), 1, STC18507.136.

nation of Argyle's troops in 1622 and a report that Tilly and Pappenheim had been killed in May 1622. Both were corrected in the following weeks. Spinola was reported to be leaving his command in March 1623, but this too was subsequently corrected. He concluded that 'considering the frailties of seventeenth-century communications, letter writers did a good job of getting the news to readers quickly and accurately'. Moreover, readers 'were made to feel they knew and understood what was happening in Germany'.[60]

Readers learned that reports of major events arrived in London over several weeks and that later reports could confirm with further detail, but accuracy and truth remained a major source of potential difficulty. Debate with readers flared up in August 1631. An editorial on 2 September, that may have been penned by Butter, given its intemperate language and use of 'we' and 'our', referred back to the disputed reports of the king of Sweden's victories over Tilly and responded with the defence that these were printed 'as wee received them from forreine parts ... without addition or subtraction'. The publishers felt they,

> deserved a more favourable construction from the most malevolently affected, yet from some it could receive no better approbation than that all was lyes, and that the King of Sweden was kild, or taken Prisoner, and his Army utterly defeated, as at this houre some shame not impudently to maintaine both here, and beyond the sea at Antwerp, Bruxels, and else-where. Wherefore wee doe now publish ... a confirmation of the Truth thereof with some circumstances not in our former, and against which, let the most barking curre open his mouth.[61]

Watts was tripped up early in his news-editing career by a report from Frankfurt that Tilly had been killed at Breitenfeld and was naive enough at that stage to defend the report, perhaps because of its somewhat convincing level of detail.

> Indifferent Reader, we promist you (in the front of our last Aviso) the Death and Internment of Monsieur Tilly, which we now performe: notwithstanding the last Antwerpian Post hath rumoured the contrary, against which you may balance each other, and accordingly believe: onely wee will propose one question unto all gaine-sayers, let them demonstrate where Tilly is and that great formidable Army which he hath raised and we will all be of the Catholike faith.[62]

As the confusion and rumour over Tilly's death illustrated, although Watts had more material at his disposal, correspondents continued to be unsure of the facts. Thus a Protestant in Prague wrote, 'we can seldome understand the certainty of things here, where all is related as the Imperialists will have

---

[60] Randall, *Credibility*, 24–30, 68–9; Schumacher, 76–8.
[61] (2 September 1631), verso of title page, STC18507.221.
[62] (20 October 1631), verso, STC18507.227; Dahl, 182; Randall, *Credibility*, 25–6.

it. But we perceive so much by their lookes and behaviours, that their last newes are not so good.' From Wimpfen another correspondent admitted, 'I can tell you no certain newes out of Bohemia, for some say and write one thing, some another'. However, Watts assessed the validity of reports and was open about uncertainties. In August 1632, he was willing to believe news that Pappenheim has been defeated at Maestricht, 'it is very probable (and letters from Lille and other places doe import no lesse out of very apparent circumstances) ... and advices ... yesterday doe confirm the same'. He improved accounts when more information became available but he also expected a high level of sophistication from his readers to compare texts and even to hold onto back issues for that purpose, inviting readers in August 1632 to compare the new text with a declaration and letters in an issue printed nearly two months earlier.[63]

However, with the benefit of more time to gather and assess information Watts could provide a greater quality assurance in *The Swedish Intelligencer*. He was able to claim he,

> trusted no written Relations, unlesse received from a knowne hand, or confirmed by personall eye, or eare-witnesse. No, I have not singly relyed, so much as upon that diligent ambassador of the Dutch Currantoes, the Gallobelgicus ... where I differ from [the French publication] I report me to those who have read both, and have been personally present in actions ... nor doe I professe myselfe to be other [than] ... the disposer of other mens materials, at my best value. I am Author of nothing, here, but of the mistakings.... If I have made my Readers wait.... I only staid, till false rumours might be contradicted, true reports, brought home to me by men present; and the passions of people a little over.

He knew this to be a counsel of perfection appropriate only for a publication that could take weeks to appear. Even so, by the summer of 1632 he was sufficiently confident that he made issues of reliability a selling feature and included on the title page, *The true state of the armies ... somewhat contradicting our last ... but plainly & truly nullifying that groundlesse report spread abroad, concerning a great defeat (and what not) of the King of Sweden and his armies*. Watts became proud of what he accomplished and defended newsbooks vigorously 'which if a man of judgement reads, he shall for the most part finde (especially those of latter times) very true, and very punctuall. Whosoever will be cunning in the Places and Persons of Germany, and would understand these warres, let him not despise Currantoes.'[64]

Watts resigned after completing Part 4 of the *Swedish Intelligencer*, though his account, reporting the conveyance of Gustavus's body to the Baltic,

---

[63] (23 August 1632), title page, STC18507.264; Dahl, 210; (3 August 1632), title page, STC18507.262; Dahl, 207; Schumacher, 199–233; (12 January 1632), 7, STC18507.237.
[64] *The Swedish Intelligencer*, Part 3 (1633), 2–5; (13 August 1632), title page, STC18507.263; *The Swedish Intelligencer*, Part 1 (1632), 4–5.

appeared in the next issue. He was responding to continuing interest and need for a definitive account. Conflicting reports from correspondence, imported news, and a witness (Dalbier, paymaster to Count Mansfield), meant that in December people were betting on whether Gustavus Adolphus was truly dead. Watts's sure hand supplied every last detail, even to where the coffin was made and who attended.[65]

Truth and accuracy were issues set to run and run as readers actively sought to separate truth from falsehood. Learning how to interpret the printed word and assess its credibility is a skill. Seeing how the editorial approach was modified issue by issue over a period, we have a privileged insight into the relationship and its evolution. Editorial comment gives information about readers and writers and was, at times, part heated disputes. Gainsford's responses to readers revealed a largely Protestant readership with keen enquiring minds, not to be fobbed off with inconclusive or incomprehensible reports. Failure to 'edit out' personal addresses and comments was sufficiently frequent to indicate that these were left because they gave a flavour of authenticity that was more important than literary skill or tidiness. But even when Gainsford was at the height of his editing career newsbooks contained much that was repetitious, or included with the caveat that it was rumour. This weakened trust, even though he explained the factors that affected reliability. The majority of reports were broadly accurate, and errors were soon corrected.

Watts and subsequent editors had an easier time, with more material and a more sophisticated readership that had developed an understanding in the 1620s or grown up with printed news. Watts appears to have had every confidence in the ability of readers to digest the news and discern the truth. His successors in the 1630s addressed an educated elite and were content to challenge them to find more accurate news if they could.

Getting the news from close to home in the 1640s did not resolve truth and accuracy concerns however. These were among the issues aired in a battle in print fought between Parliament and Royalists. Accusations of lies and slanders spread to parliamentary debate, and D'Ewes voiced exasperation that 'the very truth must not be published on either side'. In the midst of this, Butter compared his (by this stage much diminished) publication favourably with the competition. In the title, *A little true forraine newes: better than a great deale of domestick spurious false newes*, he claimed the higher ground, but others did not agree. John Cleveland's *Character of a London Diurnall*, in 1645, attacked all London newsbooks as the descendants of *Gallobelgicus*, including *Mercurius Civicus*, which was among those including continental news in their coverage. His spelling of 'Britannicus' was possibly accidental. (Two 'n's' were used by Butter and Bourne's 1625–7 publications and this had no direct connection with the 1640 series called

---

[65] *The Continuation*, Part 5 (1633), A3 recto, A2; *CandT*, 2:202–6, 210–12.

Mercurius Britanicus and *Anti-Britanicus*.) However, it suggests he was making a deliberate link between the old and the new, accusing them all of reporting lies. Similarly in the same year *The Great Assises* accused domestic and foreign news alike of reporting lies.[66]

However, the existence of a range of competing periodical newsbooks in the emerging news market meant readers could more easily make their own comparisons. Raymond has shown how the earl of Leicester compared news-books and provides evidence of many correspondents through the 1640s passing on newsbooks to men and women outside London and even as far afield as Paris, Brussels and the Colonies without criticism of the content, by implication demonstrating a belief that their recipients would find the content interesting and serviceable. By contrast, John Squier, vicar of St Leonards, Shoreditch, received and closely read and annotated news while imprisoned in Newgate. Connor has described his reading as 'a battlefield of correction, denial and repudiation' focused exclusively on domestic and Church issues, rather than the events of the wars either at home or abroad.[67]

In the Civil Wars, readers found that truth could be stretched and victo-ries embellished even with domestic news. Evidence could be presented selectively and mistakes could be made, particularly when reporting the outcome of battles. There were often as many difficulties in determining the truth when the engagement took place on English soil as overseas. Peacey has acknowledged the enthusiasm with which contemporaries consumed the news and the way readers learned about faction, parliamen-tary procedures and practice in the process. He concluded that 'pamphlets and newsbooks … were remarkably accurate in their analysis'. This may be an optimistic view, especially in relation to pamphlets and tracts, but, as we have seen, periodicity placed publishers under a discipline of responsibility towards their readership. Continuity required them to be more mindful of their relationships with their news suppliers and the authorities. O'Hara, who compared the reporting in London of Irish affairs in pamphlets and the periodical press of the 1640s, found the latter consistently more restrained. Raymond, pursuing the relationship between readers and their chosen peri-odicals, explored marginalia of the 1640s for readers' responses and revealed close and attentive reading that 'must change the way we perceive not only these readers but the newsbooks themselves'.[68]

---

[66] Cressy, *England on Edge*, 298–9, 302; (Mid January 1642), WingL2553, quoted in Dahl, 262; Raymond, 210, 216–7, 221–2.

[67] Raymond, 246–64; T. P. Connor, 'Malignant Reading: John Squier's Newgate Prison Library, 1642–6', *The Library*, 7:2 (2006), 164, 173.

[68] Raymond, 264–8; Peacey, *Politicians*, 239, 242–3, 245; D. A. O'Hara, *English Newsbooks and the Irish Rebellion, 1641–1649* (Dublin, 2006), 38–9, 47, 54; J. Peacey, 'Perceptions of Parliament: Factions and "The Public"', in *The English Civil War*, ed. J. Adamson (Basingstoke, 2009), 99–104.

Conclusions

Returning to Gainsford's claim to have 'got the start of opinion', we might ask to what extent we can discern evidence of the bookshop emerging as an early public sphere where public opinion was shaped through discussion and debate. Blanning has argued that Habermas's bourgeois public sphere is not rooted in class identity, but a bit like Noah's Ark with a meritocratic nature, socially heterogeneous and politically multi-directional, a space for all kinds of opinions. Jonson, without the benefit of Habermas's terminology, commented on a shift away from the theatre and on a fundamental change in society where everyone had an opportunity to engage in public debate. From *Bartholomew Fair* through *The Devil is an Ass* to *The Staple of News* he explored the role of the theatre audience and compared this with that of the readers of news. He blurred the demarcation between stage and auditorium, and public discussion became part of the performance. In *The Staple of News* the audience moved onto the stage and the action moved into the news office.[69]

Readership in the early 1620s and 1630s included a broad band of readers able to follow the news. They differed from Jonson's depiction of them in one key respect: they were not undiscerning and if, when they began to read, they were ignorant this did not last. The debate recorded here is about news reports as products, truth, reporting and allegiance, not high politics, nor strategy, but this change in the reach of printed news had a profound political impact. It began a process of politicising a broader range of people and giving them a degree of confidence in their understanding of major war events. The next step, to involvement in domestic politics, as witnessed in the 1640s, was almost bound to follow. Cressy wrote of 'a reading revolution that built its own audience ... within an energised public sphere'.[70] In Jonson's extended dramatic conceit, his mixed audience took to the stage.

---

[69] (13 December 1623), 1, STC18507.136; T. C. W. Blanning, *The Culture of Power and the Power of Culture: Old Regime Europe 1660–1789* (Oxford, 2002), 12; McKenzie, 171–5.
[70] Cressy, *England on Edge*, 425.

Part Three

News and its Political Implications

7

James I and Sir Francis Cottington

Sales of newsbooks were high in the early 1620s making this a valued market the publishers were determined to retain. They respected the censorship constraints placed upon them and did what they could to ensure they printed only what 'is thoroughly examin[ed and pri]nted according to the high or low Dutch [printed c]opies, or out of Letters of the best credit fro[m beyond]d the Seas'.[1] Success in periodical publication necessitated an effective working relationship with the Crown. Initially, this was through Cottington who, as James I's licenser, needed to consider the political implications of these publications in a time of complex international diplomacy and growing Protestant concern that reached a watershed with the embarkation of Charles and Buckingham for Madrid. After Charles and Buckingham returned, the relationship between the Crown and the syndicate needed to adapt to the changing political context; the prospect of war with Spain, Cottington's withdrawal from Court, and the initiation of negotiations for a marriage alliance with France.

In managing the foreign news press, James demonstrated, as with so many other things, an apparent inconsistency of the sort that has encouraged historians to repeat the remark attributed to Henry IV of France that he was 'the wisest fool in Christendom'. Between 1620 and 1622, James had made a steadily more concerted effort to stem public debate and speculation. This culminated in the proclamation of July 1621. Yet control was not draconian: as Fritz Levy noted, James was in practice more generous than his predecessors in allowing news. His approach was neither simplistic nor absolute, but was pragmatic and balanced. He allowed the trade to continue, but appointed Cottington, who understood his foreign policy and diplomatic relations with Spain, to license foreign news.[2]

The popular image of James as a king who was learned and scholarly, yet whose political judgments were poor, is undergoing revision. Scottish historians have pointed to his success in Scotland and there has been a re-examination of his record in the management of ecclesiastical affairs and

---

[1] (14 September 1622), 21, STC18507.77; (4 October 1622), 17, STC18507.81.
[2] K. Sharpe, *The Personal Rule of Charles I* (New Haven, CT and London, 1992), 152, on Cottington's judgment as a diplomat; Levy, 13, 17, 31–4.

of foreign policy. He has been shown by Fincham and Lake to have successfully reformed a number of abuses in the Church and enforced conformity,
while maintaining a degree of flexibility and scope for compromise. He
steered a middle course, distinguishing between moderates and radicals
among papists and puritans. Their verdict now is that he did well to maintain harmony for as long as he did in the face of considerable challenges.
Patterson, meanwhile, depicts James as 'shrewd, determined, flexible, and a
resourceful political leader who had a coherent plan for religious pacifica-
tion', was wholeheartedly committed to church unity and who achieved a
great deal with little physical force. James maintained balance in the Church
through strategic appointments, prepared his bishops carefully for the Synod
of Dort, forged alliances across Europe and became a respected European
peacemaker, served by a remarkably able corps of diplomats.[3] Was Cottington's appointment consistent with this interpretation and a shrewd move,
supportive of James's wider objectives of securing a diplomatic solution to
the conflict in Bohemia and the Palatinate? How far did this appointment
work domestically? Was the appointment an example of resourceful and
moderate political leadership or little more than an ineffective compromise?

James's attitude towards news publication corresponded with his attitude
towards the publication of state information generally. He displayed sensitivity to criticism of himself, his family and other governments and was quick
to suppress individual publications that offended, responding sympathetically to complaints of foreign ambassadors; and he was particularly protective of the sensitivities of Gondomar, the Spanish ambassador.[4] In 1614,
George Wither spent four months in prison for writing *Abuses Stript and
Whipt* for offending Henry Howard, the earl of Northampton, a supporter
of a Spanish marriage. In 1624, James commanded the alteration of verses
written for a masque which criticised the Spanish, while the proclamations
of 1620–1 were attempts to stem the upsurge of interest in foreign news,
but also responses to verbal attacks on Gondomar, the Spanish ambassador.[5]

Repeated proclamations against 'licentious speech' and the control
James exerted over the pulpit in 1622–3 seem to indicate an authoritarian
approach. Yet, as Tanner remarked, 'James himself did not press his own

---

[3] J. Wormald, 'James VI and I: Two Kings or One?', *History*, 68 (1983); K. Fincham and
P. Lake, 'The Ecclesiastical Policy of King James I', *JBS*, 24 (1985), 169–207; K. Fincham
and P. Lake, 'The Ecclesiastical Policies of James I and Charles I', in *The Early Stuart
Church 1603–1642*, ed. K. Fincham (1993); Patterson, ix, 3, 20, 264, 271, 198, 295–6;
K. Sharpe, *Image Wars; Promoting Kings and Commonwealths in England, 1603–1660* (New
Haven, CT and London, 2010), 117–23.

[4] C. S. Clegg, *Press Censorship in Jacobean England* (Cambridge, 2001), 178, concern for
the reputation of his mother, Mary Queen of Scots, 92–6, and the duke of Savoy, 180–1;
G. Redworth, *The Prince and the Infanta* (New Haven, CT, , 2003), 13–15, 30–1, 35–6,
45–8.

[5] Clegg, *Jacobean England*, 114, 163, 177; S. Lambert, 'Coranto Printing in England',
JNandPH, 8 (1992), 7.

premises to their logical conclusion'.[6] He presented his view of the international situation in his opening speech to the Parliament of 1621, where he expressed his great regret that the peace he had maintained for 18 years was now threatened and the Palatinate in danger of falling. In November 1621, when the collapse of the Palatinate seemed imminent, James invited Digby to explain what had happened on his summer embassy to Vienna. So, while he objected to the publication of matters of state for the 'vulgar multitude', he was willing to expose his statesmanship and invite discussion in Parliament despite the House of Commons' consternation that he was trying to interfere with their right of free speech. In addition, he and his officials sponsored numerous publications justifying and presenting his policies. Titles from the presses of the king's printer include *His Majesties Speach in the Upper House of Parliament the 26 of March 1621* and *His Majesties declaration touching his proceedings in the late Assemblie ... of Parliament.* And in 1618 he published a panegyric to peace, celebrating his achievements as a peacemaker.[7]

However, James remained protective of his authority and careful about news in circulation immediately prior to sessions of Parliament. He preferred a personal presentation of the facts in each of the Houses of Parliament to an earlier appeal in print, and he combined this silence with the appropriate measures to frustrate attempts by the opposition to publish anti-Spanish propaganda. Buckingham explained James's method in a letter of 19 October 1620 to Francis Bacon, after the king rejected his first draft of the proclamation for summoning Parliament: 'he findeth a great deal more containing matter of state and the reason of calling Parliament whereof neither the people are capable, nor is it fit for his Majesty to open now unto them, but to reserve, to the time of their assembling'. The emphasis is on timing, complexity and the mode of communication.[8] It was a cautious and coherent approach necessitated by the fact that, with the collapse of his pacific foreign policy, the question of what to do next was difficult to answer.

Simon Adams, in his study of the Parliaments of 1621 and 1624, argued that the Crown's proposals 'were either militarily, politically, or financially absurd', but there were no easy options. In January 1621, James appointed

---

[6] J. R. Tanner, *English Constitutional Conflicts of the Seventeenth Century* (Cambridge, 1966), 20.

[7] D. Colclough, *Freedom of Speech in Early Stuart England* (Cambridge, 2005), 136, 168–9; R. E. Ruigh, *The Parliament of 1624* (Cambridge, MA, 1971), 157. *His Majesties Speach ... March 1621* (1621), STC14399; *His Majesties declaration touching ... the late Assemblie ... of Parliament* (1621), STC14377 and 9241; Patterson, 305–06, 309, 296 quotes from James I, *The Peace-Maker: or, Great Brittaines Blessing* (1619), STC14387; Sharpe, *Image Wars*, 17, 28–42, 46.

[8] J. Spedding, R. L. Ellis and D. D. Heath, ed., *The Works of Francis Bacon*, 14 (1874), 128.

a council of war to compute the size and expense of an army strong enough to defend the Palatinate. The figures seemed to rule out this option and continued to make him cautious in 1624. The indirect approach of a diversionary, naval war against Spain was to attract considerable attention in both Parliaments but was a gamble that would rely on the success of Protestant allies in Germany. The alternative, diplomatic route lacked popular appeal and was difficult to justify given Spain's support for their Habsburg cousins and occupation of the Palatinate.[9] It seems James never fully comprehended the unpopularity of negotiations with Spain. His adherence to this option meant that, almost to the end of his reign, there was a continuing problem with handling the press. His proclamations in the early 1620s and increasing controls over the press reflect his failure to convince Parliament that a naval war against Spain was not the way to save the Palatinate. When the House of Commons set down views on foreign policy that were substantially different from his own, his reaction was firm and uncompromising. He replied, 'We wish you to remember that we are an old and experienced King, needing no such Lessons, being in our conscience the freest of any King alive.' But his assurance that he would 'labour, by all Means possible, either by Treaty or by Force, to restore Our Children to their ancient Dignities', and his explanation that the issue in Germany was not one of religion but due to Frederick's 'hasty and rash Resolution ... to take himself the Crown of Bohemia' did not sufficiently reassure MPs, nor stop discussion.[10]

The decision to license foreign newsbooks may have been influenced by awareness that, if publication were successfully banned in London, the Dutch could resume their export trade to the English market.[11] However, at this stage, James may well have been optimistic about both his ability to sway opinion in his favour and to control the press through an astute licenser. His pacific foreign policy had proved successful for many years. It had made him a widely admired figure in the Protestant community and brought him closer to securing peace in Europe, even after White Mountain, than most observers have recognised. Buoyed by the success of soundings from the Spanish in 1620, James had persuaded Frederick to withdraw completely from Bohemia and wait in Silesia until April 1621, while he embarked on a new round of negotiations in 1621 in a bid to spare the Palatinate.[12] Such success may also have led him to hope that if people

9   S. L. Adams, 'Foreign Policy and the Parliaments of 1621 and 1624', in *Faction and Parliament in Early Stuart History*, ed. K. Sharpe (Oxford, 1978), 139, 149–50, 160, 162.
10   E. Nicholas, *Proceedings and Debates of the House of Commons in 1620 and 1621* (Oxford, 1766), 318–33; D. Hirst, *England in Conflict 1603–1660, Kingdom, Community, Conflict* (1999), 103–04, 106.
11   Frearson, 200, 232, 240, 245; M. C. Frearson, 'London Corantos in the 1620s', in *Annual* (1993), 7–8; Clegg, *Jacobean England*, 85, 168–9, 176.
12   S. Lambert, 'Richard Montagu, Arminianism and Censorship', *PandP*, 124 (1989),

were acquainted with the facts of the military theatre of war in central and northern Europe (if not the significance of diplomatic negotiations), they might better understand his point of view. Reports of the war, if based on information (which would in any event come out sooner or later), could potentially help reduce speculation and lead to more realistic discussion. News reports could also support recruitment: Sir Andrew Gray began raising troops in London and Scotland in April 1620 to march to Bohemia. Sir Horace Vere set out shortly after, and a stream of volunteers continued to enlist to serve in the Dutch army and in the Palatinate for the remainder of James's reign.[13] Anything reported needed careful scrutiny to ensure that it stayed clear of Spanish sensitivities, given their central role in his plans for negotiating peace. The risk must have seemed manageable. He saw the Spanish position as divided over events in Bohemia and did not expect them to seek suppression of accurate news reports, so long as the reports were about what was happening in Bohemia and the Palatinate and were not critical of the Spanish government, its minister and policies. Cottington's job was to manage this risk.

Cottington's contribution

To Clegg, the appointment of Cottington marked an important shift in press control and 'represents the government's first major effort to "license" printing'. She has refuted Lambert's argument that it was simply due to the fact that clerical licensers were unable to cope with demand and depicted Cottington's service as a government effort to control news as a gesture to conciliate Gondomar. Clegg argued that licensed news published between 1621 and 1625 was 'markedly different' from what was published without licence or entry in the register of the Company of Stationers and contrasted them with A briefe description of the Ban made against the King of Bohemia, which led to the imprisonment of Edward Aldee and Thomas Archer, and which frequently returned to the role of Spain against Frederick. To her, Cottington's appointment resulted in a change of tone in reporting: newsbooks thereafter contained nothing critical of Spain or attacking the Catholic Church and she suggested that Cottington's surveillance clarified for printers what was dangerous and what could be published. Similarly, Frearson has argued that Cottington's presence curbed criticism of

36–53; Patterson, 124, 295–9, 306, 363; G. Parker, ed., The Thirty Years' War (London, Boston, MA and Melbourne, 1984/1997), 51–5; J. V. Polisensky, 'A Note on Scottish Soldiers in the Bohemian War 1619–1622', in Scotland and the Thirty Years' War, 1618–1648, ed. S. Murdoch (Leiden and Boston, MA, 2001), 113.
[13] M. C. Fissel, English Warfare, 1511–1641 (London and New York, 2001), 78, 90, 256, 271; P. H. Wilson, Europe's Tragedy: A History of the Thirty Years' War (2009), 321–2; Polisensky, 'A Note', 111.

the government's foreign policy.[14] Nonetheless, licensing by Cottington got off to a weak start from October 1621 to September 1622. A more careful approach was apparent only once the syndicate was formed and Gainsford given responsibilities to help them to avoid including troublesome material. As we have seen, Gainsford openly acknowledged the need to satisfy the authorities. He wrote about only including in the newsbooks what 'is allowable' and 'such things as are fitting for you to know and for me to relate' and which he 'dare justify in London'.[15] He frequently took care to make clear when he was copying verbatim from Dutch originals. He also showed how he was aiming to arrive at the truth.[16]

The result was a discernable change in the newsbooks, with more Catholic sources used when Cottington was in the country. However, there were many other factors influencing newsbook content: Gainsford did not edit every issue between the summers of 1622 and 1624 and, when he did, the news sources he was working with were full of reports of the Habsburg advances made in this period. Whether penned by Protestants or Catholics, these could be alarming to an English reader, so the impact of Cottington's oversight and Gainsford's editing was muted, and it would be a mistake to overemphasise government influence.

On 15 October 1622, just after Cottington arrived in England, the publishers produced a newsbook based on Spanish material. Possibly this issue arrived with Cottington and his entourage. But by the following issue the material was once again from Protestant sources and the issue of 22 October included praise for the Protestant armies while that of 30 October expressed hopes of a Protestant success. Those of 16 and 21 November were also Protestant in their sympathies. But then, in January 1623, while Cottington was still in the country, all the issues included material that was clearly from Catholic sources. In the issue of 31 January, Gainsford expressed caution over the use of those sources, quite possibly in response to criticism from readers. Part of Cottington's role may, therefore, have been to support a balance of reporting, encouraging the use of news from Antwerp. He also encouraged a moderate editorial tone. We see a similar pattern in May 1623, after Cottington returned to England: first there was an issue from Catholic sources where Gainsford expressed a qualification about whether reports could be trusted. The issues of 17 and 26 May contain news sympathetic to Spain, but by the end of the month Gainsford again criticised the emperor and included a report of Spanish soldiers pillaging.[17]

[14] Clegg, *Jacobean England*, 181–3; Frearson, 'London Corantos', 12–14; Frearson, 254–63.

[15] (4 October 1622), 17, STC18507.81; (11 December 1623), 14, STC18507.135; Chapters 5 and 6 above.

[16] (20 April 1624), 8, STC18507.147; Frearson, 200.

[17] (22 October 1622), STC18507.84; (30 October 1622), STC18507.85; (16 November 1622), STC18507.89; (21 November 1622), STC18507.90; (31 January 1623),

Cottington's role was not to oppose or edit out main Protestant sources, nor to suppress the expression of hopes for securing Frederick's hereditary lands. James and his people shared a considerable degree of common ground in their aspirations for a fair settlement to the troubles in central Europe. Cottington had acquainted the king of Spain from the outset that James was concerned that those who had taken arms in Bohemia had done so to prevent a massacre because of their religion, and Buckingham wrote to Gondomar that James was committed to do all in his power to resolve the Bohemian problem peaceably. James had reacted swiftly with embassies to Germany and the emperor intended to support Frederick through a peaceful settlement that secured the Palatinate. Negotiations were intense, complex and sensitive. Digby's visit to Brussels in early March 1621 secured an agreement with Archduke Albert to recommend a truce in the Palatinate to the Spanish government in anticipation of the ending of the Twelve Year Truce between Spain and the United Provinces, but Philip III died late in March and Albert in July. Villiers attempted to persuade Frederick to accept James's strategy while Chaworth approached Archduchess Isabella.[18] When the Palatinate was close to collapse, James called Parliament for supplies to defend the Palatinate. Digby explained to Parliament the hopes for peace but Parliament wanted war with Spain, a Protestant marriage and stronger action against Catholics at home. The differences were about how to protect the Palatinate and Spain's role rather than the goal. James and Cottington knew that Spain might not be completely committed to supporting Ferdinand given the costs that could entail.[19] However, Parliament could not know this. Its members never saw Spain as a genuine potential ally and at no point was James in a position to spell out the Spanish position since to do so would risk embarrassing Spain, thereby undermining the very agreement he aimed to secure.

Unable to fully expose his position, James instead did what he could to control information about the conflict being published. Employing Cottington with an insider's knowledge of the diplomatic situation was to ensure that nothing inappropriate or offensive to potential allies would be said about his diplomatic efforts while these remained in the balance. Throughout 1622, the public and Parliament remained ignorant of the progress James made diplomatically since this progress was negated by military leaders acting independently. Readers learned instead of the fall

---

STC18507.95; (12 May 1623), 12, STC18507.110; (17 May 1623), STC18507.111; (26 May 1623), STC18507.112.

[18] Patterson, 306–9, 302; Parker, *Thirty*, 57.

[19] Patterson, 309–19, 299, 301–2, Cottington reported to Lake, 26 September 1618, that though Spain was supporting Ferdinand with 500,000 ducats, there were concerns about the cost and that Philip III was pleased that James was willing to work for peace in Bohemia and would support his efforts in Vienna.

of the Palatinate.[20] A considerable gap was opening up between what was happening visibly, in the public eye through newsbook reports and what may, or may not, have been possible diplomatically. James, through continuing to pursue this strategy and further enforcing silence on diplomatic developments, was protecting Spain from embarrassment, but he was doing so at the cost of his own image.

Factual and reasonably accurate reporting of military activities, of levies, taxation, dearth and starvation were less sensitive than anything about the intent of leaders. James may also have hoped that the newsbooks, by focusing attention primarily on land-based military action, on the disposition of Imperial forces and on activities in Vienna, might help MPs to reach a shared view of where the need for an English military response really lay. If so, then it would be reasonable to conclude that Cottington's licensing was a success both when he was around in person and when he was abroad. However, this conclusion would overlook the fact that beneath the arguments about tactics there were deeper worldview and ideological issues at stake. Johann Sommerville has been criticised for his construction of an ideological map that places opponents into separate camps, overlooking the complexities of views and allegiances. Nevertheless, there were distinct ways of approaching foreign policy. Giving priority to the maintenance of stable monarchical government meant supporting and seeking to work with Spain and France, even though they were Catholic, since they represented social order and monarchical legitimacy. This approach remained the most influential at Court into 1624. There were also moderates at Court and in Parliament who supported Elizabeth and Frederick and who hoped to see Protestantism flourish in Europe, including the earl of Pembroke, Sir Benjamin Rudyerd and the Bedfords, but other Protestant groups were more radical and interpreted events through an apocalyptical conception of history. To them, the acceptance of the Bohemian Crown by Frederick was a step towards the final struggle between the godly and the Antichrist. Recent historians have demonstrated how James steered a middle course by allowing ambiguity and avoiding open debate about potentially fundamental differences, but Kevin Sharpe has pointed to the tensions both within and between texts, ideals, theory and practice, and showed that people did not always act according to their words. Everyone could believe in ideals like universal harmony and 'one true interpretation of God's word' and be basically conservative, yet believe that those who did not share their interpretation were either separatist or Jesuit.[21]

---

[20] The Brussels Conference began with Frederick and Isabella agreeing to a stand off. However, the offensive continued and once Heidelberg fell in September 1622 the emperor began to look for different ways of settling matters, by calling a Diet. Patterson, 312, 318; Wilson, *Europe's Tragedy*, 355.

[21] J. P. Sommerville, *Royalists and Patriots, Politics and Ideology in England 1603–1640*

Newsbooks contributed to ever-increasing discussion of foreign policy outside the formal institutions of government. Whether their content was moderated or not they provided a continual source of information, and by focusing on the more dramatic events and presenting conflict rather than consensus, they helped reinforce the more radical apocalyptic views of the struggle with the papal Antichrist. Seaver's account of the puritan Wallington shows how reading the news, reflecting on its meaning and prayer played an integral part in his spiritual life. He used the news to look for the working out of God's will in public events and interpreted what he read in a way that reinforced his beliefs. Richard Cust and Ann Hughes commented in *Conflict in Early Stuart England*, that the implications of the popular focus on foreign events in the 1620s may not have been fully understood by the revisionists. James seems to have grasped that the widening of public discussion and debate posed a real problem for him and led to the growing challenge to the royal prerogative, making it increasingly difficult for him to maintain control of decision-making on foreign policy. However, it is less likely he could have appreciated the deeper and more long-term impacts of periodical news reporting, read alongside the tracts of writers such as Thomas Scott, or interpreted with the help of puritan preachers, to support the development of a radical Protestant worldview.[22]

The Spanish match

Letting facts stand for themselves was the favoured approach, but had drawbacks. Even at the tactical level, the facts did not always produce an account that supported James. Newsbooks, through the lucrative co-operation of the syndicate and the Crown, could have been used as a vehicle for James to promote his point of view to the public, but instead they exemplified his failure to do so. At no time was this more evident than during the 1623 crisis of the Spanish match. This must go down in the annals of lost news reporting opportunities for both the Crown and publishers.

In February/March 1623 news of two major events was breaking: the one best known to English historians is the news of Charles and Buckingham's trip to Madrid to secure the hand in marriage of the infanta. The other was news of the Arminian conspiracy against the Prince of Orange, which (though posing less of an immediate threat to English puritans), nonetheless appeared to demonstrate that nowhere was entirely safe, not even in

(London and New York, 1999); K. Sharpe, 'Ideas and Politics in Early Stuart England', *History Today*, 38 (1988), 45–51.
22 C. Durston and J. Eales, ed., *The Culture of English Puritanism 1560–1700* (1996), 5–6; R. Cust and A. Hughes, ed., *Conflict in Early Stuart England: Studies in Religion and Politics 1603–42* (1989), 29; P. Lake, 'Constitutional Consensus and Puritan Opposition in the 1620s: Thomas Scott and the Spanish Match', *HJ*, 25 (1982), 805–25.

the heartland of Calvinism, the United Provinces. Yet, just when it would seem the syndicate might be in greatest need of an editor, Gainsford was not employed. Many of the reports, letters and other documents, particularly about the Dutch conspiracy, were published without any editing, while newsbooks maintained complete silence on the Madrid expedition, long after the destination and purpose of the journey were publicly known, up to the return of Charles and Buckingham.

No doubt, news of the conspiracy presented a dilemma for the publishers and for those deputising for Cottington while he travelled to Madrid with the prince. In the absence of information on James's position (which must have been torn between abhorrence for any hint of treason and regrets about the loss of any base for the development of a middle ground in the United Provinces), the syndicate seized the commercial opportunity that the conspiracy news presented. They adopted an old and familiar approach, dispensing with editorial services and printing unedited translations of the official documents. This was the speediest and most commercially viable approach, allowing them to publish issues quickly in large numbers. It was also the most prudent. Cottington's representative evidently concurred. Issues appeared with no editorial comment whatever, neither condemning the treason nor questioning the veracity of reports. Lengthy passages even repeated some of the text in Dutch. The issue of 19 February admitted to muddle:

> The last weeke we received and published certaine private Letters concerning the late intended horrible treasin ... little or nothing was knowne ... but since divers persons have beene apprehended, and some of them examined, and tortured; upon whose examination the States have permitted something to be published to the world ... assuring you, that so soone as more particulars shall come to my hand ... you shall receive it impartially.

But the following issues were little better: on 7 March two issues appeared, *A Proclamation* contains statements and letters about the conspiracy and *The Sentence and Execution* describing 'the abominable, wicked, and barbarous Conspiacie, (as was never heard of the like)'. They were not simply filling up paper: two February issues ran to over forty pages. Possibly they aimed to demonstrate authenticity. Issues then returned to normal with a final piece about one conspirator.[23]

Why did The Hague news sell well just when news was also breaking of Charles's expedition? The reports can only have amplified the sense of

---

[23] Patterson, 263–4, 271–2, 281; Fincham and Lake, 'The Ecclesiastical Policy', 201; (6 February 1623), 102, STC18507.96, (11 February 1623), STC18507.97; (19 February 1623), STC18507.98; (28 February 1623), 30–end, STC18507.99; (7 March 1623), STC18507.100; (7 March 1623), title page STC18507.101; (31 March 1623), STC18507.103.

threat and danger to readers who saw events as interconnected and studied the news for 'signs' of the Divine Plan unfolding while the Crown became ever more deeply embroiled in relations with Spain. The view represented by contemporaries Thomas Scott, James Howell, John Reynolds and others, that Gondomar, the Spanish ambassador 'had been neutralizing the English' with negotiations for a Spanish match for Prince Charles while the Spanish fleet was being reinforced, was suddenly being tested. Whether we concur with Cogswell's view that Charles was right to go because he shortened negotiations and saw for himself that the Spanish were not serious, there can be little question that the step was decisive. Charles and Buckingham broke the deadlock in negotiations, failed to conclude an agreement in Madrid, and set in motion a chain of events that was to carry through into the 1624 Parliament and bring England to war. James understood the risks involved and the extent to which he had lost the initiative. Quite possibly he felt himself at a loss to present these developments publicly in any way that would have been any better received than silence. Whatever his reasons, the undeniable fact is that he did not try, but he continued to meet Spanish ambassadors and raise the German question into 1624.[24]

Cust has described this as a period when the circulation of news became an integral part of the political process, something that those who were making the news had to make allowances for 'which they appreciated could substantially affect public attitudes'. Yet diplomatic discussions remained protected. It was impossible to see how this distinction could be maintained once the whereabouts of Charles and Buckingham were known. Cogswell's study of the sea change in English foreign policy that was precipitated by the trip to Madrid starts from the premise that if historians look only at individual courtiers or at parliamentary affairs they are 'likely to miss the full significance of the domestic turmoil over the Spanish match'. He shows how the clamour against the match had swelled from 1622.[25] Immediately after Charles departed for Spain there was an outbreak of anxious sermons. Thomas Gataker's tract, called A Memento for Christians, expressed the need for concern about the children of a king being in a strange land. The government responded by ordering the clergy to pray for Charles's safe return 'and no more'. Items circulating as far as Chester about the Spanish match included Archbishop Abbot's supposed council speech opposing it, a letter purporting to be from the king of Spain – informing Gondomar that the match was simply a ploy to keep James out of the war – and a copy of Thomas Alured's letter to Buckingham urging him to oppose the match.

[24] J. Bowle, Charles the First (1975), 64, 66–70; Cogswell, 58–60; Redworth, The Prince, 3–5, 32–4, 73–4, 136–8, for Spain's perspective in the negotiations. Ruigh, The Parliament, 384–8.
[25] Cust, 73; Cogswell, 51, 27, 32, 34, 36–48.

There was no evidence of the Court's side of the story. Only two sermons were published supporting the match.[26]

Meanwhile, the syndicate made no attempt to circumvent their understanding with Cottington and there is no evidence to suggest they attempted to renegotiate their agreement. Instead, we see a muted handling of the aftermath of the decision at Regensburg to depose Frederick. Newsbooks reported where the emperor was granting freedom of worship to Protestants and where he was not. We can read of the poverty and famine in both Bohemia and Austria, and the low value of the land in Bohemia, with the explanation that 'thus five severall Religions being in prosecution one of another ... Christendome [is] still suffering which Religion soever prevailes'. The violence of the duke of Bavaria's men was reported and his policy of reform: 'wheresoever the Duke of Bavaria is Master they goe strongly with their manner of Reformation (as they call it) causing many to forsake their former Religion, and to turne Papists'. Tilly's manoeuvres were also reported, and Mansfeld's agreement with the French. The news covered Turks moving into Poland, Silesia and Moravia and Christian's campaign defeat at Stadt-lohn. The issue of 29 August covered Italian news, while the issue of 11 October included news of devaluation and prices, with lots of misery recorded in news coming from Rome and Vienna. The 28 October issue had a discursive editorial explaining the implications of the manoeuvres of the Turks and Bethlem Gabor with a wish that he would help the Protestant cause.[27]

There is scope for speculation here: did Gainsford resign that summer through frustration with the restrictions of the licensing agreement? Or were there personal reasons or arguments about pay in negotiations for the next contract? The syndicate was missing a valuable commercial opportunity, unable to report on the progress of the visit to Madrid or act as a vehicle for any crown-inspired account of the issues at stake. Only later, in January 1624, when Bristol came home to face charges from Buckingham did the special commission learn how close James had come in both 1618 and 1623 to succeeding in securing a peaceful settlement.[28]

It has been suggested that from July to October 1623 the newsbook attacks on the Habsburg rulers were 'vitriolic'. The 16 June issue included news about rape and violence by Bavarian troops and the 10 July newsbook said there was no hope left for Bavarian Protestants. However, Bavaria was never regarded as a potential ally by the English Crown, and any link Bavaria had

[26] Cust, 72–3, 80–1; Schumacher, 119, 146–7; Sharpe, *Image Wars*, 130–1.

[27] (7 May 1623), 1, 4, 8, 14, STC18507.109; (27 August 1623), 1–3, 8–9, STC18507.123; (12 May 1623), 9, STC18507.110; (16 June 1623), 13, STC18507.115; (17 May 1623), 14, STC18507.111; Schumacher, 77; (29 July 1623), STC18507.121; (21 August 1623), STC18507.122; (29 August 1623), STC18507.124; (11 October 1623), 12–13, STC18507.130; (28 October 1623), 14, STC18507.131.

[28] Patterson, 328–9, 336.

with Spain was too many steps removed to have been a significant diplo-matic consideration. Moreover, from August through October, there is an increasing trend for misery of every kind to be reported, including devalua-tion, plague and escalating prices affecting anyone unfortunate enough to be in the way of the Turks, Bethlem Gabor or famine. It was as late as March/April 1624 before direct references to Spain were less guarded and then there was even mention of Spain's fear of war with England.[29]

The syndicate was finally free to join the clamour to celebrate the forthcoming return of the party with an announcement in their issue of 24 September 1623 under the heading A *Relation of the Journey of the High and Mighty Prince Charles ... from ... Spaine.* 'Mr S D, an English gent in Charles traine', who was sent ahead with letters for James, supplied the account. It wished Charles God speed and ends 'as once againe to enjoy the sweetnesse of his presence. Amen.' Butter also published with Henry Seile a pamphlet that reported 'the unspeakable joy of both nations: testi-fied no lesse by Triumphal Expressions of the Spanish Ambassadors (here now residing) as by the lowd Acclamations of our owne People'. Public celebrations demonstrated what Hirst has described as 'the clearest and most widespread expression of public opinion before the Restoration'. The celebrations were so great that they became an embarrassment.[30] On 25 September, James, responding to the immense popular interest in the negotiations and especially to the wave of anti-Spanish feeling unleashed, expressed his dissatisfaction with the efficiency of the various means to control discussion and dissemination of news at his disposal with A *Procla-mation against the Disorderly printing, uttering and dispersing of books, pamphlets etc.* Its target was the vigorous polemic pamphlet trade flourishing both in imports and domestic publications. For James, the pursuit of a Spanish match was not over: he raised the stakes in what Patterson describes as 'a bold and calculated attempt ... [to] keep his peace policy on track'. Correspondence continued with the papacy into November and negotiations ended only in December. While this was happening Calvert was collecting evidence about unauthorised publications, but the September proclamation had no discern-ible effect on the syndicate. Newsbooks continued to report as the emperor began to distribute Frederick's lands, devaluation and poverty devastated much of central Europe and Bethlen Gabor and the Turks manoeuvred.[31]

What is more noticeable in Gainsford's style over the winter of 1623/4, as England gradually adjusted to the abandonment of a Spanish marriage alliance and the influence of the pro-Spanish lobby dwindled, is a growth in

---

[29] Frearson, 259; (16 June 1623), STC18507.115; (10 July 1623), STC18507.118. For reports of misery and suffering (28 October 1623), 14, STC18507.131; (19 March 1624), 19, STC18507.145.
[30] (24 September 1623), STC18507.128; Schumacher, 121–2; Hirst, *Conflict*, 109.
[31] *Proclamations*, I, 583–5; Clegg, *Jacobean England*, 186–7; Lambert, 20; Patterson, 332–4.

confidence, not in the potential outcome of the conflict, nor in the justice of the Protestant cause, but, more personally, in the value of his work as editor and in his own skills. In this period he was straightforward in his condemnation of reports he did not believe and direct in his responses to readers.[32] He well understood the constraints that continued to apply. In December, he included in a report from France about their internal Protestant conflicts,

> Now what will be the issue of this, time will declare: for great Kings wil deliberate upon businesse of such importance, and the subject must not expect present dispatches in matters of such consequences; lest Princes diminish their greatnesse.

But with increased confidence came a measure of carelessness. By February, even references to Spanish diplomats seemed safe along with intimations of a change of line from the French government. A report from Paris from someone in the embassy of Lord Kensington reassured its recipient that the French were not likely to be raising arms against the Protestants and was quoted fully in the newsbook.

> There is great alteration of officers at this Court, & the Spanish Ambassador seemeth much discontented, and we know not wherefore: the Jesuits for all that they are very busie, & dare still to threaten the Protestants, but I am perswaded, you shall heare more shortly: For although the Queen mother standeth altogether for the Romane Religion, yet are all things better carried, since her reconciliation and coming to Court, then they were before. God turne all to the best: For I thinke the world went never so ill in Europe as it is now.[33]

Kensington's negotiations for a French marriage were not officially underway until the following June and Gainsford cannot have realised they had begun unofficially. He had blundered into highly sensitive matters. Gainsford was quickly reminded that James was still taking a close interest and that, contrary to any impression the syndicate may have gained from the seeming shift in foreign policy following the prince's return from Madrid, Cottington's role had not ended. On 5 March we find the last reference to Cottington acting as a licenser, and, in the issue of 6 March 1624, Gainsford noted that he could not tell readers that the Palatinate has been restored so 'you and I both must be contented with such other newes, as wee finde, and dare justify in London'.[34] This suggests that he was pulled up sharply. The

---

[32] (20 November 1623), 21, STC18507.133; (13 December 1623), STC18507.136; (19 March 1624), STC18507.145.
[33] (11 December 1623), 22, STC18507.135; (24 February 1624), 21–(misnumbered) 14, STC18507.141.
[34] Patterson, 353; Arber, vol. 4, 75; (6 March 1624), verso, STC18507.143.

licensing rules still applied and diplomatic matters remained firmly outside his remit.

James was consistent in allowing news of the war and its consequences while controlling reports of diplomatic efforts to ensure that the news neither caused offence nor embarrassment during sensitive discussions. After Gainsford's death in August 1624 there was far less editing and news-books were, as frequently claimed, straight 'out of the originals'. They were less coherently assembled yet the overall range of news remained broadly similar, further demonstrating that James's concern had been primarily to protect the diplomatic process. Cottington continued as the prince's secre-tary until James' death the following spring, upon which he surrendered the post and was asked to leave the Court.[35]

Cottington was an able administrator who established clear ground rules in 1622 that were understood by the syndicate, editor and Cottington's assistants who operated during the periods of his absence abroad. Those rules covered a requirement for publishers to co-operate to produce just one licensed series of approximately weekly issues. Editing was to make texts as coherent and accurate as possible by drawing on a wide range of reliable sources, including Catholic ones, and by avoiding speculation. Sensitive matters were to be avoided. These included reports and letters from England that appeared in publications in Germany, the United Provinces or else-where, news of embassies and overt criticism of other governments, espe-cially of Spain. Had James's diplomatic efforts been successful, the verdict today on his media policy may well have been positive. But as it failed, the only lasting effect of Cottington's vigilance was to ensure that no one knew how close it came to realisation.

It had taken time to develop a news policy and then a process of trial and error and negotiation to implement it effectively. Newsbooks published under the supervision of Cottington recounted what was happening week by week on the Continent, on the basis of reports, not only from Dutch and German publications, but also from Antwerp. They contained nothing potentially damaging to diplomatic relations with Spain. From James's point of view, they may even have performed a useful service after the failure of the 1621 Parliament to vote sufficient subsidies for effective action on behalf of Frederick in the Palatinate by helping to focus English readers upon the real military problems surrounding recovery of the Palatinate.

Although it has been argued that newsbooks were 'a thinly veiled vehicle for an oblique yet unmistakable and sustained critique of English foreign policy', in fact, newsbook content was more complex.[36] The real issue was the political and cultural impact of the fact that readers were able to follow

---

[35] M. Havran, *Caroline Courtier: The Life of Lord Cottington* (1973), 81–2.
[36] Frearson, 173, 222, 225.

events, develop and hone skills of critical analysis and apply their own interpretation to the events as they unfolded.

James was a Calvinist and, for all his efforts to establish Christian unity in Europe and a peaceful settlement to the crisis precipitated by Frederick's decision to accept the Bohemian Crown, he consistently held out for Protestant security and the restoration of the Palatinate. He also appears to have realised the true reality of the crisis. Restoring the Palatinate meant dealing with the emperor and Bavaria and from the time the Protestants were defeated and on retreat there were only two ways forward: the first was through building alliances that were sufficiently strong to wield influence in central Europe; the second was through military action, on land in Germany, on a sufficiently grand scale to draw the emperor to the negotiating table. Naval action against Spain, as favoured by many, was a less direct option. It had the merits of a lower cost and of allowing England to intervene in an arena where it already had strength and expertise, but James believed intervention was potentially unnecessary so long as he had credible reasons for believing the Spanish were open to negotiation and had something to gain from a treaty with England. Regular reporting of the war as it evolved in Germany, especially since it was edited by a soldier familiar with the realities of European warfare, had potential to direct the attention of readers to the reality of what was happening 'on the ground'. Yet it did not have the effect of converting readers to James's perspective and James was not sufficiently proactive to win the public debate.[37] Readers learned nothing of the intricacies of international negotiation. The story of international alliances and the subtle shading of different political and religious affiliations that unfolded particularly of those, like Saxony and France, whose allegiance was less committed, remained complex, however much Gainsford aimed to simplify it into a story of an uneven contest in which the defenders of Protestantism struggled valiantly against the superior Hapsburg forces.[38] Underreporting Protestant failures and heralding even minor successes would, if anything, have tended to allow readers to believe that potential Protestant allies were bigger and stronger than they were. This encouraged false hopes and made James's lack of military or naval action all the more difficult to comprehend or accept.

The wars were interpreted by many as a conflict of religions and injected an ideological element into an already vulnerable body politic. Debates in the Parliament of 1621, especially in the second session, were informed by fresh news of the suffering of the Palatinate and of Elizabeth and Frederick and revealed divisions about financing, foreign policy, the proposed military approach and the underlying religious convictions. These helped to explain

---

[37] R. Cust, 60–90; Cogswell, 27–8, 30–4, 301, 311; T. Cogswell, 'The Politics of Propaganda: Charles I and the People in the 1620s', JBS, 29 (1990), 192; Sharpe, Image Wars, 125–6, 130–2.
[38] Frearson, 342, 196.

how the nation could divide more deeply in 1642.[39] James's failure was his apparent inability to realise that if people are kept informed about current events and government policies, they apply their own interpretation to the information and can reach different conclusions. This failure was all the more unaccountable given the strength of opposition, in print and in manuscript that was simultaneously circulating at the time. He lacked the personal charm to persuade and his policy of appeasement towards Spain failed to bring any visible or sufficiently convincing results. He opened debate on sensitive subjects and, when the arguments did not go the way he anticipated, he attempted to close it again. He could exercise some control over the pulpits and, by means of the licensing system, over what might be published, but his repeated efforts to ban controversial publication demonstrate the inadequacy of the system to control illicit and imported works.

Britain goes to war

The return of Charles and Buckingham had little immediate effect on the publication of newsbooks, but a change in foreign policy was ushered in by the 1624 Parliament.

The new Parliament met in February. While bad weather was delaying the opening, the Lord Keeper recommended a proclamation to prohibit the publication and sale of any book not approved by authorised persons. Charles and Buckingham also made preparations, using their patronage, mobilising allies in both Houses. James undertook to have his Secretary disclose correspondence and Charles and Buckingham relate what had happened, then listen to Parliament's advice. Buckingham reported to Parliament on 24 February, setting the stage for change and for war with Spain by presenting detailed reports of Spanish duplicity and securing the support of important voices in the House of Commons.[40] Newsbooks had been reporting blow by blow the steady decline of the fortunes of the Protestants. At last, there was an opportunity for action. Three subsidies and three fifteenths were voted for a Spanish war, and Charles and Buckingham (against the advice of James) encouraged the impeachment of the Lord Treasurer Middlesex, who continued to oppose the war on cost grounds, for mismanagement. It was a worrying Parliament for James who saw the dangers in inviting Parliament to have so decisive a voice in royal concerns of marriage and foreign policy, allowing discussion of religion with a complaint against Richard Montague's tract A New Gag for an Old Goose that was thought to be strongly Arminian, and putting pressure on Councillors. But whatever James's misgivings, it

[39] Hirst, Conflict, 103, 106.
[40] Cogswell, 63–8; Ruigh, The Parliament, 154–5, 162–6, 35–6, 60–89, 187, 191–2, 215–16, 392.

marked a significant step with the Crown and Parliament in agreement on the decision to go to war. James prorogued Parliament at the end of May with a speech that praised 'the obedience and good respect of the Commons' and celebrated 'the happy conclusion of this session', apparently intending to recall them in the autumn, though he did not do so.[41]

Geoffrey Parker has argued that by the spring of 1622 the Catholics had 'overwhelming superiority in the Rhineland' and James 'failed to realise that the Spaniards had no intention of surrendering their footholds in the Rhineland, for they offered an invaluable link between the Netherlands and the Alps'. Conrad Russell concluded that 'James and the House of Commons shared one illusion: both thought that by their dealings with Spain they could affect the policy of the Emperor in the Palatinate and Bohemia'. If so, it was understandable: Spinola's Spanish-Walloon army together with Tilly's Catholic League troops had taken the Palatinate. Newsbook readers were well aware that a Spaniard, Don Guilielmo, occupied the Palatinate on the left bank of the Rhine. Since 1621, with the ending of the Twelve Year Truce, Spain had again been at war with the United Provinces. Action by 1624 was focused around the fortress of Breda and at sea, with Spanish efforts to damage the Dutch shipping trade in the Baltic and with the Iberian Peninsula. It is also a perspective shared by historians who have shown how the spread of the war to Germany was due to Spanish involvement. There were, however, a multiplicity of issues that separated Crown and Commons around whether this was a battle against the Antichrist or a political and dynastic issue, how the discussion and decision-making process should be conducted, what funds were needed, what preparations should be made and how funds should be spent. As Kevin Sharpe summarised 'In the euphoria of 1624, such differences were not aired and may not have been comprehended'. He saw these as rooted in fundamentally discordant attitudes to strategy, war and the conduct of foreign affairs.[42]

The most immediate and visible question in 1624 was about how England might best intervene. England and Scotland had been injecting money and forces into Germany since before the 1621 benevolence. Even for MPs who were perhaps naïve about the true costs of seventeenth-century warfare or the inadequacy of the financial mechanisms available to the Crown, it was easy to see that a great deal of money could be needed. Adams has argued that 'Parliament would not support an expedition to the Palatinate;

---

[41] Ibid., 217–27, 230, 249–55, 303–44; D. L. Smith, *The Stuart Parliaments 1603–1689* (1999), 111–12; Bowle, *Charles*, 80–1.

[42] Parker, *Thirty*, 58; C. Russell, *The Crisis of Parliaments: English History 1509–1660* (Oxford, 1971), 292; *Numb. 29* (2 May 1623), 19–20, STC18507.108; P. Brightwell, 'Spanish Origins of the Thirty Years' War', *ESR*, 9 (1979); P. Brightwell, 'Spain and Bohemia: The Decision to Intervene, 1619', *ESR*, 12 (1982), 117–41; P. Brightwell, 'Spain, Bohemia and Europe, 1619–21', *ESR*, 12 (1982), 371–99; Sharpe, *Personal Rule*, 7; Adams, 'Foreign Policy', 149.

James would not undertake any other form of military action'. Cogswell has accepted that 'the prospect of a major expeditionary force operating deep inside the Empire, and the cost of such a venture, filled the Commons with horror'. However, he has suggested that the Commons was willing to use loans to encourage princes within the Empire to start to work together again, pointing out that they were only invited to increase the defence budget. They voted a bigger subsidy than ever before and they expected to meet again, though he concedes that 'generous though the 1624 Parliament was the fact remains that it was not generous enough to underwrite the full expense of warfare'. James remained firm throughout in refusing to declare war on Spain and insisting that recovery of the Palatinate was the only justifiable reason for hostilities. He was also consistent in then dedicating funds to Mansfeld's expedition with a specific instruction not to use them in the Netherlands against Spain. Ruigh has concluded that 'the mutual distrust' between King and Commons was such that it was only the fear of a breach that prevented dissolution, plus the intervention of Charles and Buckingham that gratified Parliament and placated James. But these interventions by concealing the extent of the divergence of views between Crown and Commons, created a misunderstanding that was to undermine subsequent Parliaments.[43]

Signals about how money was to be spent were mixed. Mansfeld was in London when the subsidies were debated and his popularity was celebrated in ballads and newsbooks alike. Supporting Mansfeld offered James the prospect of using his army to unite the Protestant forces and of doing something for Elizabeth at the least possible cost, but he only agreed to payment subject to Mansfeld also getting French support. Cogswell has noted the mass of anti-Catholic material in print in the summer of 1624: it was 'a banner year for booksellers' and the fact that government was not very concerned about the printing and distribution of almost all of these could been seen as an acknowledgement that it was moving into line with popular expectations. The consensus in celebrating the end of Spanish treaties 'combined to convey to their readers a profound feeling of providential deliverance'.[44] The tracts were rather less consistent about strategy. A few, such as Leighton's *Speculum Belli* and Scott's *Vox Regis*, assumed that Parliament was called to provide for direct participation in the war. The frontispiece of *Vox Regis* even shows the Commons offering their hearts and purses for the war. D'Ewes still hoped for recovery of the Palatinate, expressed hope for direct action in Germany and believed that many shared his view. Others, including *Tom Tell-Troath* and *Vox Militis*, complained of too much peace, while John Reynolds praised Buckingham's work to restore

---

[43] Ibid., 171; Cogswell, 225, 266–8, 310–12, 318, 242–3; Ruigh, *The Parliament*, 385–7, 391, 393–4; Hirst, *Conflict*, 110–11.
[44] Cogswell, 224–5, 243, 281–99; Schumacher, 161; Cogswell, 'The Politics', 214.

the navy in *Vox Coeli* and *Votivae Angliciae*.[45] Many enthusiasts harked back to the Elizabethan era, nurturing memories of a naval war against Spain that was perceived as successful and cheap, even potentially profitable. Sir Francis Seymour stated that, 'he had heard wars spoken on, and an army, but would be glad to hear where. The Palatinate, the place intended by his Majesty. This were never thought of, nor fit for the consideration of this House, in regard of the infinite charge.' Some pamphleteers argued that a profit could be made from a naval war, but also supported an attack on Spain in the United Provinces. Meanwhile, newsbooks reported whatever came their way that was likely to be of interest and included naval and some mercantile shipping news. They were increasingly reporting news of bandits and pirates, for example, the 11 December issue covers pirate activity in the Mediterranean, shipping reports on the East and West Indian Companies and the use of Spanish bullion to support Spinola. This would have tended to support the idea that a stronger naval presence was needed.[46]

James was allowing greater freedom to the press, but, as the experience of John Reynolds showed, when Reynolds took a step too far in criticising James for failure to protect his daughter and son-in-law and was imprisoned in July 1624, James was still defining limits. On 15 August 1624, a proclamation appeared against 'seditious, popish and puritanical bookes and pamphlets' which stated that 'No person or persons whatsoever [should] presume to print any Booke or Pamphlet, touching, or concerning matters of Religion, Church government or State ... [unless it has been] perused, corrected, and allowed.' It added that no person was to import a book until it had been allowed. This proclamation coincided with the nine-day run of Thomas Middleton's *A Game at Chesse* in August, which demonstrated how Charles and Buckingham, by going to Madrid, had exposed Spanish designs for a 'universal monarchy'. It offended the Spanish ambassador, Coloma, who complained to James. A letter from Conway to the Privy Council dated 12 August asked them to investigate, but it is indicative of James's change of heart by this stage that action was taken slowly. Middleton was not severely punished and no follow-up action seems to have been taken against the printers who were making copies without licence or entry. Cogswell has suggested that this play is evidence of a new leniency or 'blessed revolution'.[47]

From March until the following September, with war the determined course, the government neglected its supervision of newsbook publication.

---

[45] J. O. Halliwell, ed., *The Autobiography and Correspondence of Sir Simonds D'Ewes*, 1 (1845), 241–4; M. A. Breslow, *English Puritan Views of Foreign Nations 1618–1640* (Cambridge, MA, 1970), quotes D'Ewes, 29; Clegg, *Jacobean England*, 174–5, 185; Schumacher, 134–5, 140–1, 148–9.

[46] Ibid., 155–60; (20 November 1623), 6, STC18507.133; (11 December 1623), 15–17, STC18507.135.

[47] *Proclamations*, 1, 599–600; Clegg, *Jacobean England*, 187–9. T. Cogswell, 'Thomas Middleton and the Court, 1624: *A Game at Chess* in Context', *HLQ*, 47 (1984), 273–88.

Cottington was out of favour as discussions with Spain deteriorated and he withdrew from Court in April 1625. Issues appeared without licence or entry, but this did not help the syndicate since the important news, both about the meeting of the Catholic League at Augsburg and the meeting between France and the United Provinces at Compiègne in June, was slow to reach them. England joined their alliance on 15 June 1624, yet three weeks later, in the last issue edited by Gainsford, he was still struggling to distinguish truth from rumour. As a result, it seems unlikely that the stronger position of the Protestant side in 1624 was fully appreciated by readers.[48] Newsbooks processed the minutiae of the war while sometimes failing to recognise bigger political pictures.

Gainsford's experience and skills had made him uniquely suitable for his role and finding a replacement when he died would not have been easy. There were also financial considerations: as the fortunes of Frederick declined and attention turned to war with Spain, sales of news of military action on the mainland were dropping. The publishers may well have concluded that they could save costs by not employing another editor. With the withdrawal of Cottington from the scene and no discernable pressure from government there was less need to collaborate. The syndicate started to fall apart in July. Gainsford referred to the newsbooks as 'our next Relations (for so I stile the newes which I write) to distinguish them from other which (as it seemeth) have not … [like us paid good money to get good quality news reports]'. The syndicate split and Archer found a new partner, Benjamin Fisher, who had a shop in Paternoster Row, and called his newsbook *A Continuation of the Former Newes*. It was a poorly translated and assembled effort which Archer clearly intended to sell as the next in the syndicate series since he numbered it 32. He also aimed to protect his title to this newsbook. Archer turned to official channels for support, approaching Thomas Worrall, the bishop of London's chaplain and rector of St Botolph's, Bishopsgate. Worrall had responsibility primarily for the licensing of religious works and was not known as a statesman with an understanding of foreign politics, but as a fairly lax licenser who readily gave his authority. Andrew Marvel wrote of 'Doctor Woral, the Bishop of London's Chaplain, Scholar good enough, but a free fellow-like man, and of no very tender Conscience' who was apt to approve 'hand over head' any copy submitted to him. He authorised more than 100 works during the last three years of James's reign and continued to work as an ecclesiastical licenser under Charles. Worrall and Warden Lownes entered Archer's newsbook on 7 September, thereby protecting Archer's copyright, albeit only for that issue.[49]

---

[48] Ruigh, *The Parliament*, 288; (3 July 1624), STC18507.149; Schumacher, 168–9.
[49] (3 July 1624), STC18507.149; (9 September 1624), STC18507.346; W. W. Greg, *Licensers for the Press* (Oxford, 1962), 289–90; Clegg, *Jacobean England*, 66; C. S. Clegg, *Press Censorship in Caroline England* (Cambridge, 2008), 39, 223.

Archer was quickly challenged. The next day, possibly due to pressure from the remainder of the syndicate, he produced a covering sheet for his newsbook with a different title *Extraordinary Newes. Three Great Invasions already attempted* and on that page the number was confusingly given as 23. In a race to establish their legitimacy, on 10 September Bourne and Butter also went to Worrall and Lownes and entered their next newsbook, which duly appeared on 11 September as *The Continuation of the weekely Newes* and bore the names of Butter, Bourne, Newbery and Sheffard. It looks very much as if Archer was trying to take over the publishing syndicate's market of readers for newsbooks, but given that Archer was the initiator and founder of this trade, he probably saw this differently and, true to pattern, was once more the first to realise the significance of the changes that were taking place at a political level and to explore new options. Sadly for Archer, he was under resourced. In his issue of 11 October, Archer used large print with only eleven pages of scraps he had assembled from a variety of sources.[50] Benjamin Fisher abandoned the enterprise after his first brush with the competition. Archer continued to register under the authority of Dr Worrall until December and to publish news from time to time until 1628, but his issues lacked the content and range of material that was available from the news networks. He doubtless also lost access to too much of the domestic distribution network. Archer lost hope of market recognition and ceded the title to Bourne and Butter. He avoided further conflict by employing a wide range of titles. His 21 October 1624 issue was called *A relation of the chiefest and last proceedings* and in November he published at least two more issues. From 1625 to 1628 Archer did not number or date his infrequent publications. His fortunes never recovered and he was soon to end his days in poverty, reliant on the charity of the Stationers' Company. A December 1630 Court Book entry recorded 'It is ordered yt Tho: Archer shall have 10s p qvter out of ye poores money'.[51]

The syndicate dissolved after Archer's challenge leaving Butter and Bourne to continue in partnership. To maintain their market, and ensure their issues were seen as the main series, the title page of almost every issue indicated the date of the previous one. From 11 September 1624 the opening words of the title of the series were standardised to *The continuation of the [or our] weekly [or weekely] newes*. This was an original idea unknown in any other series that made it abundantly clear this was one continuous series. Further standardisation occurred when the imprint, 'Printed for Mercurius Britannicus' was adopted by Butter and Bourne at the end of 1624. The new imprint signalled that this was an officially sanctioned war effort. It was probably inspired by the recruitment of forces to serve Mansfeld that

---

[50] (9 September 1624), STC18507.347; Arber, vol. 4, 84; (11 September 1624), STC18507.151; Frearson, 265; (11 October 1624), STC18507.348.
[51] (21 October 1624), STC18507.349; (10 November 1624), STC18507.351; (24 November 1624), STC18507.352; Jackson, 'Court Book C', 221, 20 December 1630.

the partnership witnessed that winter as they included men from all parts of Britain. Mansfield's army set out from Dover in January 1625 while the Anglo-Dutch brigade had been recruiting from both England and Scotland from 1624. Together these format changes produced a uniform front page, despite variations in the longer form of the title, and they confirmed their status as the official foreign news publishers.[52]

The partnership clearly placed more faith in marketing techniques and the loyalty of their established clientele than they did in any copyright established through licensing. After obtaining two authorisations from Worrall in September they must have decided that, with their readership secure and Cottington no longer breathing down their necks, they could relax. They made no entries with the Company of Stationers in October. However, this was not acceptable to the Company. On 6 November Butter was fined 6s. 9d. 'for printing a Currant without entrance', as part of what looks like a sweep by the Stationers' Company to address infringements by a number of news publishers, including Nicholas Oakes who was also fined for publishing news about Breda without licence and Thomas Archer who was given a warning.[53] This set in place a new system, not overseen directly by the state, but conforming to regular trade practices. It may also have suited James's purposes reflecting the change in foreign policy, but there is no evidence of crown involvement. Butter and Bourne continued to turn to Worrall for licences and paid for their entries in the Company register to satisfy the trade requirement for an entry fee, but they were no longer seeking authority in order to stay on the right side of the Crown, and Worrall was less effective in inspecting newsbooks than his predecessor.

The syndicate's first newsbook without Archer was completely unedited. It contained both the Jansz and Veseler corantos from Amsterdam and reflected, unmediated, the optimism of its Protestant correspondents. The formation of the anti-Habsburg Alliance is reported, but without according it the weight that might be expected had there been any appreciation of its potential significance:

> It is held for certaine and true, that the aforesaid union betwixt most mighty Kings, Princes, Potentates, Commonwealthes and Nobles, is now firmly made: and that there is such a unity, that many Lords wonder thereat, & they are resolved & meane to unsit the house of Austria, Burgundy, & the King of Spaine.
> ...
> [The] valiantest and best Souldiers and Officers [are in Bergen] ... As also above 1000 voluntaries, as well French and English, most persons of qualitie ... in the meanetime the Spainiards make great outrage, and have shamefully abused some women and maids of the towne ... stripping them naked.

---

[52] Dahl, 114, 133; There were occasional small variations such as (8 December 1626), STC18507.184; Wilson, *Europe's Tragedy*, 233; Patterson, 354–5.
[53] Jackson, 'Fine Book', 472; 'Court Book', 171.

Butter and Bourne soon showed no anxiety about reporting whatever arrived in their mailbag. Their issue of 20 October included a report from France 'that our English, as well the Ambassadours as others are used with more then an ordinary respect of courtesie in all that Kingdome' and this was not picked up either by them as an opportunity for speculation, or by the Crown as an occasion for censure.[54]

The issue of 4 December 1624 stands out for its rich combination of European and English news, showing how fully England had become engaged in European affairs and demonstrating how far the boundary had changed on what could be reported. It contained the French response to the royal marriage reported from Paris,

> there hath beene much triumphing and solemnity used in the Court, the City of Paris & generally through the Kingdome of France, for the honour of the concluded marriage betweene the high and mighty Prince Charles, Prince of Wales, and Christian of Bourbon, daughter unto Henry the fourth of famous memory.

The publishers included reports of the congratulations of many ambassadors but noted that the Spanish ambassador was less than happy. This story was complemented in February 1625 by a report from Madrid: 'Two dayes agoe made the French Ambassadour our King acquainted with the match that is concluded betwixt France and England, and the people here in generall shewed thereupon signes of Joye.' These reports even included reports that originated in England that had been routinely edited out of issues from 1621 onwards. Thus, we learn from the issue of 4 December from a report written from England, 'The like solemnityes were used upon Sunday Last in London, and other neighbouring places.' The news was welcomed by all 'except Jesuited English, who have not so much hope to accomplish their ambitious projects, allwayes hurtful to the good, and tranquility of this kingdome; by this marriage'.[55]

Through the autumn and winter of 1624/5, the siege of Breda was well reported in the sort of detail and with a level of coherence that English readers would have appreciated even though there was no London editor. Worrall allowed other news originating in England to be reprinted in London. For example, a report from a Hamburg publication recorded the assembling of German and English troops, including an account from England that,

> twelve thousand English who are appointed to meete at Dover ... to march under the command of the most illustrious Ernestus Earle of Mansfeld, a man whose commaund and worth is such that it is beyond the panegiries and stile of

[54] (11 September 1624), 5, 7, STC18507.151; (20 October 1624), 7, STC18507.155.
[55] (4 December 1624), 4–5, STC18507.158; (8 February 1625), 4, STC18507.162.

my commendation. These Troupes are to be payd one third part out of England, another third part out of Fraunce, and the last third from the Protestant . . . Cities of the German Empire. What their Design is, God he knows . . . the issue whereof we hope will prove fortunate, to us, our friends & our Country.

The report ended with, 'A list of those souldiers who are Prest out of every Shire in England for this next expedition of Count Mansfield'. The writer solemnly warned readers about the value of secrecy in laying military plans. The detail, accuracy and reference to the intended purpose and destination of the troops suggest that this could have come from an official source, possibly at the instigation of Buckingham, given his involvement in the engagement of Mansfeld. If so, it was an early signal of his willingness to court the public and gamble on military success.[56]

The partnership may have been able to dispense with an editor of note, but they still needed a translator, someone to control the length of issues and sometimes, too, to include an editorial notice. Who did these tasks after August 1624 is unknown, though John Pory may have taken on the translation on his return from Virginia. A seemingly modest note at the end of a story suggested that this new translator had less editorial control and that no one was attempting to assess the merit or significance of reports:

> I hope that none that have any sence or judgement will blame me if either hee, I, or another shall receive or publish hereafter anything contrary to this newes. For I translate only the Newes verbatim out of the Tongues or Languages in which they are written, and having no skill in Prognostication, leave therefore the judgement to the Reader, & that especially when there are tidings which contradict one another.

Other notices appear to bluntly reveal the feelings of the publishers towards Verheoeven's Antwerp news:

> May it please you to understand, that whereas we have hitherto printed (for the most part) The *Occurrances* ... from the Protestant side, which some have excepted against: wherefore to give them content, we propose to publish (as they now come into our hands) such Relations as are printed at Antwerp, Utopia, or other such ... to build their miraculous faith upon: and feede them with Milke from their owne dame, and this we doe not for profit, but to free ourselves from partiallity.

In fact, they used this material because of a shortage of other reports. The claim, that all that was being done was exact translation, was reiterated in May, 'The Translator to the Reader. Seeing that I have lately received many

---

[56] (15 November 1624), 8–9, STC18507.156; (1 February 1625), 16–17, STC18507.161; (4 December 1624), 18–19, 21, STC18507.158.

particular advices of the last two conflicts which have been made betwixt Count Mansfield and the Imperialists, I will exactly translate then, and leave the judgement of them to your discretion.'[57] An answer to complaints about multiple repetitions again claims to come from the translator, but seems to have come from Butter given its tetchy, impatient tone and the assumption that readers knew him:

> For my part I would willingly please everyone, but seeing that this is impossible, and not Jupiter himselfe could give content to everyone whatsoever weather he sent, whether it were drie or wet, I will still doe my best endevours, and please every one as farre as I can. And I hope that all men of discretion would have bourne with me, if I had lately extended our newes as farre as I could, seeing that we received none from the United Provinces in the space of 5 or 6 weekes (by reason of contrary winde, which was not seen in the space of 30 years).[58]

The strain of sustaining a periodical through a period of declining sales appears to have been taking its toll.

Sensitivity about Spain and its ambassadors was no longer relevant and Cottington's skills were no longer required so the lines of engagement between the industry and the Crown were redrawn. Satisfied that the Crown was no longer interested, the publishers brought in Worrall. The Court of the Stationers' Company supported the arrangement because it secured their continued role and income. Far fewer issues were entered in the Company's register and Butter and Bourne established a bulk reckoning system with the Company.

By December 1624 we see signs that perhaps Charles and Buckingham recognised some potential benefits in the reporting of England's new role in continental affairs. They were allowing people who were sufficiently well connected to know what was happening in diplomatic and military circles to release their accounts. It was their misfortune that constraints placed on the funds expended in 1624 exacerbated the problems of mismanagement inherent in a war, where alliances came and went, and generals often acted independently of the rulers from whom they received their commissions, preventing the effective deployment of the forces they supported. Consequently news reported in the early years of Charles's reign was uniformly bad and it would have been very difficult for readers to comprehend from the reports they received quite why the allies were failing to meet up and execute anything resembling an effective campaign. Butter and Bourne became the purveyors of news that was singularly unlikely to inspire confidence in the ability of Charles and Buckingham to manage a war effort.

---

[57] (28 June 1625), 5, STC18507.173; Dahl, 137. Dahl referred the 'rankness of the wording' of a notice, 29 March 1625 as typical of this time, verso, STC18507.164. (23 May 1626), 11, STC18507.179.

[58] (28 June 1625), 1–2, STC18507.173.

Conclusions

James's profile as an international statesman is improving. He saw himself as part of a European brotherhood of monarchs, giving himself the title 'defender of the faith', and acting as a negotiator and peace broker in Europe. His pacific foreign policy served him for many years, but he was well aware of the delicacy of the balance he strove for, and of Britain's financial weakness and consequent vulnerability should diplomacy fail. Events in Bohemia fatally strained that balance and he failed to live up to his title. He failed to satisfy English Protestants who did not believe England should stay out of the conflict and failed to keep England at peace. Nonetheless his approach, if disappointing to many, was coherent.

Similarly, his approach to the media was aimed at achieving a balance. It was far from simplistic: he was aware of the power of words and sought to influence public opinion. James was more pragmatic and experimental than is generally recognised. He also had an awareness of the emerging role of the media. He was, however, out of his depth in 1620/1, when the new international threat was accompanied by a massive upsurge in public interest and printed news, at a time when his sympathies and policies were at odds with public opinion.

Charles, far less cautious approach at the end of James's reign had all the appearances of simplifying relationships abroad, in Parliament and with the news press; so much so that Charles appears to have been lulled into a false sense of security. He was undoubtedly, at this early stage, unaware of the critical interdependences of success at home and overseas, or of the harsh ability of the news press to hold up a mirror, reporting events as they happened, for good or ill.

over simplified

8

Charles I and Georg Weckherlin

'More sad or Heavie Tydings hath not in this Age been brought since Prince Harries Death to the True Hearts of England.'[1]

It was Charles's misfortune to succeed James in place of an older brother whose early death and loss as a putative champion of Protestantism were deeply mourned, and to inherit through his sister a seemingly intractable, and humiliating, international situation for the Stuart dynasty.[2] Through most of his reign Charles pursued a range of unsuccessful diplomatic, naval and military approaches to secure the restoration of the Palatinate, while on Continent an increasingly stark contrast with Charles was provided by the example of Gustavus Adolphus, the Swedish hero of the Protestant cause. Historians now debate Charles failure to explain himself, to create a successful image or to defend himself against the arguments of others, asking to what extent this failure may have contributed to the wars within his kingdoms.[3]

Charles management of communications can be observed through his handling of Parliaments, fundraising and the recruitment of forces to support foreign policy, and through his experiments with news licensing arrangements in bids to influence reporting on European events and Britain's role in them. From his wars with Spain and France, through the Peace of Prague, to the negotiation of a Franco-British alliance in 1636/7, changes in press relationships can be related shifts in foreign allegiances. For much of the period Georg Rudolf Weckherlin, a crown official serving a succession of secretaries of state, acted as the news licenser, and he established a produc-

---

[1] John Bradshaw (later presiding judge at Charles's trial) on hearing news of Gustavus Adolphus's death, November 1632 quoted in T. Royle, *Civil War: The Wars of the Three Kingdoms 1638–1660* (2004), 3.

[2] *The True Picture* (Leyden, 1634), STC12581; K. Sharpe, *Image Wars; Promoting Kings and Commonwealths in England, 1603–1660* (New Haven, CT and London, 2010), 66–70, 273–4.

[3] Ibid., 137–8; C. Russell, *The Causes of the English Civil War* (Oxford, 1990), 198–207; R. Cust, 'Charles I and Popularity', in *Politics, Religion and Popularity in Early Stuart England*, ed. T. Cogswell, R. Cust and P. Lake (Cambridge, 2002), 235–58; R. Cust, *Charles I, A Political Life* (Harlow, 2007), 22–30, 59–62, 470–2.

tive working relationship with the publishers that survived many changes and challenges. With the introduction of a royal patent for the foreign news service at the end of 1638, Weckherlin was succeeded by Robert Reade, Secretary Windebank's nephew.

Charles came to the throne committed to a French marriage and faced with funding war with Spain in a period of economic depression with ineffective financial machinery. Of the money voted in 1625, £360,000 went to Denmark and £100,000 to troops in the Low Countries. Some £240,000 had gone to recruiting and equipping an army of 12,000 pressed men who had been transported under the command of Mansfeld from Dover to Vlissingen in January 1625. They embarked ill-equipped and under instructions from James that depended on support from France that did not materialise and this, consequently, precluded effective action. Yet Charles began his reign in a spirit of confidence and optimism. He ordered what was left of Mansfeld's troops (barely 3000 in active service after the losses from disease and desertion) to Breda to support the Dutch and turned his attention to raising funds. His experience during the Parliament of 1624 suggested that he could align foreign policy with public opinion. He also initiated a more open style of public relations, backed by his use of the pulpit and the printing press over the Spanish match and French alliance.[4]

Charles expected parliamentary support for his plan to attack Spain directly and for a naval campaign, but his confidence seems to have blinded him to the need to construct an effective court party in the House of Commons. He equally neglected to take the sorts of precautions familiar under James to ensure that the printing industry supported his policies or at least published nothing to undermine them. He seems to have been content to let the news speak for itself. A *laissez-faire* approach to the press might have worked but for the fact that events in the Low Countries and Germany went from bad to worse. Readers followed the courage and suffering of the Dutch in Breda and were left to wonder why the English troops did not arrive. As newsbooks reported outward events only, they were silent about diplomacy and strategy, including the fact that French aid was promised, but not forthcoming, and that James had wanted Mansfeld's troops to go to Germany not the Netherlands. Charles and Buckingham appear to have been oblivious of this public reading of developments, expecting continuity between the Parliaments of 1624 and 1625, despite fresh elections and the fact that the new MPs would be well informed about events on the Conti-

---

4 M. A. Breslow, *A Mirror of England Puritan Views of Foreign Nations 1618–1640* (Cambridge, MA, 1970), 30–1; C. R. Kyle, 'Prince Charles in the Parliaments of 1621 and 1624', *HJ*, 41 (1998), 603–24; P. Gregg, *King Charles I* (1981/2000), 124–5; T. Cogswell, 'The Politics of Propaganda: Charles I and the People in the 1620s', *JBS*, 29 (1990), 191–7.

nent. Worse, neither of them appears to have contemplated the possibility that they might be considered accountable for the failures reported.[5]

Charles called Parliament for June seeking help to make good his commitments in Europe and declare war on Spain. However, he did not directly address the discrepancy between the line taken, particularly by Buckingham in the Parliament of 1624 and the implementation of foreign policy under the direction of James in his last months, even though the effects were being reported for all to see. Breda was lost and the Dutch marched out on 5 June 1625. This news was broken to the assembling MPs in a gathering storm of rumours. The English loan ships sailed for France on 9 June but to present a show of force to quell the Huguenots, not to oppose Spain. Meanwhile Wallenstein moved to support Tilly, and the Protestant alliance began to crack. Readers were angry. In the issue of 28 June, the translator attempted to smooth things over, not only explaining why the newsbooks included (and repeated) rumours, but also that 'a contrary winde' had prevented them from receiving anything from the Low Countries except Antwerp reports. Unfortunately, the reports that followed from the Dutch only confirmed what they had already heard. Breda news was buried at the back of this issue, but this did not make it more palatable.[6]

As if this were not enough to challenge the mood of MPs, there was an outbreak of the plague so severe that members assembled in fear for their lives and Parliament had to be adjourned to Oxford in August. Suspicion about the terms of the French marriage agreement and Charles's decision to protect Richard Montague, following his publication of a further Arminian tract, *Appello Caesarem*, were added to complaints about Buckingham's management of the fleet and of increasing piracy. Newsbooks added fuel to the flames by leading with reports of rumours of the recovery of 'Todos los Santos' (Bahia in the West Indies) by the Spanish in March/April and the loss of two Dutch ships coming from Brazil.[7] The result was a break down in discussions in the House of Commons and early dissolution with only two subsidies voted.

So Charles began his reign levying a forced loan, pressing men and billeting them throughout the summer in order to assemble the 1625 fleet. Hirst described the wedge these actions placed between the new king and his people: 'Such burdens were not readily understood, for fear of the plague made men all over the country shun company and stop trading, and left inhabitants of clothing areas (already suffering an economic depression)

---

[5] (14 April 1625), 10–11, STC18507.166; (24 May 1625), final report from an English officer in Dortrecht, STC18507.171. T. Cogswell, 'The People's Love: The Duke of Buckingham and Popularity', in *Politics*, ed. Cogswell *et al.*, 221.

[6] Wedgwood, 201–03; (28 June 1625), 2, 19–22, STC18507.173.

[7] C. Russell, *The Crisis of Parliaments; English History 1509–1660* (Oxford, 1971), 300–2; D. Hirst, *England in Conflict 1603–1660, Kingdom, Community, Conflict* (1999), 113–14; (28 June 1625), 1–5, STC18507.173.

facing starvation.' The attack on Cadiz, in October/November 1625, resulted in another defeat. Cadiz was better defended than in Elizabethan times and the English forces were ill-equipped and inexperienced. In Germany things were no better. Only Denmark went to war in the summer of 1625. Money from England ran out and no more payments were forthcoming except for Mansfeld's troops, and they received less than a third of what was expected. Supplies for the war were missing, inadequate or too late.[8]

By the beginning of 1626, however, a fresh anti-Habsburg Alliance had been agreed at the Hague Convention that brought together Dutch, English and Danish interests and had the support of France and Bethlem Gabor. This was based on a Danish plan to eject Imperial and League troops from the Lower Saxon Circle and relieve pressure on the United Provinces. So Charles tried again to secure support at home, calling a new Parliament in February 1626, this time attempting to keep out some of the more difficult members by picking them as sheriffs. Nothing was done, however, to influence news in circulation or to explain the significance of the new alliance.

While Parliament was sitting printed news was in short supply with the number of issues falling despite the existence of a market of readers with MPs in town. The publishers blamed the damage being done by Dunkirkers to Dutch and English shipping, so even lack of news could be attributed to Buckingham's failure as admiral to command the fleet. What news did get through reflected badly on the English war effort. Butter and Bourne put the best face on it they could. For example, the front page of the issue of 18 January lists one item after another promising news of Protestant victories, but the content was primarily of Catholic origin and began with a Spanish report celebrating the safe arrival of their fleet in November having evaded the English. When news of Mansfeld's defeat by Wallenstein at Dessau Bridge in April reached England, Joseph Mead wrote to Stuteville,

> Mansfield is overthrown by Count Wallenstein, nor can gather his men together again for want of money, which he hath in vain expected from us. Wallenstein is thirty thousand strong, and proceeds. All will be lost, and they say by our fault.[9]

Blame was placed on Buckingham. He was accused of mismanagement and impeached. To protect him, Charles dissolved Parliament without gaining any further supply.

---

[8] Hirst, *Conflict*, 116; J. Bowle, *Charles the First* (1975), 94–6; Wedgwood, 203; R. G. Asch, *The Thirty Years' War; The Holy Roman Empire and Europe, 1618–48* (New York, 1997), 80–5, 88; K. Sharpe, *The Personal Rule of Charles I* (New Haven, CT and London, 1992), 8.

[9] (18 January 1626), 11, 1, STC18507.177; Harl. MS 390 fo. 8, May 1626; *CandT*, 1:100; Harl. MS 390 fo. 40, 8 April 1626, Mead wrote, 'Of foreign news we hear nothing; the Dunkirkers stop all'.

With no new money from England, bad news continued unabated. Christian of Brunswick died in June 1626 dejected. In August, Christian of Denmark lost half his army at Lutter and Tilly occupied the greater part of Lower Saxony. After defeat, the subsequent manoeuvres of Mansfeld and Bethlem Gabor through Moravia and Silesia were difficult to follow, though they were met with some short-lived initial successes. Readers lost both heart and interest. By the end of 1625, the plague had reduced the London population by twenty percent, doing considerable damage to the economy. Sales of newsbooks petered out after January 1626 and were to remain low until 1630 when Gustavus Adolphus revived the fortunes of the Protestant cause.[10]

Thus, despite the optimism with which Charles embarked upon an adversarial foreign policy in 1625, he was soon frustrated. The support he expected was not forthcoming. He did not secure an adequate vote of funds. Failure bred further failures, both on land and at sea. Charles arguments for the loan of 1626 and explanation of the dissolution of Parliament did not allay concerns and he did little to lead public opinion, either by means of censorship or by spelling out the opportunities that were offered by the formation of an anti-Habsburg Alliance. Cogswell has suggested that a division in opinion developed that owed much to the way government presented its position. He considered Charles's problems to have been entirely of his own making since he knew how to explain his case, yet chose not to. It seems Charles found it difficult to understand anyone else's perspective and had a mistrust of popularity. An education that depicted the people as irrational and unstable may have deterred Charles from considering their views, while his ideas about kingship and its dignity may have obscured the distinction between actively courting popularity (in the way that Buckingham had quite unashamedly done in 1624) and more simply presenting a compelling argument for his case.[11] By the summer of 1626, there was a breakdown in relationships. Parliament was unwilling to back failure and readers only wanted to buy newsbooks that held some hope of success for the Protestant cause.

[10] Wedgwood, 209–12; Bowle, *Charles*, 98–100; Russell, *The Crisis*, 302–3; Hirst, *Conflict*, 116–18; J. O. Halliwell, ed., *The Autobiography and correspondence of Sir Simonds D'Ewes*, 1 (1845), 288–9, 347–8; Schumacher, 179–89.

[11] R. Cust, 'Charles I, the Privy Council, and the Forced Loan', *JBS*, 24, 2 (1985), for impact of Lutter, 209–10, 218; Cogswell, 'The Politics', 191, 200; Sharpe, *Image Wars*, 157–8; Russell, *The Causes*, 207; R. Cust, 'Charles I and Popularity', in *Politics*, ed. Cogswell et al., 235–56.

Isle of Rhé 1627

After these setbacks Charles's approach to the press started to change. At first this took the form of only a minimal exercise of censorship in June 1626 when he issued a proclamation against the printing and distribution of the House of Commons' *Remonstrance*. But, by December 1626, Warwick was at sea and providing news and some privateering success against the Spanish.[12] Charles and Buckingham were soon to develop a more proactive approach to public relations in a bid to improve Buckingham's image and regain lost popularity.

Cogswell described Buckingham's use of the Rhé expedition in 1627 to win back popular acclaim. Charles decided to intervene against the French because he felt his honour was at stake after the English loan ships had been used to weaken the Huguenots in 1626. This gave Buckingham an opportunity to pose as a Protestant champion, but what might have proved a boon for Butter and Bourne did not turn out that way since they were not the chosen publishers. Possibly Charles, or a close adviser, was influenced by the criticisms of Butter, in particular, by Ben Jonson in his recent plays. If the news campaign was to be successful, it could not afford to be associated with a publisher whose credibility had been the butt of jokes.[13]

A publicity campaign was planned alongside the expedition, with publications going to Thomas Walkley, while restraints were placed on the circulation of other news, particularly on the activities of Butter. Early in 1627 Secretary Conway wrote to the Stationers' Company complaining of,

> unfitting liberties which some of your Companie do take in printing weekly for their owne privat gaine, divers false and fabulous papers under the titles of Avisoes and Courantoes which ... oftentimes raise disadvantageous and scandalous reports upon the proceedings and successes of his Majesties friends and Allies, His Majesty hath commanded me to take like course as hath been formerly used for preventing these abuses, And according to his gracious pleasure ... I have appointed my servant George Rudolf Weckherlin to have perusal and allowance of all such papers of that kind.[14]

Butter was cautioned in particular because of his association with news publication, possibly Bourne was a sleeping partner at this time.

This letter marks the official start to a long-lasting mutually beneficial relationship. Responsibility for licensing newsbooks went to Weckherlin, a gifted German poet, Swabian by birth, educated in jurisprudence, with

---

[12] *Proclamations*, II, 93–5; (8 December 1626), 13–14, STC18507.184.
[13] Cogswell, 'The People's Love', 211–34.
[14] Add MS 72439, fo 1. This draft in Weckherlin's hand is dated 25 February 1627. Jackson, 'Court Book', 193.

personal ties to the publishing business through his brother-in-law, Robert Raworth. He had entered the service of the Wurttemberg Court after leaving the University of Tübingen and worked on behalf of Elizabeth and Frederick in England in the early 1620s. As a licenser, he was a practical choice because of his relevant knowledge and skills but, unlike Cottington, he was a Lutheran whose poetry championed the Protestant cause in Germany. This does not appear to have been an obstacle to his employment. After Conway's advancement he served Dorchester, who was a strong advocate of the Palatine cause as well as a continuing channel of news between England and northern Europe. Weckherlin was a gentlemen and a paid official at the heart of Charles's intelligence service who worked from 1625 for successive secretaries, drafting, deciphering and translating official international correspondence. He never gained a high profile or visibility that associated him publicly with a particular faction at Court. He survived Dorchester's death in 1632, his friend, Thomas Roe's loss of position, and the eclipse of the Protestant faction in Charles's Council, to become a close assistant of Charles in the mid-1630s. He worked on Charles's correspondence, handling warrants and passes to travel overseas, meeting foreign state visitors and keeping Charles abreast overseas news. Among Weckherlin's surviving papers are many of his official drafts and copies of documents, plus pages from his diary showing the extent of his responsibilities.[15]

Weckherlin's correspondence was extensive. He was well connected with the news networks, particularly of Protestant Europe. He exchanged news with agencies abroad and sometimes also with gazetteers through contact with postmasters, including Johann von den Birghen. He wrote regularly to crown agents in Paris, Brussels and Turin and to Johann Joachim von Rusdorf, the Palatine diplomat. Charles may well have valued his knowledge and experience with his sister's household in Germany. His appointment, like Cottington's before him, was to make use of his expertise, while his survival in a position of trust reflects Charles's continued concern for the Palatine.

There were further signs of government scrutiny and caution: in May, the bishop of London was busy seizing books and seeking the support of the Privy Council against a contention from some stationers that they should be compensated for their losses. On 2 June, Mead wrote that,

---

[15] ODNB, Weckherline; H. Langer, *The Thirty Years' War* (Poole, 1978), 220; L. W. Forster, *Georg Rudolf Weckherlin zur Kenntnis seines Lebens in England* (Basel, 1944); L. W. Forster, 'Sources for G. R. Weckherlin's Life in England: the Correspondence', *The Modern Language Review*, 2 (1946), 353–6; A. B. Thompson, 'Licensing the Press: The Career of G. R. Weckherlin during the Personal Rule of Charles I', *HJ*, 41 (1998), 658–61; A. Schaffer, *Georg Rudolf Weckherlin* (Danvers, MA, 1918/2009), 46, 54–5, 81; Add MS 72433; Reeve, 107–17, 181, 235–7, 284; Sharpe, *Personal Rule*, 157, 201–5; Atherton, 42.

The Lords of the Counsell have of late used to seaze upon the Merchants packes & break them open both from & to their Factors whereupon they have given a generall Caveat to their Factors to write nothing of intelligence by this meanes there is no more newes of forraigne affaires upon the Exchange … whatsoever is, is from the Corranto & that so ancient as it concernes nothing done since May began & so not worth relating.[16]

Butter, however, seems to have been strangely slow to respond to this changing climate since nothing more about foreign news is recorded by the Stationers' Company for nearly three months. Then, on 19 June, Charles gave the Rhé instructions to Buckingham. That day, Butter and Bourne put their business in order at the Company of Stationers, paying the hefty sum of 15s to register newsbooks from the previous June through to 1 August. They must have been hopeful that some new business would come their way. Butter also registered a further Warwick story. This was licensed by Weckherlin and provides the first record of his involvement in the licensing of foreign news.[17]

Buckingham led 7000 English troops ashore at the Île of Rhé, a few miles from La Rochelle, and issued A Manifestation and a request for the realm's prayers. These showed Buckingham as a heroic knight, listed the ships and commanders, and advertised a map of the Citadel where the French were besieged, though none of this explained why, in the middle of a war with Spain, the country was also engaged in war with France. Secretary Coke drafted an account of the diplomatic background to the French war that was not published. Charles, unlike his father, preferred not to explain. Instead of revealing the expedition's motives, in August, Thomas Walkley published A Journall, 'by Authoritie', with accounts of the expedition's progress. This ran to a second edition and was followed, on 30 August, by A Continued Journall of All the Proceedings of the Duke of Buckingham. It imitated the newsbooks and contained an upbeat account of the English troops and of the duke leading them courageously, including a foiled attempted assassination, and it assured readers that the English forces were well supplied.[18]

By contrast, on 2 August 1627, a warrant was signed by Coke for Butter's arrest. No reason was given. It simply stated, 'A warrant to the keeper of the Gatehouse to receave into his custodie and keepe prisoner the person of Nathaniell Butter. Signed by Mr Secretarie Coke.' The timing of the arrest points to the newsbook issued on 1 August. Butter had invited members of the expedition to supply material and the issue included lengthy accounts of the attack on Rhé. Most of it was in a positive vein, with ample praise for

[16] APC, April 1628–April 1629 (1958), 396, 398, 289; Harl. MS 390. fo. 261.
[17] Arber, vol. 4, 146.
[18] Cogswell, 'The People's Love', 226–8; T. Cogswell, '"Published by Authoritie": Newsbooks and the Duke of Buckingham's Expedition to the Ile de Rhé', HLQ, 67 (2004), 5–6.

Buckingham, but there were a few details that the government would probably have preferred to exclude, for example, the fact that the people of La Rochelle had not welcomed the duke and a report of soldiers running away and being called back by the duke. The account ends with a list of English dead and injured, admitting there were many more who drowned. Overall, however, it showed Buckingham acquitting himself well. Coke had a more serious concern, the circulation of pro-Habsburg propaganda.[19]

Altera secretissima instructio falsely claimed to be a translation from Dutch and had a careful analysis the internal strains of the Hague Alliance with enough insight to give it credibility. It explained why France, Venice and Ottomans were not likely to help and dismissed the value of Sweden. It then advised Frederick to overthrow Charles I and seize his Crown. This was treason, yet small numbers of printed copies entered England. Butter explained his involvement in a revealing petition that suggested a close working relationship with Weckherlin and a belief that Coke was fully aware of it. He had sold copies only to known trustworthy customers and was lending out an imperfect copy at a high charge of 1d a day. A customer, John Balle, a Buckinghamshire lawyer, who,

> made great protestacons, that hee would but read it over, and retourne it once againe within a weeke, but did not performe his promise. So the said 3rd printed booke, I seeing it amongst mr Wakerlins papers, desired him to lend it me for Robt. Gourdon for 2. or 3. daies, promising to retorne it back againe. This being all the hand or dealing that I have had with the booke aforesaid.

As Noel Malcolm has observed, this suggests that 'the policing of these matters, far from being a black-and-white affair, might often involve some rather complicated and mutually beneficial interactions between game-keepers and poachers'.[20] There was good money to be made in illicit material. Sharing news with Weckherlin could benefit both men while potentially supporting Frederick's cause. *Instructio* would have provided compelling reading for those committed to the restoration of the Palatinate.

We do not know how long Butter was imprisoned, though it was at least sixteen days. Thomas Walkley continued to report on the expedition, while Butter was permitted to continue to publish licensed continental and Rhé news.[21] However, on 12 September he made a double mistake of publishing an issue without first showing it to Weckherlin and of including a report from Paris from early August of the siege noting that the English were expecting reinforcements. Conway wrote again to the Stationers' Company, 'I have formerly signified unto you his Majesties dislike of the Libertie

---

[19] *APC, 1627* (1938), 470; (1 August 1627), 9, 11–12, STC18507.186.
[20] Petition from Butter, 4 August 1627, Add MS 64,892, fo. 59; N. Malcolm, *Reason of State, Propaganda, and the Thirty Years' War* (Oxford, 2007), 45–70, 68–9.
[21] Add MS 69,911, fo. 87; Appendix 3; Cogswell, 'By Authoritie', 10.

taken in printinge of weekly courantos and pamphletts of newes without anie rule or warrant.' He complained that some of the Company's members had published 'manie things ... that are false and oftentimes scandalous ... nothing ... should bee printed without ... approbation of my servant Weckherlin'. On 14 September, Mead again commented,'Currantes will be scare hereafter; for there hath a check bin given the Printers'.[22]

Again, Butter was allowed to continue, but he must have felt besieged on every side. He was required to get licences, yet the partnership had no monopoly. The imprint 'Mercurius Britannicus' was dropped after 1 August, possibly in recognition of the fact that they no longer held any claim to being the sole or official publishers of periodical news from abroad. Now that profits were once again being made they were vulnerable to further competition. Another publisher, Ralph Mabbe, started a new series and registered his first issue on 28 September. Butter had evidently felt it unwise to challenge Walkley given his connections but he felt no such constraint about Mabbe and reacted promptly, complaining that 'there is another unknowne Mercurie sprung up within these few dayes' who is merely an opportunist, 'that by chance met a Pinke from Holland, twixt that and Gravesend, that wil tel strange newes'.[23]

In the midst of this, readers debated the news and its significance. Rous set news of the progress of the king of Denmark along side news of La Rochelle. Locally, he defended the Crown against men 'disposed to speake the worst of state business', but no doubt spoke for many when he wrote in the margin of his diary, 'Why did we leave the Palatinate and fall fowle with France?'[24] By October the good news from Rhé was crumbling, attempts to re-supply the forces had failed and awareness of the loss of English troops was growing. Walkley's reports continued to be upbeat, but readers had become sceptical. Butter meanwhile, deprived of official reports from the English forces, continued to rely on his usual contacts. In the end, this gave him credibility: when he reported, on 17 October, that the Citadel was taken he was able to add 'which newes was written by good hands from the Hage'.[25]

Historians are divided on the relevance of the war with France and on this attempt to manipulate the news. Failure at La Rochelle could not be disguised, but, as Cogswell conceded, while Charles made errors in allowing the Rohan publication while stifling the more helpful explanation drafted

---

[22] (17 August 1627), 5 and 6, STC18507.187; (12 September 1627), STC18507.188; Cogswell, 'The People's Love', 229–320; Thompson, 'Licensing the Press', 653–4; Add MS 72439 fo. 2; Harl. MS 390. fo. 292; Conway to the Wardens, 5 September 1627, Add MS Misc. 18, fo. 82.
[23] Arber, vol. 4, entry for Ralph Mabb, 28 September 1627, 150; (4 October 1627), 1, STC18507.189.
[24] Rous, 11–13.
[25] Harl. MS 390, fo. 299; Cogswell, 'The People's Love', 230; (17 October 1627), 11, STC18507.191.

for publication by Coke, he succeeded in 'throttling the *Mercurius* then mounting its own coverage ... never before had the government ... accorded any military or naval operation such lavish coverage'.[26] This episode may, however, say more about Buckingham and his desire for popularity than about the development of Charles's thinking. Charles could allow Buckingham to do as he wished without necessarily completely agreeing with him. This was demonstrated when Cottington was sent away from Court by Buckingham in April 1625, but provided with a pension by Charles. If Charles had an interest in reporting the Rhé campaign or in the muzzling of Butter, he did not sustain it. His only press preparation for Parliament in early 1628 was to hold up to the London Stationers *The Spy discovering the danger of Arminian heresie and Spanish trecherie*, printed in Amsterdam and proposing to advise Parliament and the Crown on the dangers of 'foreyne enemies, [the Pope and Spain and] ... domestick traitors', as an example of what they should not sell or 'meddle with'.[27]

Weckherlin continued as licenser. In May, Butter was allowed to make a bulk entry in the register for twenty-four newsbooks. Parliament was awash with petitions and, on 30 July, Bourne's pamphlets touching on relations with the Dutch following Amboyna were confiscated. Bourne quickly extricated himself and remained in good standing in the Stationers' Company. He claimed he published entirely at the behest of the East India Company and even gained compensation. George Wither castigated his countrymen for their failure to support the wars, 'War threatens us ... Yet we do nothing ... Armes, victuals, men and money we have in store; Yet we falsely cry that we are poore.'[28] But Charles began to rethink foreign policy, initiating moves for peace with Spain. Buckingham's assassination in August did not immediately curtail his hopes of redeeming honour at La Rochelle, but, after unsuccessfully sending ships to the Huguenot rescue in the spring and autumn, their capitulation in October left him little to fight for.

Criticisms of Buckingham reached a peak in 1627–8, with many rhymes and verses blaming him for failure. More perhaps even than the jibes and financial implications of loans and coat and conduct money, the effects of military involvement on the Continent reached deep into lives of Charles's subjects. Drums to recruit for one volunteer force after another had beat incessantly from 1624 to 1628. Soldiers moved through the countryside to assembly and embarkation points. There were months of billeting in Kent, Essex, Suffolk and Norfolk, and many families in all the Stuart kingdoms had sons who took up a military career. Yet this involvement had little

---

26 Reeve, 15; Thompson, 'Licensing the Press', 665, 654, fn. 3, 665, fn. 44; Henri, Duc de Rohan, *A Declaration of the duke of Rohan*, Butter (1628), 6–7; Arber, vol. 4, 161; Cogswell, 'The People's Love', 231–3; Cogswell, 'Politics of Propaganda', 188, 207.

27 C. S. Clegg, *Press Censorship in Caroline England* (Cambridge, 2008), 48–53.

28 APC, *April 1628–April 1629* (1958), 61 No. 205; Arber, vol. 4, 162; G. Whither, *Britain's Remembrancer* (1628), 239, quoted in Sharpe, *Personal Rule*, 60.

discernible impact. The Cadiz expedition, support for the Danish army, and the Rhé expedition all failed. Charles had found it difficult to raise money and support where his direction was unclear and his views at odds with the populace. Confidence was lost.[29]

In Germany, the Protestants and the Roman Catholic League considered how to respond to the increasingly dynastic moves of Ferdinand, while Wallenstein went from strength to strength. He was given Mecklenburg by Ferdinand and was only frustrated in his ambitions to establish dominion over the Baltic by failure to take Stralsund. The summer of 1629 marked a low ebb in Protestant fortunes. Newsbook sales fell to an all time low, leaving us with little evidence of the coverage of the Danish defeat at Wolgast or the Dutch successes off Cuba or at home in Flemish waters, at Wessel and Hertogenbosch.

The newsbook ban

Still more difficult times lay ahead for the publishers with a ban in 1632 on the publication of newsbooks that was to last until 1638. This ban has long bolstered the Siebert account of how 'early Stuart kings continued on their way, extending … repressive measures' and heavily censoring news. It is not difficult to find incidents that suggest censorship was tightening or to support Steinberg's explanation of the ban, that the 'undisguised enthusiasm of the editors for the success of the anti-Habsburg powers was their undoing'.[30] However, a simple analysis cannot explain the confusion caused by the ban at the time nor why Butter and Bourne were permitted to continue to publish a less frequent serial 'history' of the war under a variety of titles including, *The Swedish Intelligencer* and *The German History*.

In the period from January 1629 to the ban on news publication in October 1632 Charles's attitude towards the possibility of calling Parliament hardened and his foreign policy vacillated before settling for pro-Spanish 'neutrality' through which he hoped to develop support for the Palatine cause. A Hispanic orientation was so much at odds with popular sentiment

---

[29] A. Bellany, '"Raylinge Rhymes and Vaunting Verse": Libellous Politics in Early Stuart England, 1603–1628', in Lake, 288–9, 297–310; M. C. Fissel, *English Warfare, 1511–1641* (London and New York, 2001), 256, 109–12, 261–8; J. Eales, 'The Rise of Ideological Politics in Kent 1558–1640', in *Early Modern Kent, 1540–1640*, ed. M. Zell (Woodbridge, 2000), 287, 307; *Rous*, 14–15; A. Searle, *Barrington Family Letters, 1628–1632*, Camden Society, 4:28 (1983), 19, 79–83; J. Morrill, 'William Davenport and the "Silent Majority" of Early Stuart England', *Journal of the Chester Archaeological Society*, 58 (1975), 121.

[30] Arber, vol. 4, 528–36; *CSPD, 1631–33*, 426; Siebert, 126, 155; *CSPD, 1628–29*, 525, 539; *CSPD, 1629–31*, 202; S. H. Steinberg, *Five Hundred Years of Printing* (1955/1974), 248.

that it would not comfortably co-exist with the practical or political pressures created by news publication, but the confused nature of this switch in foreign policy and the fact that it was not publicly explained left those affected ignorant of the reason for the sudden loss of their livelihood while providing the opportunity to accommodate the *Intelligencer*.

In January 1629, Charles recalled Parliament. He was still committed to supporting Denmark and seeking to avert or at least delay Christian's peace negotiations with the emperor following defeat in September 1628 outside Wolfgast. He also still hoped to confirm the legality of the collection of tonnage and poundage. He appears to have approached the new session with optimism, instigating new commissions to investigate abuse at Court, restoring old enemies of Buckingham, and enforcing the recusancy laws. His preparations did not extend to any attempt to influence public opinion, and debate quickly deteriorated into arguments about religion and taxation. On 5 February, Viscount Dorchester, having succeeded Conway as Secretary of State, wrote to the Stationers' Company reminding members of the need to submit to Weckherlin any proposed publications 'of newes relations histories or other things ... that have reference to matters and affairs of State'. The letter noted that publishers had been negligent, but it was mild in tone and made no reference to Parliament. The session of Parliament ended in disarray on 2 March. Charles followed dissolution with two proclamations, the first explaining his motives and, on 27 March, a second, 'For suppressing of false Rumours touching Parliament'.[31]

Historians continue to debate the relationship between Parliament and foreign policy in the 1620s. While MPs represented the concerns of their localities, including concerns about increasing financial burdens and probably remained ignorant throughout the 1620s about the real costs of government and especially of war, Cust has shown that MPs were becoming more representative of public opinion, while Pauline Croft has shown the greater frequency of Parliaments allowed greater informal contact in London, facilitated shopping for goods including publications, and strengthened the role of networking in the formation of public opinion. Newsbook readers, MPs included, were better informed than ever before about political and military events in Europe, about trading concerns and tensions further afield. They now had evidence on which to base arguments about how a war should be conducted. Any gap in knowledge was due to the fact that James and Charles withheld information about diplomacy, costs and expenditure, and they did the latter at least partly because budgeting was poor. It is possible that only a privateering sea war with Spain could have satisfied the Commons. MPs were also undoubtedly concerned about the prospect of money being misspent and about the bad news from La Rochelle. Given

---

[31] Sharpe, *Personal Rule*, 52–3, 56–7; Sharpe, *Image Wars*, 170–1, 158–60; Hirst, *Conflict*, 127; Add MS72439, fo. 4; *Proclamations*, 2, 226–8; Reeve, 75–96, 106, 109–11.

these very real grounds for concern, the subsidies voted were generous and reflect the significance of foreign policy in this political awakening. Had Charles had some military or naval success, it is quite reasonable to suppose that more money would have been forthcoming.[32]

Charles and Buckingham had gambled on turning failure into success, no doubt believing fewer questions would be asked and more support would be forthcoming, but matters went from bad to worse through a mixture of failed negotiations, poor naval and military strategies, inefficient procurements and bad luck. Events on the Continent in the spring of 1629 caused further distress for Charles: news of the accidental drowning in January of Henry, the Prince Palatine and heir to the lost lands, was followed, in March, with the Edict of Restitution. Charles could see he was in no position to play a direct and influential role within Germany. He reached agreement with France but was concerned about how his withdrawal from direct action might be seen in England and took steps to influence the way in which this news was presented.

Dorchester's February letter to the Stationers' Company was followed, on 2 May 1629, after the terms of the Treaty of Susa were agreed, but before they were signed, by Weckherlin licensing two newsbook issues. One had already been published on 24 April, but the other, dated 5 May, promised *Certaine commands ... by the French King concerning ... peace betweene the two nations. Articles of peace propounded by the King of Denmarke.* However, it contained nothing about relations between France and England; only lengthy transcripts of the articles of peace offered alternately by the king of Denmark and the emperor at Lubeck, together with a scatter of news on the implementation of the Edict of Restitution. Material on the English/French negotiations had been withdrawn. Presenting these two independently negotiated treaties together would have associated them far too closely. However, details of treaties were not suppressed for long. On 27 May, Weckherlin licensed Bourne's publication of the peace with France.[33]

Meanwhile Butter was busy defending himself, along with Michael Spark and two printers, from articles relating to the publication of anti-Arminian religious works. Laud's influence was growing, and the vigilance of the Ecclesiastical Commissioners was increasing. This led to noticing that Butter's printed text of *The Reconciler* included previously deleted material. Butter's experience of the courts showed in his defence to the Commission. He challenged the licenser and persuaded the Commission that the 'judgment of two bishops ... was more to be regarded than the opinion of the Licenser'.

---

[32] Reeve, 232; R. Cust, 'Politics and the Electorate in the 1620s' and C. Thompson, 'Court Politics and Parliamentary Conflict in 1625', in *Conflict in Early Stuart England: Studies in Religion and Politics 1603–42*, ed. R. Cust and A. Hughes (1989); P. Croft, 'Capital Life, Members of Parliament Outside the House', in *Politics, Religion*, ed. Cogswell *et al.*, 65–83.
[33] Arber, vol. 4, 176–7; (5 May 1629), STC18507.200.

However, news regulation and the control of religious publications were managed separately and the former remained under the Protestant oversight of Dorchester and Weckherlin. Charles continued to support the Palatine cause in a new embassy to northern Europe and in negotiations with Spain, but he could not stop Christian of Denmark from making peace with the emperor on 12 May 1629, having looked in vain for promised support from England.[34]

Butter caught up with payments for another bulk registration of news-books, but appears to have left what was, by this stage, a struggling business, in the hands of Bourne until after the news broke that the Swedish king, Gustavus Adolphus, had entered the war and sales started to pick up. Bourne survived the downturn in business by prudently reducing newsbook output to about one issue a month. Then, from the summer 1630, with the arrival in Germany of Gustavus Adolphus, sales began to increase until, by October 1632, they were back to levels at the start of the 1620s. This change in fortunes justified Bourne's decision to invest in maintaining the business and its supply and distribution contacts through lean times. Charles supported Gustavus Adolphus as best he could without calling Parliament by letting Hamilton raise a troop of 6000 volunteers and giving £25,000 towards expenses. The men sailed in July/August 1631 for Stralsund while Charles sent Sir Robert Anstruther to Vienna and Sir Henry Vane to negotiate with Gustavus Adolphus and welcomed home and knighted the messenger, John Caswell, sent by Gustavus Adolphus to announce his victory at Breitenfeld. His report subsequently appeared in the printed news.[35]

Butter and Bourne became confident that there was now no need for a subtle or implicit Protestant voice. This period was a high point in the development of Thirty Years War news reporting in England for content and quality. There was a creative co-operation between the trade and those in authority based on a belief that newsbooks could serve the policy objectives of the Protestant pro-Palatine family faction in Whitehall.

The cumulative effect of successive British recruitments meant that, by 1631 and 1632, soldiers from the Stuart kingdoms were serving in large numbers in north Germany and the Netherlands, including many in senior positions, especially in the Swedish army. Though numbers are difficult to establish, there may have been nearly 10,000 British mercenaries in the Dutch army and over 20,000 in Gustavus Adolphus's army by December 1631, including survivors from Mansfield's recruitment in 1625 who had joined the Danes then transferred to Sweden. These were augmented by Hamilton's men in 1631. Thomas Barrington wrote to his father in June 'the drum beates in London dayley and forces increase', and Hamilton's tents

---

[34] Reeve, 113, 237, 242–9; Sharpe, *Personal Rule*, 66–8; Clegg, *Caroline England*, 87–9, 108; CSPD, 1628–9, 525, 539.
[35] Arber, vol. 4, 20 June 1629, 182; CandT, 2, 139, 140.

were up in Islington.[36] There were many opportunities to obtain news and considerable demand for it at home. There was also a sense (as in Antwerp in 1620) that there was a need for proactive news reporting to harness public opinion in support of military commitment. Fortunately for Butter and Bourne, Dorchester remained Secretary of State and among those in Court who had been waiting for the political tide to turn in favour of proactive engagement to restore the Palatinate, and Weckherlin was the licenser.

It seems as if from the beginning Weckherlin was content to trust the publishers. His secretarial responsibilities were extensive and the task of reading newsbooks carefully every week would have been time-consuming. So, despite the fact that his knowledge could provide a valuable check on sensitivity, he seems to have been too busy to do justice to this role. Even in 1627, in the height of interest in controlling the news of the Rhé expedition, Weckherlin caught up with the news only after there was a problem and, even then, he did not inspect every issue. Repeated complaints between 1627 and 1632 that the publishers were not presenting their newsbooks for scrutiny suggest that Weckherlin let the publishers police themselves at their own risk. Whatever the informal arrangements, the publishers found them workable. Butter was later to compare Weckherlin with succeeding licensers and describe him as 'more understanding in these forraine affaires, and ... more candid'. By the summer of 1631, despite the upturn in business, they appear to have had no foreign publications officially inspected since approval of their Bermuda news in April 1630 while, in February 1630, even with a risk of a read-across to English negotiation with Spain, he had approved *Three severall treatises*, that argued against the Dutch making at truce with Spain.[37]

Once again, a trustworthy editor was needed to support the upturn in business, to avoid mistakes and political gaffes, and to present news well enough to appeal to a broad spectrum of readers. Watts was appointed. He may have known Weckherlin from his time in the Palatinate in 1620 and he appears to have been the ideal candidate. Protestant but not a Puritan, connected to Laud and with his connections to the Court growing, he

---

[36] Arblaster, 41, 44–51; Fissel, *English Warfare*, 270; A. Grosjean, *An Unofficial Alliance: Scotland and Sweden 1569–1654* (Leiden and Boston, MA, 2003), 55–62, 76, 88–95, 325; A. Grosjean, 'A Century of Scottish Governorship in the Swedish Empire, 1574–1700', in *Military Governors and Imperial Frontiers c. 1600–1800*, ed. A. Mackillop and S. Murdoch (Leiden and Boston, MA, 2003), 57–61; S. Murdoch, *Britain, Denmark-Norway and the House of Stuart, 1603–1660* (East Linton, 2003), 50, 56–7, 60; P. H. Wilson, *Europe's Tragedy: A History of the Thirty Years' War* (2009), 321–2; S. Murdoch, ed., *Scotland and the Thirty Years' War, 1618–1648* (Leiden and Boston, MA, 2001), 8–12, 19; J. V. Polisensky, 'A Note on Scottish Soldiers in the Bohemian War 1619–1622', in *Scotland*, ed. S. Murdoch, 111–12; Searle, *Barrington*, 195, 197.
[37] Add MS 72439, fo. 2; 5 February 1628/9, fo. 4; 30 January 1631/2, fo. 6, also fn. 79 above. Arber, vol. 4, 195, 198, 222, 376; *Three severall treatises*, B&B (1630) STC24258; (11 January 1641), STC18507.343, quoted in Dahl 251.

carefully omitted almost all criticisms of the British forces, and their lack of supplies, and any inappropriate hint of discussions that were going on behind the scenes between Gustavus Adolphus and Charles. There is a case for suggesting that Watt's editorship, with its almost unprecedented access to privileged news, signified a court attempt to influence news coverage to support the Crown, making him a possible forerunner to Berkenhead. The Swedish king represented an acceptable, monarchical face of Protestantism in Europe, and it was acceptable to be visibly pro-Palatine in 1631.[38]

That year, Massinger's *The Maid of Honour* was licensed even though it was unmistakably about the Palatine family and began with a scene that recreated events in 1620/21 when James did not rush to the aid of Frederick. However, *Believe as You List* was rejected by the Master of Revels because it dealt critically with Spain's relations with Portugal, then passed once re-written with a Syrian setting. If writers found intervention unpredictable, it was probably because of Charles's changing allegiances.[39]

It had taken time to negotiate peace with Spain because Charles held out for support for the restitution of the Palatinate. Encouraged by Spanish defeats in the Low Countries, he simultaneously pressed the Dutch through Carlisle and Vane for troops for the Palatinate, but finally settled for vague promises of help. The Treaty of Madrid, signed in November 1630, did no more than restore the balance of 1604, but Charles continued to pursue his objectives of retrieving honour and reclaiming the Palatinate. In addition to negotiating with Sweden, he began to restore the fleet, recognising the need for a strong navy to protect Britain's growing mercantile interests against piracy and to counter the growing Dutch fishing fleet presence of British shores. Spain might benefit from English naval protection in the Channel, and might perhaps even pay for it through diplomatic intervention in Vienna, thus sparing Charles from direct engagement in the war in Germany. Undecided, through 1631 and 1632, he explored options, including one of siding with the Dutch to stir up rebellion in the Spanish Netherlands and another, with Spain, to launch a joint attack on the Dutch. A turning point came in the winter of 1631/2 when Swedish forces advanced on Heidelberg. Charles had to decide whether to form an alliance with Sweden as the price for a commitment to the restoration of Frederick. Despite the obvious popular appeal of such an alliance, he hesitated then decided not to call Parliament for funding. Dorchester died in February 1632, leaving Weston to continue the negotiations. Thereafter the emphasis shifted towards Spain in what Reeve has called the 'masked end of an era in the history of Anglo-continental Protestantism'. Vane was recalled from

---

[38] Schumacher, 202–03, 205–07, 212–15; Sharpe, *Personal Rule*, 284–5.
[39] A. Worden, 'Literature and Political Censorship in Early Modern England', in *Too Mighty to be Free: Censorship and the Press in Britain and the Netherlands*, ed. A. Duke and C. Tamse (Zutphen, 1987), 53–7.

negotiations with Sweden in the summer of 1632 and Windebank, rather than Roe, was appointed Secretary of State.[40]

Still, the partnership remained confident. When, in May, John Bartlett attempted to profit from interest in the Swedish campaign by publishing *The Swedish Devotion*, his competition was speedily addressed with the cooperation of both Weckherlin and the Stationers' Company. His entry in the register was deleted and a new one substituted in favour of Butter and Bourne 'under the handes of master Weckherlyn and both wardens'. Butter and Bourne's *Swedish Discipline* explained,

> having beene heretofore by promise engaged to give you all three parts of the Swedish Discipline, wee are here enforced to present you with the first onely, and that dismembered from the other two ... Tis done to prevent your being abused by another: who ayming ... more at his owne profit, then the benefit of his Reader ... is about to thrust these following prayers upon the world.

It robustly dismissed the competing volume in terms of 'uselessnesse': his translator had not recognised the connections between the Swedish and English *Common Prayer Book*, nor referenced his text to scripture.[41]

However, Charles was becoming annoyed by 'the pernicious publishing ... dayly practiced, of divers pamphlets', so he wrote to the Stationers' Company reminding them of the need for licences. Weckherlin's role continued: he was by this stage working for Sir John Coke, an aging diplomat with a strict Protestant and anti-Spanish views, who trusted him to carry out most of his duties unsupervised, but who seems to have had less personal authority at Court, as Windebank took responsibility for relations with Spain, Italy and Flanders. In June and July, Butter, realising he had mistakenly spoken too freely to a customer in his shop who turned out to be Thomas, agent to the Archduchess Isabella, resumed taking newsbooks to Weckherlin for licensing. By then issues were appearing often, more than once a week, and there was no possibility that Weckherlin could scrutinise them all effectively. After licensing five more issues, it seems he did not try: no further newsbooks were entered in the register after July leaving them exposed to a tumble of events that led to abolition.[42]

In the issue of 3 October, Butter included a report that Olivares and Legnares had been imprisoned in Spain for storing up personal treasure. This mistake was spotted quickly: while the press was still running the passage

---

[40] Sharpe, *Personal Rule*, 57–9; Cust, 'Charles I and Popularity', 246–7; Reeve, 207, 256–9, 277–89; C. Carlton, *Charles I: The Personal Monarch* (London and New York, 1995), 172.

[41] Arber, vol. 4, 243, 244; *The Swedish Discipline* (1632), A2-verso, STC23519.5.

[42] Carlton, *Charles I*, 160; Sharpe, *Personal Rule*, 155–6; Letter 9 June 1632, in *Pory*, Micro. 272; Add MS 72439, fo. 8; Arber, vol. 4, entries for 26 June and 2 July 1632, 246, 248.

was removed. However, it was shortly followed by an issue devoted to the Dutch taking Maastricht. This was one unfortunate news report too many for Isabella's agent and its timing could not have been worse. Arrangements had been negotiated for the coining in London of Spanish silver to pay the army in Flanders. Shipments had just begun to arrive bringing with them a percentage for Charles for their safe passage. Charles listened sympathetically to Thomas's complaints, but the ready opportunity to mollify Spain by giving London news a pro-Spanish gloss through the use of Verhoeven's Antwerp news had just been lost because victory at Maastricht allowed Frederick Henry to sever the news link between Antwerp, Brussels and western Germany.[43]

The resulting ban on news publication in London, on 17 October, by order of the Star Chamber, was to last for six years. The Order was prompted directly by Charles to address,

> the great abuse in the printing of gazettes, and pamphlets of news from Foreign parts, and upon signification of his Majesty's express pleasure and command to the Board for the present suppressing of the same, it was ordered that all printing of the same be suppressed and inhibited; and that as well Nathaniel Butter and Nicholas Bourne, booksellers, under whose names the said gazettes have been usually published, as all booksellers, presume not from henceforth to print, publish, or sell any of the said pamphlets.[44]

Pory wrote to Lord Brooke, 25 October, repeating the order listing those involved in the decision and adding,

> They say the occasion of this order was the importunity of the Spanish and arch-duchess's agents, who were vexed at the soul to see so many losses and crosses, so many dishonours and disasters, betide the House of Austria ... but this smothering of the corantos is but a pallation, not a cure, of their wounds. They will burst out again one of these days.

The coining of Spanish money in England is mentioned in this letter. Pory's letter to John Scudamore, 20 October, confirms that 'printing newes is wholly suppressed', and his letter, 27 October, also referred to the ban and offence to Spain. Sabrina Baron supported her argument that Pory translated for Butter and Bourne with the comment that his reaction to the ban was that 'of a man who had just lost a significant portion of his livelihood'. Pory probably had more at stake. He was well placed to supply news to the continental networks to which the partnership subscribed and, as we

---

[43] (3 October 1632), STC18507.273; Dahl, 219; (16 October 1632), 12, STC18507.276; Reeve, *Charles I*, 256; G. M. D. Howat, *Stuart and Cromwellian Foreign Policy* (1974), 44; Sharpe, *Personal Rule*, 91; H. Taylor, 'Trade, Neutrality, and the "English Road", 1630–1648', *EHR*, 2:25:2 (1972), 241–5.

[44] *CSPD, 1631–33*, 426; Arber, vol. 4, 528–36.

saw with the incident over *Altera secretissima* manuscript, copying and print trade in foreign news were intimately connected in Butter's shop. We see this again when, in February 1633, Butter held on to a report about Lutzen and Gustavus Adolphus's death, thinking he would get permission to print, only to find he was warned not to circulate it, even in manuscript.[45]

Despite warning signs, the ban came as a surprise to Butter who thought that, whatever the problem, it could be fixed. He told Pory,

> a gentleman of his acquaintance having dined this day sennight in the company of Mr Taylor, the arch duchesse's agent, and asked him the reason of calling in the Currantos, he answered the newes was so ill, as the lords would not have it known ... Besides he is getting to be translated divers Antwerp Currantos, to show their lordships how they lie upon us and our friends, and we in the meantime must be muzzled and our mouths stopped. But yesternight I met him at Whitehall, after he had been in Mr Secretary Coke's chamber: and he told me he hoped ere long his Currantos would be revived.[46]

Butter's relationship with Weckherlin had endured the dramas of news production for five years, but matters were not settled quickly. A further reassurance was given in December after the deaths of the king of Sweden and Frederick, and the partners published eulogies to both the kings, but Pory noted that the market for printed news was faltering, 'next week, Currantos shall be permitted ... but some men say, now that incomparable king is dead, they will buy no more'.[47] The war ceased to be about the Protestant cause and became a dynastic war without clear confessional alignments while, at home, Weckherlin found himself having to cope with increasingly complicated relationships, surrounded by Laud, Weston, Cottington and Windebank.

Nevertheless, Butter and Bourne persisted. In September 1633, the partnership petitioned again, pleading their livelihood:

> a great part of the King's subjects content by the Gazettes and weekly news, they therefore pray, that on promise of being careful in time to come, that nothing dishonourable to princes in amity with his Majesty should pass the press, they may, like the subjects of all other states, be permitted the publishing of the said news again.

This was endorsed with a statement that these are published in all other countries, and 'at Brussels and Antwerpe are corrected and licensed by the

---

[45] *CandT*, 2: 185–6, 225–6, Gresley to Puckering, 6 February 1632; *Pory*, Micro. 309 and 311; S. A. Baron, 'The Guises of Dissemination in Early Seventeenth-century England', in DandB, 46; Raymond, 90–1.

[46] *CandT*, 2:188, to Sir Thomas Lucy, 1 November 1632.

[47] Ibid., 210, from Pory, 13 December 1632; F. Schloer, *The Death of the two renowned kings ... a sermon*, B&B (1632), STC21819; Wedgwood, 327, 332.

Jesuits'. A further note suggested the partnership was willing to 'settle it in some fitting course'. In December, they thought their petition had been granted and paid seven shillings in arrears for registering the newsbooks at the Stationers' Company, but still they were disappointed.[48]

The new arrangements must have suited the now, more vulnerable, Weckherlin quite well. Publication had become so frequent that it must have been difficult to keep an adequate oversight. The war was being covered in the lengthier and less frequent *Swedish Intelligencer*, where there was time to tell the story coherently, to edit and check with a level of care that was appropriate given Charles's closer relations with Spain. However, others also believed that renewed weekly publication was a possibility. Walter Wardner and George More petitioned unsuccessfully and a proposal the following year, offering greater surveillance by setting up an office to check that nothing was added to books after they were licensed, similarly failed.[49] Meanwhile imported news was available for those who could afford it.[50]

Despite Buckingham's experiment to woo the press, a number of warnings given to the Stationers' Company, licensing, and the 1632 ban, in practice, Charles had paid little real attention to news publication and put little true effort into communications. He intervened sporadically. The forced loan was justified by reference to Lutter and the need to support the Palatines, and ship money by naval defence arguments. Recruitment drives were accompanied by news coverage. Watts's espoused the Swedish invasion but this support was abandoned at Gustavus Adolphus's death. Charles left news licensing in the hands of Weckherlin who shared his concern for the Palatinate and was happy to allow a Protestant foreign news press to thrive under nominal supervision in politically sensitive times. There were many brushes with the Crown over this period, yet none saw the ban as part of any strategy, only as a temporary setback to avoid a passing embarrassment with Spain. Petitions were commended, and Weckherlin continued to license compendiums of news that were sufficiently infrequent to allow more effective editing. The ban reduced day-to-day political pressure on Weckherlin, whose position was weakening as Laud and Windebank gained influence. Cust tells us Charles needed 'a steady stream of pamphlets and declarations, justifying his actions in terms that were intelligible to the political nation'.[51]

---

[48] CSPD, 1633–1634, 222; Arber, vol. 4, 283, entry 6 December 1633.

[49] CandT, 2:193, Gresley to Puckering, 14 November 1632; CSPD, 1634–1635, 418; S. Lambert, 'Coranto Printing in England', JNandPH, 8 (1992), 6, dates the Wardner/More petition in James's reign.

[50] (Amsterdam, 1633), STC18507.359; (Amsterdam, about February 1633), STC18507.360; (Amsterdam, February 1633), STC18507.361; H. Hexham, A Journal of the taking of Venlo, ... the memorable siege of Maastricht (Delph, 1633), STC13236; Dahl, 280–3; M. E. Bohannon, 'A London Bookseller's Bill: 1635–1639', The Library, 4:18 (1938), 423.

[51] Cust, Charles I, 170, 195.

But the decision to turn towards Spain would have been difficult to explain, and only a much more coherent effort could have redirected the impact of news on the formation of public opinion.

Charles's peace and the Peace of Prague

The initial decision to ban weekly publication may well have been pragmatic and symptomatic of a vacillating foreign policy with Charles playing cards held close to his chest. However, the mid-1630s were marked by steps designed to improve the Crown's influence over newsprint, while the Thirty Years War reached a critical watershed with the Peace of Prague.

A proclamation, in 1626, to address religious controversy by constraining the expression of 'opinions' and a declaration, in 1628, limiting the interpretation of the Articles of Religion made it more difficult for Calvinists to obtain ecclesiastical licenses, while increased surveillance, the involvement of the High Commission in printing cases, and the replacement of Archbishop Abbott's licensers by those supporting Laud, resulted in a further shift in the balance. Anthony Milton argues that in the 1630s Laudians were 'aggressive and effective combatants'. Licensers allowed the publication of works with Arminian sympathies and had a decisive influence over what appeared in print as mainstream orthodoxy. The result was a gradual and significant change in the content of religious printing in London.[52]

The Star Chamber Decree, in 1637, tightened trade control, integrating existing mechanisms, addressing trade concerns while encompassing the reprinting of previously licensed material. It tackled loopholes in control over imported books, and extended licensing to law books and ephemeral material usually left to the discretion of the Stationers' Company. Lambert has depicted the Decree as primarily a trade mechanism, while Sharpe, recognising that 'some contemporaries felt the sharpness of the wind of change', denied that the Decree had anything new. He concluded 'England in the 1630s was not a country in which men were free to publish or read what they saw fit. Nor, however, was it a realm in which all criticism and dissent were stifled.' But censorship became an issue that people talked about, and 1630s changes contributed to a culture of censorship where the punishments of Prynne, Bastwick and Burton were seen as emblematic of a clamp down on puritan works.[53]

[52] A. Milton, 'Licensing, Censorship and Religious Orthodoxy in Early Stuart England', *HJ*, 41, 3 (1998), 623–51; Clegg, *Caroline England*, 45, 48, 84–92, 103, 108, 134–48; S. Mutchow Towers, *Control of Religious Printing in Early Stuart England* (Woodbridge, 2003), 163–4, 189, 210–11, 232–5, 277.
[53] *CSPD, 1637–1638*, 72; S. Lambert, 'State Control of the Press in Theory and Practice: The Role of the Stationers' Company before 1640', in *Censorship and the Control of Print in England and France 1600–1910*, ed. R. Myers and M. Harris (Winchester, 1992), 1–32;

Ecclesiastical licensers were not, however, directly involved in the news nor with what came to be called 'histories', which were permitted when 'news' was not. Nonetheless, Figure 4 shows a drop in surviving publications on continental affairs from the end of 1634.[54] Close scrutiny of news content also reveals a shift in perspective.

Year	Publication	Impressions
1632	*The Swedish Intelligencer* Part 1 (January), revised three times. *The Swedish Intelligencer* Part 2 (July), surviving variants suggest at least three impressions. *The Swedish Discipline* (May) two issues *Swedish Devotion* for J. Bartlet *A Short Survey of the Kingdome of Sweden*, J. Storey, for M. Spark[55]	10+
1633	*The Swedish Intelligencer* Parts 3 and 4 (February), surviving variants suggest two+ impressions *The Continuation of the German History* Part 5 (October), two issues	4+
1634	*The Swedish Intelligencer* Part 1, 4th revise *The Swedish Intelligencer ... 4 parts with the Discipline* *The Relation of that great Generalissimo*[56] *A True Relacon of the Duke of Ffreidlands death*[57] *The History of the Present Warres* Part 6 (June) *A supplement to the sixth part* (June) *Arrest of the Court of Parliament* *The German History Continued* Part 7 (November) two variants *Two famous pitcht battels*[58]	10
1635	*The forme of the agreement made at Strumsdorff*[59] *The Modern History of the World* Part 8 (November)	2
1636	None known	0

Figure 4: Output of *The Swedish Intelligencer* and it successors 1632–6

Were there other factors at play here? For many readers there were more immediate concerns: plague spread through the country, emptying London in the summer of 1636, closing palaces, fairs, theatres and paper mills. An

M. Mendle, 'De Facto Freedom, De Facto Authority: Press and Parliament, 1640–1643', *HJ*, 18, 2 (1995), 310; Clegg, *Caroline England*, 92, 95, 110–12, 121, 194–207; Towers, *Control*, 213–16; K. Sharpe, 'A Commonwealth of Meanings: Languages, Analogues, Ideas and Politics', in *Politics and Ideas in Early Start England*, ed. K. Sharpe (1989), 9; Sharpe, *Personal Rule*, 644–54.

[54] Clegg, *Caroline England*, 120, 140–2, 164, 191, 202.

[55] J. Storey, *A Short Survey of the Kingdome of Sweden* (1632), STC23517.5, 23518.

[56] T. Helfferich, *The Thirty Years War* (Indianapolis, IN and Cambridge, 2009), Doc. 21, 144–50; STC24956.

[57] Arber, vol. 4, 289.

[58] J. Russell, STC21460.

[59] Text in Latin and English of the Swedish/Polish agreement, names Sir George Douglas as a mediator acting for Charles, B&B, STC23366.

invoice in the Barrington family letters for bookshop purchases in 1636–9 shows that Sir Thomas, a keen follower of contemporary issues foreign and domestic, purchased orders for the plague in 1636 but only bought *The Modern History* in February 1637, fifteen months after publication when interest in the war was revived by the return of Arundel's 1636 embassy to the emperor.[60] So, even those who could afford these lengthier publications may have been less inclined to buy by the mid-1630s. With the death of Gustavus Adolphus, the fortunes of the Protestants faltered. Military action became confusing as internal differences between the Protestant forces impeded the development of a coherent strategy. Sweden was losing its grip in northwest Germany while the part played by the French was unclear, as were the implications for Charles.[61]

After Watts resigned, interest in Europe was sustained temporarily by the death of Wallenstein, though the partnership reported this in a way that suggested they did not know what perspective to adopt:

> on the lamentable death of him, who by the actions of his life hath often times afforded us many a discourse. Therefore wee will present unto you a short view, of … the murther committed on the person and friends of that great Imperiall Generalissim.… About such time of the Duke of Friedland pretended a peace with the Swedes and Prince of the Union, (whereof we have spoken in our fifth part).

Catholic accounts of the murder were provided from *Mercurius Gallobelgicus* and Brussels, with details of his Scots and Irish assassins without comment or speculation.[62]

The partnership proceeded cautiously, appointing 'another author' for the seventh part of *The German History* who appears from his learned approach, littered with classical references and moralistic judgements, to have completely satisfied any possible court requirements at that time to reflect the image of pacific, discriminating, chivalry espoused in Shirley's *Triumph of Peace*.[63] The new editor aimed to set a high tone, referring to Livy and Quintilian, and expressing the hope that the text would work 'as well upon English spirits, as Xenophons Cyropadie upon African Scipio'. Moralistic stories were included, such as that of a Swedish soldier who went ashore to drink and whose ship sailed without him. When found, he was hanged.

---

[60] P. Gregg, *King Charles I* (1981/2000), 261; Sharpe, *Personal Rule*, 620–5; Bohannon, 'A London Bookseller's Bill', 433, see pp. 237–8.

[61] Wilson, *Europe's Tragedy*, 520–35; Wedgwood, 352, 370.

[62] *The History of the Present Warres of Germany*, Part 6 (1634), 134, 136, 138–60, 159, STC23525.5.

[63] J. Adamson, 'Chivalry and Political Culture in Caroline England', in Lake, 170–4; Sharpe, *Image Wars*, 199, 213, 263; R. Cust, *Charles I*, 169–70; *The German History*, Part 7 (1634), 'To the Reader', STC23525.7.

The account concluded 'An excellent piece of justice … wilful negligence in matters of importance' is almost as bad as treason. An account that Horn demolished fortifications and hanged a governor (having found he could not trust him nor afford a garrison) ended 'This was good justice, and required by the law of Armes, for that he doth not punish such faithlessnesses, openeth a gap to all perfidiousnesse.' This was 'lawfull for an Enemy'.[64]

The initials 'N. C.' at the end of the editorial in Part 7, probably short for 'nota censoria' or the mark of the censor or licenser, are highly suggestive of the continuing handiwork of Weckherlin who used the expressions 'Nota-Non licet' and 'Nota – Nondum licet' to record Charles's decisions to refuse licences. It seems Weckherlin was, somewhat tongue in cheek, acknowledging the inescapable expectation of mid-1630s' licensing conditions that texts would bear signs of the licenser's handiwork. He may also have been responsible for the eulogy, inserted in chapter 11, telling readers how fortunate England was:

> the blessed fruits of peace … wee our selves cannot thinke of it, without thankfulnesse to God, by whose mercy: and to his Vice-gerent our Soveraigne by whose wisdome, of justice religiously grounded in himselfe … ministered to us, divinely blessed … wee reape that Harvest, which other Realmes would faine but see.[65]

This packaged reports of Swedish defeat at Nordlingen and the subsequent disarray of the Protestant League, without any recognition of its significance. However, these superficial tweaks were evidently not enough, in November 1634, to assuage government concerns as news was breaking of the negotiations in Pirna that were to lead to the Peace of Prague and ship money writs were being issued in London. Butter and Bourne must have acted on a tip-off as they rushed a mass of material (running to sixteen chapters and about 200 pages, painstakingly assembled and in the process of editing for two or three intended future publications) to the press. They used four different printers and hastily produced one disordered publication, which makes fresh starts with numbering from page 1 in five places. This marks the dawn of a new, and far more restrictive, era.[66] There was only one further *History* (Part 8) in over two years.

Part 8 appeared just in time for the arrival, in England, in late November 1635, of the new Palatine Elector, Charles Louis. In this, the roll call of Protestant heroes lost at Nordlingen was belatedly presented after an editorial extolling the benefits of peace and Charles's governance:

---

[64] Ibid., Ch. 1, 9–10; Ch. 2, 12, 18, 26.
[65] Ibid., verso, 'To the Reader', Ch. 11, 1; Thompson, 'Licensing the Press', 668; Clegg, *Caroline England*, 134–5; Schumacher, 241, 254.
[66] *The German History*, Part 7, the second and the last batch went to Harper, other printers were Dawson, Fletcher and Eliz Allde (?).

Germanie, which so long hath felt the misery of warre, famine and the plague, doth not onely continue … in the same condition, but the flame therof hath set the neighbour countreys on fire; Italie, France and the Valtoline … onely we divided from the rest of the Christian world by the Ocean do (by the blessing of God) enjoy the contrary vertue of peace and tranquillity under a happy government.[67]

This issue updated readers on the Peace of Prague and on the efforts of Ferdinand and Saxony to encourage Protestant allies to join it. News, that the Peace made no provision for the restitution of the Palatinate, follows plainly in the Articles.[68]

Both issues drew heavily on Catholic sources: a commentary on Nordlingen, from a 'Catholike Gallant with a large preface of himselfe, [who] writes gloriously of his owne adventure', described Nordlingen as a 'victory'. It referred to the recapture of Regensburg by the Imperialists as a 'happy surrendering', and ended with 'our souldiers will make good booty'.[69] If readers were outraged by either the news or the editorial perspective (as they most surely would have been in earlier years) we have no record. Readers were probably well aware of the situation. D'Ewes missed very little: he recorded Nordlingen as the loss of all Gustavus Adolphus's victories at one blow, then followed the subsequent progress of the Imperial forces, the treachery of Saxony for abandoning Sweden, and the error (in his view) of Brandenburg and Luneburg settling on poor terms at Prague; and the more encouraging news of the Struhmsdorf truce between Sweden and Poland. He built his own network of correspondents to supplement printed news. John Rous noted the arrival of Charles Louis as well as news covered in *The Modern History*. He noted, too, the subsequent departure of Charles Louis and Rupert and, in 1637, the revival of hopes for the Protestant cause and the punishments of Prynne, Bastwick and Burton, without comment. Fielding's account of the diary of Robert Woodford, a Northamptonshire steward who frequently visited London and acted as a channel for news, shows that, like Rous, he fought hard to think well of the king but espoused concerns that emerged in the 1620s about Charles's involvement with papists and enemies of England. Fielding argues that Woodford tended to keep a low profile, typical of puritans before 1640, and his silence suggests that, in practice, there were restrictions on discussion socially and locally.[70]

---

[67] *The Modern History of the world*, Part 8 (1635), 'To the Reader' [misn'd 3 and verso], 2-A3, STC23525.9.
[68] Ibid., Sec 2. 1–4, 50–1, final section, 40–5; P. H. Wilson, *The Thirty Years' War: A Sourcebook* (2010), 194–211.
[69] *The German History*, Part 7, Ch. 4, 52, 60, 61–2.
[70] *Autobiography D'Ewes*, vol. 2, 85, 110–11, 128, 223–8; *Rous*, 72–5, 81–2; J. Fielding, 'Opposition to the Personal Rule of Charles I: The Diary of Robert Woodford, 1637–1641', *HJ*, 31:4 (1988), 777–88.

With the exception of Lambert who ascribes the absence of news in 1636 to the plague, historians focusing on the 1632 ban have not asked what prompted a further drop in reporting from late 1634 to the end of 1636. However, we have seen before how the embarrassments of rulers and shifts in policy were reflected in changes in the treatment of the press. Ferdinand negotiated from strength at Pirna and invited all German princes to join a Catholic peace. Charles was unwilling accept the diplomatic outcome of the Peace of Prague, so he began making preparations for a more active foreign policy. Ship money provided a means for strengthening the fleet to deal with the problems suffered by English trading vessels at the hands of the Turks, French, Venetians and Dutch, and giving England a stronger hand internationally.[71]

Progress with the fleet in 1635 was encouraging. In January 1636, Prince Rupert joined his brother in England and, by the spring, Charles had sent out embassies to Madrid and Paris, and to Regensburg where a diet for the election of the king of Hungary as Imperial successor was convening. The support of England was, in Sharpe's words, 'on offer to whoever came up with the proposition most likely to aid the young Elector'. The French-Swedish pact was renewed that spring and Bernard of Saxe-Weimar accepted the pay of France. By summer, negotiations with Paris were progressing and Charles halted the minting of Spanish bullion at the Tower.[72]

Most historians would probably agree with Howat that at the heart of Charles's foreign policy was 'the perennial issue of the Palatinate: the wolf in the web of all his endeavours' and that, when the cause of Protestantism and the cause of the Palatinate coincided, he and his people were in agreement. Charles had achieved neutrality, security and lucrative opportunities for the English shipping trade in this period, but at the cost of a humiliating settlement for the Palatine family at Prague. He had achieved stringent news press control only when the Palatine cause looked all but lost and domestic pressures to publish were limited. Charles worked with Spain, ever hopeful of a diplomatic solution because Spain occupied much of the Palatinate and needed supply lines to Flanders. However, people distrusted Charles because the peace was Spanish and Catholic, and because of connections they saw with Laud's policies and Arminianism. Public opinion remained staunchly anti-Spanish. Spain symbolised values, including the papacy, ritual and spiritual tastes that were rejected by many. Because Charles and Laud denied papal authority, they do not appear to have recognised that others did not make the same distinctions. Charles did not allow for the feelings of others or consider that these might have any basis. Nor is there

---

[71] Lambert, 'Coranto', 13; *The German History*, Part 7, Ch. 5, 70; Sharpe, *Personal Rule*, 509–13, 549–53, 598–9; Wilson, *Europe's Tragedy*, 554; G. Parker, ed., *The Thirty Years' War* (London, Boston, MA and Melbourne, 1984/1997), 127–9; Wedgwood, 381, 388–91.

[72] Sharpe, *Personal Rule*, 518–26.

any hint of understanding how people might interpret the punishment of argumentative clerics when this coincided with a period when reporting on European affairs, and current events involving British soldiers abroad, unaccountably disappeared from the streets only to be replaced by costly volumes with reports from Imperialist soldiers.[73]

The boom in newsbook sales, and the enthusiasm with which publishers responded to even the smallest of Charles's pro-Protestant steps in the early 1630s, are indicative of an open door that he could have walked through to be in sympathy with his people. Instead, he failed to reveal his thinking or to act decisively or effectively in the interests of his sister, and he silenced the press that supported her cause. He entertained the Papal Agent, Con, joked about his religion, and appears to have been oblivious of the impression he created or the nervousness and fear liable to underlie the news vacuum he created.

Negotiations with France

As negotiating initiatives began to bear fruit, Charles started to rethink both the merits of peace and the accompanying news controls. An offensive and defensive alliance with France was to bring Britain directly into the continental conflict.

A first public sign of change was the licensing by Coke, on 23 December 1636, of Monro's *Expedition*, based on his continental military experience. This heroic epic displayed the glories of 'vertue', praising piety, courage and self-sacrifice. Like the publications of 1634 and 1635, it expressed indignation at breaches in the code of military standards but was dedicated to Charles Louis and his mother, 'Queene of Bohemia, Jewell of her sex', and it encouraged military engagement.[74]

We do not know how sincere Charles was in his negotiations with France, but he may well have been willing to go to war after receiving news from Arundel that he was slighted by the Habsburgs. Sharpe has pointed out that 'The best informed ... read the king's mind as bent on belligerent courses.'[75] However, even if all Charles wanted was to secure a seat at the peace negotiations, then he needed to convince those closest to him. Weck-

---

[73] Howat, *Stuart and Cromwellian*, 40–1, 44, 46; Reeve, *Charles I*, 183–7; Sharpe, *Image Wars*, 160, 176; J. S. Keppler, 'Fiscal Aspects of the English Carrying Trade', *EHR*, 2:25:2 (1972), 264–7; Taylor, 'Trade, Neutrality', 240–6.

[74] Arber, vol. 4, 343; R. Monro, *Monro his Expedition with the worthy Scots Regiment* (London, 1637), 2, 7; G. Mortimer, *Eye-Witness Accounts of the Thirty Years' War, 1618–48* (Basingstoke and New York, 2002), 154–61.

[75] P. Gregg, *King Charles I* (1981/2000), 262–3; Carlton, *Charles I*, 174; Cust, *Charles I*, 129–30; Sharpe, *Personal Rule*, 535–6.

herlin and Coke were part of the pro-French alliance faction at Court at that time supported by Henrietta Maria. Weckherlin's diary reveals close collaboration with the king and a carefully orchestrated change of direction using print to support the alliance.[76] Secret negotiations could be denied and reversed, but a successful war initiative demanded men and support, and therefore publicity. If this was a game of bluff, then Charles was probably the most seriously deluded player, ignoring the political consequences of promoting war while (once again) intending to rely on volunteers.

In January, Weckherlin licensed William Crowne's journal of the progress of Arundel's embassy along the Rhine and via Frankfurt to Vienna. It provided a grim catalogue of abandoned villages, plague, leprosy, poverty, starvation, fires and destruction, capped off with an account of gruesome executions in Linz. For Butter, he licensed the start a new series, *Numb.1. The Principall Passages of Germany*. Described as 'History confirmed by authenticall persons of good credit', it covered news from July 1636, with the attempted defence of Hanau by the Landgrave, Ramsay and Leslie, and many details about the gathering to elect Ferdinand's successor, including fascinating details of dealings with the Elector of Triers (ally of France and held as a Habsburg prisoner). It reported the successes of Duke Bernard and the Swedes following victory at Wittstock and ended with confidence that there would be further issues, 'there is yet much … remaining, which we shall within few weekes describe'.[77] In February, Coke licensed a translation of Justus Stella's *A Bewailing of the Peace of Germany … touching the Peace of Prague*, which took its text from Jeremiah: 'They have healed the hurt of the daughter of my people slightly, saying, Peace, peace, when there is no peace.' Also that month, Coke licensed Rusdorf's *In Causa Palatina* and the Prince Elector's *Protestation*, which Weckherlin then circulated to contacts on the Continent. Weckherlin also sent Butter papers that were probably on the *History of Henry IV of France*, entered in the Stationers' register on 13 February.[78] After years of silence this was a notable and powerfully presented change.

The proposed treaty with France provided for England to declare war on the Habsburgs, contribute thirty ships, and let France recruit in Britain. In

---

[76] I. Atherton, *Ambition and Failure in Stuart England: The Career of John, First Viscount Scudamore* (Manchester, 1999), 178, 191–7; Add MS 72,433, Counsel 22 January 1663, fo. 4, Paris correspondence February and July, fos 5–7; M. Smuts, 'Religion, European Politics and Henrietta Maria's Circle, 1625–41', in *Henrietta Maria, Piety, Politics and Patronage*, ed. E. Griffey (Aldershot and Burlington, VT, 2008), 27–31.

[77] *A True Relation of … the Travels of … Arundell* in Helfferich, *The Thirty Years War*, Doc. 26, 180–90; Arber, vol. 4, 382, 343, 344, 345; *Numb.1. The Principall* (1637), 'To the Reader', 2–3, 16–23, 24–40, 119–20, STC4293.

[78] Arber, vol. 4, 347, 350, 355; J. Stella, (1637), title page, STC23245; Add MS 72433, 13/14 February, fo. 5, verso, 1 February, fo. 4, 5 February 1637, fo. 5, 24/6 March 1637, fo. 27.

the event, negotiations slowed down in the spring and the terms were not ratified after news spread of the riots in Edinburgh, in July, over the new Prayer Book. But Scottish troubles did not result in an immediate withdrawal from a more active involvement in Germany nor in a reduction in publications with a continental focus. Military officers serving on the Continent came and went. Warrants and passes were signed. At Court it must have seemed as if England was already engaged. Lord Craven raised a force of volunteers and Charles Louis was given command of the small fleet that sailed for the United Provinces under the Palatine flag. Frederick Henry welcomed 'a great train of English noblemen and gentlemen', all volunteers who paid their own costs.[79]

Butter and Bourne brought out further parts to their new series in May and October 1637, and two more by February 1639. Thus, when, in July 1637, the Star Chamber Decree allowed the publication of histories 'or any other Booke of State affaires ... licenced by the principall Secretaries of State' this was no more than an acknowledgment of a return to the 1632–4 status quo. In reality, the pendulum had already begun to swing towards still greater permissiveness.[80] Breda was at once recognised as a notable victory, regained from the Spanish after 12 years amid much celebration. Publications included A *True experimentall discourse upon the ... recovery of Breda*, by William Lithgow, and Butter and Bourne's *Short description of the marching forth of the enemie out of Breda*. Before the end of the year the Stationers' Company had registered a number of other titles with contemporary European themes with several stationers now associated with this market.[81]

However, this was a false dawn for the revival of a policy of engagement for the Protestant cause. As troubles in Scotland deepened, Charles began casting around to raise arms and money for war in Scotland. The need to avoid war abroad plus some suspicion that the French could be supporting rebels in Scotland led him to revive discussions with Spain. Charles was now simultaneously negotiating with France and Spain while relationships nurtured by the queen brought proximity to Parisian court intrigue and to Spain's efforts to destabilise France.[82] Butter, Bourne and Raworth (a

---

[79] Wilson, *Europe's Tragedy*, 594; Sharpe, *Personal Rule*, 533–5, 825–7; *Autobiography D'Ewes*, vol. 2, Weckherlin to D'Ewes 27 May 1637, 232; Cust, *Charles I*, 129; R. B. Manning, *Swordsmen: The Martial Ethos in the Three Kingdoms* (Oxford, 2003), 128–9; Add MS 72433, fo., 4, 6, 7 verso, 10, 15, 26, 33, 34; ODNB, Lord Craven.

[80] *Numb.2. The Continuation*, (1637), STC4293.2; *Diatelesma*, Part 3 (1637), STC4293.4; *Diatelesma*, Part. 2 (1638), STC4293.6; *Diatelesma*, Part 5 (1639), STC4293.8; Arber, vol. 4, 358, 369, 370.

[81] Arber, vol. 4, 350, 358, 364, 369, 375; STC3597.8; Wedgwood, 416; Add MS 72,433, fo. 13, 14, 15; J. Dunton, *A true journal of the Sally fleet* (1637), STC7357.

[82] Arber, vol. 4, 301; Wilson, *Europe's Tragedy*, 489–90, 521–2, 664; Wedgwood, *The King's Peace 1637–41* (1955), 225–8; Sharpe, *Personal Rule*, 826–9; Atherton, *Ambition*, 180, 183, 196; Smuts, 'Henrietta Maria's Circle', 32–7.

printer and Weckherlin's brother-in-law) became incidental victims in these shifting sands. They were imprisoned for the publication (back in 1634) of *Arrest of the court of parliament* as a result of an official complaint on behalf of the duchy of Lorraine. Weckherlin resolved the issue and secured their release, and Coke sent a masterly diplomatic response defending the licensing system robustly and Weckherlin's role.[83] But though Weckherlin's diary shows his work at Court continuing as normal after this, he and Coke stepped down from licensing. Masters of the Company of Stationers now entered news publications in the register without reference to state licences. Butter and Bourne, perhaps feeling exposed, produced little. Their confusingly titled *Diatelesma: The second part of the moderne history of the world*, was, in fact, Part 4 of the series being passed off as a second part of *Diatelesma Nu. 3*. It was not registered, presumably to avoid any questions about licensing in the Stationers' Hall.[84]

That year Nicholls published *A True … Relation of the Bloudy Battel between Bernard Van Wymerin (victour) and John de Weerdt*. Rothwell published a well-edited history of the war from 1618 to 1638, including a map of Germany with the locations of battles and quality engravings of renowned officers. Attention was increasingly also drawn to 'the misery of Germany' that 'no heart can believe, except those that have seene, and felt the bitternesse of it … your Country is desolate, your Cities burnt with fire'.[85] Ballads, recorded in the register of the Stationers' Company, show that songs about the lives of soldiers had entered into popular culture with titles such as *Brittaines Valour*, *The Northern Pheonix*, *The Soldiers Delight* and *A Soldiers Resolution*. Others, such as *The Complaint of Germany* and *A lamentable list of certaine hideous signes*, indicate that news of the devastation of parts of Germany was also reaching many people.[86]

Accounts of military professionalism and valour vied with those of plunder and horror. The confessional divide was no longer clear and Sweden, too, was now fully implicated, while Protestant territories suffered as the Imperial and Spanish armies advanced through Franconia, Swabia and Wurttemberg. *The History*, Part 6, noted the burning of Saltzkotten, casting Protestants into the Elbe, and cruelty in the taking of Munden. Part 7's report of 'The outrages done by the Imperialists at Hochstatt in Swaben' itemised tortures and cruelty, noting that 'the best relation is ful of horror'. *A breefe disection of Germanies affliction*, by Martin Parker, was published by Francis Grove in February 1638 – just weeks after what is probably the best known of publications in this genre for its graphic depiction of murder and

---

[83] Sharpe, *Personal Rule*, 829–30; *CSPD, 1637–8*, 117, 223–4; Add MS 72,433, fos 19, 20, 21; Thompson, 'Licensing the Press', 674–5.

[84] (1638) STC4293.6.

[85] Arber, vol. 4, 393, 395; *The Invasions of Germanie* (1638), A3-verso, STC11791.

[86] Arber, vol. 4, 277 (1633), 286 (1634), 308 (1635), 382 (1638), 402 (1638), 438 (1639).

mutilation, Philip Vincent's *Lamentations of Germanie. Lacrymae Germainiae* also appeared in 1638.[87]

The shocking nature of the atrocity reporting at this time can only have heightened fears of war and popery in England. Sharpe has suggested that in the early 1630s the temperature of paranoia was lowered by the success of Gustavus Adolphus and, from 1634, by the strengthening of the fleet. But military interest had remained strong with up to sixty-one percent of Scottish peers, fifty-eight percent of Irish peers and sixty-five percent of English peers having military experience in 1635, and numbers continuing to rise into the early 1640s. Barbara Donagan has argued that the 'halcyon days' of Charles I were not so much an idyll as a period of 'nervous and knowledgeable awareness of the nature of contemporary war … that prepared the country … for its own war'. The late 1630s offered 'neither pacifism nor isolation'. Military manuals were published and soldiers gained experience that was to become available to both sides in the Civil War. 'Men and officers came and went … Veterans and the maimed were familiar sights.' All this made war 'vividly present' and 'conditioned the English for their own war'. The calamitous literature deserves attention for it 'formed expectations as to the character of war, [and] … contributed to war-education, in its broader social sense'.[88]

Gratitude for continuing peace was a possible response, but Gataker's sermons instructed readers to be mindful of the misery of others, especially their Protestant 'brethren in forraine parts, either assaulted, or distressed or surprised by Popish forces'. The king's failure to champion Protestantism in the Thirty Years War was witnessed alongside the spread of Laudian ritual and the high profile of Henrietta Maria and other court Catholics. Nehemiah Wallington labelled a section in his journal 'The Bitterness of War' and referred to 'the miserable estate of Germany, wherein … you might see the mournful face of this our sister nation now drunk with misery', hoping it might 'serve as a strong motive to stir us all up with speed to turn unto God, that he may turn … from us this fearful calamity'. Seaver notes that the news confirmed to Wallington the many warnings of wrath to come for

---

[87] *The History*, Part 6, 100–03; *The German History*, Part 7, Ch. 2, 11, 21, Ch. 4, 50–1, 56, 60, Ch. 6, 20, Ch. 8, 9, 26, Ch. 11, 15; M. Parker, *A breefe disection of Germanies affliction* (1638), STC19222; P. Vincent, *The Lamentations of Germany* (1638), STC24760.5; *The Warnings of Germany* (1638), STC3758; *Lacrymae Germainiae* (1638), STC11791; H. Werner, '"The Lamentations of Germanie": A Probable Source for Heywood's "Londini Status", 484–486', in *Notes and Queries* (December 1994), 626–7.

[88] Manning, *Swordsmen*, 18; Sharpe, *Personal Rule*, 608–11; C. Hibbard, 'The Theatre of Dynasty', in *The Stuart Court and Europe; Essays in Politics and Political Culture*, ed. M. Smuts (Cambridge, 1996), 161; B. Donagan, 'Halcyon Days and the Literature of the War: England's Military Education before 1642', *PandP*, 147 (1995), 68–78.

England's sins and conveyed 'a lesson the government should have been more reluctant to assist the saints in learning'.[89]

Resumption of weekly foreign news

By late 1638, Charles was pressing forward with plans for a show of force against the Scottish Covenanters and was increasing preoccupied with their pamphlets which were reaching England in considerable numbers. He brought the years of the foreign news ban to an end, authorising the partnership to resume weekly publication on 20 December 1638.

The brewing war with Scotland presented an international print control challenge. Though some of the Scottish Covenanters propaganda emanated from Edinburgh, Amsterdam printers produced a torrent of covenanting propaganda. Alistair Mann has suggested this was 'surely the most concerted and effective use of media ... in the early modern period'. Williamson has described the media campaign as part of what many contemporaries perceived as an expansion of the theatre of the Thirty Years War. The Crown responded through Sir William Boswell, English ambassador in the Netherlands, who succeeded in bringing some of the chief perpetrators into court. At least seventeen books were stopped, but, by the end of 1638, they had simply driven much of the business from Amsterdam to Rotterdam where a network of merchants then distributed the works via London, Norwich and Yarmouth.[90]

In December, in London, John Bartlett was detained in the Fleet for selling Burton and Bastwick's works and receiving 'Scottish news'. Charles's proclamation, on 27 February 1639, commanded his 'loving subjects' that 'they receive no more ... seditious Pamphlets sent from Scotland, or any other place'. The seriousness of his concern can be gauged by his measures to stamp out circulation: the proclamation was to be read out in every church and 10,000 copies were printed. Altogether, Charles's last significant effort at censorship involved four proclamations and two declarations in less than two years, with efforts to track down anyone handling Scottish propaganda. It may well have been the failure to stem the tide of puritan polemic and a growing awareness that he was in danger of loosing the argument by

---

[89] Gataker, quoted in J. Raymond, *Pamphlets and Pamphleteering in Early Modern Britain* (Cambridge, 2003), 145; Cust, *Charles I*, 145; P. S. Seaver, *Wallington's World: A Puritan Artisan in Seventeenth-Century London* (Stanford, CA, 1985), 157–61.

[90] A. J. Mann, *The Scottish Book Trade 1500–1720: Print, Commerce and Print Control in Early Modern Scotland* (East Linton, 2000), 83–4, 90; A. Williamson, 'Scotland: International Politics, International Press', in *Agent of Change: Print Culture after Elizabeth L. Eisenstein*, ed. S. A. Baron, E. Lindquist and E. Shevlin (Amherst and Boston, MA, 2007), 196, 200–01; K. L. Sprunger, *Trumpets from the Tower* (Leiden, New York and Koln, 1994), 116, 119–24, 157.

default that led Charles to allow Butter and Bourne to resume newsbook publication.[91] What we do not know is how far he saw this as the establishment of an official government reporter along the lines of the news press operating in Paris by this stage, nor to what extent he hoped Butter and Bourne, by monopolising the foreign news, might use their contacts abroad and position in London to assist with the suppression of Scottish material.

News from the Continent was improving from a Protestant perspective. The success of Bernard of Saxe-Weimar on the Rhine put Alsace into the hands of troops in the pay of France, and Swedish fortunes were reviving in the east. In this time of heightened anxiety, licensed news reporting must have been more attractive to Charles than the increasing output sanctioned by the Stationers' Company, but Butter and Bourne were to pay dearly for the patent. In addition to the regular fees for licensing, Charles's project to improve St Paul's was to be supported for the term of 21 years, by payments 'yearly towards the repair of St Paul's the sum of 10£'. In return, the patent was extensive and superseded Article III of the 1637 Star Chamber Decree, covering 'all matter of History or Newes of any foraine place or Kingdome since the first beginning of the late German warres to this present. And also for ... all Newes, Novells, Gazetts Currantos or Occurrences that concerne forraine pts &c.'[92] It meant that none of the publishers who had become involved since the beginning of 1637 would be able to continue.

The agreement was far from 'business as usual'. Neither the Stationers' Company nor Weckherlin were to play a part. Windebank's pro-Spanish interest in licensing was officially acknowledged and his nephew, Robert Reade, inspected issues individually. The words 'With privilege' or 'permission' in each imprint signified their new status. Instead of permission to produce fifty issues over a period of approximately one year, the new system took them to a hundred issues in about eight months. Any potential complexity in scrutiny was eliminated by removing all editorial discretion. After a first issue that caught up on news going back as far as the previous summer, they produced short 'currantoes' (four sides of print to a slightly larger format), which were simply translations of continental originals.[93]

This was a feeble exercise in control, not a public relations initiative. As the partnership already knew, a good editor was needed to tell a good story. Instead, this tightly constrained series suffered from licensing interference. Butter later told readers that the licenser '(out of partial affection) would not oftentimes let passe apparent truth, and other things (oftentimes) so crosse and alter which made us almost weary of Printing'. The result was a low quality product that did not even eliminate reports that were least likely

[91] Clegg, *Caroline England*, 207–12; Cressy, *England on Edge*, 288–9; Sharpe, *Personal Rule*, 652–3.

[92] *CSPD, 1638–1639*, 182, quoted in Dahl, 223.

[93] Arber, vol. 4, 422; Dahl, 223–60; (20 December 1638), STC18507.277. Plate, p. 244.

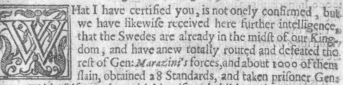

Num. 84. 337 54

The NORIMBERG Curranto of this week.

The confirmation of the defeat of the remainds of Marazini's Army, and taking him prisoner. The people of Tabor make away space to Vienna, and to Gratz, and so to the Mountains, by reason of the Swedes approach. Generall Bannier is drawing his forces from all parts to Brandeis, 3 leagues from Prague, where Hatzfeld is now joyned with Gallas; whereupon another battell is like to follow.

Prague the 2: 12 of May.

What I have certified you, is not onely confirmed, but we have likewise received here further intelligence, that the Swedes are already in the midst of our Kingdom, and have anew totally routed and defeated the rest of Gen: *Marazini's* forces, and about 1000 of them slain, obtained 28 Standards, and taken prisoner Gen: *Marazini* himself, together with his wife and children, the yong Count of Shlick, and other Officers, which causeth great fear, not onely in this City, but even at Vienna: Gen: *Hatzfeld* is comming with his troops, to succour Gen: *Gallas*, but the Swedish Gen: Major *King* followeth him upon the foot; if this conjunction be hindred, our Kingdom will be in the highest danger; and it is to be feared, that we shall not be rid again so soon of these guests: Gen: *Gallas*, Fieldmarshall Baron of Hoffkirck, the old Count of Shlick, Count of Furstenburg, and Count of Colleredo, are here in this City very much perplex'd, and their forces intrench themselves upon the White-Hill.

Norimberg the 7: 17 of May.

The Hatzfeldish troops, which are arrived hereabouts, and lye at Furt, are to break-up again to morrow, or next day after, with whom certain Bavarian troops are to joyn, and go together into Bohemia, they have very bad weather to march, and are likely to come too late: At this instant we receive the Letters from Prague, it seemeth the poor people dare not write what they know, yet this they certifie, that the Swedes at their own pleasure straggle all the Country over, and play the master in the field; the Imperialists, except the Hatzfeldish succour, which consists of brave horsmen, but the foot are not 1500 strong, and in all, both horse and foot, not above 5000; the Imperialists themselves begin already to pillage in the Cities of Prague; the passage towards Dresden and Silesia is stopp'd, and it seemeth that the War will be very hot this yeer in Bohemia and Silesia; if so be that Gen: *Bannier* gives one blow more to the Imperialists, he will go a great way: the Swedes go about to salute the Hatzfeldish troops, afore they come into Bohemia; many

Rrrr of

Plate 5. This shows the front page (337) of a curranto (21 June 1639), from the tenth series, covering reactions to Bannier's advance into Bohemia after defeating Marazzino in April. Translated from German, it is similar to the Dutch corantos of 1620/1, except for its quarto booklet format and continuous page numbering. On the same day, a further two issues appeared. Issue 86, from the Netherlands, started with page 345.

to prove true. Dillingham, arguing to Lord Montagu the superiority of his newsletters, claimed 'they print all, and ours seldom proves false'.[94]

This patent came at a time when, to quote Sharpe, the foreign committee was most 'paralysed by uncertainty'. Raymond has questioned why Charles did not follow the French example more closely and concluded that his experiences of public exchanges with the 1628 Parliament made him cynical about the use of propaganda. Baron has argued that Charles failed to control manuscript news because he 'completely miscalculated', believing the upper orders of society impervious to the politically polarising effects of news, that the regime exhibited insularity and insensitivity, and Charles was 'out of step with popular political opinion in his realm'.[95] Charles's reluctance to court popularity or to explain his reasons for doing anything is sufficient to account for the distance he maintained from the press, but what shaped the 'on–off' nature of the controls exercised, and made it impossible for court officials to work with the partnership to develop a consistent foreign policy voice, had a deeper root: it was the absence of a sufficiently coherent and consistent foreign strategy to inform or provide editorial direction. No one knew from one month to the next what the story line should be.

Conclusions

From the time he ascended the throne, Charles's choices were constrained on all sides. He was faced with the prospect of an unaffordable war in Germany or an indirect naval engagement that depended on having convincing allies on the mainland. Charles explored many options and made mistakes. Each time his efforts failed or he encountered an impasse he tried something else, often working with different officials simultaneously on conflicting approaches. Frequently playing one interest off against another, he never seemed to reap any benefits. To find some basis for a diplomatic solution, he needed a bargaining tool. The fleet offered this, but his loan ships were used against Protestants, then he engaged in war with France and Spain simultaneously. When Charles rediscovered the attractions of alliance with Spain as a tactical and potentially economical approach to the recovery of the Palatinate he also found, like his father in 1623, he did not have sufficient leverage, even with an improved fleet. His expectation of loyalty and his tendency to see opposition as no more than small groups of malcontents prevented him from recognising the importance of cultivating public opinion. While he was playing the French and Dutch against Spain, or being strung along by one or another, Charles was unable to engage in

[94] Clegg, *Caroline England*, 207–12; Cressy, *England on Edge*, 288–9; Sharpe, *Personal Rule*, 652–3; (11 January 1641), STC18507.343; Raymond, 211.
[95] Ibid., 95–100; Sharpe, *Personal Rule*, 833; S. A. Baron, 'Guises of Dissemination', in DandB, 52; Cust, 'Charles I and Popularity', 235–56, 254–5.

effective public relations at home. When the opportunity came, in 1631, to adopt a more popular foreign policy for a relatively low cost, the news industry, working in co-operation with its friends at Court, was ready and able to respond, but Charles hesitated.

He seems not to have recognised that ideologically, concepts of a vast conflict of religion were set against his worldview of monarchy and stability, and that not only the objective (restoration of the Palatine family), but also the means by which this was achieved, mattered deeply to others. In a period recognised by many as marking a high watermark in censorship and press control through the 1637 Decree, heightened activity by Laudian licensers and the cases of Prynne, Bastwick and Burton, the evidence points to relationships between government and the news press that followed a very different trajectory. Laud was able to resource licensing, and he influenced the content of religious publications through time-consuming editorial effort because he could draw upon a large ecclesiastical team of licensers. The approach to news of the Thirty Years War was subject to vacillations in the fortunes of different court groups, and influenced more by immediate and transitory tactics of foreign policy than by any longer term or strategic view of the goals or by a generic attitude to print. As far as we can tell, both Weckherlin and then Reade worked with the news press single-handedly, while a growing press confronted government with issues of significance, and a scale of change in society and politics, that would not have been easily comprehended, even by a much more open and communicative monarch. The press was beginning to equip people to form their own views while Charles vacillated, willing to allow publication when it appeared to suit his immediate objectives, whether these were to support recruitment for war in Germany in an Anglo-French alliance or to distract from an expanding Covenanter's print campaign. Charles did not argue is own views in the way that James had done, and he was seemingly oblivious of any 'bigger picture' or, indeed, of the impact on the lives of those most involved through faith, family, trade or the military.

Readers were aware of government interference in the news, which (by analogy with what they saw happening to Calvinist literature) they could imagine to be more effective than in reality it was. This, in itself, would have created a degree of paranoia and mistrust. However, as Charles's reign progressed, with one failed initiative after another, and the impact of successive waves of recruitment and taxation were experienced, news of the resulting devastation experienced in parts of Germany reached London, further fuelling fears.

9

War in Britain and Peace at Westphalia

The impact of foreign news during the turbulent years that were heralded by the Bishops' Wars is perhaps best understood in terms of reaping the effects of twenty years of war reporting, diplomacy and recruitment. Readers followed the Thirty Years War as a single conflict, and we can track some of the effects as the lines of engagement within the Stuart kingdoms took shape. Charles had set out in 1637 preparing the nation for one war. In 1639, he set out upon a different one, with royalist forces arraigned against veterans who had fought in the Protestant armies of Europe. The deal with Spain to help transport bullion for the Spanish war effort on the Continent was to help with his finances. To many people, it must have seemed as if the war had finally crossed the Channel. Soldiers came home to fight, naval engagement took place in offshore waters, and reports of atrocities against Protestants came from Ireland. It was only after the royalist defeat at Naseby in 1645 that the situation in London became sufficiently settled for a new approach to reporting on the European conflict to emerge and, by this time, with delegates gathered in Munster, the end of the Thirty Years War was finally in sight.

The Bishops' Wars and Battle of the Downs

Charles's lack of understanding of popular opinion was dramatically demonstrated through military engagement in the north involving many of the soldiers that the London press had reported upon as warriors for the Protestant cause in Germany and the Netherlands, and by a humiliating naval stand off in the Channel. The response of the military and the public was to have practical and pressing implications.

To draw upon the military experience of those serving in the wars on the Continent, Charles issued a circular letter calling for their return to support his stand against the Covenanters. The response was meagre by contrast with the exodus to Scotland. The Swedes agreed to release men to support the Covenanters in large numbers and supplied arms. Scottish merchants procured munitions in Zealand and the Baltic with loans from puritan Englishmen, then shipped them to Scotland with the connivance of sympathetic Protestant powers. By contrast, Charles had to divert many of

his Channel fleet to Newcastle to obstruct the flow of support to the Covenanters via the Baltic and North Sea, while Christian IV negotiated with
Charles to allow him to recruit troops in Denmark at his own expense, and
providing his own transport. This left Charles with opportunities to recruit
Catholic support from Spain, Flanders and Ireland that could only be taken
up at the risk of drawing Britain fully into the European war. Even at home,
the response to royal recruitment was taken up by Catholics and Charles
had to resort to pressing men. He was, after all, in Fissel's words, turning
'English strategy on its head' by attempting to suppress Protestant Scots who
proclaimed their loyalty. Some of the officers he appointed for the Scottish
offensive were men who, in 1631/2, had filled newsbooks with reports of
action in Germany, but Leslie, Montrose and Lorne joined the Covenanters
and there were enough soldiers with military experience from Germany all
over Scotland to ensure that their troops were trained.[1]

While Charles was raising money and impressing men to serve in the
north, and during his expedition to York in March 1639, foreign news sales
were strong enough to justify something in the order of 150 separate issues
of currantoes, running through to the twelfth series that began in February
1640. Bleak reporting from Nuremburg through the summer of 1639 told
of Swedish progress into Bohemia 'which causeth fear ... even at Vienna'.
Dutch publications covered the French campaign. From Cologne, in May,
came the confirmation, with the taking of St Claude, in Alsace, that the
'passage is now stop'd, that the Spaniards can bring no troops into the
French-country'.[2]

Even at his late stage Charles might have accepted the opportunity to
divert warfare away from Britain had he supported the Elector Palatine, who
had come to England with a plan to take leadership of the Saxe-Weimar
troops at Breisach. Instead, with the 'Spanish Road' closed and the English
Channel route to Flanders now vital to Spain, but less secure, the king
returned to London in August to find Spanish officers in London requesting
safe passage for their troops landed on the south coast en route for Flan-

---

[1] S. Murdoch, 'Scotland, Scandinavia and the Bishops' Wars: 1638–40', in *The
Stuart Kingdoms in the Seventeenth Century: Awkward Neighbours*, ed. A. I. MacInnes
and J. Ohlmeyer (Scarborough, ON, Dublin and Portland, OR, 2002), 114–5, 118–9;
S. Murdoch, *Britain, Denmark-Norway and the House of Stuart, 1603–1660* (East Linton,
2003), 90–2; J. S. Keppler, 'Fiscal Aspects of the English Carrying Trade during the
Thirty Years' War', EHR, 2:25:2 (1972), 269; M. C. Fissel, *English Warfare, 1511–1641*
(London and New York, 2001), 79, 112, 272–4, 294; I. Gentles, *The English Revolution
and the Wars in the Three Kingdoms 1638–1652* (Harlow, 2007), 13–32; A. I. MacInnes,
'The "Scottish Moment", 1638–45', in *The English Civil War*, ed. J. Adamson (Basingstoke, 2009), 128–31; D. Cressy, *England on Edge; Crisis and Revolution, 1640–1642*
(Oxford, 2006), 73–80.
[2] (21 June 1639), 337–8, 340, STC18507.312; (21 June 1639), 345, 347–8,
STC18507.313; P. H. Wilson, *Europe's Tragedy: A History of the Thirty Years' War* (2009),
611, 647.

ders. Charles agreed to their transportation in English ships, to the hire of English merchant ships to defend the coasts of Biscay from the Dutch and French, and for an escort for its fleet with troops, money and supplies for the Spanish Netherlands. Pennington was instructed to protect them. In September, the Spanish fleet put into Dover for safety from the Dutch, while Charles, seeking the best deal he could get, negotiated with both sides. Meanwhile, the Prince Palatine left in early October, sailing past the Dutch, English and Spanish fleets off the English Downs, all waiting on the outcome of negotiations in London. What followed exemplified the confused state of the Crown's foreign policy and the uncomfortable position of Butter and Bourne with their news monopoly. On 11 October the Dutch fleet, with a combined force of seventy ships and thirty transporters, attacked and defeated the Spanish ships while Pennington, with thirty ships of the English fleet, stood by, and the local populace looked on.[3]

Rumours would have reached London with speed. After years of foreboding it could have seemed that Spain was ready to invade with royal support. Angela McShane, tracking the increase in political ballad production from 1639 onwards, noted that balladeers seemed more concerned about renewed threats to Protestantism from Spain than by any news from Scotland. Nearly half of that year's output was devoted to Dutch sea-battles against Spain. Charles's position was, at best, completely inexplicable. There was no way of turning this into a story to bolster the Crown's reputation. Butter and Bourne were chosen to defuse gossip and panic by setting out the facts. Reade licensed *An Extraordinary Curranto wherein is related the Late Sea Fight betixt the Spaniards and the Hollanders*. This described the encounter, including how the Dutch blew up a Spanish ship which had on board,

> 100 of our Englishmen, which the admiral had hired for money at half a Crown a day. The Spanish seamen performed their service and fought bravely, as long as there was any hope; yet at last, most part of the Fleet was destroy'd.

It reported an attempt by the Dutch to follow and pillage the fleeing Spaniards on the English shore, but said Pennington 'gave fierce fire upon the said two Hollanders', then ended with a comment that there was bravery on both sides. There was no mention of the joyful English crowds on the shore celebrating Spanish defeat. Kentish plunder of the fleeing Spanish was airbrushed into hints that possibly not all coastal residents were as hospitable as they might have been, and a story about a minister's horse catching a stray bullet.[4]

---

[3] C. Hibbard, *Charles I and the Popish Plot* (Chapel Hill, NC, 1983), 131–5; Wilson, *Europe's Tragedy*, 662–3; Wedgwood, 429–30; C. V. Wedgwood, *The King's Peace 1637–41* (1955), 271–4.

[4] K. Sharpe, *The Personal Rule of Charles I* (New Haven, CT and London, 1992), 843–6; A. McShane Jones, 'The Gazet in Metre; Or the Rhiming Newsmonger' The English

Charles acted as if oblivious to the depth of feeling against accommo-
dating Spanish demands and did so in full view on English soil and in the
English Channel. Then, as with the Rhé expedition, he allowed the description of external events while failing to explain anything. However, it would
be a mistake to see many parallels with that reporting experience. Here
there was no plan, and at no point was there hope of positive publicity,
simply a need to stop rumour and allay anxiety. Sharpe argues that it was
after 1638 that popish fears began to escalate, suggesting that if Charles
had signed a treaty with the French and gone on the offensive his kingdom
may have been saved because the fear of popery would have been addressed.
Instead, relations with France deteriorated into hostility, with Richelieu
ordering the arrest of the Elector Palatine as he travelled through France en
route to the siege at Breisach.[5]

This event brought the long collaboration of the publishing partnership
to an end. Butter and Bourne had never before been called upon to act
so blatantly as mouthpiece for the Crown. Nor had they previously been
so closely monitored and regulated. Neither Cottington's parameters in the
early 1620s, nor later understandings with Weckherlin, reduced the periodicals to a government news vehicle. Bourne prudently dropped out of
the partnership after the *Extraordinary* issue.[6] Customers at his shop at the
Royal Exchange included the Dutch mercantile community based around
the Dutch Church and his stock was in Bills of Lading in English, French,
Italian, Dutch and Indentures for Virginia. He needed to respect potentially
conflicting local sensitivities due to the fact that, with French entry into the
war, English shipping had benefited from neutrality, an increased demand
for commodity transport, especially of textiles (as well as silver shipments),
and from the protection given by the English fleet.[7]

Spanish troops had now been given safe passage across the south of
England to avoid German Protestant defences on the Rhine, with the
Dutch pursuing the Spanish onto the English coast. It was evident that
England could not pursue a policy for the restoration of the Palatinate and
simultaneously take action against the Scots. Charles's need for Spanish
gold and customs revenues meant that the transportation of Spanish troops,
and negotiations, continued even as the Short Parliament met. After June

---

Broadside Ballad as Intelligencer, a New Narrative', in Koopmans, 137; (18 October
1639), 166–7, STC18507. 315.

[5] Sharpe, *Personal Rule*, 953; Wedgwood, *Peace*, 302–03; Wedgwood, 424; Hibbard,
Charles I, 124–8; H. Werner, '"The Lamentations of Germanie": A Probable Source for
Heywood's "Londini Status", 484–486', in *Notes and Queries* (December 1994), 628–9.

[6] Bourne's name appears only on one further issue, probably by mistake (24 March
1640, STC18507.326); L. Rostenberg, 'Nathaniel Butter and Nicholas Bourne, First
Masters of the Staple', *The Library*, 5:12 (1957), 30.

[7] Keppler, 'Fiscal Aspects', 265–8; H. Taylor, 'Trade, Neutrality, and the "English
Road", 1630–1648', *EHR*, 2:25:2 (1972), 237–9, 246, 251–5.

1639, only two other currantoes have survived for the year, a sure sign of the struggle that Butter had to keep going alone. The brief hope of a renewed Protestant alliance had been snuffed out and, with it, what remained of public interest. Butter signed over most of his stock to Master Flesher. The news that winter was all of manoeuvres, speculation about where armies might go and levies for the next season. Reports were repetitious and the currantoes must have been virtually unsaleable to all but newsletter writers. There were only glimpses of interesting detail such as the enthusiastic letter from Frankfurt referring to 'smoak'd Beefe and Bacon ... Pullets & Geese they have found in great store' and a well composed summary from Hamburg, from late January, that showed the disposition of the forces and concludes 'The Swedes grow still stronger and stronger. ... The destruction ... can with no pen be described because of the Imperial enquartering, they spare no man ... everyone must run away from his house and goods'.[8]

Irish Rebellion and civil war in England

Two Parliaments were called in 1640 and the assembly of the Long Parliament in November heralded major changes for the London news press. People became involved in politics to an unprecedented extent, while initial signs of a refreshed Protestant alignment for foreign policy only briefly renewed hopes.

In April 1640, shortly after he might reasonably have hoped for a boost in sales once MPs arrived in London for the opening of the Short Parliament, Butter announced his return to a single, weekly publication. He hoped this would give better value to customers, but he could not afford to employ an editor and did no more than add the Frankfurt to the Nuremburg reports, most of which simply tracked Bannier's progress and the trail of destruction left in his wake. Sales did not pick up. The Short Parliament was dismissed before it had hardly begun and England turned in upon itself with civil unrest and riots in London and elsewhere. Charles once again travelled north to engage with the Scots.[9]

Only fifteen issues appeared in the following six months despite the opening of the Long Parliament in November. Readers would have been aware of the forthcoming Diet in Regensburg and could pick up some Parisian propaganda from Renadot's *Gazette*. Reports from May, for example, told of French forces restoring peasants' goods that had been plundered by the Spanish and of Parisian celebrations for victory in Italy. Meanwhile, the

---

[8] Arber, vol. 4, 440–1; (24 February 1640), 304, STC18507.323; (24 February 1640), 306–08, STC18507.324; (31 March 1640), 46, STC18507.329; (20 April 1640), 70, STC18507.335.

[9] (23 April 1640), STC18507.337.

name of Philip Minutelius had replaced that of Robert Reade as licenser, and the licensing relationship broke down quickly.[10]

Public engagement in domestic political affairs peaked in this period. Huge petitions were organised. The crowds who escorted Bastwick, Burton and Prynne into London after their release from prison demonstrated the extent to which the muting of the press, in the 1630s, had caused concern. After the start of the Long Parliament, despite worries about inaccurate reporting, MPs quickly saw the benefits of publication and the need to influence public opinion. Many speeches were circulated as a form of political activism. Copies of declarations and parliamentary documents of the sort that had been available in manuscript in large numbers in 1629 were now printed, and further spates of printing marked other events in 1641 and 1642 in much the same way as major events in other countries, such as the Imperial Ban against Frederick, had generated 'pamphlet wars'.[11] Then, once the Long Parliament went into continuous session, the London print industry adapted quickly to produce weekly proceedings that complemented copies of speeches already available in print. Raymond has described the way editors learned to present news and how they subsequently moved from non-controversial narrations of parliamentary proceedings into aggressive factional writing. It was, of course, easy to produce domestic newsbooks on a fixed day of the week since the supply of material was not dependent on a Channel crossing. Issues were distributed using the methods established by Butter and Bourne. The newsbook format was adopted and largely anonymous editors digested material for publication, while Humphrey Blunden in his effort to produce a distinctive periodical also copied the issue number and consecutive pagination methods adopted by Butter and Bourne from 1622 and 1639 respectively. Like the partnership in 1639 these domestic news publishers conserved space by abandoning the full title page.[12]

Hopes for a more favourable, Protestant foreign policy revived in December with talk of plans for the Prince of Orange's only son to marry one of the English princesses. Charles depicted it as a change intended to support the queen of Bohemia and, as previously, more favourable treatment for the foreign news accompanied a shift in Crown policy towards an agenda

---

[10] Dahl, 242–50; (6 June 1640), 120, 123, STC18507.338.

[11] P. Burke, *Popular Culture in Early Modern Europe* (Cambridge, 1978), 263; D. Hirst, *England in Conflict 1603–1660, Kingdom, Community, Conflict* (1999), 173–4; Love, 16–17; M. Mendle, 'News and the Pamphlet Culture of Mid-seventeenth-century England', in DandB, 59–61; W. Notestein and F. Relf, ed., *Commons Debates for 1629* (Minneapolis, MN, 1929), Introduction; Raymond, 13, 101–02.

[12] Ibid., 20–39, 105–10; J. Raymond, *Making the News: An Anthology of the Newsbooks of Revolutionary England 1641–1660* (Moreton-in-Marsh, 1993); S. A. Baron, 'Licensing Readers, Licensing Authorities in Seventeenth-Century England', in *Books and Readers in Early Modern England: Material Studies*, ed. J. Andersen and E. Sauer (Philadelphia, PA: PA, 2002), 220. Plates, pp. 244 and 262.

likely to find favour with advocates of a Protestant alliance. The context had, however, changed significantly.

A jubilant and seemingly irrepressible Butter could hardly contain his relief: on the title page of the issue of 11 January 1641 he announced it was 'Examined and Licensed by a better and more Impartial hand than heretofore'. Inside, he explained, 'Courteous Reader ... the Licenser ... being vanished (and that Office fallen upon another, more understanding in these forraine affaires, and as you will finde more candid.).' The licenser was once again Weckherlin, Windebank and Reade having fled to France. Weckherlin's fortunes, like those of the foreign news publications, were tracking vacillations in foreign policy. He had survived dark times of internal struggles within the Court that accompanied the shift from a French to a Spanish orientation, and difficult times accompanying the king to Newcastle and Berwick managing his correspondence. He had been working for Vane since Coke's retirement at the end of 1639. He described the arrangement to Sir Thomas Roe as 'a great grace, yet affords no benefit nor comfort at all for my great toil in all foreign affairs'. To Oxenstierna, he wrote more bluntly of having been treated as a 'posthorse under so many postmasters' and asked for Swedish employment.[13]

However, as the Long Parliament took an increasingly independent role, the structure of press control changed. Still with Vane, Weckherlin found himself working for both Crown and state. Butter reflected this shift, 'We are again (by the favour of his Majestie and the State) resolved to goe on in Printing'. Weckherlin and the clerics who continued to work as licensers after 1640, were appointed in the 1643 *Order... Regulating Printing*, to continue in their role by the House of Commons. Then, in 1644, Weckherlin was appointed secretary for foreign affairs to the Committee for both Kingdoms, a post he occupied until 1649 and returned to again in 1652 (to assist John Milton who needed help due to his blindness).[14]

Weckherlin's name appears on newsbooks as 'Imprimatur' from January to July 1641 and reappears in the Stationers' Company register as licenser for other pamphlets of foreign news published in this period. By the summer, however, this became unnecessary: the Court of Star Chamber and the High Commission were gone and the House of Commons had embarked upon what Mendle described as a 'largely laissez-faire course'.[15]

---

[13] (11 January 1641), STC18507.343; *CSPD, 1639*, 180, 268, 271–2; *CSPD, 1639–40*, 434; A. Schaffer, *Georg Rudolf Weckherlin* (Danvers, MA, 1918/2009), 48.

[14] Baron, 'Licensing Readers', 218–19, 223, 229, 231; M. Mendle, 'De Facto Freedom, De Facto Authority: Press and Parliament, 1640–1643', *HJ*, 18:2 (1995), 320–1; Clegg, *Press Censorship in Caroline England* (Cambridge, 2008), 226–28; (11 January 1641), 'to the reader' STC18507.343; Schaffer, *Weckherlin*, 47.

[15] Dahl, 223–60; H. R. Plomer, ed., *Transcript of the Stationers' Company Registers 1640–1708*, 1 (1913), 11, 14, 15, 29; Clegg, *Caroline England*, 218–22; Mendle, 'De Facto', 322.

In the winter of 1640/1, the Diet of Regensburg convened. In the face of ever growing devastation in many areas of Germany, its rulers were obliged to strive for peace, but for quite a while progress looked unlikely. Ambassadors agreed to make large contributions to maintain the Imperial army, 'which is' one report asserted, 'to cut their own throats'. The surprise arrival of the Swedish army outside the walls of Regensburg was reported in February.[16] If Stuart interests were to be heard at Regensburg, it was important for Charles to position himself with allies now. The popular royal marriage between the twelve-year-old Prince of Orange and his nine-year-old bride took place in May, just two weeks after Strafford's death. While few in Britain may have appreciated the significance of the step towards a peace in Germany taken by the emperor in abrogating the Edict of Restitution, they could appreciate that the mission of Thomas Roe to the Diet had resulted in the release of Rupert. Charles was finally prepared to act publicly on behalf of his nephew, pursuing his cause in Edinburgh and publishing a manifesto arguing that he, and his father before him, worked for twenty years for peace in Germany and the restoration of the Palatinate. He explained in detail his policy and the history of disappointed negotiations:

> Wee have been led on, and invited thereunto by divers promises and assurances ... both from the late Emperour, and King of Spaine; and other usurpers of the Inheritantes of the Electorall House Palatine.... Our pious Negotiations have beene eyther delayed or deluded ... and our Patience and Piety thereby abused.[17]

Though this was welcomed in Scotland, they mistrusted Charles's plea to raise an army for the Palatinate. The response was similar in London. A *Speech delivered in the House of Commons ... in the Palatine cause* by Sir Simonds D'Ewes recounts the history of the fraught relationship between Crown, Parliament and the European conflict, concluding 'wee have greater encouragements then ever to concurre with our sacred soveraigne'. Calybute Downing's closely argued letter urged support for the Elector and linked troubles in Europe with plots in Britain. His *Discoverie of the false Grounds the Bavarian Party have layd* returned to the theme of plots.[18] However, the

---

[16] (11 January 1641), 425, 430–1, STC18507.343; (11 February 1641), 12, STC18507.345; (8 April 1641), 133, 139, 239 (misno'd), 142, 146, N&S64.409; Wedgwood, 436–42, 446–7.

[17] Wedgwood, *Peace*, 360–1, 379–80, 389, 413–14; C. Carlton, *Charles I: The Personal Monarch*, (London and New York, 1995), 221; P. Gregg, *King Charles I* (1981/2000), 325, 332–3; *Newes from Scotland. His Majesties Manifest touching the Palatine Cause* (Edinburgh and London,1641), N&S997, E.171(17); *CandT*, 2:280, Edward Rossingham to Puckering, 14 February 1637.

[18] J. R. Young, 'The Scottish Parliament and European Diplomacy 1641–1647: The Palatine, the Dutch Republic and Sweden', in *Scotland and the Thirty Years' War, 1618–1648*, ed. S. Murdoch (Leiden and Boston, MA, 2001), 77–90; *A Speech* (1641), 15,

Manifesto that was prepared in the winter of 1636/7, as part of the preparations for a French alliance, was now too late to quell fears and mistrust. Similarly, Charles failed to convince diplomats in Regensburg. Butter's trade did not revive. He could not afford subscription renewals that summer. Thereafter his foreign news publications ceased to constitute a series and were, in any case, upstaged that autumn by news of the Irish Rebellion.

From November 1641, many pamphlets appeared claiming to describe in lurid detail the cruelty and atrocities being perpetrated by Catholic Irish against Protestant settlers as refugee's stories fed fears of popish plots. The religious alignments in this conflict closely resembled the outset of the Thirty Years War, with Protestantism and Catholicism in direct opposition. Meanwhile, London writers already had a mine of reports of bloody massacres from Germany to hand to recycle and stir imaginations. David O'Hara uses the term 'Foxean reasoning' to describe the fear and hatred of Catholicism reflected in the reporting of the rebellion, tracing this back to the Marian persecutions. This 'disposed people to believe anything evil about the Catholics' including an expectation that the rebels would receive money and arms from Spain and Flanders. The arrival of Catholics from continental military service further proved the international scope of the threat. Fast sermons linked the rebellion with events in Rochelle, Bohemia and the Palatinate. The news emphasised the spiritual significance of Protestant suffering and drew parallels with Germany to highlight the dangers faced by the godly in Europe. Wallington bleakly recorded in his journal 'all these plots in Ireland are but one plot against England'.[19]

Just as German historians have questioned the extent to which the reporting of atrocities in the Thirty Years War was politically motivated, we too can question the extent to which Irish Rebellion news was manipulated by politicians to encourage popular preconceptions and prejudices. It added to the pressures on Charles and helped to ease the difficult passage of the Grand Remonstrance through Parliament. Sharon Achinstein traces the impact of this reporting on parliamentarians who 'took it as evidence of the international conspiracy to enslave England in popish chains'. Numbers of reported Protestant deaths multiplied. Even recognising that some accounts could be questionable, MPs in Westminster realised that a new army would be needed to bring order so there was a pressing concern about and the control of these forces. News, even mistrusted, was of greater significance

---

E.198(38), WingD1253; C. Downing, *The Copy of a Letter* (1643), E.87(15), WingD2848; C. Downing, *A Discoverie of the false Grounds* (1641), E.160.

[19] D. A. O'Hara, *English Newsbooks and the Irish Rebellion, 1641–1649* (Dublin, 2006), 27–38; J. Cope, *England and the 1641 Irish Rebellion* (Woodbridge, 2009), 89–103, 113; P. S. Seaver, *Wallington's World: A Puritan Artisan in Seventeenth-Century London* (Stanford, CA, 1985), 166, 192.

than facts since it stoked fears that Ireland would become a springboard for a foreign Catholic invasion.[20]

The years 1641 and 1642 were a fertile period for ephemeral contemporary publications. While there is debate among historians about the extent to which this can be ascribed to the impact of the lapse of licensing as well as a debate about the scale of change and whether this can reasonably be depicted as an 'explosion of print', there is little doubt that there was a proliferation of small cheap pamphlets. Printers switched from substantial productions to more slender, topical and fast-selling items.[21] Butter was consequently competing for custom in a market for news that was dominated by the coverage of unprecedented domestic events. Issues for the thirteenth series were produced cheaply and edited inconsistently.

Butter did what he could to become part of the new wave of public interest in domestic news. In late 1641, he published several Irish Rebellion pamphlets and he briefly collaborated with Samuel Pecke, but Butter's real interest remained with the news on which he had built his reputation. So he continued as best he could with a fourteenth series.[22] In January 1642, he had shown he understood the 'faire opportunity being now offered to recover the Palatinate' as a result of Swedish successes, but he also recognised the unlikelihood of English support, adding, 'if friends were both ready and willing'. In March he tried to sell his foreign news by referring to domestic upheaval on the front page, *Newes from Forraigne Parts ... very fitting for this State to take notice in this time of division and Distraction. Especially the great councell of the kingdome, the Parliament*, but it was only scraps. *The Most Remarkable Passages* was a substantial, seventy-page publication spanning January to April 1642, but it was unedited and failed to pick up the potential domestic significance of a report that the Dunkirkers would not be supporting the Irish rebels. He could not protect his foreign news monopoly and was arguing with other booksellers who he claimed 'doe

20 J. Peacey, *Politicians and Pamphleteers: Propaganda during the English Civil Wars and Interregnum* (Aldershot and Burlington, VT, 2004), 37, 239–42; S. Achinstein, 'Texts in Conflict: The Press and the Civil War', in *Writing of the English Revolution*, ed. N. H. Keeble (Cambridge, 2001), 59–60; Cressy, *England on Edge*, 5, 28–9, 47, 317; Gentles, *The English*, 33–8, 56–62.

21 O'Hara, *English Newsbooks*, 35–6; Mendle, 'De Facto', 323; Cressy, *England on Edge*, 292–3; S. Lambert, 'State Control of the Press in Theory and Practice: The Role of the Stationers' Company before 1640', in *Censorship and the Control of Print in England and France 1600–1910*, ed. R. Myers and M. Harris (Winchester, 1992), 1–32; D. F. McKenzie, 'Printing and Publishing 1557–1700: Constraints on the London Book Trades', in Barnard, 557–61; Clegg, *Caroline England*, 218, 223–6.

22 Raymond, 20–4; C. J. Sommerville, *The News Revolution in England: Cultural Dynamics of Daily Information* (New York and Oxford, 1996), 35, 39–40; O'Hara, *English Newsbooks*, 39–41; *Worse and Worse* (27 November 1641), E.180(15); *The State of Dublin* (27 December 1641), E.181(38); *Warranted Tydings* (16 January 1642), E.132(37); *Good and Bad Newes* (28 February 1642), E.137(31).

(out of envie or ignorance) ... obscure and vilify the said Avisoes'. In late May, after a disagreement (possibly sparked by the publication of *News from Holland* by Edward Blackmore), he was no longer able to sell through other bookstores. He advised London customers to establish terms directly with him at his shop in St Austin's Gate.[23]

Butter had demonstrated a belief in the alignment of his work with the Protestant cause in Europe and royal interests from 1622 when he displayed the Palatine coat of arms in his newsbooks and, in 1627, in his petition to Coke for release from prison, when he asserted that he 'never published any ... but such as both stoode for the honor of his Majestie ... and allied the good of this state'.[24] During this period, he used his trade connections with Oxford and the distribution methods developed for the periodical publication of the foreign news for the Royalists, printing and dispersing proclamations, letters and books. Then, sometime before January 1643, Butter was among several people arrested and sent to the Fleet for offending Parliament who suffered unusually harsh sentences. That month he was taken to Windsor, under the charge of being an 'Intelligencer and Spy'. Finally, he was committed to Southwark prison where he remained until some time in 1644. On release, he did not resume the news trade, but was later to petition for a place in Sutton Hospital, claiming he had risked his life in service for the royal cause.[25]

The demise of his periodical made it more difficult to follow European news. Coverage was reduced and continuity lost but the great variety of pamphlets on sale included much to remind readers of the international context. There was satire such as *A Conference Between the two Great Monarchs of France and Spaine* on events in England and 'the Runaways' now living in their realms, and cautionary accounts of the Anabaptists and Jesuits in Germany. Johnson, Matthews and Underhill published foreign news later in the year.[26] Many publications revealed continuing fears of papal plots at home and abroad and of potential military alliances. The message from the press in London was that discord at home created opportunities for the Crown or the Irish rebels to bring in Catholic (particularly Spanish) forces.[27]

---

[23] *A cruell and bloody battaile* (end January 1642), title page, E.135(2), WingC7416; *The Most Remarkable Passages*, Butter (1642), 21, WingM.2915; (5 March 1642), title page, Wing N597A; (4 June 1642), 114, quoted by Dahl, 265; *News from Holland* (20 May 1642), WingN967.

[24] (23 August 1622), verso, STC18507.72; Add MS 69,911 fo.87.

[25] Mendle, 'De Facto', 328–9; Rostenberg, 'Nathaniel', 33; *CSPD*, 1660–1, 168.

[26] *A Conference* (1641) E.160; *Newes from Dunkirke* (1642), WingH33; *Newes from France* (1642), WingS200.

[27] *The Hollanders Embassage* (1642), E.131(31); *The Royal Message from the Prince of Orange* (1642), E.135(43); *Matters of great consequence*, (1642), E.135(7); Mendle, 'De Facto', 328–9; *A Message... touching letters lately intercepted* (1642), E.135(6).

War relationships

Through the twists and turns of the English Civil Wars there was an ever-present fear of foreign intervention. The withdrawal of Charles from London and the advent of war posed Parliament with questions about how to manage international relationships. Diplomacy became a complex and urgent issue for everyone caught up in the conflicts in all three kingdoms.

European news coverage for this period has attracted less interest among historians than the development of press concerns with domestic war news. Nonetheless, the new generation of periodicals that blossomed under the newly regenerated registration system established by Parliament between August 1642 and June 1643 reflected many familiar international themes with an added sense that England had become fully integrated into the European war zone: *Speciall and Late Passages* reported, from Utrecht, in September 1642, the deployment of men from the Prince of Oranges forces to England and, from Cologne, that Captain Flood was imprisoned in Dort for conducting soldiers to England for the king. A *Perfect Diurnall* reported that the French wanted to bring forces to England in support of Charles, while a calm voice came from *Speciall Passages* referring to 'Great talke of France and Spanyards, that are to come to England, but whether either of them be at leasure to afford any ayde to England or no, is a question, for they have irons enow of their owne'. However, the same issue suggested royalist collaboration with the Dunkirkers, reporting that twenty ships were being prepared to be sent by the Jesuits to Newcastle and to take any English ships that do not have a royal warrant. Memories of the battle of the Downs were fresh: the report continued 'but if Von Trompe the Dutch Admirall meets with them, he will soon scatter them, as he did the Navy of Spaniards 3 or 4 yeers since'. The editor was even able to jest about whether the Pope would send his 'gallant Army' to Ireland 'for the advance of the Protestant Religion'. *The Parliament Scout* suggested that Ireland 'will be so accommodated from forrain parts, that neither the King nor Parliament will have any interest there, but they will kick at both, if not drive out both'.[28]

London news editors in the 1640s had access to a good range of news sources from the growing market on the Continent. Had the conflicts there reflected divisions on straightforward confessional lines, no doubt the press could have made more of them. There was, however, some attempt to draw direct analogies. *A true and perfect relation of the great and bloody battell ... betwixt the King and the Lord Generall Earle of Essex ... the Emperours army ... and the Swedish army* covered Edgehill and the second battle of Breitenfeld

---

[28] Mendle, 'De Facto', 329–30; Raymond, 29–30; *Speciall and Late*, T. Underhill (6 October 1642), A2, 60, WingS4836, E.240(24) A *Perfect Diurnall* (22 May 1643), 206, N&S513.50A, E.249(10); *Speciall Passages* (4 April 1643), 289, 290, N&S605.35, E.96(2); *Parliament Scout* (19 September 1644), 527, N&S485.66, E.10(13).

with bulletins of news from Leipzig, Frankfurt, Bremen and other cities. But the realities of 1640s international relationships were far too complex and, with no consistent periodical coverage foreign news, it was more difficult for readers to follow the war's progress. It is also more difficult for us to gauge the extent to which readers could have recognised the significance of Brietenfeld for the Imperial cause, or the destruction of the army of Flanders at Rocroy. *Certaine Informations*, however, followed the progress of the French as they closed down routes from Flanders into Germany and we can see many editors starting to express their views on the way in which national and international concerns interlaced.[29]

Complexities in the story line for international news started close to home. Parliament recruited Dutch, Walloon and German officers throughout the 1640s, and many Scots from Marston Moor onwards. Charles had four regiments of French mercenaries, in 1643–5, and 9000 men from Ireland, mostly serving in Wales.[30] Their practical help was probably outweighed by their public relations cost. But what was a Parliamentary press to make of Prince Rupert's role in Charles' army? It was met with sarcasm: 'Prince Rupert is grown so famous for pillaging of Waggons: he is like to be called into Germany to be a Generall'. The arrival of forces in Gloucestershire 'will leave us with nothing but skin and bones', Rupert 'is requiting us for all the moneys we gave legally and illegally to redeeme his and his Fathers lands in Germany'. But, when Parliament was considering what relief it might send to Elizabeth and the Prince Elector, the emphasis in *The Parliament Scout* was on pity for them, suggesting that all the money given for their restoration had fallen into the hands of the Spanish faction around the king.[31]

A Catholic country, France, was now simultaneously a potential threat and the strongest ally of Sweden. Dillingham, editor of *The Moderate Intelligencer*, put it succinctly, 'Poore Protestants of Germany. France will doe more for you, then those that professe the same Religion.' Meanwhile, disputes over tolls and shipping in the Baltic between Sweden and Denmark were deteriorating into war. *The Parliament Scout* commented 'it proves harder to work out Denmarke then was imagined'. How would this affect England? Dillingham again, in *The Parliament Scout*, referred to the Chancellor of Sweden, 'many yeares since', saying 'there was no trusting England for Spanish faction ... would never leave off until they had introduced Popery, and therefore there was no relying on the state'. More optimistically, *Mercurius Civicus* reported that 'the Swedes are sending an Embassie to the

---

[29] *A true and perfect relation* (1642), E.127(30), WingT2539; *News from Germanie* (10 December 1642), 2–5, WingN959, E.127(27); *A Coranto*, H. Tuckey (9 June 1643), N&S77, E.105(20), 3–4; *Certaine Informations* (19 June 1643), 128, N&S36.23, E.56(2); Wilson, *Europe's Tragedy*, 638–9, 669; Wedgwood, 449–50, 455–9, 465, 467.

[30] Gentles, *The English*, 100–01.

[31] *Speciall Passages* (4 April 1643), 289, N&S605.35, E.96(2); *The Parliament Scout* (23 May–30 May 1644), 391, E.49(33).

Parliament of England: wherein they desire they may associate themselves with the Kingdomes of England and Scotland, for the defence of the Protestant Religion, against the Popish party in any part of the World'. *Mercurius Britanicus* reminded readers of the 'ancient amity between the Crownes of England and Scotland, and that Kingdome of Swethland ... interested in the same Cause (the defense of the Gospel)'. Readers were told that the queen's 'zeale sparkles ... to devoure Popery here, as her Fathers did in Germany'. Looking at the potential threat from the other side, *A Perfect Diurnall* in May 1643 reassured readers that 'the King of Denmarkes formidable Army of 300000 men and 30 or 40 saile of Ships' is 'not intended for England, as was supposed' while assuring them that Warwick's fleet continued to be actively protecting the seas.[32]

Both sides of the conflicts in all three kingdoms stood to benefit or suffer as a result of international relations. The Covenanters, whose international aspirations led to the establishment of their own Dutch printing press even before the outbreak of the Bishops' Wars, were pressing ahead with their proselytising agenda. The Scots had established relationships with the Dutch and Swedish and were in discussions with Denmark and France. From England ambassadors for the Crown and Parliament sought assistance in the Netherlands. For Parliament, there was a search for munitions and recognition, while Henrietta Maria sought refuge in The Hague hoping this would encourage support for the royal cause. The United Provinces shared many Baltic trading interests with the Swedes, so Frederick Henry's support for the British Crown, plus the alliance with France, had the effect of isolating him within the Netherlands. None of this was lost on the editor of *Speciall Passages* who reported on how they each 'claw the other' and commented they could 'pay as dear for their suffering or conniving at Popery as we in England have'.[33]

For the Irish, too, the confessional divide and earlier military involvement in continental armies gave both sides natural support networks reaching as far as Rome and the Papacy itself. *The Parliament Scout* reported a Bull sent from the Pope to the Irish, pardoning their sins and encouraging them to root out Protestantism. The arrival of the papal nucio, Rinuccini, in Ireland to help ensure free exercise of Catholicism there, was widely reported in London periodicals even before he landed. *The Exchange Intelligencer*,

---

[32] *The Moderate Intelligencer* (8–15 May 1645), 83, N&S419.011, E.284.6; *The Parliament Scout* (13 June–20 June 1644), 420, E.51(18); *Parliament Scout* (29 September–6 October 1643), 138, E.69(27); *Mercurius Civicus* (7 March 1644), 435, N&S298.042; *Mercurius Britanicus* (6 January 1645), 516, N&S286.065; *A Perfect Diurnall* (22 May 1643), last page (260?) N&S513.50A, E.249(10).
[33] Young, 'The Scottish', 87–94; P. Geyl, *History of the Dutch Speaking Peoples 1555–1648* (1961), 424–9; *Speciall Passages* (21 February 1643), 238, N&S605.29, E.91(5).

commenting on news from Paris on the installation of bishops in Ireland, warned that the Irish 'are but Spaniards in their hearts'.[34]

The press was facing completely new editorial challenges about the inter-pretation of foreign news in a transformed, evolving, and tense political landscape. This evoked a lively and diverse response to the complexities of international relationships. Yet news press developments in London in the years 1640 to 1645 can be seen as different primarily only in scale to the transitions experienced in other European cities, especially in the 1630s and 1640s. Brendan Dooley has observed that the first papers in most places were entirely concerned with foreign news, but, as they began providing more and more information, they began to turn to local affairs. It is the 'unparalleled vitality of the English media landscape' with over 350 titles of news publications, from 1641 to 1659, that distinguishes it.[35]

Peace negotiations

The battle of Naseby in June 1645 was a military and political disaster for Charles. Secret diplomatic correspondence, captured then published a month later, showed that paranoia about invasion had a continuing basis in reality and demonstrated the need to pay attention to international devel-opments. Once negotiations for peace were underway, there was an interest in parallel negotiations in Germany. *The Moderate Intelligencer* provided weekly coverage of the final stages of reporting the Thirty Years War.

During the Civil War, periodicals had branched out in a variety of direc-tions demonstrating some of the lessons learned from Butter and Bourne. Charles had finally recognised the need for a news press to 'turn the hearts of the nation' towards him. From 1643, with the aid of Peter Heylin and Sir John Berkenhead, a series from Oxford under the title *Mercurius Aulicus* put forward the Crown's case. Cogswell notes that 'some of the staff involved in the [Walkley] experiment figured in Charles's later efforts' and that 'Buck-ingham doubtless would be delighted to learn that the journalistic laurels that scholars have long accorded Richelieu and Renaudot more properly belong to the brows of Mr Walkley and the duke'. Thomas Audley and Marchamont Needham replied for Parliament with a series named *Mercurius Britanicus* in ironic recognition of Butter and Bourne's *nom de plume* from the same period. In 1645, a further publication, *Mercurius Anti-Britanicus*, completed the honours more scathingly, referring to the work of Captain Gainsford. They had all learned about the need to form and develop public

---

[34] *Parliament Scout* (23 May–30 May 1644), 395, E.49(33); O'Hara, *English Newsbooks*, 124–5; Hirst, *Conflict*, 231; *The Exchange Intelligencer*, 2 (22 May 1645), 16, E.285(5).
[35] B. Dooley, in DandB, 296, 11.

(551)

Numb. 72.

THE
Moderate Intelligencer:

Impartially communicating Martiall
Affaires to the KINGDOME of

ENGLAND.

From Thurfday, July 16. to Thurfday, July 23. 1646.

Rinces who neighbour to other, that they may enjoy their own with fafety, and if poffible enlarge ; conceive it good policie to foment differences in the adjacent countries to them : there are a hundred prefidents, befides thofe on foot at this day. That thefe ftrifes may continue, once fet on foot, they undertake to interpofe, and therefore preffe unity, peace and concord between them at difference, but the contrary is ufually meant, and they at difcord ufually brought at greater feud : For as on the one fide nothing can take but the pretence of reconciliation, fo nothing fo prejudicial to the others end as that : therefore is hinted a ftanding upon punctilio's to the one party, (and thats private) to which affiftance fhall be given, on the other a condefcenfion, affuring all readines in the oppofite, but in heart wifhes it not. This way of fomenting troubles under colour of accommodation, as its eafie to be feen, yea forefeen, fo is it not difficult to prevent by thofe that are Victors, not by fluggifhnes, retarding, falling back, demurring, or withdrawing from action. We have examples in our eyes (to paffe by the moft obvious and neer) the

Cccc   Diet

Plate 6. The first page (551) of *The Moderate Intelligencer*, No. 72 (16–23 July 1646): the half page title, positioning of the issue number and the use of continuous page numbering and dating were familiar by this stage. Here the editor leads with a reflection on the complexity and frustrations of peace negotiations that might be applied equally at home and abroad to introduce news from Germany.

opinion around their standpoint, and recognised that a clear structure and a direct form of speech was most effective.[36]

Bourne still had both capital and good credit within the industry. He used his position in the Stationers' Company (appointed as master twice and as a warden three times) to police his more lucrative copyrighted publications and publish popular religious works. This brought him into service on behalf of the House of Commons. He ventured again into periodical publication, in June 1644, targeting an export market with *Le Mercure Anglois*. He addressed 'all merchants and others that are desirous weekely to impart beyond seas the certain conditions of affairs here and the proceedings of the war'. It was short (only three to four pages), and usually appeared at weekly intervals. As it was especially for those of the Reformed Church who wanted to understand what was happening in England and its Parliament, it began by recounting who was on which side and naming all the commanding officers in the Civil War. Bourne's market niche avoided local competition while building upon his mercantile contacts and customer base. *Le Mercure Anglois* outlived the death of its first editor late in 1645. For a while distribution appears to have been handled by the printer, Thomas Fawcett, from Old Fish Street. It continued into 1648.[37]

Bourne's second series, *Generall Newes from all parts of Christendome* took the more traditional form of an English translation of datelined European news. Like *The Exchange Intelligencer*, it aimed cautiously for a narrowly defined market, 'among so many Bookes that come out weekly, to find some acceptance, chiefly amongst them that are well acquainted with forraigne Countries'. The first issue ended, 'if it be to your liking, I shall have the presenter encouragement to continue the same weekley'. This series appears to have ended after only four issues. It was based on Paris news with a high proportion of Mediterranean shipping news covering the Ottoman war with the Venetian Republic over Crete.[38]

The royal diplomatic papers captured at Naseby were deciphered by Weckherlin and published in *The King's Cabinet Opened* with an editorial commentary by Henry Parker, one of Parliament's 'great clerks' and a friend of Viscount Saye. Confirming many fears, they deepened distrust by showing

[36] Raymond, 26, 87; Peacey, *Politicians*, 127; T. Cogswell, '"Published by Authoritie": Newsbooks and the Duke of Buckingham's Expedition to the Ile de Rhé', *HLQ*, 67:1 (2004), 3, 24; Raymond, *Pamphlets*, 137; N. Brownlees, 'Polemic and Propaganda in Civil War News Discourse', in *News Discourse in Early Modern Britain*, ed. N. Brownlees (Bern, 2006), 17–19, 24–32, 37.

[37] *ODNB*, Bourne; Rostenberg, 'Nathaniel', 30–1; D. Freist, *Governed by Opinion; Politics, Religion and the Dynamics of Communication* (London and New York, 1997), 98, 105; Raymond, 37–8, 146; *Le Mercure Anglois* (June 1644), 1, E.1252(1); (13 November–4 December 1645), 1, E.1252(64); (9–16 August 1646), 129, E.1253(1).

[38] *Generall Newes* (6–26 May 1646), 1, 8, E.336(4); (6–13 May 1646), E.337(14); (21–6 May 1646), E.338(6).

Charles's determination to bring whatever help he could secure from France, Denmark, the Netherlands, Lorraine and the Irish Catholic Confederation. *Mercurius Britanicus* then used this evidence to oppose negotiations with Charles whose series of defeats that year and the dismissal of Rupert led to capitulation in March 1646. In this breathing space for London editors we see attention turning more effectively to European news. *The Phoenix of Europe*, *The Exchange Intelligencer* and *The Moderate Intelligencer* ventured into foreign news publication more seriously. Of these, only *The Moderate Intelligencer* was successful. Dillingham had the necessary experience as a news correspondent. His recent experience with *The Parliament Scout* had given him a taste for the London periodical market. He had lived in Paris where he provided news for Lord Montagu from 1639 to 1643. He was able to establish relations with correspondents and news networks. Sales of *The Moderate Intelligencer* were sufficient to fund the purchase and translation of a regular supply of continental news, and to allow enough space in each issue to cover foreign events consistently.[39]

Dillingham had the ability to summarise a situation cogently, for example, three knotty international situations are captured in two sentences, 'the Netherlands, their Army attempts nothing, the Ambassador of Denmarke doth as yet nothing but settle and agree the tolls of Norway. The Agent of Poland hath made no progresse in his negotiation.' He confidently interpreted the news explaining, for example, that a further two years of alliance between the French and Dutch 'inclines to fall in with England, and to prosecute a Protestant interest, which is like to prove more advantageous and safe'. He also firmly advocated the restoration of the Palatinate: when the question was asked in the Munster negotiations whether the Prince Elector Palatine should be restored, he commented, 'there was but 23 for him, and 39 against him'; adding 'an Army of 10000 Scots, and as many English, which may be spared this summer would make them vote a little eavener'. Two weeks later he reported on troublesome disbanded cavaliers in the Bristol area and commented pragmatically, apparently in response to readers, 'Why may it not be good to make an army of them and send them with others into Germany, to serve the Prince Elector, for the recovery of his countrey? They will do more hurt, here by evill wayes then the money and pay will amount unto.'[40]

[39] R. Cust, *Charles I, A Political Life* (Harlow, 2007), 400–13; Baron, 'Licensing Readers', 230–1; J. Peacey, 'The Exploitation of Captured Royal Correspondence and Anglo-Scottish Relations in the British Civil Wars', *The Scottish historical Review*, 89:2 (2000), 215–20; Peacey, *Politicians*, 95, 104–9, 260; ODNB, Dillingham, Cotgrave; Raymond, 45–9, 53, 147–8.

[40] *Moderate Intelligencer* (3–9 September 1646), 642, N&S419.079, E.353(18); (16–22 April 1646), 398, N&S419.059, E.334(2); (26 March–2 April 1646), 368, N&S419.056, E.330(14); (9–16 April 1646), 392, N&S419.058, E.333(15).

From February 1646, with the benefit of several pages per issue to dedicate to foreign news, he could select the material from Parisian and Dutch
publications most likely to speak to readers' concerns, and cut and paste
chosen reports, using to the tried and tested dateline sub-headings of the
past. The voices of individual correspondents, once again, brought publications to life: writing indignantly from Flanders, a correspondent denied 'the
reports of the ridiculous disorders imputed by the enemy to our countrymen'
while a French negotiator wrote, 'You would not wonder at the tediousness
of our Treaty, did you but understand what difficulties ... have arisen.' *The
Moderate Intelligencer* could use problems in other cities to cast light on more
local concerns: a detailed report about how the Venetians are funding their
war effort revealed the struggle to get people to part with their money, and
would have been read with great interest in 1647 London as it attempted to
address years of tax arrears and pay its soldiers. It was also able to follow the
last stages of the continuing French and Swedish campaign against Bavaria
with considerable eyewitness detail.[41]

Dillingham was a moderate in religion who began with the patronage of
Montagu. He remained pro-army but had a strong belief in the educative
role of his work and promoted flexibility and tolerance to create a favourable atmosphere for negotiations. The main ongoing international story of
these years was the peace negotiations that began in 1643/44 in Munster
and Westphalia. All along Dillingham was able to report and interpret what
was happening in terms of how this might affect the Palatine cause. He
explained why a cessation, rather than a peace, 'may be good for France and
the Swedes, but the Princes and Nobles of Germany are like to get nothing
by it, because there will be no restitution'. As Parliament, the army and the
Scots negotiated with Charles, readers could also learn of the difficulties
of negotiations from Osnabruck. In January 1647, he reported that France
was demanding more from Spain, including territory in Italy and Burgundy.
Full terms of the ceasefire at Ulm between Bavaria, Sweden and France
quickly reached London and, by mid-October 1648, the first reports of the
full terms concerning the Palatine appeared, as the Newport negotiations
with Charles were about to collapse.[42]

---

[41] *Moderate Intelligencer* (1–8 October 1646), 680, N&S419.083, E.356(8); (11–18
March 1647), 966, N&S419.105, E.381(3*); (15–22 April 1647), 1026, N&S419.110,
E.385(1); (22–9 April 1647), 1037–8, 1045, N&S419.111, E.385(8); G. Parker, ed., *The
Thirty Years' War* (London, Boston, MA and Melbourne, 1984/1997), 156. Plate 6 on
peace negotiations on both sides of the Channel.

[42] Raymond, 30, 40; O'Hara, *English Newsbooks*, 122–3; *Moderate Intelligencer* (17 April
1645), 58, N&S419.008, E.278(26); (21–8 January 1647), 872, N&S419.099, E.372(15);
(15–22 April 1647), 1027–9, N&S419.187, E.468(17); (12–19 October 1647), 1693,
N&S419.187, E.468(17); Gentles, *The English*, 352–62; Cust, *Charles I*, 442–7, 464;
Hirst, *Conflict*, 242.

It is difficult to assess the impact of the news of the Westphalian settlement in a year when London was barely recovering from the shocks of rebellion, an upsurge in the propaganda war waged by both sides, and further civil war. Hamilton's army was defeated at Preston in August, and the hero of the Palatine cause in the 1630s was brought to London as a prisoner. As the trial of Charles was contemplated there was a new possibility of escalation, recruiting mercenaries from among the forces released by the Treaty of Westphalia. It may have seemed a better option to work with the existing king than provoke foreign intervention, if possible, but against that was the fear that so long as the king lived, so too did the possibility of plotting on his behalf.[43]

Preliminary agreements were signed at Munster on 24 October 1648. The signing of the Peace of Westphalia was reported in *The Moderate Intelligencer* in November 1648. This described how it was marked by a 108 shot salute and the appearance of a stork flying about the lodgings of the Imperial Lords. 'The next day was so cleer a Sun-shine without any clouds, that it seemed, Heaven it self was well pleased with this general Peace: in the Churches thanks was given to God.' The council house was hung with ensigns and trumpets and kettledrums played, but the report concluded:

> amongst other harsh conditions of this Peace to the Calvinists, The Prince Elector Palatine, and his Brothers are to renounce for themselves, & their heires their right to the Upper Palatinate ... There are also some lands (Fees) of the Lower Palatinate, bestowed by the Emperour and the Duke of Bavaria upon foure Noblemen, their Counsellors, who have beene always the greatest enemies to the House Palatine.... Let all take notice of the different disposition and affection ... in England now, and 30 yeeres, when Prayers, Fasts, Men and Money was offered in abundance.[44]

Though taken into account by the emperor in his negotiating strategy, England was not a signatory to Westphalia. The fate of the Palatinate had been settled in the winter of 1646 when Charles Louis, weakened by the collapse of Charles's power in England, had resigned himself to loss, though to the end he was supported by Sweden and Spain against Bavaria and France; a fact that, in different circumstances, might have helped shed light on Charles's ever mistrusted negotiations with Spain.[45] It was a partial restitution and the Palatine family began to make preparations for celebration, and a return to the Rhine, when the news reached them of the execution of Charles in Whitehall at the end of January.

---

[43] M. Kishlansky, *A Monarchy Transformed, Britain 1603–1714* (1977), 179–80; Gentles, *The English*, 328–49; Cust, *Charles I*, 331, 373, 386, 412, 449.

[44] Quoted in Raymond, *Making*, 263–6.

[45] P. H. Wilson, *The Thirty Years' War: A Sourcebook* (2010), 286, 290–1; Wedgwood, 454–9, 498, 501, 488–9, 491, 524.

Neither the execution of Charles nor the Peace of Westphalia marked a final ending of hostilities. The execution in Whitehall was carried in the face of the diplomatic efforts of the Dutch to save him and turned England into an outlawed nation. Settlement was still needed in both Ireland and with the Scots. Meanwhile English shipping became 'fair game' for all.[46]

News of the execution aroused a storm of indignation in Germany and elsewhere on the Continent, with numerous pamphlets written in protest.[47] It alarmed other rulers when it reached Munster. So many countries were experiencing unrest due to the war. Delegates at Westphalia soon reassembled at Nuremberg for a conference to supervise the paying off and demobilisation of soldiers. This difficult operation was protracted and the congress remained in session until July 1651 with a Spanish garrison in Frankenthal until 1653. Charles of Lorraine did not leave Hammerstein until early 1654. Most of the Imperial forces were withdrawn to the Hungarian borders, though in breach of the agreement the emperor also sent men to Italy and the Netherlands. The Swedish were the last hostile garrison to withdraw from Vechta to the Baltic in May 1654, five and a half years after signing the peace.

After the introduction of further censorship legislation in London in September 1649, it was left to yet another new generation of newsbooks to cover demobilisation and the Dutch War.[48]

Conclusions

Little attention has been given to the implications of the Thirty Years War during the period of wars in the Stuart kingdoms. This perspective allows us to observe continuities from the 1620s and 1630s and to recognise the extent to which international news interwove with domestic concerns.

Charles retained his interest in the restoration of the Palatinate but was slow to recognise the political potential of a shared concern with his people. Just as he did not issue the explanation of why England went to war with France in the 1620s, he stalled publication of the *Manifesto* from 1637 to 1641, only issuing it when it was already too little, and too late. Ignored in Prague and then Regensburg, he had built up his international negotiating capital through non-parliamentary taxation for a fleet intended to make other countries take Britain more seriously. Yet its inept use culminated in a humiliating encounter off the Downs that Butter and Bourne's *Extraordinary Curranto* could not explain away. His preference for a show of

---

[46] Gentles, *The English*, 375; Cust, *Charles I*, 460.

[47] G. Waterhouse, *The Literary Relations of England and Germany in the Seventeenth Century* (Cambridge, 1914), 80–4; Peacey, *Politicians*, 119.

[48] H. Langer, *The Thirty Years' War* (Poole, 1978), 259–61; Parker, *Thirty*, 167–9; Wedgwood, 507–10; Peacey, *Politicians*, 228–30.

force was similarly apparent when he attempted to impose the new Prayer Book in Scotland through the Bishops' Wars. In his response to Covenanter literature, similarly Charles relied far more heavily on attempts to suppress than any attempt to explain his own position or to use the patent granted to Butter and Bourne in 1638 to provide a voice for government policy. It seems that, despite the fact that the reporting of the Ile of Rhé and the Battle of the Downs demonstrated that government had the capability to work in collaboration with the press in London, right up until the start of *Mercurius Aulicus* Charles simply did not appreciate the desirability of telling his side of events, nor see the need to persuade.

The Thirty Years War did not lead directly to calling Parliament in 1640, yet it contributed to the anxieties that attended the 1640s Parliaments, and Charles's willingness to try every means to support the Palatine (including working with Spain) contributed to the mistrust between Charles and his Parliaments. Securing votes for funds in the 1620s had been a problem because of differences over whom to fight and how. In the 1640s, the fears went deeper and the dangers were closer. Spanish and French soldiers were on English soil and the Irish Rebellion was interpreted as a confessional war, while reporting styles developed on the Continent, in the 1630s, amplified the horrors and destruction of the conflict.

Reporting upon the Thirty Years War involved handling complexity, with many armies, manoeuvres and allegiances to comprehend, many of which conflicted with religious affiliations. Effective coverage therefore required a specialist commitment that was lost with the demise of Butter's periodical, so that it became difficult to follow the events in print. But all of the combatants in the Stuart kingdoms had networks in Europe and they exported the domestic conflicts through competition for support between royalist and parliamentary sympathies, particularly in Paris and The Hague. This, in turn, increased anxieties about whether the involvement of other countries might lead to a further escalation of hostilities. An uneasy aware-ness of this dimension of the conflicts was followed by a resumption of consistent and continuous Thirty Years War reporting after Naseby.

Meanwhile, MPs and the news trade in London had learned much from the Thirty Years War and its news coverage about the value of print to prom-ulgate points of view and woo public opinion. Parliamentarians provided a fertile source of material for the press. The printing trade quickly adapted to periodicity to cover the Long Parliament in continuous session, using the form, format, dating and numbering techniques developed over the previous decades. This expansion into the domestic market acknowledged, through periodical names and references, its foreign news forebears while Nicholas Bourne attempted to revive a version of the 1620s newsbooks himself, and he successfully recreated, in *Le Mercure Anglois*, a curranto that reported back to Europe on London in much the same way as the Dutch corantos of 1620 first reported to English speakers.

Conclusions

The Thirty Years War generated demand for news. It led to a Europe-wide expansion in printed periodicals that started in the Protestant northwest and gradually spread. A great deal of public news was shared across confessional and dynastic communities and the flow of news allowed its readers to construct a coherent view of events.[1] News crossed the Channel into London so that, by the 1620s, there was a thriving and popular interest with more news available and available more quickly than ever before. Publishers in London began combining material culled from a number of publications from Germany and the Netherlands, making England one of the early countries to have its own series(the first printed news periodicals thus became established in Jacobean England.)

Periodical news reporting was not, in itself, revolutionary since the news networks that were to supply the presses during the Thirty Years War had been connecting cities across Europe and developing for over a century. However, the step into print made the whole enterprise more visible. This drove forward the development of the industry because periodical publication needs to be sustained with settled and effective relationships with suppliers, the authorities, within the trade (London booksellers, distribution connections and carriers), and with readers. Publishers drove the development of these relationships. It involved a far greater level of responsibility and entrepreneurial risk taking than ever before. This expansion of their role was recognised at the time and led to the use of the term 'publisher' in dialogue with the reader.[2]

The news series established by the syndicate of publishers in 1622, after false starts the year before, meant a commitment to continuity and recognition of a need to steer a careful course between the Crown (and later Parliament), licensers and the Stationers' Company. This allowed them to maintain working relationships and to stay in business week after week, weathering the storms of sensitive times, changes of approach to control, and political uncertainty as foreign policies changed. The publishers built news supply relationships and a distribution infrastructure. Supply needed to be as steady as possible and dissemination networks needed to reach towns

---

[1] P. Arblaster, 'Posts, Newsletters, Newspapers: England in a European System of Communications', in *News Networks in Seventeenth Century Britain and Europe*, ed. J. Raymond (London and New York, 2006), 19; DandB, 31, 279, 275, 277, 286–7.

[2] (16 July 1630), 14, STC18507.205; Dahl, 167–8.

and rural communities on a consistent basis. The distribution network they built facilitated the development of the printed periodical reporting of the Long Parliament while their trade innovations, learning about how to speed up production and dissemination, and their experimentation with form and format in order to create a recognisable ordered series, stimulated and informed domestic news press developments from 1640/1.

The printing figures show that very large numbers of copies were likely to have been in circulation in busier periods. Print runs of over one thousand copies were not uncommon in the early seventeenth century for ballads and the more popular pamphlets. Since we know the number of issues produced each month for much of the period, it is possible to conclude that there could easily have been over six thousand copies of Thirty Years War news in circulation in a month in 1622/3 and again in 1631/2. Calculations of output based on survival rates yield similar findings and help to demonstrate that what made periodical newsbooks so significant, especially in times of high demand, was the frequency of their appearance. This gave an overall output that was remarkable but we also know copies were shared and news was read aloud. Correspondents and diarists refer to issues they had seen (or had a summary of) but could not buy. The presence of periodical news was experienced keenly and continuously, and was consequently explored in contemporary literature and correspondence, especially in the periods when sales peaked in the early to mid-1620s and again in the early 1630s.

Financing demanded the underpinning of these sales through the establishment of a subscription base of committed customers and this constantly needed to be refreshed with new buyers. This meant that publishers had to listen to their readers and be attentive as their readership evolved. To try to meet readers' demands they explored editing and reached out to extend their readership to the newly literate of the middling classes who needed to be cultivated and trained to be able to assess and understand the reports and so participate in the news culture that gripped society from the outset of the Thirty Years War. They had to account for their sources and for how they were handling the material they received. In parallel, publishers were also looking out for new sources of interest and information. As soldiers headed to the Île de Rhé in 1627, and as trade grew in 1630/1, they took early steps in the creation of a new craft of active investigative journalism, inviting officers, soldiers and merchants to send back their reports, soliciting families and friends for copy, and scrutinising and comparing the accounts they received.

By the end of the 1630s a generation of readers had grown up with a taste for periodical news within a culture of active and conscientious reading that, for many, was a way of searching for signs of God's work in the world. The periodical press provided the means for following the war in a challenging and engaging way that called for the honing of skills of discernment, and learning about the Counter-Reformation and the suffering of Protestants in Europe. Readers had a capacity for following political and military

opinions established

events, and learned to compare reports to discern the 'truth' from rumours and opinions. The stage was set for the step change in the domestic news media from the circulation of several hundred copies of domestic separates and newsletters to printing. The process of integrating domestic and foreign news reporting then followed.

Readers learned lessons from living on the periphery of a war zone where the issues spoke to them deeply and the events reported challenged their concepts and fostered tensions. Readers experienced fear and the frustration of the impotence of Britain, and witnessed the unexplained and seemingly confused policies of the Crown as they unfolded in failure after failure. The press was also a vehicle for recruitment. Those who volunteered, or were conscripted, had first-hand experiences, but all the readers (and those who listened in alehouses across the nation) learned the conventions of war and formed views on how to conduct war. Then, when war came to Britain, experienced officers and men and the Swedish government, in particular, helped to make it a reality. Several historians have considered whether military news encouraged readers to view conflicts in terms of military solutions, legitimised violence, and prepared the public for years when war became a reality for the Stuart kingdoms. The news generated excitement. Weckherlin read the news with fading hope for his homeland and ultimately switched allegiances. Scudamore read widely for an overall understanding and a bigger picture of events while Wallington read avidly for an insight into Divine Providence at work in the world. By 1643, he wished for revolution and had learned to see politics in terms of a European religious struggle.[3]

The public sphere got its start through the formation of public opinion based on evidence provided by the press. People gained confidence in their understanding. They could have a view because they knew about what was happening. We do not at this stage see the full Habermasian model of public discourse falling into place behind unprecedented access to information. The greatest importance was attached to the identification of truth rather than the pursuit of reason, and that truth was frequently related to the necessity for supporting a Protestant alliance in Europe. Opinion forming and debate found a fuller expression in the print of the early 1640s in reaction to the repression of the mid-1630s that began building in 1637. There was self-awareness about the process that found its expression in the work of Gainsford and Dillingham who actively engaged with readers in the

---

[3] B. Donagan, 'Halcyon Days and the Literature of the War: England's Military Education before 1642', *PandP*, 147 (1995), 65–100. J. Raymond, 'Irrational, Impractical and Unprofitable: Reading the News in Seventeenth Century Britain', in *Reading, Society and Politics in Early Modern England*, ed. K. Sharpe and S. N. Zwicker (Cambridge, 2003), 198, 201; K. Sharpe, *Reading Revolutions: The Politics of Reading in Early Modern England* (New Haven, CT, 2000), 56, 115; Frearson, 345, 344; P. S. Seaver, *Wallington's World: A Puritan Artisan in Seventeenth Century London* (Stanford, CA, 1985), 156–7, 192.

formation of public opinion. As the 1640s progressed, Dillingham observed the debates in London bookstores and elsewhere and probed the impact of opinion formation on society.[4]

There is already ample evidence from contemporary diaries and correspondence of the development of political consciousness. The work of uncovering county and family archive material is progressing and, as further archives are explored, they will no doubt yield more evidence of news exchange and its impact. Historians are exploring the effect of political opinion on elections and can no longer afford to ignore the media, yet knowledge of what people knew and read tends to remain a preserve of social and cultural history rather than influencing the way the political history is written. Sharpe complained in 2000 that revisionists ignore the wider formation of public opinion. Still only a minority of historians provide political histories that weave public opinion into their fabric.[5]

The Thirty Years War drove forward the political agenda. It put an end to James's government without Parliament. Charles's reign began with war and was, at all times, shadowed by a sister in exile, a Protestant faction anxious to see him do something effective to address this and a press that provided constant reminders of the dilemma. Unlike his father, he was neither pacific nor inclined to use the tools of persuasion. Rather, he was haughty and combative. Yet, for all but two brief periods, the first early in Charles's reign and the second in the early 1630s when there was some prospect of an effective Protestant alliance with Sweden, the Crown favoured messages about the benefits of peace and prosperity. These were unlikely to appeal greatly to a news industry built on war reporting, selling to a Protestant readership suckled on stories of the Spanish Armada and keen to see action in support of the queen of Bohemia. Neither James nor Charles developed an effective communications strategy that worked with the new media or operated, as earlier historians and bibliographers believed, through suppression and censorship. It would be anachronistic in the extreme to blame either monarch for their failure to fully grasp the power and potential of the media as a vehicle for the cultivation of public opinion or to manage it effectively to promulgate their own views.

James's approach was far from simplistic: he was aware of the power of words and sought to influence public opinion.[6] More pragmatic and

---

4 (13 December 1623), 1, STC18507.136; (6 March 1624), 1, STC18507.143; *The Moderate Intelligencer*, 53 (5–12 March 1646), front page, N&S419.053, E.327(25).
5 K. Sharpe, *Remapping Early Modern England: The Culture of Seventeenth-Century Politics* (Cambridge, 2000), 15; K. Sharpe, *The Personal Rule of Charles I* (New Haven, CT and London, 1992); Cogswell; R. Cust, *The Forced Loan and English Politics 1626–28* (Oxford, 1989).
6 K. Sharpe, *Image Wars; Promoting Kings and Commonwealths in England, 1603–1660* (New Haven, CT and London, 2010), 28, 35, 46.

experimental than generally recognised, James's profile as an international statesman is improving, seeing himself as part of a European brotherhood of monarchs, giving himself the title 'defender of the faith', and acting as a negotiator and peace broker in Europe. He was well aware of the delicacy of the balance he strove for, and of Britain's financial weakness and consequent vulnerability should diplomacy fail. He also had an awareness of the emerging role of the media. He was however out of his depth in 1620/1, when the new international threat was accompanied by a massive upsurge in public interest and printed news at a time when his sympathies and policies were at odds with public opinion.

From late 1621, pragmatism, negotiation and accommodation resulted in compromises with the publishers, some of which have been more widely misunderstood than others, especially in the 1630s where the role of later publications in *The Swedish Intelligencer* series and the significance of the position of Secretary Weckherlin have largely been missed. The Protestant, pro-Palatine, faction at Court retained a voice throughout the 1630s, reflecting Charles's continuing sympathy and concern for the Palatinate and his sister's plight. Well before Berkenhead, Charles had Buckingham, then William Watts, Coke and Weckherlin, who were interested in working with the press and had co-operative working relationships within the trade. Butter was to end his days claiming his loyalty but the foreign news press never became an effective mouthpiece for the Crown.[7] Charles was largely inattentive and negligent of the press from 1627 to 1630 when Gustavus Adolphus's successes forced it to his attention. His subsequent initiatives with both press control and privileged publication were inadequately resourced. Weckherlin and Reade worked with the news in addition to their secretarial responsibilities at Court and without the benefit of a team of officials to scrutinise and amend texts in the way that Laud's ecclesiastical licensers worked with religious texts. Moreover, their efforts were undermined by successive failures in foreign policy. These faced Charles with monsters in the form of the press and public opinion which government was unable to address. Charles worked secretively with factions within his Court, often on mutually contradictory initiatives, and he persistently chopped and changed tack, gambling on finding a way to restore the Palatinate while often also striving to save (or even make) money from his relationship with Spain. Had the outcome of his efforts been successful there could have been a very different story for the press and for historians to tell, but he failed and there was never any back-up plan for damage limitation.

The real failure, recognised and felt keenly at the time, was the failure of foreign policy to defend Protestantism and to avert the advancing tide of the Counter-Reformation. The news consequently provided a week-by-week window on the working out of this failure. Readers learned of military

---

[7] CSPD, 1660–1, 168.

defeats, failed alliances, and the application of measures to re-convert Protestants and penalise those who refused to co-operate. News of the suffering of fellow Protestants and of the devastation of war added to fears and forebodings, while intrigue at Court, the presence of high profile Catholics, including Con and Marie de Medici, and the awareness of press control initiatives bred mistrust. Ironically, in so far as news was controlled and censored to avoid political embarrassment through the reporting of embassies and negotiations on politically sensitive matters, there was a perverse effect that made most readers largely unaware of sustained diplomatic efforts to restore the Palatinate. Readers were increasingly mystified and alarmed by Charles's tactics to avoid the costs of war and reap benefits from dealings with Spain. Reports of the progress of re-catholicisation amplified the fears of Protestants for their own security especially when, in the 1630s, Charles began to enforce a religious conformity that seemed popish. Thus seeds of distrust were sown by the late 1630s and these grew strong by the time of the Parliaments of 1640. The telling verdict of Wallington, willing finally to support war against Charles and ultimately even his execution, was built on the fact that he read the news avidly and from this knew Charles had turned on the Huguenots and failed Elizabeth. To him, this made Charles's execution seem like a working out of Divine Providence.[8]

News of the Thirty Years War can be seen as a contributory element to the causes of the Civil War, and the Civil War as a rebellion in a series that included the one in Bohemia that began the Thirty Years War and a similar Calvinist rebellion in Scotland twenty years later. Many in England tried to work within the establishment but became more and more convinced that this was not possible. In *England's Troubles*, Scott challenged the anglocentric focus of historians of the early seventeenth century. It is understandable that English historians would resist an approach that depicts the Civil War as what Arblaster has described as 'a sideshow in the final crises of the Thirty Years' War'. There is, nonetheless, a need to recognise the broad European culture of the educated and the awareness of international events that penetrated into English society and set the context for conflict. There is scope for further work on the 1630s, exploring the development of public opinion through archive records of news readers, avoiding being thrown off course by the 1632 news ban, since *The Swedish Intelligencer* continued as did the activities of news correspondents, while the Dutch resumed news imports. Many returned from the Continent in the 1630s and played roles on both sides in the Bishops Wars and subsequently.[9]

By the 1640s, many different lessons had been learned by many people. Charles acted publicly on behalf of his Palatine nephew. He issued his

---

8   Seaver, *Wallington's World*, 81, 143–4, 158, 160–1, 167–9.
9   J. Scott, *England's Troubles: Seventeenth Century English Political Instability in a European Context* (Cambridge, 2000), 15, 21; Arblaster, 'Posts', 30.

Manifesto explaining his foreign policy and secured a Dutch and Protestant marriage for his daughter.[10] The Long Parliament had members who were fully aware of the benefits of a good press and they were able to work with stationers who had seen how printed periodicals could work very successfully, given sufficient public interest. The London trade quickly spotted opportunities and adapted to the continuous session of Parliament applying the skills of periodicity, series formatting, and dissemination.

After a period of aggressive rivalry and propaganda, the balancing of reporting and opinion forming were mastered more effectively for both domestic and foreign news in the 1640s. Despite the demise of currantoes, the international dimension was not forgotten, but the Long Parliament was heir to a confused foreign policy with issues that were quickly compounded by the English Civil War itself. The Europe-wide threat to Protestantism loomed large and the Irish Rebellion captured imaginations, fulfilled fears, and gave them a tangible vehicle for expression. Memories were long. Years of recruitment and payments for forces in Germany were remembered, and the sight of the Dutch and Spanish fleets fighting off the English coast was recalled, but much early 1640s reporting was speculative about the prospects of aid and foreign intervention or referred to the activities of those who had either fled England or were otherwise in direct dialogue from overseas. A serious commitment to foreign news coverage could only be made with the benefit of trade contacts, arrangements for importing, translating and interpreting reports of military and diplomatic activities. The new news press was initially unsure of how well European news might sell when there was so much happening at home, and editors were often perplexed by news that included conflict between Denmark and Sweden, and cast France in the defence of Protestants. These concerns were reflected in the tentative comments that accompanied overseas news reports.

However, news networking was a two-way process and Nicholas Bourne used his contacts to establish a successful news market niche exporting English parliamentary and Civil War news to European Protestants and traders. Then, after Naseby, as negotiations for peace on both sides of the Channel proved lengthy and fraught with difficulties, and throughout Europe governments faced questions about how to pay armies and disband them, the synergies between overseas and domestic events became more apparent. Once again, the rooted conviction that the war in Europe was a single conflict against the forces of popery was easier to sustain. The international periodical news legacy was inherited by John Dillingham after an apprenticeship as a news correspondent in Paris. Relying on the import of Dutch corantos and the Parisian *Gazette*, his experience equipped him with

---

[10] *Newes from Scotland. His Majesties Manifest touching the Palatine Cause* (Edinburgh and London, 6 September 1641), N&S997, E.171(17), WingC2525.

contacts, understanding and the confidence necessary to relate the news to the concerns of readers in London. He ended the reporting of the Thirty Years War speaking with a calm voice of religious moderation and with a desire for peace.

Appendix 1

Typographical and imprint analysis of earliest English corantos

STC 18507	Date	Imprint	Typeface	Bibliographical comments	Last news	Conclusions
1	2 Dec 1620	Amsterdam, G. Veseler, by P. Keerius	small roman with subtitles in italics	No heading. Dahl: GV series began in Amsterdam in 1618 with title in roman, text in Dutch blackletter. VH took over in Aug 1620	Cologne	genuine
2	23 Dec 1620	Amsterdam, G. Veseler, by P. Keerius	blackletter with subtitles in roman	**Corrant out of** Hanson: same font as Dutch *Courante uyt Italien* printed by GV 25 Nov 1619 and 12 Feb	Cologne	genuine 2 copies survive
3	4 Jan 1621	Amsterdam, G. Veseler, by P. Keerius	blackletter	*Corrant out of*	Cologne	genuine
4	21 Jan 1621	Amsterdam, G. Veseler, by P. Keerius	blackletter	*Corrant out of*	Copenhagen and Paris letters after Heidelberg	genuine
5	31 Mar 1621	Amsterdam, G. Veseler, by P. Keerius	blackletter	*Corant out of* Dahl: BJ issue of 27 March with 34 lines of news from England missing	UP	genuine
6	9 Ap 1621	Amsterdam, G. Veseler, by P. Keerius	blackletter	*Corant out of* Dahl: translation from BJ corantos STC mistakenly identifies this as in Harl.MS. (See 18)	Palatinate Poland, Denmark, Sweden	genuine
7	25 May 1621	Amsterdam, G. Veseler	blackletter with datelines in roman	Courant Newes out of Italy Mead Harl. MS 389/79	UP	probably only genuine Veseler issue in Harl. MS

No.	Date	Printer	Font	Title / Notes	Origin	Status
8	13 June 1621	Amsterdam, Joris Veselde	roman font, datelines italic	*Corante, or newes from* STC says probably printed in England	Amsterdam news via Cologne?	London
9	20 June 1621	Amsterdam, Joris Veselde	roman font Identical to the BJ ones, e.g. 24 but with different imprint	*Corante, or newes from* Dahl: translation from Van Hilten corantos Mead Harl. MS 389/107 STC has this as Harl. MS 389/106	Cologne	London
10	5 July 1621	Amsterdam, G. Veseler,	blackletter	*Courant out of*	Cologne	genuine
11	9 July 1621	Amsterdam, G. Veseler,	blackletter	*Courant out of* Dahl: translation from BJ coranto	France and Flanders	genuine
12	15 July 1621	Amsterdam, G. Veseler,	blackletter	*Courant out of*	The Hague	genuine
13	9 Aug 1621	Amsterdam, Joris Veseler,	roman	**Newes from**	Cologne followed by ruling then Brussels, La Rochelle, Venice	London
14	6 Sept 1621	Amsterdam, G. Veseler,	blackletter	*The Courant out of*	Cologne followed by ruling then France, Sweden, Denmark, Arnhem and Utrecht	genuine
15	12 Sept 1621	Amsterdam, G. Veseler,	blackletter	**The Courant out of** Dahl: translation from BJ coranto. (2 different texts, translations of the 2 different corantos published in Amsterdam that day)	UP	London?
16	12 Sept 1621	Amsterdam, G. Veseler,	blackletter	*The Courant out of* This version is a translation of GV's VH original	Cologne with France and Poland added after ruling	genuine

No.	Date	Place, printer	Font	Title / Notes	Content	Verdict
17	18 Sept 1621	Amsterdam, G. Veseler,	blackletter	*The Courant out of* Dahl: translation from BJ coranto	Amsterdam includes news from France and Italy	genuine
18	9 Ap 1621	Amsterdam No printer No name	roman font, italic datelines	**Corante, or, newes from** Dahl: printed by BJ Hanson: Same as GV content plus 2 paras. No reason for Jansz to use GV's copy, too reputable to do this Mead Harl. MS 389/56 STC. does not identify this as in Harl. MS instead it shows GV's issue of same date (6) as in this collection	Amsterdam News of the UP declaring war on Spain and the Archduke	London
19	22 April 1621	Amsterdam	roman font very like 18	*Courrante, Or, Newes from* STC: probably printed in England, possibly for Archer. Dahl: printed by BJ Mead Harl. MS. 389/68 Amsterdam news includes 'His Maiestie of Bohemia with our Lady the Queene are...come to the Hage ... [entertained by] our Lord Ambassador Sir Dudley Carleton'	The Hague	London
20	6 June 1621	Amstelredam, B. Jonson	roman font italic datelines Identical to 21 and 23	*Corante, or, newes from* STC: probably printed in England, possibly for Archer. Hanson: roman 144 heading is not like the heading BJ used. BJ also used gothic for his corantos, and spelled his name Jansz, even in French edits Dahl: translation of BJ corantos Mead Harl. MS 389/87 STC has this as Harl. MS 389/82	Cologne and France	London

	Date	Printer/Place	Font	Title / STC notes	Coverage	Location
21	25 June 1621	Amstelredam, B. Jonson	roman font italic datelines Identical to 22 but not the same as 18	*Corante, or, Newes from* STC: probably printed in England, possibly for Archer Mead Harl. MS 389/82 STC has this as Harl. MS 389/83 (Harl. MS 389/81, and therefore in the same bundle of news sent by Mead as this coranto, is a roman type transcript of Letters Patent to the West India Co. Also claiming Dutch origins and also likely to be from a London press) Hanson: dating in text suggests it took 3 weeks from Hage to Amsterdam; more likely to be trans from a Frankfurt coranto	Cologne including news from Brussels	London
22	3 July 1621	Amstelredam B. Jonson	roman font very like 21 but type face a little wider	*Corante, or, Newes from* STC: probably printed in England, possibly for Archer Mead Harl. MS 389/83 STC mistakenly has this as Harl. MS 389/84	Denmark, Brabant, France	London
23	9 July 1621	Amstelredam B. Jonson	roman font identical to 21	*Corante, or, newes from* STC: probably printed in England, possibly for Archer Mead Harl. MS 389/84 STC mistakenly has this as Harl. MS 389/87	The Hague, Bon, Zealand	London
24	20 July 1621	Amstelredam B. Jonson	roman	**Corante, or, newes from** STC probably printed in England, possibly for Archer Dahl: translation of BJ corantos Mead Harl. MS 389/104	Miscellany from Turkey, Poland, France and Sweden probably gathered in UP	London 2 copies survive
25	2 Aug 1621	B. Jonson	roman	*Corante, or, newes from* STC probably printed in England, possibly for Archer	Augsburg? Covering Ostend news	London
26	29 July 1621	Altmore MH	blackletter, same font as 27	*Newes from* STC: probably printed in London, Hanson: No known stationer. blackletter font available in England, not like Dutch font probably printed by N. Oakes	Cologne	London

27	6 Aug 1621	from Altmore MH	blackletter, same font as 26	*Corrant or Newes from* STC probably printed in London, Hanson: No known stationer. blackletter font available in England, probably printed by N. Oakes	London
28	10 Aug 1621	The Hage, A. Clarke	roman Similar in title and look to 21–25	*Corante, or, newes from* STC probably London Hanson: No known stationer. blackletter font available in England, same press as 'NB' London issues of 2 and 11 Oct 1621, probably printed by J. Dawson. Content makes it unlikely to have been printed in The Hague	Cologne / London
36	1622	The Hage		*Newes from Turkie and Poland* STC London, E. Allde?	London
37	1622	The Hage		*Newes from the Palatinate* STC London, E. Allde?	London
38	1622			*More Newes from the Palatinate*	London?
49 and 50	3 June 1622	W. Jones for Butter and Sheffard		*More Newes from the Palatinate* 2 issues – sold well Hanson: probably meant to be a sequel to 37 (with false imprint)	London
				The Continuation of More Newes from the Palatinate No copy remaining	London
151	11 Sept 1624	Same miss spellings, Joris Veseler, Broer Janson The title 'Currantier to the Prince of Orange' with 'formerly' omitted from the text in the Dutch original.		*Sept 11. Numb. 32 The Continuation* STC E. Allde?	London

Abbreviations
BJ   Broer Jansz
GV   George Veseler
UP   United Provinces
VH   Van Hilten

Notes: Hanson's main contention was that many of the 1621 corantos were in London print and therefore had false imprints.[1] STC reflects this. Unfortunately, the STC has some referencing errors.

Dahl disputed Hanson's findings in particular the suggestion that some of the originals came from Germany rather than from Amsterdam. He demonstrated that many were translations of Broer Jansz issues (see table above).[2] Dahl may have been unaware of how linked Dutch and Cologne sources were and that Jansz was exporting corantos to Cologne. He studied the first two disputed corantos and concluded 'on typographical grounds and from the fact that the second one is a translation from one of (Broer Jansz's) own Dutch originals, I do not hesitate in declaring them to have been printed by him'. Dahl does not resolve the question Hanson raised about the 9 April issue, which was almost identical to Veseler's English coranto of that date. Hanson argued that Jansz would not have pirated work from Veseler. Hanson further argued that Jansz usually used blackletter for corantos. The English series are in a print generally available in both England and Europe at that time: five of them have roman 81 which Jansz probably didn't possess; the other is in roman 94, but it is not like his roman 94. Hanson noted the significance of the fact that the names Amsterdam and Jansz are distinctively anglicised and misspelt as 'Amstelradam' and 'Jonson', 'Jansen' or 'Johnson'. A further anomaly is that Broer Jansz is described as Currantier to the prince of Orange. This is a title that ended in 1619. Jansz himself when using it always used the word 'formerly' and this is omitted in these translations. Dahl did not answer Hanson's points about the fonts used in this series, which Jansz did not possess, nor the distinctive misspellings.

A confirmation that both the Broer Jansz and the misspelt Veseler issues came from London presses is to be found in a later newsbook which was undoubtedly published in London in 1624 and part of the officially recognised continuing series running at that time. This has many of the typographical hallmarks of the disputed 1621 issues, including the distinctive misspellings 'Joris Veseler', 'Broer Janson' and was printed by Edward Allde.[3] This suggests that all the corantos identified by Dahl in his bibliography as coming from the press of Broer Jansz are most likely to have been printed in

---

1   L. Hanson, 'English Newsbooks 1620–1641', *The Library*, 4·18 (1938).
2   F. Dahl, 'Amsterdam- The Cradle of English Newspapers', *The Library*, 5·4 (1945), 171.
3   STC18507.152.

London and up to four of those attributed in their imprints to Veseler may also have had a London publication (where Veseler's name is misspelled and the text is roman).

If we accept that all the corantos stating that they were printed by George Veseler and in a font used by him are genuine, but that others (with imprints for George Veseler but with roman text, imprints for Broer Jansz, and those from 'Altmore' and The Hague) were published and printed in London with false imprints, we get a single series of surviving genuine Dutch imports until 9 April 1621, followed by 8 surviving genuine Veseler printed corantos after that. Surviving corantos with false imprints then run from 9 April to 10 August 1621, culminating with one claiming to be for Adrian Clarke at The Hague. This brings the potential number of surviving issues with false imprints which appeared in London between December 1620 and August 1621 to up to fifteen. This conclusion could also help to explain the disappearance of de Keere's name from the imprints of the Veseler series after 9 April. That day, two issues, almost identical except for the imprints, appeared and the one was almost certainly pirated. De Keere would have been aware of developments in London.

Appendix 2

Transcripts in Harl. MS. 389 for 1621

Folio no.	London summaries of foreign and domestic news	Transcripts from corantos	Printed corantos	Other content details
2	26 Jan 1621			
3–4		Cullen 29 Feb 1621		'All of this is contradicted by other letters from Cullen' NB the use of 'other' here suggests he may have been referring to another coranto
5				parliamentary speech extract not in Mead's hand
7–8	2 Feb 1621			
9				letter signed by Mead includes datelined reports
11				letter from Mead 9 February 1621 says he got Cologne transcripts from an unnamed clergyman in the City, '(as being not so continual yet better then those of the Hague) he having an opportunitie of neighbourhood'
13				transcribed anti-Spanish satirical verse.[4]
16–17		Cullen 12 and 19 Feb 1621		letter from Mr Pettie in Venice is added at end. Also margin note in Mead's hand referring to 'a postscript' added by the translator
18	23 Feb 1621 from Dr Meddus, on verso, from Mr F.			
24				from Dr Burgess Frankendale 26 Feb
25–6	On verso of 26 from Dr Meddus			from Mr Heape, Frankendale
27		16 March 1621		

4 F. G. Stephens, *Catalogue of Political and Personal Satires in the British Museum*, 1 (1978), 41–3.

Folio	Source / Date	Note	Description
28	2 March 1621 summary of news mostly foreign		
30			letter from Mead includes extract from king's speech
32–3	Cullen 4 March 1621		4 March from Holland on second sheet
34–5	9 March 1621		first 2½ sides direct from corantos, followed by London news then letters from Hamburgh
43–4	30 March 1621		refers to letter from Henry Balam from Berlin
45			Mead's letter includes list of Acts of Parliament
50–1	6 April 1621		summary of foreign news reports with a little from London
52			letter from Mead quotes letter from Cullen on verso
54–5	13 April 1621		all foreign
56		9 April	
57–8	20 April 1621		news that Union has dissolved. Letter from Dr Burgess
61		See note	letter from Mead, Then in a later Courrante, then this I send you, I have seen it but I could not be the owner…'
63–6	Cullen 29 April, Amsterdam 1 May 1621	domestic news begins at the bottom of fo. 65	margin notes refer to another from Cullen
67			letter from Mead describes news from Dr Meddus, including transcript of a letter from The Hague
68		22 April	
70–1			transcript of a speech in a different hand
72–3	11 May 1621	on verso fo. 73 'Out of a printed Corrante'	refers to letter from The Hague
74	18 May	See note	margin notes refer to this week's letter, a letter from Amsterdam, and 'the corranto'

	More out of the coranto from Amsterdam 24		
75			
77–8	25 May 1621		ends with letter from The Hague
79		25 May	mostly foreign news
80	28 June 1621		
81			printed letters patent
82		25 June	
83		3 July	
84		9 July	
85			short letter with foreign news snippets
87		6 June	
88–9	1 June		a little foreign new summarised
92	8 June		'We have not had anything (save from Fraunce) since this day fortnight, & therefore can write nothing of Germany, Denmark or the Low Countries'
96–7	22 June 1621		
104		20 July	
106		20 June	
112	2 Aug 1621		message from the Palatinate
114	7 Sept		starts with news from The Hague
116–17	10 Sept 1621		news arrived at St Katherine's from Antwerp, after domestic news there is news of a royal birth and death in Spain
120	Sept 1621		includes E. India Co. news
123	28 Sept 1621		
124	5 Oct 1621		Heidleberg – scrappy addition
145		See note	letter from Mead 16 Feb1622 'the corrantoes now confirm'
151		See note	PS. 'I forgot to tell you out of a corranto…'
218			verso 'partly out of printed newes'

Notes: Transcripts are clearly identifiable; they are on smaller paper with a left hand margin. Columns 2 and 3 identify the source of Mead transcripts.

Columns 2 transcripts summarise news from a variety of sources, including letters and corantos from Europe and domestic news. Mead appears to be transcribing summaries assembled in London.

Column 3 transcripts have datelines and text apparently word for word from European originals. Other transcriptions referring to foreign sources, whether included in the London Summaries (Column 2) or in Mead's letters, are less likely to have datelines and text in a form that suggests they have been copied directly.

Mead's letters are not included unless they have evidence of a coranto or foreign news source as shown in column 5.

Appendix 3

Licensing and registration from August to November 1627

2 August to November 1627 entries in Company register, Arber, vol. 4, 148–52	'printed by authoritie'	Issues known to have been published
7 August		8 August
16 August		17 August
20 August issue numbers 30 & 31		NE
25 August		NE
		12 September
22 September issue number 35		NE
4 October issue number 36		4 October
		9 October
	yes	17 October
23 October issue number 39	yes	24 October
30 October	yes	1 November
	yes	7 November

Abbreviations

NE   No known surviving issue

Select Bibliography

Manuscripts

British Library

Add MS 64,892 and 69,911, British Library, Coke Papers, miscellaneous correspondence and petitions from January 1627 to August 1627

Add MS 72,433, British Library, Trumbull Papers, Weckherlin Diary, 16 December 1633 to 17 May 1642

Add MS 72,439, British Library, correspondence including letters to Elizabeth Trumbull from G. R. Weckherlin, Trumbull Papers, 1626–1631

Harleian MSS 389–390, British Library, correspondence of Joseph Mead to Sir Martin Stuteville 1621–1625

The National Archives

PROc115/M.35/8406 and 8415, Pory correspondence with John Scudamore

Printed sources

Corantos and newsbooks, listed by date

Amsterdam

The new tidings, Veseler (Amsterdam, 2 December 1620), STC18507.1

Corrant out of Italy, Germany etc, de Keere, Veseler (Amsterdam, 23 December 1620), STC18507.2

Corrant out of Italy, Germany, de Keere, Veseler (Amsterdam, 4 January 1621), STC18507.3

Corrant out of Italy, Germany, de Keere, Veseler (Amsterdam, 21 January 1621), STC 18507.4

Courant out of Italy, Germany, de Keere, Veseler (Amsterdam, 31 March 1621), STC 18507.5

Courant out of, G. Veseler (Amsterdam, 5 July 1621), STC18507.10

Courant out of, G. Veseler (Amsterdam, 9 July 1621), STC18507.11

Courant out of, G. Veseler (Amsterdam, 15 July 1621), STC18507.12

Courant out of, G. Veseler (Amsterdam, 6 September 1621), STC18507.14

Courant out of, G. Veseler (Amsterdam, 12 September 1621), STC18507.16

Courant out of, G. Veseler (Amsterdam, 18 September 1621), STC18507.17

Amsterdam – Resumption

Briefe relations from merchants letters, with some other occurences ... printed publiquely in the Low Countries and nowe translated... (Amsterdam, 1633), STC18507.359

The Continuation of newes from diverse parts (Amsterdam, about February 1633), STC18507.360)

The last weekes letters (Amsterdam, February 1633), STC18507.361

London

Corante, or, newes from, false imprint (9 April 1621), STC18507.18

Courante, Or, Newes from, false imprint (22 April 1621), STC18507.19

Corante, or, newes from, false imprint (6 June 1621), STC18507.20

Corante, or, newes, false imprint (13 June 1621), STC18507.8

Corante, or, newes from Italy, false imprint (20 June 1621), STC18507.9

Corante, or, Nevves from, false imprint (25 June 1621), STC18507.21

Corante, or, Nevves from, false imprint (3 July 1621), STC18507.22

Corante, or, newes from, false imprint (9 July 1621), STC18507.23

Corante, or, newes from, false imprint (20 July 1621), STC18507.24

Newes from, false imprint (29 July 1621), STC18507.26

Corante, or, newes, false imprint (2 August 1621), STC18507.25

Corrant or Newes from, false imprint (6 August 1621), STC18507.27

Newes from, false imprint (9 August 1621), STC18507.13

Corante, or, newes from, false imprint (10 August 1621), STC18507.28

The Courant out of, false imprint (12 September 1621), STC18507.15

Corante, or, newes from Italy, Germany, N.B. (24 September 1621), STC18507.29

Newes from Poland, Wherein is enlarged the Turks, B.D. and W. Lee (after 4 October 1621), STC18507.35A

Corant or weekly newes, N.B. (9 October 1621), STC18507.33

Corant or weekeley newes, N.B. (22 October 1621), STC18507.35

The Certaine and True Newes, from all Parts of Germany and Poland, B. Downes and W. Lee (after 29 October 1621), STC18507.35C

Newes from Turkie and Poland, false imprint (1622), STC18507.36

Newes from the Palatinate, false imprint (March 1622), STC18507.37

More newes from the Palatinate, false imprint (late March 1622), STC18507.38

Good newes for the King of Bohemia, false imprint (17 April 1622), STC18507.40

It is certified from Palmero, Bourne and Archer (14 May 1622), STC18507.45

A true relation of all such battles, Bourne and Archer (27 May 1622), STC18507.47

More newes from the Palatinate the 3. of June, Butter and Sheffard (3 June 1622), STC18507.49

A true and ample relation of all such occurrences … in the Palatinate since first of June Stilo Antique. Truely Related in a Letter, received from Doctor Welles the tenth of Iune 1622, John Bartlet (14 June 1622), STC25233

The True Copies of two especial letters, Bourne and Archer (21 June 1622), STC18507.55

The safe arrival of Christian Duke of Brunswick, Bourne and Archer (3 July 1622), STC18507.59

A true relation of the murther, Butter (4 July 1622), STC18507.60

The strangling and death of the great Turke, Bourne and Archer (15 July 1622), STC18507.62

A continuation of more newes, Bourne and Archer (26 July 1622), STC18507.66

The certaine newes of this present weeke, Butter (23 August 1622), STC18507.72

The ninth of September, Count Mansfields proceedings, Bourne and Archer (9 September 1622), STC18507.76

The 14. of September. A relation of many memorable passages, Butter, Downes and Sheffard (14 September 1622), STC18507.77

The 25. of September. Newes from most parts, Butter and Sheffard (25 September 1622), STC18507.79

The 27. of September, Butter and Archer (27 September 1622), STC18507.80

The 4 of Octob. 1622. A True relation, B&B (4 October 1622), STC18507.81

Nou. 3. A relation of the weekely occurrences, Butter, Downes and Sheffard (22 October 1622), STC18507.84

No. 4. A Continuation, Butter and Downes (30 October 1622), STC18507.85

A Continuation of the weekly newes from Bohemia, Butter and Downes (30 October 1622), STC18507.86

A Continuation of the newes, Downes and Archer (1622), STC18507.87

A Coranto. Relating, B&B (7 November 1622), STC18507.88

Numb. 7. A Continuation, Butter, Bourne and Sheffard (16 November 1622), STC18507.89

Numb. 8. A Continuation, Butter, Downes and Archer (21 November 1622), STC18507.90

Weekly Newes, containing, Butter, Bourne and Downes (28 January 1623), STC18507.93

Weekly Newes, containing, Butter, Bourne and Sheffard (30 January 1623), STC18507.94

Weekely Newes, containing, Butter, Bourne, Sheffard (31 January 1623), STC18507.95

Numb. 23. A New Survey of the Affaires, Butter, Downes and Archer (6 February 1623), STC18507.96

Numb. 18 Weekely, Butter, Bourne and Sheffard (11 February 1623), STC18507.97

Numb. 19. A Relation of the Late Horrible Treason, Butter, Downes and Archer (19 February 1623), STC18507.98

Numb. 20. The Newes of forraine partes, Butter, Bourne and Sheffard (28 February 1623), STC18507.99

Numb. 21. A Proclamation by the States of the Province of Utrecht, Butter, Bourne and Archer (7 March 1623), STC18507.100

Numb. 22, The Sentence and Execution, Butter and Sheffard (7 March 1623), STC18507.101

Numb. 24. Weekly Nevves, From forraine Parts, Butter, Bourne and Sheffard (31 March 1623), STC18507.103

Numb. 26. The Continuation of our former newes from Aprill the 8 untill the 17, Butter, Bourne and Archer (17 April 1623), STC18507.105

Numb. 29. The Continuation, Butter and Sheffard (2 May 1623), STC18507.108

Numb. 30. A Relation of the Duke of Brunswicks, Butter, Bourne and Archer (7 May 1623), STC18507.109

Numb. 31. The Newes of this present weeke, Butter, Bourne and Sheffard (12 May 1623), STC18507.110

Numb. 32. The Last Newes, Butter and Sheffard (17 May 1623), STC18507.111

Numb. 33. A Relation of Count Mansfields, Butter, Bourne and Sheffard (26 May 16230), STC18507.112

Numb. 35. More newes of the affaires of the world, Butter and Archer (10 June 1623), STC18507.114

Numb. 36. The Affaires of the World, B&B (16 June 1623), STC18507.115

The Last Newes Continued, Butter and Sheffard (10 July 1623), STC18507.118

Numb 40. The weekely newes continued, B&B (18 July 1623), STC18507.119

Numb. 42. More Newes of the Good Successe of the Duke of Brunswick, B&B (29 July 1623), STC18507.121

Numb. 44. Our last Weekly Newes, B&B (21 August 1623), STC18507.122

Numb. 45. More Newes for this Present Weeke, Butter and Sheffard (27 August 1623), STC18507.123

Numb. 46. Ital: Gazet. More Nevves from Europe, Butter and Archer (29 August 1623), STC18507.124

Numb. 49. More Newes for this Present Weeke, Butter and Sheffard (24 September 1623), STC18507.128

Numb. 50. Our Last newes containing, Butter and Archer (2 October 1623), STC18507.129

Numb. 1. Our Last weekely newes, Butter and Archer (11 October 1623), STC18507.130

Numb. 2. A Most True, Butter and Sheffard (28 October 1623), STC18507.131

Number 3. The Wonderfull resignation of Mustapha, B&B (11 November 1623), STC18507.132

Numb. 4. The Affaires of Italy, Butter (20 November 1623), STC18507.133

Number 6. First from Constantinople, B&B (2 December 1623), STC18507.135

Numb. 7. Weekely Newes from Germanie, B&B (13 December 1623), STC18507.136

Numb. 9. The Newes and Affaires of Europe, B&B (7 January 1624), STC18507.137

Number 10. The Newes and Affaires of Europe, Butter and Sheffard (15 January 1624), STC18507.139

Numb. 14. The affaires and generall businesse of Europe, Butter (24 February 1624), STC18507.141

The Newes and Affaires of Europe, B&B (6 March 1624), STC18507.143

Numero 17. Newes of Europe, Butter and Sheffard (12 March 1624), STC18507.144

Newes From Europe, Butter (19 March 1624), STC18507.145

Numb. 24. Extraordinary Newes, Butter (7 April 1624), STC18507.146

Numero. 21. The Newes of Europe, B&B (20 April 1624), STC18507.147

More Newes and Affaires of Europe, B&B (6 May 1624), STC18507.148

Numb. 30. Late Newes or true Relations, B&B (3 July 1624), STC18507.149

Numb. 32. The Continuation, Butter, Bourne, Newberry and Sheffard (11 September 1624), STC18507.151

Numb. 38. The Newes this present weeke continued, B&B (20 October 1624), STC18507.155

Numb. 41. The Continuation, B&B (15 November 1624), STC18507.156

Numb. 43. The Continuation, B&B (4 December 1624), STC18507.158

Numb. 6. The Continuation, MB (1 February 1625), STC18507.161

Numb. 7. The Continuation, MB (8 February 1625), STC18507.162

Numb. 1. Good and true tidings, MB (29 March 1625), STC18507.164

Numb. 16. The Continuation, MB (7 April 1625), STC18507.165

Numb. 17. The Continuation, MB (14 April 1625), STC18507.166

Numb. 18, The Continuation, MB (21 April 1625), STC18507.167

Numb. 23. The Continuation, MB (24 May 1625), STC18507.171

Numb. 28. The Continuation, MB (28 June 1625), STC18507.173

Numb. 49. The Continuation, MB (18 January 1626), STC18507.177

Numb. 13. The Continuation, MB (23 May 1626), STC18507.179

Numb. 26. The Continuation, MB (4 August 1626), STC18507.181

Numb. 42. The third newes continued for this moneth of December, MB (8 December 1626), STC18507.184

June 8. The Continuation, MB (8 June 1627), STC18507.185

Numb. 25, The Continuation, MB (1 August 1627), STC18507.186

Numb. 29. The Continuation, Butter (17 August 1627), STC18507.187

Numb. 32. The Continuation, Butter (12 September 1627), STC18507.188

The Continuation of our weekly Newes from the 26 of September, Butter (4 October 1627), STC18507.189

Numb. 38. The Continuation, Butter (17 October 1627), STC18507.191

Numb. 39. The Continuation, Butter (24 October 1627), STC18507.192

Numb. 19. The continuation, Butter (28 October 1628), STC18507.198

Numb. 32. Newes of Certaine commands lately given, Bourne (5 May 1629), STC18507.200

Numb.34. The Continuation, Bourne (4 June 1629), STC18507.201

Numb. 9. The Continuation, Bourne (16 July 1630), STC18507.205

Numb. 23. The Continuation, B&B (14 March 1631), STC18507.209

Numb. 27. The Continuation, B&B (9 May 1631), STC18507.213

Numb. 31. The Continuation, B&B (25 June 1631), STC18507.218

Numb. 37. The Continuation, B&B (2 September 1631), STC18507.221

Numb. 43. The Continuation, B&B (13 October 1631), STC18507.226

Numb. 44. The Continuation, B&B (20 October 1631), STC18507.227

Numb. 46 The Continuation, B&B (9 November 1631), STC18507.228

Numb. 1. The Continuation, B&B (29 November 1631), STC18507.233

Numb. 6. The Continuation, B&B (12 January 1632), STC18507.237

Numb. 8. The Continuation, B&B (24 January 1632), STC18507.238

Numb. 9. The Continuation, B&B (30 January 1632), STC18507.239

Numb. 10. The Continuation, B&B (8 February 1632), STC18507.240

Numb. 14. The Continuation, B&B (6 March 1632), STC18507.242

Numb. 15. The Continuation, B&B (15 March 1632), STC18507.243

Numb. 18. The Continuation, B&B (14 April 1632), STC18507.246

Numb. 19. The Continuation, B&B (24 April 1632), STC18507.247

Numb. 20. The Continuation, Bourne and Butter (28 April 1632), STC18507.248

Numb. 26. The Continuation, B&B (6 June 1632), STC18507.254

Numb. 29. The Continuation, B&B (23 June 1632), STC18507.256

Numb. 38. The Continuation, B&B (3 August 1632), STC18507.262

Numb. 39. The Continuation, B&B (13 August 1632), STC18507.263

Numb. 40. The Continuation, B&B (23 August 1632), STC18507.264

Numb. 41. The Continuation, B&B (30 August 1632), STC18507.265

Numb. 42. The Continuation, B&B (1 September 1632), STC18507.266

Numb. 43. The Continuation, B&B (4 September 1632), STC18507.268

Numb. 48. The Continuation, B&B (3 October 1632), STC18507.273

Numb. 1. October 16. A journal of all the principall passages, B&B (16 October 1632), STC18507.276

London – Archer

A Continuation of the Former Newes, Archer and Fisher (9 September 1624), STC18507.346

Extraordinary Newes (9/10 September 1624), STC18507.347

Two Wonderful and Lamentable accidents, Archer (11 October 1624), STC18507.348

A relation of the chiefest and last proceedings, Numb 3, Archer (21 October 1624), STC18507.349

In this weekes newes, Numb. 5, Archer (10 November 1624), STC18507.351

The weekely newes containing, Archer (24 November 1624), STC18507.352

A Certaine and Perfect Relation of the Encounter and Bloodey, Archer (November 1625), STC18507.353

A True and Very Memorable relation, Archer (late June 1628), STC18507.355

Numb. 6. The Continuation of our weekly newes, Archer (7 August 1628), STC18507.357

Numb. 7. The Continuation of our weekly newes, Archer (15 August 1628), STC18507.358

The Swedish Intelligencer and successors

The Swedish Intelligencer. The first part, B&B (9 January 1632), STC23521

The Swedish Intelligencer. The first part, Newly revised, and corrected, for B&B (1632), STC23522

The Swedish Intelligencer. The first part, ed. 3, B&B (1632), STC23523

The Swedish Intelligencer, The second part, B&B (1632), STC23524

The Swedish Discipline (1632), STC23519.5

The Swedish Intelligencer: The third part, Unto which is added the fourth part, B&B (1633), STC23525

The Swedish Intelligencer, The Fourth Part, B&B (1633), STC23525.1

The Continuation of the German History, The Fifth Part, B&B (1633), STC23525.3

The History of the Present Warres of Germany, A sixth part, B&B (1634), STC23525.5

A supplement to the sixth part of the Germane history, B&B (1634), STC23525.6

The German History Continued. The seventh part, B&B (1634), STC23525.7

The Modern History of the World. Or, an historicall relation since the beginning of 163, The eight part, B&B (1635), STC23525.9

Numb.1. The Principall Passages of Germany, Italy, France, and other places, B&B (1637), STC4293

Numb.2. The Continuation of the actions, B&B (1637), STC4293.2

Diatelesma. Nu.3. The moderne history of the world, B&B (1637), STC4293.4

Diatelesma. The second part of the moderne history, B&B (1638), STC4293.6

Diatelesma. The fifth part or number, B&B (1639), STC4293.8

London – Resumption

Numb. 1. An abstract, B&B (20 December 1638), STC18507.277

Numb. 6. From Norimberg. Ordinary avisoes from severall places, B&B (1 January 1639), STC18507.278

Numb. 7. Ordinary weekly currantoes from Frankford, B&B (1 January 1639), STC18507.279

Numb. 8. Ordinary weekly currantoes from Holland, B&B (1 January 1639), STC18507.280

Numb. 9. The articles and other circumstances and particulars of the taking of Brisack by the Duke of Weymar, B&B (1 January 1639), STC18507.281

A true and particular relation, B&B (between 22 and 27 May 1639), STC18507.308

Numb. 84. The Norimberg Curranto, B&B (21 June 1639), STC18507.312

Numb. 86. The Curranto ... from Holland, B&B (21 June 1639), STC18507.313

An Extraordinary Curranto, B&B (18 October 1639), STC18507.315

Cent. 2. Numb. 86. The Curranto this weeke from Norimberg, Butter (12 February 1640), STC18507.316

Cent. 2. Numb. 94. The Curranto for this weeke from Frankeford, Butter (24 February 1640), STC18507.323

Cent. 2. Numb. 95. The Curranto for this weeke from Holland, Butter (24 February 1640), STC18507.324

Cent. 3 Numb. 11. A true narration of the late sea fight, Butter (27 March 1640), STC18507.328

Cent. 3. Numb. 12. The Curranto for this weeke from Norimberg, Butter (31 March 1640), STC18507.329

Cent. 3. Numb. 18. The Curranto for this weeke from Franckford, Butter (20 April 1640), STC18507.335

Cent. 3. Numb. 19. The Curranto for this weeke from Holland, Butter (20 April 1640), STC18507.336

Century 3. Numb. 20. The News for this Week, Butter (23 April 1640), STC18507.337

Cent. 3. Numb. 27. Newes of the present, Butter (6 June 1640), STC 18507.338

A true relation, Butter (12 June 1640), STC18507.339

Cent. 3. Numb. 48. The Continuation of the forraine occurrents for 5 weekes last past, Butter (11 January 1641), STC18507.343

Cent. 3. Numb. 48. The Continuation, Butter (11 January 1641), STC18507.343

Cent. 4. Numb. 1. The Forraine Aviso's, Butter (11 February 1641), STC18507.345

Cent 4. Numb. 9 From Hamborough, From Wolfenbutle (8 April 1641), N&S64.409

London – 1642–9

A little true forraine newes, Butter (mid-January 1642), WingL2553

A cruell and bloody battaile, Butter (end January 1642), E.135(2), WingC7416

Nevves from Forraigne Parts, Butter (5 March 1642), WingN597A

Speciall Passages and Certaine Informations from Severall Places, 29 (21 February 1643), N&S605.29, E.91(5)

35 (4 April 1643), N&S605.35, E.96(2)

A Perfect Diurnall of the Passages in Parliament, 50 (22 May 1643), N&S513.50A, E.249(10)

The Parliament Scout, Dillingham, 1 (10–27 June 1643), N&S485.1, E.56(7)

15 (29 September–6 October 1643), N&S485.15, E.69(27)

49 (23–30 May 1644), N&S485.49, E49(33)

52 (13–20 June 1644), N&S485.52, E51(18)

66 (19–26 September 1644), N&S485.66, E.10(13)

Certaine Informations from Severall Parts of the Kingdome, R. White, 23 (19 June 1643), N&S36.23, E.56(2)

The Military Scribe, 1, G. Bishop (20–27 February 1644), N&S404.1, E.34(16)

3 (5–12 March 1644), N&S404.3, E.37(4)

4 (12–19 March 1644), N&S404.4, E.38(4)

5 (19–26 March 1644), N&S404.5, E.39(11)

The Weekly Account, 37 (6–13 March 1644), N&S671.137, E.37(6)

67 (4–11 December 1644) N&S671.167, E.21(12)

Mercurius Civicus, 42 (7 March 1644), N&S298.041

Le Mercure Anglois, 1, Bourne (June 1644), N&S258.101, E.1252(1)

1 (13 November–4 December 1645), N&S258.201, E.1252(64)

33 (30 July–16 August 1646), N&S258.233, E.1253(1)

Mercurius Britanicus, 65 (6 January 1645), N&S286.065

The Moderate Intelligencer, 8 (17 April 1645), N&S419.008, E.278(26)

11 (8–15 May 1645), N&S419.011, E.284.6

53 (5–12 March 1646), N&S419.053, E.327(25)

56 (26 March–2 April 1646), N&S419.056, E.330(14)

58 (9–16 April 1646), N&S419.058, E.333(15)

59 (16–22 April 1646), N&S419.059, E.334(2)

72 (16–23 July 1646), N&S419.071, E.345(16)

79 (3–9 September 1646), N&S419.079, E.353(18)

83 (1–8 October 1646), N&S419.083, E.356(8)

99 (21–28 January 1647), N&S419.099, E.372(15)

105 (11–18 March 1647), N&S419.105, E.381(3*)

110 (15–22 April 1647), N&S419.110, E.385(1)

111 (22–29 April 1647), N&S419.111, E.385(8)

187 (12–19 October 1647), N&S419.187, E.468(17)

191 (9–16 November 1648), N&S419.191, E.472(11)

The Exchange Intelligencer, 1 (1 May 1645), Wing145.1, E284(12)

Generall Newes from all parts of Christendome, 1, Bourne (6 May 1646), N&S167.1, E.336(4)

2 (6–13 May 1646), N&S167.2, E.337(14)

4 (21–26 May 1646), N&S167.4, E.338(6)

Other printed primary sources

A briefe description of the reasons (the 'Hayf', probably London, 1621?), STC11353

A Conference Between the two Great Monarchs of France and Spaine (1641) E.160

A continuation of a former relation concerning the entertainment given to the prince, W. Barret (1623), STC5033

Acts of the Privy Council, 1542–1631, 46 vols (1890–1964)

A declaration of the causes (Middleburg, probably London?, 1620), STC11351

A message from Parliament sent to the King touching letters lately, J. Hunscott (21 February 1642), E135(6)

A most true relation (Dort? London?, 1620), STC3210

A plaine demonstration of the unlawful succession … Emperour Ferdinand the second because of the incestuous marriage of his parents (The Hague, 1620?), STC10814

A Relation of all matters, trans. R. Boothe for W. Welby (1614), STC20862

A relation of all matters passed… since March last to the present 1614 (1614)

A relation of the funerall pompe, in which the body of Gustavus the great, was carried, T. Walkley (1633), STC12537

A relation of the glorious triumphs, Butter (15 May 1625), STC5029

Arelius, Abraham, *In nuptus illustrissimus principis Frederici V* (1613), STC960

Aretius, Jacobus (pseud.), *Primula veri spanegerics,..Palatinum* (1613), STC736

A True and ample relation of all such occvrrences… in the Palatinate since first of Iune Stilo Antique. Truely Related in a Letter, received from Doctor Welles the tenth of Iune 1622, J. Bartlet (14 June 1622), STC25233

A true and perfect relation of the great and bloody battell… betwixt the King and the Lord Generall Earle of Essex…the Emperours army…and the Swedish army (1642), E.127(30), WingT.2539

A true discourse of all royal passages, tryumphs and ceremonies, at the marriage of Charles, W. Barret (1625), STC5030

A True Relation of that which Lately Hapned to the Great Spanish Fleet, Butter, Bourne, Sheffard (1623), STC23009

Bacon, Francis, *The Works of Francis Bacon*, 7 vols (1874), ed. J. Spedding, R. L. Ellis and D. D. Heath

Barrington family, Searle, A., *Barrington Family Letters, 1628–1632*, Camden Society, 4:28 (1983)

Beaumont and Fletcher, 'The Fair Maid of the Inn', ed. A. R. Waller, in *Cambridge English Classics*, 10 (Cambridge, 1911)

Beller, E. A., *Propaganda in Germanys during the Thirty Years' War* (Princeton, NJ, 1940)

Bogel, E. and Bluhm, E., *Die Deutschen Zeitungen des 17 Jahrhunderten, Ein Bestandsverzeichnis mit historichen u. bibliographischen Angaben*, 2 vols (Bremen, 1971)

Bohemica jura defensa. The Bohemian lawes or rights defended (London? 1620), STC3205

Bohemiae regnum electivum. That is a plaine relation of the proceeding (1620), STC3206

Brathwaite, R. *Whimzies: or a new cast of characters* (1631), STC3591

Chamberlain, John, *The Chamberlain Letters*, ed. E. Thomson (1965)

Charles I, *Newes from Scotland. His Majesties Manifest touching the Palatine Cause* (Edinburgh and London, 6 September 1641), N&S997, E.171(17), WingC2525

Clarendon, E. Hyde, *The History of the Rebellion and the Civil Wars in England*, I, ed. W. D. Macray (Oxford, 1888)

Clark, A. ed., *The Shirburn Ballads 1585–1616* (Oxford, 1907)

Cobbett, W. *Parliamentary History of England*, 1 (1806)

Coppies of letters sent from personages of accompt for J. Bartlet (21 June 1622), STC18507.56A

Crosfield, Thomas, *The Diary of Thomas Crosfield, fellow of Queen's College Oxford*, ed. F. S. Boas (1935)

Dahl, F., *Short-title Catalogue of English Corantos and Newsbooks 1620–1642* (Bibliographical Society, 1938)

Dahl, F., *Dutch Corantos 1618–1650, A Bibliography and an Introductory Essay on Seventeenth-Century Stop Press News* (The Hague, 1946)

Dahl, F., *A Bibliography of English Corantos and Periodical Newsbooks 1620–42* (1952)

Davies, J. and Holland, A., *A Scourge for Paper – Persecutors...With a Continu'd Just Inquisition* (1625), STC6340

Declaration des causes (London?, 1619), STC11350.7

D'Ewes, Sir Simonds, *A Speech delivered in the House of Commons, July 7ᵗʰ 1641... in the Palatine cause* (1641), E.198(38), WingD1253

D'Ewes, Sir Simonds, *The Autobiography and correspondence of Sir Simonds D'Ewes During the Reigns of James I and Charles I*, 2 vols, ed. J. O. Halliwell (1845)

D'Ewes, Sir Simonds, *The Diary of Sir Simonds D'Ewes 1622–24*, Littérature 5, ed. E. Bourcier (Paris, 1974)

Dunton, John and Parks, S., *John Dunton and the English Book Trade* (1976)

Gardiner, S. R., *The Fortescue Papers*, Camden New Series, 1 (1871)

Downing, C., *A Discoverie of the false Grounds the Bavarian Party have layd* (1641), E.160

Downing, C., *The Copy of a Letter written to Mr Alexander Hinderston, Oct 1641* (1643), E.87(15), WingD2848

Earle, J., *Micro-Cosmographie. Or, A Peece of the World Discovered: In Essayes and Characters* (1628) STC11308

Franchis, Giovanni Maria de, *De auspicatissimis nuptiis* (1613), STC11308

A Marriage Triumph, Of the Most Auspicatious Marriage (1613), STC11309

Gallants, to Bohemia, G. Eld (1620?) STC3207

Green, M. A. E., Bruce, J. et al., ed., *Calendar of State Papers Domestic*, 27 vols (1857–97)

Grimmelshausen, J., *The Adventures of Simplicius Simlicimuss* (1668), trans. M. Mitchell (Sawtry, Cambridgeshire, 2009)

Heavens Joy, or, heaven begun upon earth, J. Harrison (1616), STC13019

Helfferich, T., *The Thirty Years War, A Documentary History* (Indianapolis, IN and Cambridge, 2009)

Heywood, Thomas, *A Marriage Triumph, Solemisized* (1613), STC13355

Howell, John, *Epistolae … Familiar Letters* (1645), Wing3071

James I, *The Peace-Maker: or, Great Brittaines Blessing*, Thomas Purfoot (1619) [first published 1618], STC14387

James I, *His Majesties declaration touching… the late Assemblie … of Parliament*, Bonham Norton and John Bill (1621), STC14377 and 9241

James I, *His Majesties Speech … 26 of March 1621*, Bonham Norton and John Bill (1621), STC14399

Jonson, Ben, 'Execration upon Vulcan', 1623 or 24, in *Ben Jonson: The Man and His Work*, ed. C. H. Herford and P. Simpson, 11 vols (Oxford, 1925–54)

Jonson, B., 'The Magnetic Lady', in *Ben Jonson: The Complete Plays*, 2 (Everyman, 1970)

Jonson, B. 'The Staple of News' (London, 1625), *Ben Jonson's Plays*, 2 vols (Everyman, 1910)

Jonson, B., 'Newes from the New World Discover'd in the Moon', in *The Works of Benjamin Jonson*, 2 (1640)

Lacrymae Germainiae (1638), STC11791

Larkin, J. and Hughes, P., ed., *Stuart Royal Proclamations*, 2 vols (Oxford, 1973)

Letter written by a French Gent, STC10812

Malcolm, N., *Reason of State, Propaganda, and the Thirty Years' War: An Unknown Translator by Thomas Hobbes* (Oxford, 2007)

Matters of great consequence, F. Coules and T. Bankes (11 February 1642), E.135(7)

May, Thomas, *The Heire, A Comedie as it was acted* (1620), STC17713

McKerrow, R. B., *A Dictionary of Printers and Booksellers in England, Scotland and Ireland and of foreign printers of English Books 1557–1640* (1910)

Middleton, Thomas, 'A Game at Chesse', in *The Revels Plays*, ed. T. H. Howard Hill (Manchester, 1993)

Monro, Robert, *Monro, His Expedition with the worthy Scots Regiment (called MacKeyes Regiment)* (1637)

Moore, Dorothy, *The Letters of Dorothy Moore, 1612–64: The Friendships, Marriage and Intellectual Life of a Seventeenth-century Woman*, ed. L. Hunter (Aldershot and Burlington, VT, 2004)

Moxon, Joseph, *Mechanic Exercises in Printing*, ed. H. Davis and H. G. Carter (1962)

Newes from Bohemia, R. Rounthwaite (1619), STC3211

Newes from Bohemia, a true relation of the warres, R. Rounthwaite (1619), STC3211.5

Newes from divers countries, V. Sims (1597), STC18504.5

Newes from Dunkirke, J. Johnson (1642), WingH33

Newes from France, A True Relation of the Great losses which happened by the Lamentable accident of fire in the city of Paris, for R.R. (November 1621), STC11279.2

Newes from France, J. Matthewes (1642), WingS200

News from Holland, E. Blackmore (20 May 1642), WingN967

Newes from Poland. Wherein is truly inlarged, for B. D. and William Lee (after 4 October 1621), STC18507.35A

Newes from Rome, Venice, for T. Gosson (1595), STC21294

Newes from... Spaine, Antwerpe, Collin, Venice, printed by Valentine Sims (1597), STC18504.5

News out of East India of the cruell and bloody usage of our English merchants and others ... by the Netherlandish Governour (1624)

Nicholas, E., *Proceedings and Debates of the House of Commons in 1620 and 1621* (Oxford, 1766)

Nixon, Anthony, *Great Brittaines generall joyes* (1613), STC18587

Parker, Martin, *A breefe disection of Germanies affliction* (1638), STC19222

Peacham, Henry, *The period of mourning...Together with nuptial hymnes* (1613), STC19513

Plaine Demonstration (1620), STC10814

Plomer, H. R., *A Dictionary of the Booksellers and Printers who were at work in England, Scotland and Ireland from 1641 to 1667* (1907)

Plomer, H. R., ed., *Transcript of the Stationers' Company Registers 1640–1708*, 1 (1913)

Pory, John, *CandT*

Questier, M. C., *Newsletters from the Caroline Court, 1631–38: Catholicism and the Politics of the Personal Rule*, Camden Society, 5:26 (2005)

Rohan, Henri, Duc de, *A Declaration of the duke of Rohan*, Butter (1628), STC21252

Russell, John, *The Two famous pitcht battells of Lypsich and Lutzen* (1634), STC21460

Schloer, F., *The Death of the two renowned kings of Sweden and Bohemia...a sermon at the Hague*, B&B (1632), STC21819

Shirley, J., *Love Tricks: or, the School of Complements* (1631/1667)

Short Survey of the Kingdome of Sweden, Michael Spark (1632), STC23517.5, 23518, 23518.5

Speght, R., *Mortalities Memorandum* (1621), STC23057

Steele, R. R., *Tudor and Stuart Proclamations 1485–1714*, 2 vols (Oxford, 1910)

Stella, Justus, *A Bewailing of the Peace of Germany* (1637), STC23245

Stephens, F. G., *Catalogue of Political and Personal Satires in the British Museum*, vols 1–4 (1978)

Swedish Devotion, John Bartlet (1632), STC23519

Taylor, Augustine, *Epithalamium upon the all-desired nuptials of Frederike* (1613), STC23722

Taylor, J., *Heavens Blessing, And Earth's Ioy* (1613), STC23763

Taylor, J., *An English-man's Love to Bohemia* (Dort, 1620), STC23751

Taylor, J., *Taylor his Travels from the Citty of London in England, to the Citty of Prague* (1620), STC23802

Taylor, J., *Taylor his Travels from London to the Isle of Wight* (1648), Wing520

Teares of Ioy shed At the happy departure, Thomas Archer (1613) STC385

The Declaration and information of the King of Bohemia (1620), STC11350

The Forme of the Agreement made at Strumsdorff, B&B (1635), STC23366

The 4 of November. The Peace of France of the Edict with the Articles of Peace, N. Newbury (1622), STC16841

The Golden Bull, for Nathaniel Newbery (1619) STC13611

The Hollanders Embassage to England, John Smith (18 January 1642), E.131(31)

The Invasions of Germanie, (1638), STC11791

The joyfull returne, of the most illustrious prince, Charles, Butter (13 October 1623), STC5025

The Last Newes from Bohemia (1620), STC3208

The Late Good Successe, STC3209/11356

The Magnificent, princely and most royall entertainments, Butter (1613), STC11357

The Marriage of Prince Fredericke...second time imprinted, W. Barley (1613), STC11359

The Marriage of two great princes, Wright (1613), STC11358

The Most Illustrious Prince, G. Waters (Dort, 1619), STC11360

The reasons which compelled the states of Bohemia, G. Waters (Dort, 1619), STC3212

The Royal Message from the Prince of Orange to the Peeres and Commons, J. Thomas (1642), E.135(43)

The True Picture and Relation of Prince Henry (Leyden, 1634), STC12581

Three severall treatises, B&B (1630), STC24258

Vincent, P., *The Lamentations of Germany wherein as in a Glasse, we may behold her miserable condition*, for J. Rothwell (1638), STC24760.5

Webbe, George, *The Bride Royall, or The Spirituall Marriage* (1613), STC25157

Wither, George, *Britain's Remembrancer* (1628), STC25899

Epithalima: or nuptuall poems (1612/13), STC25901

Withers Mottos (1621), STC25924

Yonge, Walter, *The Diary of Walter Yonge*, Camden Society, 1:41 (1848), ed. G. Roberts

Printed secondary sources

Achinstein, S., *Milton and the Revolutionary Reader* (Princeton, NJ, 1994)

Achinstein, S., 'Texts in Conflict: The Press and the Civil War', in *Writing of the English Revolution*, ed. N. H. Keeble (Cambridge, 2001), 50–68

Adams, S. L., 'Captain Thomas Gainsford, the "Vox Spiritus" and the "Vox Populi"', *Bulletin of the Institute of Historical Research*, 49 (1976), 141–4

Adams, S. L., 'Foreign Policy and the Parliaments of 1621 and 1624', in *Faction and Parliament in Early Stuart History*, ed. K. Sharpe (Oxford, 1978), 139–71

Adamson, J., 'Chivalry and Political Culture in Caroline England', in *Culture and Politics in Early Stuart England*, ed. K. Sharpe and P. Lake (Basingstoke and London, 1994), 161–97

Adamson, J., ed., *The English Civil War* (Basingstoke, 2009)

Allen, E. J. B., *Post and Courier Service in the Diplomacy of Early Modern Europe* (The Hague, 1972)

Andersen, J. and Sauer, E., ed., *Books and Readers in Early Modern England: Material Studies* (Philadelphia, PA, 2002)

Arblaster, P., 'London, Antwerp and Amsterdam: Journalistic Relations in the First Half of the Seventeenth Century', in *The Bookshop of the World: the Role of the Low Countries in the Book-trade 1473–1941*, ed. L. Hellinga, A. Duke, J. Harskamp and T. Hermans (t Goy-Houten, The Netherlands, 1999), 145–50

Arblaster, P., *Antwerp and the World: Richard Verstegan and the International Culture of the Catholic Reformation* (Leuven, 2004)

Arblaster, P., '"Dat de boecken vrij sullen wesen" Private Profit, Public Utility and Secrets of State in the Seventeenth-century Habsburg Netherlands', in *News and Politics in Early Modern Europe 1500–1800*, ed. J. W. Koopmans (Leuven, Paris and Dudley, MA, 2005), 79–95

Arblaster, P., 'Posts, Newsletters, Newspapers: England in a European System of Communications', in *News Networks in Seventeenth-Century Britain and Europe*, ed. J. Raymond (London and New York, 2006), 19–34

Asch, R. G., *The Thirty Years' War: The Holy Roman Empire and Europe, 1618–1648* (New York, 1997)

Ashley, M., *England in the Seventeenth Century* (1952/1977)

Atherton, I., *Ambition and Failure in Stuart England: The Career of John, First Viscount Scudamore* (Manchester, 1999)

Aylmer, G. E., *The King's Servants* (London and Boston, MA, 1961)

Baron, S. A., 'The Guises of Dissemination in Early Seventeenth-century England', in *The Politics of Information in Early Modern Europe*, ed. B. Dooley and S. Baron (London and New York, 2001), 41–56

Baron, S. A., 'Licensing Readers, Licensing Authorities in Seventeenth-Century England', in *Books and Readers in Early Modern England: Material Studies*, ed. J. Andersen and E. Sauer (Philadelphia, PA, 2002), 217–42

Baron, S. A., Lindquist, E. and Shevlin, E., ed., *Agent of Change: Print Culture after Elizabeth L. Eisenstein* (Amherst and Boston, MA, 2007)

Barry, J., 'Bourgeoise Collectivism? Urban Association and the Middling Sort', in *The Middling Sort of People, Culture, Society, and Politics in England 1550–1800*, ed. J. Barry and C. Brooks (Cambridge, 1991), 84–112

Barry, J., 'Literacy and Literature in Popular Culture: Reading and Writing in Historical Perspective', in *Popular Culture in England c1500–1850*, ed. T. Harris (Basingstoke and London, 1995), 69–94

Baumann, G. ed., *The Written Word: Literacy in Transition* (Oxford, 1986)

Bayne, R., 'Religion', in *Shakespeare's England*, 1 (Oxford, 1916)

Bellany, A., '"Raylinge Rhymes and Vaunting Verse": Libellous Politics in Early Stuart England, 1603–1628', in *Culture and Politics in Early Stuart England*, ed. K. Sharpe and P. Lake (Basingstoke and London, 1994), 285–310

Bellany, A., *The Politics of Court Scandal: News Culture and the Overbury Affair, 1603–1660* (Cambridge, 2002)

Bellany, A., 'The Embarrassment of Libels: Perceptions and Representations of Verse Libelling in Early Stuart England', in *The Politics of the Public Sphere in Early Modern England*, ed. P. Lake and S. Pincus (Manchester, 2007), 144–167

Bennett, H. S., *English Book and Readers 1603 to 1640* (Cambridge, 1965)

Bevan, J., 'Scotland', in *The Cambridge History of the Book 1557–1695*, vol. 4, ed. J. Barnard and D. F. McKenzie (Cambridge, 2002), 687–700

Bidwell, D., 'French Paper in English Books', in *The Cambridge History of the Book 1557–1695*, vol. 4, ed. J. Barnard and D. F. McKenzie (Cambridge, 2002), 583–601

Blake, N. F., *Caxton: England's First Publisher* (1976)

Blanning, T. C. W., *The Culture of Power and the Power of Culture: Old Regime Europe 1660–1789* (Oxford, 2002)

Bohannon, M. E., 'A London Bookseller's Bill: 1635–1639', *The Library*, 4:18 (1938), 417–46

Bowle, J., *Charles the First* (1975)

Breslow, M. A., *A Mirror of England Puritan Views of Foreign Nations 1618–1640* (Cambridge, MA, 1970)

Brewer, J. and Porter, R., *Consumption and the World of Goods* (1993)

Bridenbaugh, C., *Vexed and Troubled Englishmen* (Oxford, 1968)

Brightwell, P., 'Spanish Origins of the Thirty Years' War, *ESR*, 9:4 (1979), 409–31

Brightwell, P., 'Spain and Bohemia: The Decision to Intervene, 1619', *ESR*, 12:2 (1982), 117–41

Brightwell, P., 'Spain, Bohemia and Europe, 1619–21', *ESR*, 12:4 (1982), 371–400

Brooks, C., 'Apprenticeship and Social Mobility and the Middling Sort', in *The Middling Sort of People, Culture, Society, and Politics in England 1550–1800*, ed. J. Barry and C. Brooks (Cambridge, 1991), 52–83

Brownlees, N., 'Polemic and Propaganda in Civil War News Discourse', in *News Discourse in Early Modern Britain*, ed. N. Brownlees (Bern, 2006), 17–39

Brownlees, N., ed., *News Discourse in Early Modern Britain* (Bern, 2006)

Brownlees, N., 'Spoken Discourse in Early English Newspapers', in *News, Networks in Seventeenth-Century Britain and Europe*, ed. J. Raymond (London and New York, 2006), 67–81

Burke, P., *Popular Culture in Early Modern Europe* (Cambridge, 1978)

Butler, M., 'Ben Jonson among the Historians', in *Culture and Politics in Early Stuart England*, ed. K. Sharpe and P. Lake (Basingstoke and London, 1994), 91–115

Calhoun, C., ed., *Habermas and the Public Sphere* (Cambridge, MA and London, 1992)

Carlton, C., *Charles I: The Personal Monarch* (London and New York, 1995)

Clair, C., *A History of European Printing* (1970)

Clark, S., *The Elizabethan Pamphleteers* (1983)

Claydon, T., 'The Sermon, the "Public Sphere" and the Political Culture of Late Seventeenth Century England', in *The English Sermon Revised: Religion, Literature and History, 1600–1750*, ed. L. A. Ferrell and P. McCullough (Manchester, 2000), 208–34

Clegg, C. S., *Press Censorship in Jacobean England* (Cambridge, 2001)

Clegg, C. S., 'Censorship and the Courts of Star Chamber and High Commission in England to 1640', *Journal of Modern European History*, 3 (2005), 50–79

Clegg, C. S., *Press Censorship in Caroline England* (Cambridge, 2008)

Cogswell, T., 'Thomas Middleton and the Court, 1624: "A Game at Chess" in Context', *HLQ*, 47 (1984), 273–88

Cogswell, T., 'The Politics of Propaganda: Charles I and the People in the 1620s', *JBS*, 29 (1990), 187–215

Cogswell, T., 'Underground Verse and the Transformation of Early Stuart Political Culture', in *Political Culture and Politics in Early Modern England*, ed. S. D. Amussen and M. A. Kishlansky (Manchester, 1995), 277–300

Cogswell, T., 'The People's Love: The Duke of Buckingham and Popularity', in *Politics, Religion and Popularity in Early Stuart Britain*, ed. T. Cogswell, R. Cust and P. Lake (Cambridge, 2002), 211–34

Cogswell, T., '"Published by Authoritie": Newsbooks and the Duke of Buckingham's Expedition to the Ile de Rhé', *HLQ*, 67:1 (2004), 1–25

Cohn, H. J., 'The Territorial Princes in Germany's Second Reformation, 1559–1622', in *International Calvinism, 1541–1715*, ed. M. Prestwich (Oxford,1895), 135–63

Colclough, D., *Freedom of Speech in Early Stuart England* (Cambridge, 2005)

Connor, T. P., 'Malignant Reading: John Squier's Newgate Prison Library, 1642–6', *The Library*, 7:2 (2006), 154–86

Cope, J., *England and the 1641 Irish Rebellion* (Woodbridge, 2009)

Coupe, W. A., *The German Illustrated Broadsheet in the 17th Century* (Baden-Baden, 1966–7)

Cramer, K., *The Thirty Years' War and German Memory in the Nineteenth Century* (Lincoln, NE and Oxford, 2001)

Cressy, D., *Literacy and Social Order: Reading and Writing in Tudor and Stuart England* (Cambridge, 1980)

Cressy, D., 'Literacy in Context: Meaning and Measurement in Early Modern England', in *Consumption and the World of Goods*, ed. J. Brewer and R. Porter (1993), 305–18

Cressy, D., *England on Edge: Crisis and Revolution, 1640–1642* (Oxford, 2006)

Croft, P., 'The Reputation of Robert Cecil: Libels, Political Opinion and Popular Awareness in the Early Seventeenth Century', *Transactions of the Royal Historical Society*, 6:1 (1991), 43–69

Croft, P., 'Libels, Popular Literacy and Public Opinion in Early Modern England', *Historical Research*, 68 (1995), 266–85

Croft, P., 'Capital Life, Members of Parliament Outside the House', in *Politics, Religion and Popularity in Early Stuart Britain*, ed. T. Cogswell, R. Cust and P. Lake (Cambridge, 2002), 65–83

Croft, P., *King James* (Basingstoke and New York, 2003)

Cust, R., 'Charles I, the Privy Council, and the Forced Loan', *JBS*, 24:2 (1985), 208–35

Cust, R., 'Politics and the Electorate in the 1620s', in *Conflict in Early Stuart England: Studies in Religion and Politics 1603–42*, ed. R. Cust and A. Hughes (1989), 134–62

Cust, R., *The Forced Loan and English Politics 1626–28* (Oxford, 1989)

Cust, R., 'Charles I and Popularity', in *Politics, Religion and Popularity in Early Stuart England*, ed. T. Cogswell, R. Cust and P. Lake (Cambridge, 2002), 235–58

Cust, R., *Charles I, A Political Life* (Harlow, 2007)

Cust, R., 'The "Public Man" in Late Tudor and Early Stuart England', in *The Politics of the Public Sphere in Early Modern England*, ed. P. Lake and S. Pincus (Manchester, 2007), 116–43

Cust, R. and Hughes, A., ed., *Conflict in Early Stuart England: Studies in Religion and Politics 1603–42* (1989)

Dahl, F., *Amsterdam – the Earliest Newspaper Centre of Western Europe* (The Hague, 1939)

Dahl, F., 'Amsterdam – the Cradle of English Newspapers', *The Library*, 5:4 (1949), 166–78

Davies, G., 'English Political Sermons 1603–1640', *HLQ*, 3 (October 1939), 1–22

Davies, G., *The Early Stuarts 1603–1660* (Oxford, 1959)

Donagan, B., 'Halcyon Days and the Literature of the War: England's Military Education before 1642', *PandP*, 147 (1995), 65–100

Duke, A., 'The Ambivalent Face of Calvinism in the Netherlands, 1561–1618', in *International Calvinism, 1541–1715*, ed. M. Prestwich (Oxford, 1895), 109–32

Durston, C. and Eales, J., ed., *The Culture of English Puritanism 1560–1700* (1996)

Eales, J., *Puritans and Roundheads: The Harleys of Brampton Bryan and the Outbreak of the English Civil War* (Cambridge, 1990)

Eales, J., *Women in Early Modern England 1500–1700* (1998)

Eales, J., 'The Rise of Ideological Politics in Kent 1558–1640', in *Early Modern Kent, 1540–1640*, ed. M. Zell (Woodbridge, 2000), 279–313

Eccles, M., 'Thomas Gainsford, "Captain Pamphlet"', *HLQ*, 45 (1982), 259–70

Eriksen, E. O. and Weigard, J., *Understanding Habermas: Communicative Action and Deliberative Democracy* (London and New York, 2003)

Ettinghausen, H., 'The News in Spain: Relacions de sucesos in the Reigns of Philip III and IV', *ESR*, 14:1 (1984), 1–20

Ettinghausen, H., 'Politics and the Press in Spain', in *The Politics of Information in Early Modern Europe*, ed. B. Dooley and S. Baron (London and New York, 2001), 199–215

Febvre, L. and Martin, H-J., *The Coming of the Book* (1976)

Ferrell, L. A. and McCullough, P., ed., *The English Sermon Revised: Religion, Literature and History, 1600–1750* (Manchester, 2000)

Fielding, J., 'Opposition to the Personal Rule of Charles I: The Diary of Robert Woodford, 1637–1641', *HJ*, 31:4 (1988), 769–88

Fincham, K., 'Prelacy and Politics: Archbishop Abbot's Defence of Protestant Orthodoxy', *Historical Research*, 61 (1988), 36–69

Fincham, K., *Prelate as Pastor* (Oxford, 1990)

Fincham, K. and Lake, P., 'The Ecclesiastical Policy of King James I and Charles I', *JBS*, 24:2 (1985), 169–207

Fincham, K. and Lake, P., 'The Ecclesiastical Policies of James I', in *The Early Stuart Church 1603–1642*, ed. K. Fincham (Basingstoke, 1993), 23–49

Fischer, T. A., *The Scots in Germany: Being a Contribution towards the History of Scots Abroad* (Edinburgh, 1902)

Fish, S., *Is There a Text in This Class? The Authority of Interpretive Communities* (Cambridge, MA, 1980)

Fissel, M. C., *English Warfare, 1511–1641* (London and New York, 2001)

Forster, L. W., *Georg Rudolf Weckherlin zur Kenntnis seines Lebens in England* (Basel, 1944)

Forster, L. W., 'Sources for G. R. Weckherlin's Life in England: The Correspondence', in *The Modern Language Review*, 2 (Cambridge, 1946), 186–9

Forster, L. W., 'Kleine Schriften zur Deutschen Literatur im 17. Jahrhundert', *Daphnis: Zeitschrift fur Mittlere Deutsche Literatur*, 6:4 (1977), 193–231

Fox, A., 'Ballads, Libels and Popular Ridicule in Jacobean England', *PandP*, 145 (1995), 47–83

Fox, A., *Oral and Literate Culture in England 1500–1700* (Oxford, 2000)

Fraser Mitchel, W., *English Pulpit Oratory from Andrewes to Tillotson; A Study of Literary Aspects* (1932)

Frearson, M. C., 'London Corantos in the 1620s', in *Annual* (1993), 3–17

Frearson, M. C., 'The Distribution and Readership of London Corantos in the 1620s', *Serials and their Readers 1620–1914*, ed. R. Myers and M. Harris (Winchester and New Castle, DE, 1993), 1–25

Freist, D., *Governed by Opinion; Politics, Religion and the Dynamics of Communication in Stuart London, 1637–45* (London and New York, 1997)

Friedman, J., *The Battle of the Frogs and Fairford's Flies* (New York, 1993)

Gaskell, P., *A New Introduction to Bibliography* (Oxford, 1972)

Gentles, I., *The English Revolution and the Wars in the Three Kingdoms 1638–1652* (Harlow, 2007)

Geyl, P., *History of the Dutch Speaking Peoples, 1555–1648* (1961)

Gillespie, R. and Hadfield, A., ed., *The Irish Book in English 1550–1800* (Oxford, 2006)

Goode, L., *Jurgen Habermas, Democracy and the Public Sphere* (London, 2005)

Greg, W. W., *Licensers for the Press* (Oxford, 1962)

Greg, W. W., *A Companion to Arber* (Oxford, 1967)

Gregg, P., *King Charles I* (1981/2000)

Griffey, E., ed., *Henrietta Maria, Piety, Politics and Patronage* (Aldershot and Burlington, VT, 2008)

Groenveld, S., 'The Mecca of Authors? States Assemblies in the Seventeenth-Century Dutch Republic', in *Too Mighty to be Free: Censorship and the Press in Britain and the Netherlands*, ed. A. C. Duke and C. A. Tamse (Zutphen, 1987), 63–86

Grosjean, A., 'A Century of Scottish Governorship in the Swedish Empire, 1574–1700', in *Military Governors and Imperial Frontiers c. 1600–1800*, ed. A. Mackillop and S. Murdoch (Leiden and Boston, MA, 2003), 53–78

Grosjean, A., *An Unofficial Alliance: Scotland and Sweden 1569–1654* (Leiden and Boston, MA, 2003)

Grosjean, A. and Murdoch, S., ed., *Scottish Communities Abroad in the Early Modern Period* (Leiden and Boston, MA, 2005)

Habermas, J., *The Structural Transformation of the Public Sphere: An Inquiry into a Category of Bourgeois Society*, trans. T. Burger (Cambridge, MA, 1989), originally published as *Strukturwandel der Offentllichkeit* (Neuwied/Berlin, 1962)

Hammer, P., 'The Smiling Crocodile: The Earl of Essex and Late Elizabethan "Popularity"', in *The Politics of the Public Sphere in Early Modern England*, ed. P. Lake and S. Pincus (Manchester, 2007), 95–115

Handover, P. M., *Printing in London 1476 to Modern Times* (1960)

Hanson, L., 'English Newsbooks, 1620–41', *The Library*, 4:18 (1937–8)

Harris, T., 'The Problem of Popular Culture in Seventeenth-Century London', *History of European Ideas*, 10:1 (1989), 43–58

Harris, T., ed., *Popular Culture in England c1500–1850* (Basingstoke and London, 1995)

Harris, T., ed., *The Politics of the Excluded, c.1500–1850* (Basingstoke and New York, 2001)

Harthan, J., *The Illustrated Book* (1981)

Havran, M., *Caroline Courtier: The Life of Lord Cottington* (Basingstoke and London, 1973)

Hellinge, W. G., *Copy and Print in the Netherlands* (Amsterdam, 1962)

Herford, C. H. and Simpson, P., ed., *Ben Jonson: The Man and His Work* (Oxford, 1925/1954)

Hibbard, C., *Charles I and the Popish Plot* (Chapel Hill, NC, 1983)

Hibbard, C., 'The Theatre of Dynasty', in *The Stuart Court and Europe: Essays in Politics and Political Culture*, ed. M. Smuts (Cambridge, 1996), 156–76

Hill, C., *Puritanism and Revolution* (1958)

Hill, C., *The Collected Essays of Christopher Hill*, 3 vols (Brighton, 1985)

Hirst, D., *England in Conflict 1603–1660, Kingdom, Community, Conflict* (1999)

Horsbroch, D., '"Wish You Were Here?" Scottish Reactions to "Postcards" Home from the "Germane Warres"', in *Scotland and the Thirty Years' War, 1618–1648*, ed. S. Murdoch (Leiden and Boston, MA, 2001), 245–69

Howat, G. M. D., *Stuart and Cromwellian Foreign Policy* (1974)

Huffman, C. C., *Elizabethan Impression: John Wolfe and his Press* (New York, 1940)

Hughes, A., *Politics, Society and Civil War in Warwickshire, 1620–1660* (Cambridge, 1987)

Johns, A., *The Nature of the Book* (Chicago, IL, 1998)

Johnson, F., 'Notes on English Retail Book – Prices 1550–1640', *The Library*, 5:5 (1950), 83–112

Johnson, P., *Habermas: Rescuing the Public Sphere* (London and New York, 2006)

Jones, P. H., 'Wales', in *The Cambridge History of the Book 1557–1695*, vol. 4, ed. J. Barnard and D. F. McKenzie (Cambridge, 2002), 719–34

Jouhaud, C., 'Power and Literature: The Terms of the Exchange 1624–42', in *The Administration of Aesthetics: Censorship, Political Criticism and the Public Sphere*, ed. R. Burt (Minneapolis, MN and London, 1994), 34–82

Keeble, N. H., ed., *Writing of the English Revolution* (Cambridge, 2001)

Keppler, J. S., 'Fiscal Aspects of the English Carrying Trade during the Thirty Years' War', *EHR*, 2:25:2 (1972), 261–78

Kerrigan, J., *Archipelagic English: Literature, History and Politics 1603–1707* (Oxford, 2008)

Kishlansky, M., *A Monarchy Transformed, Britain 1603–1714* (1977)

Kishlansky, M., 'Turning Frogs into Princes', in *Political Culture and Politics in Early Modern England*, ed. S. D. Amussen and M. A. Kishlansky (Manchester, 1995), 338–60

Kyle, C. R., 'Prince Charles in the Parliaments of 1621 and 1624', *HJ*, 41 (1998), 603–24

Kyle, C. R., 'From Broadside to Pamphlet: Print and Parliament in the Late 1620s', in *The Print Culture of Parliament, 1600–1800*, ed. J. Peacey (Edinburgh, 2007), 17–29

Lake, P., 'Constitutional Consensus and Puritan Opposition in the 1620s; Thomas Scott and the Spanish Match', *HJ*, 25 (1982), 805–25

Lake, P., 'Anti-Popery: The Structure of Prejudice', in *Conflict in Early Stuart England*, ed. R. Cust and A. Hughes (1989)

Lake, P., 'Deeds against Nature: Cheap Print, Protestantism and Murder in Early Seventeenth-Century England', in *Culture and Politics in Early Stuart England*, ed. K. Sharpe and P. Lake (Basingstoke and London, 1994), 257–83

Lake, P., '"The Politics of "Popularity" and the Public Sphere: The "Monarchical Republic" of Elizabeth I Defends Itself', in *The Politics of the Public Sphere in Early Modern England*, ed. P. Lake and S. Pincus (Manchester, 2007), 59–94

Lake, P. and Pincus, S., 'Rethinking the Public Sphere in Early Modern England', *JBS*, 45:1 (2006), 270–92

Lake, P. and Pincus, S., 'Rethinking the Public Sphere in Early Modern England', in *The Politics of the Public Sphere in Early Modern England*, ed. P. Lake and S. Pincus (Manchester, 2007), 1–30

Lake, P. and Pincus, S., ed., *The Politics of the Public Sphere in Early Modern England* (Manchester, 2007)

Lake, P. and Questier, M., 'Puritans, Papists and the "Public Sphere" in Early Modern England: The Edmund Campion Affair in Context', *The Journal of Modern History*, 72:3 (2000), 587–627

Lake, P. and Questier, M., *Antichrist's Lewd Hat* (New Haven, CT, 2002)

Lambert, S., 'Richard Montagu, Arminianism and Censorship', *PandP*, 124 (1989), 38–68

Lambert, S., 'Coranto Printing in England', *JNandPH*, 8 (1992), 1–33

Langer, H., *The Thirty Years' War* (Poole, 1978)

Lankhorst, O., 'Newspapers in the Netherlands in the Seventeenth Century', in *The Politics of Information in Early Modern Europe*, ed. B. Dooley and S. Baron (London and New York, 2001), 151–9

Lesger, C., *The Rise of the Amsterdam Market and Information Exchange: Merchants, Commercial Expansion and Change in the Spatial Economy of the Low Countries c 1550–1630*, trans. J. C. Grayson (Aldershot and Burlington, VT, 2006)

Leth, G., 'A Protestant Public Sphere: The Early European Newspaper Press', in *Annual* (1993), 67–90

Levy, F. J., 'How Information Spread among the Gentry, 1550–1640', *JBS*, 21 (1982), 11–34

Long, G., *Books Beyond the Pale: Aspects of the Provincial Book Trade in Ireland before 1850* (Dublin, 1996)

Love, H., *Scribal Publication in Seventeenth-Century England* (Oxford, 1993)

Love, H., *The Culture and Commerce of Texts* (Boston, MA, 1998)

MacInnes, A. I., 'The "Scottish Moment", 1638–45', in *The English Civil War*, ed. J. Adamson (Basingstoke, 2009), 125–52

MacInnes, A. I. and Ohlmeyer, J., *The Stuart Kingdoms in the Seventeenth Century: Awkward Neighbours* (Scarborough, Dublin and Portland, OR, 2002)

Mackillop, A. and Murdoch, S., ed., *Fighting for Identity: Scottish Military Experience c. 1550–1900* (Leiden and Boston, MA, 2002)

Mackillop, A. and Murdoch, S., ed., *Military Governors and Imperial Frontiers c1600–1800* (Leiden and Boston, MA, 2003)

Maclure, M., *The St Paul's Cross Sermons 1534–1642*, 1 (Toronto and Oxford, 1958)

Mandelbrote, G., 'From the Warehouse to the Counting-house: Booksellers and Bookshops in Late Seventeenth-century London', in *Genius for Letters*, ed. R. Myers and M. Harris (Winchester and New Castle, DE, 1995), 49–84

Mann, A. J., *The Scottish Book Trade 1500–1720: Print, Commerce and Print Control in Early Modern Scotland* (East Linton, 2000)

Manning, R. B., *Swordsmen: The Martial Ethos in the Three Kingdoms* (Oxford, 2003)

McKenzie, D. F., 'The Staple of News and the Late Plays', in *A Celebration of Ben Jonson*, ed. W. Blissett *et al.* (Toronto, 1973), 83–126

McKenzie, D. F., *The London Book Trade in the Later Seventeenth Century* (Sandars Lectures, 1976)

McKenzie, D. F., 'Printing and Publishing 1557–1700: Constraints on the London Book Trades', in *The Cambridge History of the Book 1557–1695*, vol. 4, ed. J. Barnard and D. F. McKenzie (Cambridge, 2002), 553–67

McKenzie, D. F., 'The London Book Trade in 1644', in *Making Meaning: Printers of the Mind and Other Essays*, ed. P. D. McDonald and M. F. Suarez (Amherst and Boston, MA, 2002), 126–43

McKerrow, R. B., 'Edward Allde as a Typical Trade Printer', *The Library*, 4:10 (1929), 121–62

McKitterick, D., *A History of Cambridge University Press: Printing and the Book Trade 1534–1698*, vol. 1 (Cambridge, 1992)

McShane Jones, A., '"The Gazet in Metre; Or the Rhiming Newsmonger" The

English Broadside Ballad as Intelligencer, A New Narrative', in *News and Politics in Early Modern Europe 1500–1800*, ed. J. W. Koopmans (Leuven, Paris and Dudley, MA, 2005), 131–46

Mears, N., *Queenship and Political Discourse in the Elizabethan Realms* (Cambridge, 2005)

Mendle, M., 'De Facto Freedom, De Facto Authority: Press and Parliament, 1640–1643', *HJ*, 18:2 (1995), 307–32

Mendle, M., 'News and the Pamphlet Culture of Mid-seventeenth Century England', in *The Politics of Information in Early Modern Europe*, ed. B. Dooley and S. Baron (London and New York, 2001), 57–79

Milton, A., 'Licensing, Censorship and Religious Orthodoxy in Early Stuart England', *HJ*, 41:3 (1998), 625–51

Morgan, P., 'Letters Relating to the Oxford Book Trade Founding Bindings in Oxford College Libraries c1611–1647', *Studies in the Book Trade*, 18 (Oxford Bibliographical Society, 1975), 71–89

Morrill, J., 'William Davenport and the "Silent Majority" of Early Stuart England', *Journal of the Chester Archaeological Society*, 58 (1975), 115–29

Morrill, J., 'The Religious Context of the English Civil War', in *Nature of the English Revolution*, ed. J. Morrill (1993)

Morrill, J., *Revolt in the Provinces: The People of England and the Tragedies of War 1630–48* (London and New York, revised 1999)

Morris, E. C., 'Allegory in Middleton's "A Game at Chesse"', *Englische Studien*, 38 (1907), 39–52

Morrison, S., *The Origins of the Newspaper* (1954)

Mortimer, G., *Eye-Witness Accounts of the Thirty Years' War, 1618–48* (Basingstoke and New York, 2002)

Mousley, A., 'Self, State, and Seventeenth-century News', *The Seventeenth Century*, 6:2 (1991), 149–68

Muldrew, C., *The Economy of Obligation* (Basingstoke and New York, 1998)

Mumby, F. A., *Publishing and Bookselling*, 1 (1974)

Murdoch, S., ed., *Scotland and the Thirty Years' War, 1618–1648* (Leiden and Boston, MA, 2001)

Murdoch, S., 'James VI and the Formation of a Scottish-British Military Identity', *Fighting for Identity: Scottish Military Experience c. 1550–1900*, ed. A. Mackillop and S. Murdoch (Leiden and Boston, MA, 2002), 3–31

Murdoch, S., 'Scotland, Scandinavia and the Bishops' Wars: 1638–40', in *The Stuart Kingdoms in the Seventeenth Century: Awkward Neighbours*, ed. A. I. MacInnes and J. Ohlmeyer (Scarborough, Dublin and Portland, OR, 2002), 113–34

Murdoch, S., *Britain, Denmark-Norway and the House of Stuart, 1603–1660* (East Linton, 2003)

Mutchow Towers, S., *Control of Religious Printing in Early Stuart England* (Woodbridge, 2003)

Myers, R. and Harris, M., ed., *Censorship and the Control of Print in England and France 1600–1910* (Winchester, 1992)

Myers, R. and Harris, M., ed., *Serials and their Readers 1620–1914* (Winchester and New Castle, DE, 1993)

Myers, R. and Harris, M., ed., *Genius for Letters* (Winchester and New Castle, DE, 1995)

Myers, R. and Harris, M., ed., *Spreading the Word, the Distribution of Print 1550–1850* (Winchester and Delaware, DE, 1998)

Nelson, C. and Seccombe, M., 'The Creation of the Periodical Press, 1620–1695', in *The Cambridge History of the Book 1557–1695*, vol. 4, ed. J. Barnard and D. F. McKenzie (Cambridge, 2002), 533–50

Nevitt, M., 'Ben Jonson and the Serial Publication on News', in *News, Networks in Seventeenth-Century Britain and Europe*, ed. J. Raymond (London and New York, 2006), 51–62

Norbrook, D., 'Areopagitica, The Early Modern Public Sphere', in *The Administration of Aesthetics: Censorship, Political Criticism and the Public Sphere*, ed. R. Burt (Minneapolis, MN and London, 1994), 3–33

Notestein, W. and Relf, F., ed., *Commons Debates for 1629* (Minneapolis, MN, 1921)

O'Hara, D. A., *English Newsbooks and the Irish Rebellion, 1641–1649* (Dublin, 2006)

Ohlmeyer, J., *Civil War and Restoration in the Three Stuart Kingdoms: The Career of Randal MacDonnell, Marquis of Antrim, 1609–1683* (Cambridge, 1993)

Ormrod, D., *The Dutch in London: The Influence of the Immigrant Community 1550–1800* (1973)

Orwell, G., ed., *British Pamphleteers from the 16th Century to the French Revolution*, 1 (1948)

Pagés, G., *The Thirty Years' War, 1618–1648* (1970)

Pantzer, K. F., 'Printing the English Statutes, 1484–1640: Some Historical Implications', in *Books and Society in History*, ed. K. E. Carpenter (1983), 69–114

Parker, G., ed., *The Thirty Years' War* (London, Boston, MA and Melbourne, 1984/1997)

Parmelee, L. F., 'Printers, Patrons, Readers and Spies: Importation of French Propaganda in Late Elizabethan England', *Sixteenth Century Journal*, 25 (1994), 853–72

Patterson, A., *Censorship and Interpretation* (Madison, WI and London, 1984)

Patterson, A., *Reading between the Lines* (1993)

Peacey, J., 'The Exploitation of Captured Royal Correspondence and Anglo-Scottish Relations in the British Civil Wars', *The Scottish Historical Review*, 89:2 (2000), 213–32

Peacey, J., *Politicians and Pamphleteers: Propaganda during the English Civil Wars and Interregnum* (Aldershot and Burlington, VT, 2004)

Peacey, J., 'Print Culture and Political Lobbing during the English Civil Wars', in *The Print Culture of Parliament, 1600–1800*, ed. J. Peacey (Edinburgh, 2007), 30–48

Peacey, J., ed., *The Print Culture of Parliament, 1600–1800* (Edinburgh, 2007)

Peacey, J., 'Perceptions of Parliament: Factions and "The Public"', in *The English Civil War*, ed. J. Adamson (Basingstoke, 2009), 82–105

Pierce, H., *Unseemly Pictures: Graphic Satire and Politics in Early Modern England* (New Haven, CT and London, 2008)

Pincus, S., *Protestantism and Patriotism: Ideologies and the Making of English Foreign Policy, 1650–1668* (Cambridge, 1996)

Pincus, S., 'The State and Civil Society in Early Modern England: Capitalism, Causation and Habermas's Bourgeois Public Sphere', in *The Politics of the Public Sphere in Early Modern England*, ed. P. Lake and S. Pincus (Manchester, 2007), 213–31

Polisensky, J. V., *The Thirty Years' War* (1970)

Polisensky, J. V., 'A Note on Scottish Soldiers in the Bohemian War 1619–1622', in *Scotland and the Thirty Years' War, 1618–1648*, ed. S. Murdoch (Leiden and Boston, MA, 2001), 109–15

Popkin, J. D., 'New Perspectives in Early Modern European Press', in *News and Politics in Early Modern Europe 1500–1800*, ed. J. W. Koopmans (Leuven, Paris and Dudley, MA, 2005), 1–27

Powell, W. S., *John Pory, 1572–1636, 1572–1636: The Life and Letters of a Man of Many Parts* (Chapel Hill, NC, 1977)

Prestwich, M., ed., *International Calvinism, 1541–1715* (Oxford, 1985)

Randall, D., 'Joseph Mead, Novellante: News, Sociability, and Credibility in Early Stuart England', *JBS*, 45:2 (2006), 293–312

Randall, D., *Credibility in Elizabethan and Early Stuart Military News* (2008)

Raven, J., 'The Economic Context', in *The Cambridge History of the Book 1557–1695*, vol. 4, ed. J. Barnard and D. F. McKenzie (Cambridge, 2002), 568–82

Raymond, J., 'The Great Assises Holden in Panassus: The Reputation and Reality of Seventeenth-Century Newsbooks', in *Annual* (1994), 3–17

Raymond, J., 'The Newspaper, Public Opinion, and the Public Sphere in the Seventeenth Century', in *News, Newspapers, and Society in Early Modern Britain*, ed. J. Raymond (London and Portland, OR, 1999), 109–40

Raymond, J., 'Irrational, Impractical and Unprofitable: Reading the News in Seventeenth-Century Britain', in *Reading, Society and Politics in Early Modern England*, ed. K. Sharpe and S. Zwicker (Cambridge, 2003), 185–212

Raymond, J., *Pamphlets and Pamphleteering in Early Modern Britain* (Cambridge, 2003)

Raymond, J., ed., *News Networks in Seventeenth Century Britain and Europe* (London and New York, 2006)

Reade, H. G. R., *Sidelights on the Thirty Years' War* (1924)

Reay, B., *Popular Cultures in England 1550–1750* (New York and Harlow, Essex, 1998)

Redworth, G., *The Prince and the Infanta* (New Haven, CT, 2003)

Rostenberg, L., 'Nathaniel Butter and Nicholas Bourne, First Masters of the Staple', *The Library*, 5:12 (1957), 23–33

Rostenberg, L., *Literary, Political, Scientific, Religious and Legal Publishing, Printing and Bookselling in England 1551–1700: Twelve Studies*, 2 vols (New York, 1965)

Rostenberg, L., *The Minority Press and the English Crown* (New York, 1971)

Roy, I., 'The Army and its Critics in Seventeenth-Century England', in *War and Society, A Yearbook of Military History*, 2, ed. I. Roy and B. Bond (1977), 141–50

Royle, T., *Civil War: The Wars of the Three Kingdoms 1638–1660* (2004)

Ruigh, R. E., *The Parliament of 1624* (Cambridge, MA, 1971)

Russell, C., *The Crisis of Parliaments; English History 1509–1660* (Oxford, 1971)

Russell, C. S. R., *The Causes of the English Civil War* (Oxford, 1990)

Sawyer, J., *Printed Poison: Pamphlet Propaganda, Faction Politics and the Public Sphere in Seventeenth-Century France* (Berkeley, CA and Oxford, 1990)

Schaffer, A., *Georg Rudolf Weckherlin* (Danvers, MA, 1918/2009)

Scheele, C. H., *A Short History of the Mail Service* (Washington, DC, 1870)

Schroder, T., 'The Origins of the German Press', in *The Politics of Information in Early Modern Europe*, ed. B. Dooley and S. Baron (London and New York, 2001), 123–50

Scott, J., *England's Troubles: Seventeenth-Century English Political Instability in a European Context* (Cambridge, 2000)

Scott-Warren, J., 'Reconstructing Manuscript Networks: The Textual Transactions of Sir Stephen Powle', in *Communities in Early Modern England*, ed. A. Shepard and P. Withington (Manchester, 2000), 18–33

Scribner, R. W., 'Is a History of Popular Culture Possible?', *History of European Ideas*, 10:2 (1989), 175–91

Scribner, R. W., *For the Sake of Simple Folk: Popular Propaganda for the German Reformation* (Oxford, 1994/2000)

Seaver, P. S., *Wallington's World: A Puritan Artisan in Seventeenth-Century London* (Stanford, CA, 1985)

Sellin, P. R., 'The Performances of Ben Jonson's "Newes from the New World Discover'd in the Moone"', *English Studies*, 61:6 (1980), 491–7

Sellin, P. R., 'The Politics of Ben Jonson's "Newes from the New World Discover'd in the Moone"', *Viator: Medieval and Renaissance Studies*, 17 (1986), 321–37

Shaaber, M. A., 'The First English Newspaper', *Studies in Philology*, 29 (1932), 551–87

Shagan, E. H., 'Rumours and Popular Politics in the Reign of Henry VIII', in *The Politics of the Excluded, c.1500–1850*, ed. T. Harris (Basingstoke and New York, 2001), 30–59

Shapiro, B. J., *A Culture of Fact: England 1550–1720* (Ithaca, NY and London, 2000)

Sharpe, K., *Faction and Parliament in Early Stuart History* (Oxford, 1978)

Sharpe, K., 'Ideas and Politics in Early Stuart England', *History Today*, 38 (1988), 45–51

Sharpe, K., *Politics and Ideas in Early Stuart England* (London and New York, 1989)

Sharpe, K., *The Personal Rule of Charles I* (New Haven, CT and London, 1992)

Sharpe, K., 'The King's Writ: Royal Authors and Royal Authority in Early Modern England', in *Culture and Politics in Early Stuart England*, ed. K. Sharpe and P. Lake (Basingstoke and London, 1994), 117–38

Sharpe, K., *Reading Revolutions: The Politics of Reading in Early Modern England* (New Haven, CT, 2000)

Sharpe, K., *Remapping Early Modern England: The Culture of Seventeenth-Century Politics* (Cambridge, 2000)

Sharpe, K., *Image Wars; Promoting Kings and Commonwealths in England, 1603–1660* (New Haven, CT and London, 2010)

Sharpe K. and Zwicker, S. N., *Reading, Society and Politics in Early Modern England* (Cambridge, 2003)

Shepard, A. and Withington, P., *Communities in Early Modern England* (Manchester, 2000)

Siebert, F. S., *Freedom of the Press in England 1476–1776* (Urbana, IL, 1952)

Simmons, R. C., 'ABCs, Almanacs, Ballads, Chapbooks, Popular Piety and Textbooks', in *The Cambridge History of the Book 1557–1695*, vol. 4, ed. J. Barnard and D. F. McKenzie (Cambridge, 2002), 504–13

Skelton, R. A., 'Pieter Van Den Keere', *The Library*, 5:5 (1950), 130–2

Smith, D. L., *The Stuart Parliaments 1603–1689* (1999)

Smith, W., *A Dictionary of Greek and Roman Antiquities* (Boston, MA, 1859)

Smuts, M., ed., *The Stuart Court and Europe; Essays in Politics and Political Culture* (Cambridge, 1996)

Smuts, M., *Culture and Power in England 1585–1685* (1999)

Smuts, M., 'Religion, European Politics and Henrietta Maria's Circle, 1625–41', *Henrietta Maria, Piety, Politics and Patronage*, ed. E. Griffey (Aldershot and Burlington, VT, 2008), 13–37

Solomon, S., *Public Welfare, Science and Propaganda in Seventeenth-Century France: The Innovations of Theophraste Renaudot* (Princeton, NJ, 1972)

Sommerville, C. J., *The News Revolution in England: Cultural Dynamics of Daily Information* (New York and Oxford, 1996)

Sommerville, J. P., *Royalists and Patriots, Politics and Ideology in England 1603–1640* (London and New York, 1999)

Sprunger, K. L., *Trumpets from the Tower* (Leiden, New York and Koln, 1994)

Spufford, M., 'First Steps in Literacy: The Reading and Writing of the Humblest Seventeenth-century Spiritual Autobiographers', *Social History*, 4 (1979), 407–35

Spufford, M. *Small Books and Pleasant Histories: Popular Fiction and its Readership in Seventeenth-Century England* (1981)

Stallybrass, P., '"Little Jobs": Broadsides and the Printing Revolution', in *Agent of Change: Print Culture after Elizabeth L. Eisenstein*, ed. S. A. Baron, E. Lindquist and E. Shevlin (Amherst and Boston, MA, 2007), 315–41

Steinberg, S. H., *Five Hundred Years of Printing* (Harmondsworth and Baltimore, MD, 1955)

Steinberg, S. H., *The 'Thirty Years' War' and the Conflict for European Hegemony 1600–1660* (1971)

Stephens, M., 'Which Communication Revolution is it Anyway?', *Journalism and Mass Communication Quarterly*, 75:1 (1998), 9–18

Streckfus, R., 'News before Newspapers', *Journalism and Mass Communication Quarterly*, 75:1 (1998), 84–97

Tanner, J. R., *English Constitutional Conflicts of the Seventeenth Century* (Cambridge, 1966)

Taylor, H., 'Trade, Neutrality, and the "English Road", 1630–1648', *EHR*, 2:25:2 (1972), 236–60

Thomas, K., *Religion and the Decline of Magic* (1970)

Thomas, K., 'The Meaning of Literacy in Early Modern England', in *The Written Word: Literacy in Transition*, ed. G. Baumann (Oxford, 1986), 97–122

Thomas, P. W., *Sir John Berkenhead 1617–1679: A Royalist Career in Politics and Polemics* (Oxford, 1969)

Thompson, A. B., 'Licensing the Press: The Career of G. R. Weckherlin during the Personal Rule of Charles I', *HJ*, 41 (1998), 653–78

Underdown, D., *A Freeborn People* (Oxford, 1996)

Vittu, J-P., 'Instruments of Political Information in France', in *The Politics of Information in Early Modern Europe*, ed. B. Dooley and S. Baron (London and New York, 2001), 160–78

Von Klarwill, V., *The Fugger Newsletters 1568–1606* (1926)

Walsham, A., *Providence in Early Modern England* (Cambridge, 1999)

Waterhouse, G., *The Literary Relations of England and Germany in the Seventeenth Century* (Cambridge, 1914)

Watt, T., 'Publisher, Pedlar, Pot-Poet: The Changing Character of the Broadside Trade, 1550–1640', in *Spreading the Word, the Distribution of Print 1550–1850*, ed. R. Myers and M. Harris (Winchester and Delaware, DE, 1998), 61–81

Wedgwood, C. V., *The King's Peace 1637–41* (1955)

Wedgwood, C. V., *Seventeenth-Century English Literature* (1970)

Welch, R., 'The Book in Ireland from the Tudor Reconquest to the Battle of the Boyne', in *The Cambridge History of the Book 1557–1695*, vol. 4, ed. J. Barnard and D. F. McKenzie (Cambridge, 2002), 701–16

Werner, H., 'The Hector of Germainie, or The Palsgrave, Prime Elector and Anglo-German Relations of Early Stuart England: The View from the Popular Stage', in The Stuart Court and Europe; Essays in Politics and Political Culture, ed. M. Smuts (Cambridge, 1996), 113–32

Werner, H., '"The Lamentations of Germanie": A Probable Source for Heywood's "Londini Status", 484–486', in Notes and Queries (December 1994), 624–9

Williamson, A., 'Scotland: International Politics, International Press', in Agent of Change: Print Culture after Elizabeth L. Eisenstein, ed. S. A. Baron, E. Lindquist and E. Shevlin (Amherst and Boston, MA, 2007), 193–215

Wilson, P. H., Europe's Tragedy: A History of the Thirty Years' War (2009)

Wilson, P. H., The Thirty Years' War: A Sourcebook (2010)

Wood, A. à, ed. P. Bliss, Fasti Oxoniense, 4 vols (1813–20)

Woodfield, D. B., Surreptitious Printing in England 1550–1640 (New York, 1973)

Woolf, D., 'News, History and the Construction of the Present in Early Modern England, in The Politics of Information in Early Modern Europe, ed. B. Dooley and S. Baron (London and New York, 2001), 80–118

Worden, A. B., 'Literature and Political Censorship in Early Modern England', in Too Mighty to be Free: Censorship and the Press in Britain and the Netherlands, ed. A. C. Duke and C. A. Tamse (Zutphen, 1987), 45–62

Wormald, J., 'James VI and I: Two Kings or One?', History, 68 (1983), 187–207

Worthington, D., ed., British and Irish Emigrants and Exiles in Europe 1603–1688 (Leiden and Boston, MA, 2010)

Wright, B., 'Propaganda against James I's "Appeasement of Spain"', HLQ (1943), 149–92

Young, J. R., 'The Scottish Parliament and European Diplomacy 1641–1647: The Palatine, the Dutch Republic and Sweden', in Scotland and the Thirty Years' War, 1618–1648, ed. S. Murdoch (Leiden and Boston, MA, 2001), 77–104

Zagorin, P., The Court and Country (1969)

Zaller, R., The Parliament of 1624 (Berkeley, CA, 1971)

Zaret, D., 'Religion, Science and Printing in the Public Spheres in Seventeenth-century England', in Habermas and the Public Sphere, ed. C. Calhoun (Cambridge, MA and London, 1992), 212–30

Zaret, D., Origins of Democratic Culture: Printing, Petitions, and the Public Sphere in Early-modern England (Princeton, NJ, 2000)

Zell, M., Early Modern Kent, 1540–1640 (Woodbridge, 2000)

INDEX

Page numbers in bold type refer to illustrations and their captions.

STUDIES IN EARLY MODERN CULTURAL,
POLITICAL AND SOCIAL HISTORY